D1432257

Narcissism and Politics
Dreams of Glory

In this age of narcissism, the proliferation of politicians with significant narcissistic personality features is dramatic. Driven by dreams of glory, they seem to find irresistible the spotlight that the arena of politics provides. This book analyzes narcissism and politics and systematically explores the psychology of narcissism – the entitlement, the grandiosity and arrogance overlying insecurity, the sensitivity to criticism, and the hunger for acclaim – illustrating different narcissistic personality features through a spectrum of international and national politicians. It addresses the power of charismatic leader–follower relationships, as well as the impact of age and illness on leaders driven by dreams of glory.

Dr. Jerrold M. Post is professor of psychiatry, political psychology, and international affairs and director of the Political Psychology Program at the George Washington University. Dr. Post previously worked with the Central Intelligence Agency, where he was the founding director of the Center for the Analysis of Personality and Political Behavior. He played the lead role in developing the Camp David profiles of Menachem Begin and Anwar Sadat for President Jimmy Carter, and he initiated the U.S. government program for the study of the psychology of terrorism. In recognition of his leadership at the Center, Dr. Post was awarded the Intelligence Medal of Merit in 1979. He received the Nevitt Sanford Award from the International Society of Political Psychology in 2002 for distinguished professional contributions to political psychology. He has testified before the Senate and the House on his political psychology profile of Saddam Hussein and on the psychology of terrorism, and he has presented to the United Nations International Atomic Energy Agency on the psychology of weapons of mass destruction terrorism. He is a member of the National Academy of Sciences' Committee on Deterrence in the 21st Century.

Narcissism and Politics

Dreams of Glory

JERROLD M. POST
The George Washington University

CAMBRIDGE
UNIVERSITY PRESS

CAMBRIDGE
UNIVERSITY PRESS

32 Avenue of the Americas, New York NY 10013-2473, USA

Cambridge University Press is part of the University of Cambridge.

It furthers the University's mission by disseminating knowledge in the pursuit of education, learning and research at the highest international levels of excellence.

www.cambridge.org
Information on this title: www.cambridge.org/9781107401297

First published 2015

A catalogue record for this publication is available from the British Library

Library of Congress Cataloguing in Publication data
Post, Jerrold M.
Narcissism and politics : dreams of glory / Jerrold M. Post, The George Washington University.
    pages   cm
ISBN 978-1-107-00872-4 (hardback)
1. Personality and politics.   2. Political psychology.   3. Narcissism – Political aspects.   4. Charisma (Personality trait) – Political aspects.   I. Title.
BF698.9.P6P67   2015
320.01'9–dc23   2014011959

ISBN 978-1-107-40129-7 Paperback

To my wife Carolyn, a spectacular woman, with unbounded gratitude, for your steadfast support and nurturance

and

To my three wonderful daughters: Cindy, Merrie, and Kirsten, whose love and caring I always felt during the long voyage of bringing this book to closure

Contents

Preface

If one were to strip from the ranks of political figures all those with significant narcissistic personality traits, those ranks would be perilously impoverished. It seems that scarcely a day goes by that we are not greeted by a headline trumpeting that Senator X or Governor Y, noted for strongly espousing family values, has been caught in a sordid affair. Typically, a televised news conference, with the wife loyally by his side in a show of support, follows. This seems to be a bipartisan affair. And although the punditocracy regularly bemoans the blatant hypocrisy of such miscreants, I would suggest that another factor is at work: namely, that this behavior reveals significant narcissism in the character of the newly revealed sinner, that he somehow considers himself above the law and not subject to the usual moral, ethical, and legal constraints governing behavior.

But this apparent epidemic of narcissism is not confined to politicians. The rise of the "me generation" has been the subject of frequent commentary. There is growing concern that, intensified by the social media use of the "Facebook generation," an exaggerated concern with self and narcissism is increasingly widespread in society: College students' scores on the Narcissistic Personality Inventory rose twice as fast in the five years from 2002 to 2007 as in the decades between 1982 and 2006.[1]

It has been estimated that upward of 10 percent of the American public have significant narcissistic features, so much so that consideration was given to eliminating narcissistic personality disorder (NPD) from the revised version of the American Psychiatric Association's (APA) *Diagnostic and Statistical Manual of Mental Disorders*, the diagnostic bible of psychiatric and psychological clinicians, because it was rapidly becoming "the new normal."

Social psychologists Jean Twenge, author of *Generation Me*, and Keith Campbell, co-author (with J. D. Miller) of *The Handbook of Narcissism and Narcissistic Personality Disorder: Theoretical Approaches, Empirical Findings, and Treatments*, have written a book provocatively entitled *The Narcissism*

Epidemic: Living in the Age of Entitlement, commenting on the acceleration of this phenomenon within American culture.[2] They observe, for example, that in the past decade the frequency of cosmetic plastic surgery has increased fivefold and that, in preschool, children sing "I'm special; look at me," a song their adoring mothers have taught them.

Arrogant, vain, egocentric, extremely ambitious, entitled to succeed and to be followed by throngs of admirers, the narcissist believes he is a very special person; he is full of himself. He is so entranced by himself that there is little room for genuine, mutual loving relations with others; his relations are regularly distorted and difficult to sustain.

In support of their provocative title, *The Narcissism Epidemic*, Twenge and Campbell provide convincing social psychological data on the increasing prevalence of individuals with narcissistic traits in our society, especially among the young, and discuss some of the dangerous implications. After all, if our globalized society requires collaboration, how can individuals consumed with themselves work creatively on collaborative teams?

Epidemics have foci, places where the infection is especially widespread and nearly everyone is infected, as with the Black Plague during the Dark Ages in Europe. The epidemic of individuals with significant narcissistic traits seems to have reached pandemic proportions among politicians. This is not to say that all politicians are narcissistic but that the arena of public service and its limelight is particularly attractive, indeed irresistible, to individuals with narcissistic propensities.

In saying this, I am speaking about narcissism writ large, about individuals with many narcissistic traits in their personalities. I am not – repeat not – saying that these political figures are suffering from NPD. Indeed, to have features that warrant a diagnosis of severe NPD is probably inconsistent with being able to sustain a political career in a democracy, although, as discussed later in this volume, a number of dictators unconstrained by democratic systems seem to manifest the characteristics of a particularly severe form of NPD – malignant or primitive narcissism.

This book, for the most part, then, is not concerned with political figures with NPD but rather is about the ubiquity of narcissistic features in the world of politics in the broader sense of the word. After all, at one level, to have abundant self-confidence and ambition combined with ability and opportunity is to have the ingredients for success. The ranks of executives and academics are disproportionately weighted with healthy, ambitious individuals with significant narcissistic traits.

Psychoanalyst Helen Tartakoff has written of the Nobel Prize Complex, describing individuals who, from early on, are driven to pursue the highest honors.[3] Although Shakespeare, in Act II Scene 5 of *Twelfth Night*, has observed that "some are born great, some achieve greatness, and some have greatness thrust upon them," in fact, without reaching for the stars, without pursuing dreams of glory, greatness is rarely achieved. Some who seek the Nobel Prize will, after all, have the gold medal draped around their necks in Stockholm, Sweden, or, if dreaming of the Nobel Peace Prize, in Oslo, Norway.

I take pains to emphasize that I am not proffering a clinical diagnosis, and perhaps a word of explanation for this caution is necessary. I discuss a number of contemporary politicians in this book as I review the overrepresentation of narcissistic personality traits in the population of political leaders. I offer my impressions as a political psychologist, educated as a psychiatrist to be sure, but these impressions do not constitute a clinical diagnosis that a forensic psychiatrist would offer in courtroom testimony.

Questions concerning what makes leaders "tick" have often led journalists to turn to social scientists, including psychiatrists, to offer commentary on public figures.[a] Such questions include, for example, the effects of health and alcoholism on Boris Yeltsin's decision making; the mind of the Unabomber; the psychology and decision-making process of Saddam Hussein of Iraq (who was initially characterized by the U.S. government as "the madman of the Middle East"); the psychology of David Koresh and the Branch Davidians who were involved in an extended siege with the Bureau of Alcohol, Tobacco, and Firearms and the Federal Bureau of Investigation that ended tragically on April 19, 1993; and the psychology of the 19 al-Qaeda terrorists responsible for the tragic events of September 11, 2001, in which they claimed thousands of lives while giving their own, "killing in the name of God," and of their charismatic leader, Osama bin Laden.

In weighing whether and how to respond, psychiatrists find themselves caught between the Scylla of public service and public education and the Charybdis of the ethical prohibitions spelled out in Section 7 "The Principles of Medical Ethics, with Annotations Especially Applicable to Psychiatry." This principle, a masterpiece of internal contradiction, states that:

A physician shall recognize a responsibility to participate in activities contributing to an improved community.

Psychiatrists are encouraged to serve society by advising and consulting with the executive, legislative, and judiciary branches of the government.

Psychiatrists may interpret and share with the public their expertise in the various psychosocial issues that may affect mental health and illness. Psychiatrists should always be mindful of their separate roles as dedicated citizens and as experts in psychological medicine.

On occasion psychiatrists are asked for an opinion about an individual who is in the light of public attention, or who has disclosed information about himself/herself through public media. It is unethical for a psychiatrist to offer a professional opinion unless he/she has conducted an examination and has been granted proper authorization for such a statement.[4]

---

[a] This historical background is drawn from a chapter I prepared for a book on psychiatric ethics: J. Post, "The Psychiatric Clinics of North America," in vol. 25, no. 3 of *Ethics in Psychiatry*, edited by Glen Gabbard, Philadelphia: Saunders, 2002.

Because I have devoted my career to the application of psychiatry to international affairs and the field of political psychology, and because I wish to conduct my professional activities in an ethical manner, this principle has regularly concerned, confused, confounded, and constrained me. But the opportunity to offer public commentary on public figures often arises for mainstream psychiatrists. Because of my background as the founding director of the Center for the Analysis of Personality and Political Behavior at the Central Intelligence Agency (CIA), which prepared political personality profiles on world leaders to assist the president, secretary of defense, secretary of state, and other senior officials before summit meetings and other high-level negotiations and to assist in crisis situations, I have often been called on to testify before Congress and the United Nations and invited to offer commentary by mainstream media. Consequently, a discussion of my reactions to the quandary posed by the principles enunciated in Section 7 of the *American Psychiatric Association Code of Ethics* is in order.

THE DILEMMA

The dilemma was no more dramatically and absurdly evidenced than during the Persian Gulf crisis of 1990–91. On the basis of a political personality profile that I developed of Saddam Hussein from my base at the George Washington University, one that was widely featured in print and electronic media, in late 1990, I was invited to testify before two congressional committees holding hearings on the Gulf Crisis – Les Aspin's House Armed Services Committee and Lee Hamilton's House Foreign Affairs Committee.[b] Saddam Hussein had been widely characterized as "the madman of the Middle East," and there was considerable perplexity concerning what made him tick.

Policies were being developed that, in my judgment, were insufficiently informed by an accurate picture of Saddam Hussein's political psychology. This was an extraordinary opportunity for a political psychologist to present the principal conclusions of Hussein's profile to legislators charged with the responsibility for the policy-development process and to contribute to their understanding of the complex cultural, historical, political, and psychological influences on Saddam Hussein's decision making. After this testimony was presented, in a public forum, the president of the U.S. Institute of Peace cited the profile as a "contribution of the highest order to the national welfare." It assuredly was a career high point.

---

[b] This was a notable occasion for the discipline of political psychology, being the first time that a political personality profile of a foreign leader was presented in testimony to Congress. The testimony can be found in the Congressional Record, December 5 and 12, 1990, under the title "Saddam Hussein of Iraq: A Political Psychology Profile." It has also been printed in *Political Psychology* (Post, 1991). The testimony was cited by several congressmen as having contributed to their decision making during the crisis.

But my moment of pride was short-lived. When the chair of the APA's Council of Psychiatry and International Affairs, on which I served, called, indicating that he wished to speak to me about the profile, I was anticipating a compliment for my contribution to American psychiatry. You can only imagine my consternation when he dolefully intoned, "Jerry, the APA has received letters about your profile of Saddam, and there is reason to believe you may have violated the Canons of Ethics of the American Psychiatric Association."

Apparently, as he went on to explain, a "profile of the profiler" article about personality profiling, one that drew on the Saddam Hussein profile, had appeared in the Science News section of the *New York Times*. This led to several letters complaining that I had violated Section 7 of the Canons of Ethics of the APA because I had presented publicly a professional opinion about Hussein without interviewing him and without his authorization.

I nearly exploded. "Have you read the profile?" I asked.

"Well, no," he acknowledged.

"Then perhaps you should before rendering such judgments. The profile is not a psychiatric expert opinion. It is a political personality profile, an art form I have crafted, informed, to be sure, by my education as a psychiatrist, but concerned with such matters as leadership style, crisis reactions, negotiating style, relationship with leadership circle, etc.

"Moreover," I went on, "I think there is a duty to warn, involving a kind of Tarasoff principle,[c] for the assessments of Saddam's political personality and leadership that are guiding policy seem to me to be off – he had been widely characterized as 'the madman of the Middle East' – and policy decisions are being made based on errant perceptions, which could lead to significant loss of life. In fact he is a rational decision maker who, however, often miscalculates.

"Accordingly," I continued, "it would have been unethical to have withheld this assessment. I believed I had a duty to warn." I faxed the profile to him and heard no more on the matter, but the conversation continued to trouble me.

How can it be that a presentation deemed to be "a contribution of the highest order to the national welfare" could simultaneously raise questions concerning an ethical violation? Other academic specialists from the ranks of psychology, political science, and history regularly contribute to public discourse on political figures without having interviewed the subject, but for psychiatrists to do so is considered an ethical violation. The ethical principle seemed extreme and overdrawn.

---

[c] The Tarasoff principle derives from a controversial case (*Tarasoff v. State of California*) in which a client in counseling told his therapist that he was obsessed with a co-ed and that if she would not go out with him, he would kill her. She would not, and he killed her. In the trial, the therapist claimed that he could not warn her because to do so would violate confidentiality. The California Supreme Court overruled this previously all-encompassing principle of confidentiality, indicating that when specific danger emerged in the course of counseling, there was a "duty to warn."

To understand the severity of the principle requires examining its development. As is often the case, bad cases make bad law. The historical background for this ethical prohibition can be traced to the Lyndon Johnson–Barry Goldwater election of 1964. During the 1964 presidential election campaign, *Fact Magazine*, which had somehow acquired an APA mailing list, surveyed the membership of the APA asking whether the Republican candidate, Barry Goldwater, was psychiatrically fit for office. The results led to a front-page headline: "1189 Psychiatrists Say Goldwater Is Psychologically Unfit to Be President." Mr. Ginzburg, editor of the magazine, said that "over a quarter of a million words of professional opinion were received; never in history has a political figure been the subject of such an intensive character analysis." The article was littered with juicy quotes, including comments from prominent academic psychiatrists. Among the internationally prominent American psychiatrists who responded to the survey was Jerome Frank, chair of the department of psychiatry at the Johns Hopkins University School of Medicine, who wrote that the "ill-considered, impulsive quality of many of Goldwater's public utterances is, in my mind, sufficient to disqualify him from the presidency."[5] A number of psychiatrists, in whose opinion Goldwater was not psychologically fit to serve as president, cited his apparent paranoid tendencies. Dr. Carl B. Young of Los Angeles addressed the danger of this apparent impulsivity in combination with his paranoid tendencies: "The main factors which make me feel Goldwater is unfit to be president are: (1) His impulsive, impetuous behavior. Such behavior in this age could result in world destruction. This behavior reflects an emotionally immature, unstable personality. (2) His inability to dissociate himself from vituperative, sick extremists. Basically, I feel that he has a narcissistic character disorder with not too latent paranoid elements."[6]

The poll gave American psychiatry a black eye. In a column entitled "Psychiatric Folly," James Wechsler of the *New York Post* wrote that while the survey provided no new insights about Goldwater, "it reveals a good deal about a segment of the psychiatric profession. It is a simultaneous affront to responsible psychiatry and journalism."[7] In a press release from the APA medical director, the APA disavowed the survey and criticized both *Fact Magazine* and the naiveté of those members who responded, citing embarrassment to the profession. It was observed that "[a] physician can properly render an opinion on the psychological fitness or mental condition of anyone only in the traditional doctor-patient relationship in which findings are based on a thorough clinical examination."[8]

Reaction from its members and from the press created a public relations nightmare for the APA, which attempted to put a positive spin on the story by citing the overwhelming majority of its membership that did not respond to the poll. The headlines that appeared after public repudiation of the poll by both the American Medical Association and the APA were brutal and continued the humiliation: "5 of 6 Psychiatrists Won't Comment on Barry 'Fitness,'"

"Headshrinkers Shrink from Opinion on Barry," "Psychiatric Profession Damaged by Mail Order Analysis of Goldwater," "New Era Dawns: Instant Psychiatry."[9]

This, then, was the background of the formulation in 1973 of the Annotation in the Ethics Code relating to public statements. As Lazarus has observed, "Those who drafted the first edition of the Annotations in 1973 still had a good memory of the dramatic events of the 1960s and wanted to include a clear statement in the Code to remind psychiatrists of their ethical duties related to public statements regarding public figures."[10] The initial wording of the Annotation proscribed rendering a diagnosis without examination. It was subsequently broadened in later editions from diagnosis to professional opinion.

While the ethical prohibition in Section 7.3 was prompted by the damage to the individual under consideration, as well as to the reputation of the psychiatric profession, the prohibition as developed did not specify the intended audience. It is unequivocal: "On occasion psychiatrists are asked for an opinion about an individual who is in the light of public attention, or who has disclosed information about himself/herself through public media. It is unethical for a psychiatrist to offer a professional opinion unless he/she has conducted an examination and has been granted proper authorization for such a statement."

By then, however, programs had been developed within the FBI and the CIA that made use of psychological data to produce classified psychological profiles. These profiles were developed, in the case of the FBI, to assist criminal investigations and, in the case of the CIA, to provide assistance to U.S. government foreign policy officials conducting summit meetings and other high-level negotiations with foreign leaders, as well as to assist in dealing with political-military crises. The CIA studies were conducted by the Center for the Analysis of Personality and Political Behavior, of which, as previously noted, I was the founding director. Insofar as the Annotation did not make a distinction concerning such psychological profiles, it would seem that these efforts also fell within the scope of the ethical prohibition – a matter of considerable concern to me.

As a consequence of the unresolved questions in this area, the APA appointed a task force on "The Psychiatrist as Psychohistorian," lumping together within its purview the psychological profiles developed by U.S. government security agencies as well as psychohistories and psychobiographies.

In the course of examining the use and potential for abuse of psychiatric profiles, the Psychohistory Task Force carefully considered the use of profiles in national security. The report made an exception for psychiatric profiles that were prepared for the use of the government, not only indicating that they were not considered unethical, but also singling them out as positively contributing to the national welfare. The task force determined that profiles of significant international figures could be helpful – and were in fact necessary in some cases – to the national interest. They made positive reference to the profile "The Mind of Adolf Hitler" prepared during World War II by psychoanalyst

Walter Langer at the request of Bill Donovan, the director of the Office of Strategic Services, the predecessor organization to the CIA.[d]

This judgment was of great comfort to me in my national security role, but provided no comfort when I assumed my position as director of the Political Psychology Program at the Elliott School of International Affairs at the George Washington University. There, part of my role was to contribute to the national dialogue from the perspective of political psychology, as exemplified by my testimony concerning Saddam Hussein.

Thus, on several occasions when I believed I had something useful to contribute, I did not, constrained by the ethical canon. One such occasion, which I continue to regret, was the FBI siege of the Branch Davidian compound in Waco, Texas, in 1993. Based on a profile of David Koresh by an FBI consulting psychologist who had judged Koresh to be a psychopath, the FBI employed a strategy of increasing escalation of pressure, with sound bombardment and flashing lights going around the clock. I had been following Koresh for several years, and I had come to see him, like many charismatic cult leaders, as a narcissistic borderline. I was concerned that these FBI tactics could drive him "over the border" and lead him to seek martyrdom. I was interviewed by Sam Donaldson on ABC's *Prime Time Live,* and, although I expressed concern about the possibly counterproductive effects of the FBI tactics, I did not provide my at-a-distance personality profile assessment of David Koresh, which would have given substance to my concerns.

Troubled by the constraints posed by overly broad ethical guidance, I sought an audience with the APA ethics committee. Although they reassured me that they considered my contributions to be positive and not ethical violations, they suggested that I formally seek guidance from the committee in terms of submitting a question.

So, in 2008, I submitted the following question:

Question: Does the ethical prohibition embodied in Section 7, Paragraph 3 of the Annotations apply to psychologically informed leadership studies based on careful research that do not specify a clinical diagnosis and are designed to enhance public and governmental understanding?

This is the response, which is now included in the commentary designed to clarify ambiguities:

Answer: The psychological profiling of historical figures designed to enhance public and governmental understanding of these individuals does not conflict with the ethical principals outlined in Section 7, Paragraph 3, as long as the psychological profiling

---

[d] A detailed history of the manner in which the U.S. government has employed leader personality studies, beginning with the pioneering work of Walter Langer, is found in my chapter "The Use of Personality Studies in Support of Government Policy," in *The Psychological Assessment of Political Leaders, With Profiles of Saddam Hussein and Bill Clinton,* Jerrold Post (ed.), Ann Arbor: University of Michigan Press, 1993a.

does not include a clinical diagnosis and is the product of scholarly research that has been subject to peer review and academic scrutiny, and is based on relevant standards of scholarship.[11]

For many years, a book on the topic of narcissism and politics has been percolating within me. I believe narcissistic traits are associated with many of the behaviors of political leaders, especially those contradictory behaviors that highlight a contrast between words and deeds. I believe that these behaviors are consistent with narcissistic traits and that a book on this topic will be of great interest to the well-educated public. Knowing of my interest in narcissism and politics, Stanley Renshon, a distinguished presidential scholar, during his service as the editor of *Political Psychology*, invited me to write a review article on "Current Concepts of Narcissism: Implications for Political Psychology,"[12] but I felt constrained from writing a comprehensive book on this topic by the overly broad ethical prohibitions in the Canons of Ethics. However, with the clarifying answer provided by the APA Ethics Committee just cited, I now feel able to address the pervasive influence of narcissistic personality traits on political behavior. Many political leaders will be cited as examples in this book: this does not imply that I am providing a clinical diagnosis of NPD for them, but only that the behaviors discussed would seem to reflect narcissistic personality traits.

This book is designed to explore the manner in which narcissistic personality traits are abundantly represented (indeed, overrepresented) in the world of national and international politics. It should not be so surprising, after all, that narcissism would flourish in the political environment and that narcissistic individuals would find irresistible the attractions of the public life.

After presenting two cases of narcissistic grandiosity in its extreme – individuals with delusions of grandeur – I then consider the formative influences on narcissistic personalities and explore what generates their dreams of glory. I discuss profoundly wounded individuals such as Saddam Hussein, who developed compensatory dreams of glory after a very traumatic childhood and the tendency for retaliatory narcissistic rage when those dreams of glory were shattered. I consider those leaders who were selected to be vehicles of their parents' success, whose parents had "great expectations" for their special children, such as President Woodrow Wilson and General Douglas MacArthur. Two South Asian women – Indira Gandhi, prime minister of India, and Benazir Bhutto, prime minister of Pakistan – who also followed the paths set by their parents and grandparents, are then considered.

Benazir Bhutto, in particular, had a remarkably charismatic relationship with the wounded Pakistani people. Using this example, the powerful phenomenon of charismatic leader–follower relationships is examined, emphasizing the lock-and-key fit between two postures of narcissistically wounded individuals: "mirror-hungry" individuals as leaders and "ideal-hungry" individuals as followers. Distinctions are made between reparative charismatics, such as Mohandas Gandhi, Martin Luther King, and Nelson Mandela, and destructive charismatics, including Adolf Hitler, Ayatollah Khomeini, and Osama bin Laden.

This emphasizes that leaders with narcissistic personality traits have not only been associated with some of history's most violent and evil episodes, but also with some of history's most heroic moments, when remarkable leaders with self-confidence and persistence have overcome formidable obstacles to change their nation's history, whether it was Mohandas Gandhi's role in liberating India from its colonial status under the British Empire through nonviolent resistance or Martin Luther King's heroic nonconstituted leadership of the civil rights movement in the United States.

An observation that weaves a thread throughout this book is that the narcissist's surface grandiosity overlays great insecurity, which can lead to sycophantic relationships with key advisers who tell the leader what he *wants* to hear rather than what he *needs* to hear. Saddam Hussein is an important exemplar of this phenomenon. Wives can play a similar role, "for better or for worse." The concept of the wife or adviser as *selfobject*, a concept developed by psychoanalyst Heinz Kohut, is also discussed, which elaborates the manner in which narcissists do not relate to individuals around them as separate individuals but rather incorporate them within their own psychology to complete them, reassure them, and provide a sense of stability.

I then consider and illustrate narcissistic entitlement and the exceptional conscience, with a summary review of political figures who made exceptions of themselves while righteously emphasizing the necessity for maintaining exemplary moral standards while in public office. Case studies of an international exemplar of this trait, Silvio Berlusconi, and of a U.S. politician, Governor Arnold Schwarzenegger, follow.

The effects of ill health and aging on narcissistic leaders, for whom there never is enough glory, is then reviewed, including such examples as King Hussein of Jordan, the Shah of Iran, Jaafar Nimeiri of the Sudan, Israeli Prime Minister Menachem Begin, and, as the most recent example, Hugo Chávez of Venezuela.

Some narcissistic leaders who played important and heroic founding roles are unable to leave the position of leadership, leading to extremities of behavior, such as becoming "president for life." Often, such behaviors have tragic results for their nations, as exemplified by Habib Bourguiba of Tunisia and Robert Mugabe of Zimbabwe. Declaring oneself "president for life" is one way of ensuring that the throne of power is not abandoned, with the narcissistic leader holding on to life by holding on to power. Another is to seek immortality through one's progeny, as Saddam Hussein attempted to do and as North Korea's founding father, Kim Il-sung did with his son Kim Jong-il, who in turn designated his son Kim Jong-eun as his successor only after suffering a severe stroke shortly before his death. This is followed by a chapter discussing the psychological consequences of being leader by default – the "second-choice sons," which describes a group of leaders who were not their parents' first choice to bear the family honor: John F. Kennedy, Benjamin Netanyahu, Rajiv Gandhi, and Bashar al-Assad.

This book is designed to shed light on the manner in which narcissistic personality traits, overrepresented among domestic and international political leaders, can affect political behavior. It is all too easy to be hypnotized by the allure of the grandiose surface and neglect the insecurity that lies beneath. The dreams of glory that drive narcissists have been associated with some of the most heroic moments in history, but frustrated dreams of glory have also been associated with violent adventures and mass movements of hatred.

I would be remiss if I did not acknowledge with gratitude the contributions of five young scholars to this work: Ruthie Pertsis, Kristen Moody, Jessica Chaudhary, Jennifer McNamara, and Jessica Zayas. It has been a pleasure mentoring you; your research, writing, and administrative skills have enriched this study. And to the excellent team at Cambridge University Press, first Lewis Bateman, who shepherded this work through an often difficult process, to Sathishkumar Rajendran for his fine editorial touch, and to Mark Fox, for his care and discrimination in bringing the book to final production.

Notes

1. Jean Twenge et al., "Egos Inflating Over Time: A Cross-Temporal Meta-Analysis of Narcissistic Personality Inventory," *Journal of Personality,* 76:4 (2008): 875–902.
2. American Psychiatric Association, "The Principles of Medical Ethics: With Annotations Especially Applicable to Psychiatry," last modified 2009 Revised, http://www.psych.org/mainmenu/psychiatricpractice/ethics/resourcesstandards/ principlesofmedicalethics.aspx.
3. Helen Tartakoff, "The Normal Personality in Our Culture and the Nobel Prize Complex," in R. M. Loewenstein, L. M. Newman, M. Schur, and A. J. Solnit (eds.), *Psychoanalysis: A General Psychology* (New York: International Universities Press, 1966), 222–252.
4. "The Principles of Medical Ethics."
5. Jeremy Lazarus, "Ethical Constraints in Leadership Profiling" (prepared for the annual meeting of the American Psychiatric Association on "Psychiatric Contributions to the Study of Leadership," 1994).
6. Ibid.
7. Ibid.
8. Ibid.
9. Ibid.
10. Ibid.
11. "The Principles of Medical Ethics."
12. Jerrold Post, "Current Concepts of Narcissism: Implications for Political Psychology," *Political Psychology,* 14:1 (1993b): 99–121.

I

Narcissism in Full Bloom

Mirror, mirror on the wall
Who is the fairest of them all?

Who can forget the look of murderous rage distorting the face of the Wicked Queen in Walt Disney's remarkable animation of the classic fairy tale "Snow White" when she looks in the mirror after asking this question in her daily ritual of reassurance and, instead of her own face, sees reflected the image of the even more beautiful Snow White? The popularity of this fairy tale reflects the universality of a theme central to political psychology: the narcissistic ruler clinging to power who is threatened by pretenders to the throne. Reflecting the ruler's underlying insecurity, Arthur Feiner,[1] in an especially insightful contribution to the volume *Narcissism and the Interpersonal Self*, mischievously notes and archly asks in his parenthetical to the epigraph that introduces both his and this chapter, "Maybe, it's you, oh beautiful queen, but Madam, why do you think you need to ask?"[2]

A fatal example of this dynamic is reflected in the life of serial bomber Theodore Kaczynski. The target of one of the FBI's most costly investigations, Kaczynski became known to that agency as UNABOM (*UN*iversity and *A*irline *BOM*ber), and, until his identity was eventually discovered, he was popularly known as the Unabomber. Intellectually precocious and mathematically gifted but a social isolate because of his obvious intellectual gifts and peculiar interpersonal style, Kaczynski skipped several grades in school, which served to isolate him further from his peers. His passage through school was characterized by a major imbalance between prodigious intellectual gifts and a major deficit in interpersonal skills. He has been described as a mathematical genius and an emotional cripple. At age 10, he took with him on a family camping vacation a book entitled *Romping through Mathematics from Addition to Calculus*.

In high school, Kaczynski experimented with explosives, and he was regarded by his peers as alien, a nerd, and was ignored. He was teased and isolated. According to media interviews with classmates, "He wasn't in our world. He was in his own world." "He was never seen as a person. He was seen as a *walking brain.*"

Kaczynski graduated high school at 15 and entered Harvard at the age of 16, where he majored in mathematics. There, he was considered a "wonk." On the one occasion when he attempted to ask a young woman out on a date, it was so clumsily done that he was rejected out of hand.

In 1962, he began graduate studies in mathematics at the University of Michigan, receiving his doctorate in 1967 and winning the prize for the outstanding dissertation. One teacher said that only two or three people in the world were capable of understanding the concepts he was exploring. Interestingly – and tellingly – an unusual feature of his dissertation was the absence of any acknowledgment of the role of mentors.

In 1967, he became an assistant professor of mathematics at the University of California at Berkeley. At the time, Berkeley was in the midst of social ferment and student activism, but Kaczynski did not seem to notice, remaining totally preoccupied with his mathematics. He seemed to be on the fast track to tenure, publishing several important articles. He was considered gifted but was totally unavailable to his students, and he resigned abruptly in 1969, at the age of 26.

After living for several years with his family, who supported him financially, in the summer of 1971, he moved into a remote cabin in Montana, one without electricity or running water, to lead an ascetic, schizoid lifestyle. There, he apparently became increasingly obsessed with the desecration of the wilderness by the encroachment of modern society. Totally isolated, he had withdrawn into himself, and the manifesto on which he privately labored was his attempt to make sense of a world from which he was increasingly alienated. He had made his own personal struggle the basis of an ideology that he was going to force on society.

As revealed later, in what came to be known as the "Unabomber Manifesto," a 50-page essay on *Industrial Society and Its Future*, Kaczynski came to see the need to bring down the techno-industrial system and believed that violent collapse was the only way to accomplish this. The industrial system, as he saw it, was "robbing individuals of their autonomy, reducing their rapport with nature, and becoming increasingly remote from the natural pattern of human behavior."[3] Nothing less than a revolution against technology was called for.

In 1978, Kaczynski's lethal psychological development led to the creation of his first homemade bomb, sent to a materials engineering professor at Northwestern University. Over the next 17 years, he made a series of increasingly sophisticated bombs that killed 3 Americans and injured 24 more.

But, until 1995, there was no written message designed to inflict terror on the public, no ideological motivation expressed. He was the primary and most important audience for his own disordered thoughts and deeds. He thus was not a terrorist, seeking to inflict terror on a broader audience through violence or the threat of violence designed to accomplish a religious, ideological, or political goal through fear or intimidation. There was no sense-making message accompanying these missives. Until 1995, Kaczynski was not a terrorist – he was a serial bomber, successfully eluding authorities as he carried on his deadly, but private, campaign.

I summarized my understanding of Kaczynski in the political personality profile I prepared at the request of *The Washington Post* in June 1995, after Kaczynski's 35,000-word manifesto was delivered to its offices.[a,4] Like the Wicked Queen in Snow White, each day, Theodore Kaczynski looked into his metaphorical mirror (he did not have one in his remote cabin) and asked,

> Mirror, mirror on the wall
> Who is the most dangerous serial bomber of them all?

His most important audience was himself. And each day, like the Wicked Queen, he was reassured to see his own image and hear the answer, "You are, Unabomber." How he exulted in outwitting the authorities in his serial bomb spree! The tenor of the notes accompanying his bombs conveyed a mocking arrogance, a superiority over the FBI, which he tauntingly characterized as incompetent. "How superior I am," he seemed to convey, "being able to thwart the entire law enforcement establishment! How powerful I am!"

Kaczynski sent no bombs between 1987 and 1993. In considering this hiatus, the FBI speculated that perhaps UNABOM was burning out. But with the explosive event of February 26, 1993 – grim augury of September 11, 2001 – this was all to change.

On February 26, 1993, the first World Trade Center attack occurred when a truck bomb was detonated below the North Tower. A 1,500-pound fertilizer bomb was intended to knock the North Tower into the South Tower, bringing them both down and killing thousands of people. Had it been placed closer to the World Trade Center's concrete foundation, the plan might have succeeded. As it was, it killed 6 people and injured 1,042.

The attack was all too quickly forgotten by the American people, armed as they were with their characteristic sense of denial that "It can't happen here." But it was not ignored by the Unabomber. It seems likely that Kaczynski was challenged by the World Trade Center bombing and needed to act to regain his position as the most feared bomber in the land because, in June 1993, he resumed his letter bomb campaign.

But a date of even greater significance for the Unabomber was April 19, 1995, the day of the massive explosion of the Alfred P. Murrah Federal Building in

---

[a,4] The profile was prepared as background information to assist *The Washington Post* in its decision on whether to publish Kaczysnki's manifesto. The profile was later published in *Psychiatric Times* after Kaczysnki's identity was revealed.

Oklahoma City, causing the loss of 168 lives, including 19 children, and injuring more than 680. Three hundred twenty-four buildings within a 16-block radius were severely damaged or destroyed, causing more than $652 million in damages. Timothy McVeigh was arrested within 90 minutes of the explosion and identified as the prime suspect on April 20. And on April 20, when Theodore Kaczynski asked his customary question of the mirror,

> Mirror, mirror on the wall
> Who's the most dangerous bomber of them all?

the devastating answer came back: "Timothy McVeigh."

The third week in April 1995 was a week of prodigious activity for the Unabomber, a week that marked a major departure from his previous pattern. On April 24, the president of the California Forestry Association was killed opening a mail bomb. That same day, the Unabomber wrote a letter to the *New York Times* indicating that if it or another "respectable" periodical would publish his manifesto, he would desist from terrorism. This was taking the academic dictum "publish or perish" to a new level. Demonstrating a precise turn of mind, in his letter, he distinguished between terrorism and sabotage, characterizing terrorism as "actions motivated by a desire to influence the development of a society and intended to cause injury or death to human beings." In contrast, sabotage was characterized as "similarly motivated actions intended to destroy property without injuring human beings." The Unabomber clarified that "the promise we offer is to desist from terrorism. We reserve the right to engage in sabotage."[5]

ANDERS BREIVIK OF NORWAY: FOLLOWING THE PATH OF THE UNABOMBER

The Unabomber Manifesto was to be the basis for "2083: A European Declaration of Independence," a rambling 1,500-page document posted online by Anders Breivik just before he carried out his murderous rampage on July 2011.

On Friday, July 22, 2011, 32-year-old Anders Behring Breivik, disguised as a policeman, coldly and calculatedly perpetrated a deadly attack in Oslo by detonating a bomb outside the Norwegian prime minister's office, killing 8 and wounding 26. He then carried out a murderous rampage at a political youth camp on Utoya Island organized by the youth division of the ruling Norwegian Labor Party, killing 69.

Breivik preceded the bloody twin attacks by publishing online hours earlier a rambling 1,500-page manifesto focusing on the year, entitled "2083: A European Declaration of Independence." The author identified 2083 as the date when the author believed a European civil war would end with the execution of cultural Marxists and the deportation of Muslims (2083 is the 200th anniversary of the death of Karl Marx). According to the Norwegian anti-Islamic citizen journalist website *Document.no*, to which Breivik frequently contributed, "large parts of the Manifesto are copied directly from 'Unabomber' Ted Kaczynski's own manifesto, with minor changes such as replacement of the word 'leftist' by the phrase 'cultural Marxist' or 'multi-culturalist.'"[6] Detailing the plagiarism, Kristen Wyatt, writing in the *Huffington Post*, compares, as an example, this passage from the Unabomber's manifesto in which he lambasts leftist "feelings of inferiority" with an almost identical passage in Breivik's manifesto: "One of the most widespread manifestations of the craziness of our world is leftism, so a discussion of the psychology of leftism can serve as an introduction to the discussion of the problems of modern society in general." Breivik wrote: "One of the most widespread manifestations of the craziness of our world is multiculturalism, so a discussion of the psychology of multiculturalism can serve as an introduction to the problems of Western Europe in general."[7] There are numerous passages in which Breivik substitutes "multiculturalism" or "cultural Marxism" for "leftism." In addition, Breivik's manifesto had a section entitled "Documenting EU's Deliberate Strategy to Islamise Europe."

The manifesto begins with an entry for April/May 2002, in which Breivik identifies himself as a Knight Templar. In particular, he claims to have been "ordinated as the 8th Justiciar Knight for the PCCTS, Knights Templar Europe," the "resistance movement" that, in other parts of his manifesto, he claims was established to combat the "Islamisation" of Europe. "Our primary objective is to develop PCCTS, Knights Templar, into becoming the foremost conservative revolutionary movement in Western Europe [in] the next few decades."[8] Breivik saw himself as "the point of the spear" of Christian resistance against the Islamisation of Europe and indicated that there were tens of thousands throughout Europe to whose feelings he was giving voice. Breivik criticized his government for permitting "thousands of Muslims to stream in each year through the asylum, institutions or family connections in Norway."[9] He saw himself as protecting Christian European values against Muslims, Marxists, and multiculturalists, and, in effect, anyone different. The editor of the website on which the manifesto was posted, Hans Rustad, surmised that Breivik hoped the document would become "an organ of a cultural conservative revival."[10]

The event had long been prepared for: in his manifesto, Breivik indicated that he had undertaken a period of fund-raising between 2002 and 2006. He spent 2006–2008 researching and writing his manifesto, then moved into the next phase. In July 2010, Breivik wrote that he had "successfully finished the armor acquisition phase."[11]

Breivik's father, a diplomat, divorced Breivik's mother when his son was one year old. There was little contact between father and son in the intervening years – an annual visit – but the relationship broke down completely when Anders was a teenager and was arrested for spray-painting graffiti. There had been no contact since. When Breivik was four, social welfare workers considered removing Breivik from his home because of his disturbed behavior. As a boy, he was quiet but friendly, but was the victim of bullying.

In his writing, Breivik extrapolates from his own experiences and deplores the decline of the family: "To truly reverse the decline of the family, the momentum must be carried forward to confront the current matriarchal policies that have institutionalized 'broken family' policies. Our current system produces broken families and prevents traditional norms based on discipline." He goes on to decry the feminization of boys by a dominant maternal influence. "I do not approve of the super-liberal, matriarchal upbringing as it completely lacked discipline and has contributed to feminizing me to a certain degree." According to a boyhood friend, Breivik did not have any girlfriends and never dated. Interestingly, although his father in many ways abandoned him early in life and had very little contact with his son, it was his mother who Breivik blamed. He extends the lessons from his childhood to all of Western Europe, insisting that the father/patriarch must be given considerably more influence because this is the only way to ensure the survival of the nuclear family and enhance family integrity: "This matriarchal supremacy within the modern households must cease to exist." After this diatribe, remarkably, he then says: "I consider myself privileged and I feel I have had a privileged upbringing. . . . I haven't really had any negative experiences in my childhood in any way."

As a teenager, Breivik exercised compulsively and took steroids to aid his bodybuilding efforts. He expressed no apparent interest in the world of politics at that time. It was apparently in his late 20s that Breivik turned to right-wing extremism, joining a neo-Nazi group. In his first statement after his 2011 arrest, Breivik, through his lawyer, stated that the attacks were "atrocious, but necessary"[12] to defeat liberal immigration policies and the spread of Islam. The court-appointed psychiatrists found that Breivik was suffering from paranoid schizophrenia and recommended that he be confined to a mental hospital.

At his February 6 preliminary hearing, Breivik was visibly upset with this diagnosis, denying that he was mentally ill and instead asserting that he should be awarded a medal of valor for his heroic leadership against the Islamisation of Christian Europe. At the hearing, he claimed that his bombing attack in Oslo and subsequent murderous rampage at the Norwegian Labor Party youth camp were designed as a "preventive attack on traitors,"[13] and he pleaded self-defense on behalf of his culture. The Labor-led government, which he blamed for the "deconstruction of Norwegian culture," was also blamed for promoting the "Islamic colonization of Norway." "Ethnic Norwegians will become the minority in ten years. Indigenous people subject to genocide have the right to defend themselves," he claimed. It should be noted that both his parents supported the policies of the Norwegian Labor Party, the object of his violent attack.

That he was held to be criminally insane angered Breivik. His self-designated narcissistic title as 8th Justiciar Knight for the PCCTS, Knights Templar Europe was far grander than the broken, isolated life he was leading. By labeling him criminally insane, Breivik was denied the compensatory grandiose reality he had created. Instead, his dreams of glory were identified as a delusional psychotic symptom. He was angered by the psychiatric diagnosis because it had deprived his murderous acts of meaning.

On April 10, 2012, a second forensic psychiatric assessment report made at the request of the family of his victims was released, contradicting the initial assessment that he was suffering from paranoid schizophrenia and finding him sane. During the investigation, it emerged that Breivik had considered detonating a bomb in the square next to Oslo City Hall during the 2008 Nobel Peace Prize ceremony for Barack Obama. Because of security, the attack would have been largely symbolic, but, with hundreds of millions watching, he believed it would have been a perfect way to promote his anti-Islamic message and ensure his international prominence as a leader of the crusade to preserve Christian Europe.

In his mind's eye or, perhaps more accurately, in his grandiose mind's "I," Breivik was a hero, deserving of a medal for his dramatic leadership role in calling international attention to the dangers of the Islamisation of Europe. In fact, investigations found no evidence of a group or organization supporting Breivik; instead, he apparently was acting entirely on his own, despite claiming that he represented tens of thousands of Christian Europeans. His legions of followers existed entirely in his mind. His paranoid delusion of grandeur – that he headed the Knights Templar Europe in their resistance against the Muslim invasion – was far grander than his bleak reality.

Breivik was relieved that he had been declared sane by the second forensic psychiatric team. In a letter he sent to the Norwegian tabloid *Verdans Gang*, he declared that to be sent to a psychiatric ward would be a "fate worse than death. ... To send a political activist to an asylum is more sadistic and more evil than killing him."[14] Now, he said, he would have his day in court, where the two contradictory evaluations would both be entered into evidence, and he could use the legal platform to again proclaim his grandiose self-assigned role in protecting Christian Europe against Muslim colonization.

In his statement at the original November 2011 hearing, Breivik portrayed himself as a resistance leader, as "the commander" of a Norwegian resistance movement before the judge cut him off. Forensic psychiatrist James L. Knoll IV[15] characterized Breivik as a "pseudo-commando." Citing Park Dietz's 1986 article, "Mass, Serial, and Sensational Homicides," he observed that the term "pseudo-commando" was first used to describe the type of mass murderer who plans his actions "after long deliberation" and who kills indiscriminately in public during the daytime. Such individuals have the intent to die "in a blaze of glory" and have made no escape plans. These individuals are "injustice collectors" who are driven by strong feelings of anger against the system and seek revenge.[16] They then externalize their self-hatred and identify an external enemy who must be destroyed. In the process, the fragmented self has been reassembled as an exalted avenger, leader of a collective quest for revenge.

This was true of both Breivik and Kaczynski: in addition to their strong paranoid traits, they also possessed powerful narcissistic traits, especially grandiosity. Their individual internal distress had been transformed into a grand crusade of which they were leaders, and, in carrying out this now exalted revenge mission, they sought honor and came to believe that their violent acts would bring them fame and glory. Knoll observes that, after his capture, Breivik requested that he be evaluated by Japanese forensic specialists because "the Japanese understand the concept of honor better than the Europeans."[17]

Breivik had for the most part withdrawn from society into the dark crevices of his mind. His estranged father declared that "I couldn't believe my eyes. It was totally paralyzing, and I couldn't really understand it.... He must live in another world."[18] He indicated that, with the exception of one phone call, he had had no contact with his son since 1995. "I don't feel like his father. How could he just stand there and kill so many people and just seem to think that what he did was OK? He should have taken his own life too. That's what he should have done.... I will have to live with this shame for the rest of my life. People will always link me with him," he bitterly declared.

On August 24, convicted of killing 77 victims, Breivik was sentenced to 21 years in prison. Showing not an iota of remorse, Breivik apologized to Christian militants, expressing regret that he had not killed more. He entered court on the 24th making a fascist salute, his right fist clenched, and smiled when the verdict was announced.

If Breivik had for the most part withdrawn from the world around him, Kaczynski had totally withdrawn, having essentially no contact with other human beings since 1971 and living in a remote cabin in Montana, with no power or heat. He had withdrawn into himself, leaving behind what he believed to be a hostile rejecting world. He was not simply paranoid: he felt socially persecuted by a world into which he did not fit because of his own social peculiarities. More profound than rejection, he was simply ignored. But his violent actions ensured that the world would ignore him no longer.

FREUD'S EARLY CONCEPT OF PSYCHOSIS AS TOTAL NARCISSISTIC WITHDRAWAL INTO THE SELF

As Sigmund Freud conceptualized it in his libido theory, in individuals like Kaczynski and Breivik, the psychological energy invested in the world of people, the world of objects, is redirected and totally absorbed into the self. In the Greek myth of Narcissus, the source of Freud's clinical term *narcissism*, the youth Narcissus becomes totally transfixed by the beautiful image of himself reflected in the still waters of a pond. Besotted with (self) love, he cannot tear his eyes away:

> Am I the lover
> Or beloved? Then why make love? Since I
> Am what I long for, then my riches are
> So great they make me poor.   (Ovid, AD 8)

There is a total loss of boundaries between the world and the self: the individual so self-absorbed becomes his own entire universe. Freud[19] considers the psychology of the totally self-absorbed person, the patient with schizophrenia, who

seems really to have withdrawn his libido from people, and things in the external world without replacing them by others in fantasy. ... The question arises: What happens to the libido which has been withdrawn from external objects in schizophrenia? The megalomania of these states points the way. ... The libido that has been withdrawn from the external world has been directed to the ego, and thus gives rise to an attitude which may be called *narcissism*.[20]

In his classic analysis of the paranoid illness of the distinguished jurist Daniel Paul Schreber, Freud characterized Schreber as being "under the influence of visions" that, in Schreber's own words, "were partly of a terrifying character but partly too of an indescribable grandeur."[21] Convinced of "the imminence of a great catastrophe," as his paranoid illness peaked, he came to believe that this catastrophe had occurred and that he was the only man left alive, thus projecting his own psychological disintegration onto the entire world. He then developed the restitutive delusion that God had given him the mission of saving the world from annihilation and recreating Eden, a delusion of messianic grandiosity of cosmic scope, an expression of the ultimate narcissism.[22]

It is the breakdown of the narcissistic defensive armor that leads to psychosis. The feeling of lack of control, of being overwhelmed by powerful emotions is overwhelming. Grotstein[23] has likened this inner turmoil to the black holes in the universe hypothesized by astrophysicists. In the physical universe, these black holes, so called because they emit no light, have such extraordinary density and such powerful gravity that they swallow up everything in their paths. Grotstein, who characterizes man as "meaning-obsessed," describes the terror of experiencing psychological disintegration of the self as a psychological black hole. It is dissolution into nothingness, into a state of meaninglessness. So overwhelming is this terror of meaningless that man is impelled to make meaning, to create compensatory delusions, as Schreber did.

It is almost a hydraulic model that Freud employs as an analogy in characterizing increasing narcissism, the physical model of a U-shaped tube: as the libido is withdrawn from the world of objects, it flows into the self. Like Narcissus, in withdrawing from the external world, the narcissist is so consumed with self-love that there is no psychological energy left to love or connect with others. This explains the failure of empathy characteristically observed in narcissistic persons. Love, in this way of thinking, as Freud would have it, is a zero-sum game. Neat! But wrong.[b] For, as numerous

---

[b] The psychohistorian Peter Loewenberg (1988) has observed the importance of the evolutionary shift from libidinal-drive theory, Freud's earliest formulations, to ego psychological and object relations paradigms in applying psychoanalysis to history and biography.

psychoanalytic scholars have taken pains to point out, self-love is a requisite for love of others.[c]

The relationship between Ted Kaczynski's paranoid world and that of narcissism is not readily apparent. After all, Kaczynski was diagnosed as a paranoid schizophrenic and is now confined to a hospital for the criminally insane. The disparity between his prodigious intellectual gifts and his interpersonal peculiarities led some to raise the question of whether he did not suffer from Asperger's syndrome, considered part of the autistic spectrum. But even though there are genetic and psychobiological roots to Kaczynski's psychotic illness, nevertheless, the resultant disordered thoughts and feelings are organized in the mind.

Paranoid feelings of narcissistic grandiosity and persecution are intended to overcome an inner sense of inferiority, unworthiness, and unlovability. What could be more important, after all, than to be the center of a plot, in contrast to the ignominy of being ignored and insignificant? Thus, paranoia can be considered a primitive form of narcissistic pathology. The narcissistic triad consists of (1) narcissistic entitlement, which inevitably leads to (2) disappointment and disillusionment, which in turn produces (3) retaliatory rage due to the rejection of the "entitlement." This rage is strongly associated with the frustration of narcissistic entitlement and insatiable narcissistic needs.[24] We discuss narcissistic rage in greater detail in Chapter 2.

A clinical example may be helpful to illustrate the compensatory value of paranoia, referred to as the "restitutive" function of delusions. During my service in the National Institute of Mental Health unit in Saint Elizabeth's Hospital in Washington, D.C., I was responsible for clinically evaluating the so-called White House cases, those individuals who tried to break into the White House, the symbol of ultimate power to the powerless, to determine whether their acts were the product of mental illness and, if so, if the patient should be confined in a locked or an open ward.

An unemployed man was apprehended by the U.S. Secret Service when he tried to gain access to the White House by driving his white pickup truck through the White House gates – a direct approach to be sure – and he was sent to Saint E's for evaluation. From social services, we learned that he had been fired the day before as a dishwasher (which takes a certain amount of application). In our

---

[c] In his 1947 *Man for Himself*, Erich Fromm observes that "Selfishness and self-love, far from being identical, are actually opposite . . . the selfish person does not love himself too much, but too little; in fact he hates himself . . . it is true that selfish persons are incapable of loving others, for they are not capable of loving themselves either" (p. 131). Thus, the selfish person, the self-absorbed person, does not love himself too much but too little! Indeed, the façade of self-love masks what is truly underneath – self-hatred.

Narcissism can be viewed as a pattern of defense of the fragile self. The pathology of narcissism is tied up with the pathology of the self, especially with the regulation of self-esteem (Bacciagaluppi, 1993). Freud characterized narcissism as a quality of "perfection" (1914, p. 94). Anything that threatens that perfection must be defended against at all costs, which is the theme of Arnold Rothstein's 1980 *The Narcissistic Pursuit of Perfection*.

interview, he haughtily indicated at the onset that he was King of the World. He knew this, he explained, because a black cloud was following him wherever he went. "And why," I asked, "were you trying to get into the White House?" Barely able to conceal his impatience at this unnecessary question when the answer should have been self-evident, he explained that the White House was the seat of power and that was where his throne was. I indicated that this made sense to me, but that there was a problem: someone else was already sitting on the throne.

"You mean, Mr. Johnson?," he queried. (This event occurred during the Lyndon Johnson presidency.)

"Right," I responded, "and I get the sense he kind of likes sitting on that throne. I mean, he was elected, after all. So, what would you do?"

"Well," he said, "I would explain to him he would have to move over, because he was only the president and I was the King."

"But what if he wouldn't be persuaded?" I continued.

"If necessary," he said, his voice dropping to a chilling tone, "I would persuade him with force." At that moment, I was convinced that he needed to be on the locked ward.

Like the protagonist in *The Little Prince*, the 1943 novella by French aviator Antoine Saint-Exupery, the narcissist lives in splendid isolation. The little prince lives on an asteroid where he discovers a rose, which he believes is quite unique, only to weep inconsolably when he discovers on a subsequent visit to Earth that it is, in fact, rather commonplace. So, too, the consummate narcissist believes he or she is quite unique in this world, occupying a place at once quite splendid but dreadfully lonely.

The narcissist's exaggerated sense of self-importance tends to be manifested as extreme self-centeredness, egocentricity, and self-absorption. Abilities and achievements tend to be unrealistically overestimated, but setbacks can give a sense of special unworthiness. There is a preoccupation with fantasies involving unrealistic goals. These goals may include achieving unlimited power, wealth, brilliance, beauty, or fame. These fantasies frequently substitute for realistic activity in pursuit of success. Even satisfying these goals is usually not enough. There is a constant search for admiration and attention and more concern with appearance than substance.

The certainty of ultimate success, to which narcissists feel entitled, leads to both a sense of omnipotence and a feeling of invulnerability, a sense that they cannot go wrong. This underlies the narcissist's capacity for risk-taking; he behaves as if someone is watching over him, as if divine protection or a charmed fate will ensure his success and well-being. But under this surface appearance of the narcissist – vain, arrogant, egocentric – lies a sea of insecurity, empty and void.

In the Preface, I took pains to emphasize that the subject matter of this volume is the relationship between narcissism and politics, that individuals with significant narcissistic personality traits are inevitably drawn to the world of politics, like a moths to a flame. But, especially in democratic societies, individuals displaying the full gamut of narcissistic traits, whose personalities reflect a thorough self-oriented narcissistic organization, the narcissistic personality disorder (NPD), rarely succeed in sustaining effective leadership. Although initially they can be quite charming and persuasive, inevitably the fact that their basic loyalty is to themselves shines through. Having said that, NPD can be seen as an exaggerated version of the narcissism of everyday life. So, the distinction between full-blown narcissism and the narcissism of everyday life is not as great as it appears.[d]

Accordingly, the full-blown characteristics of NPD, as described in the *Diagnostic and Statistical Manual of Mental Disorders* (DSM) of the American Psychiatric Association, are presented here to illuminate narcissism in full. But this should not be taken to imply that the political leaders described in this volume are being diagnosed as suffering from NPD.

The description of the NPD in the DSM captures the essential features of this character disorder:

> a grandiose sense of self-importance or uniqueness, e.g. exaggeration of achievements and talents, focus on the special nature of one's problems; preoccupation with fantasies of unlimited success, power, brilliance, beauty or ideal love; exhibitionistic need for constant attention and admiration; cool indifference or marked feelings of rage, inferiority, shame, humiliation, or emptiness in response to criticism, indifference of others, or defeat; and troubled interpersonal relationships, characterized by a lack of empathy, interpersonal exploitiveness, a sense of entitlement or expectation of special favors, and a tendency to fluctuate between extremes of idealization and devaluation.
>
> (American Psychiatric Association, 1980, p. 317)

The overall description of NPD in the fourth edition of the DSM (DSM-IV, currently undergoing revision) is of "a pervasive pattern of grandiosity (in fantasy or behavior), need for admiration, and lack of empathy, beginning in early adulthood and present in a variety of contexts, as indicated by five (or more) of the following:

1. has a grandiose sense of self-importance (e.g., exaggerates achievements and talents, expects to be recognized as superior without commensurate achievements)
2. is preoccupied with fantasies of unlimited success, power, brilliance, beauty, or ideal love
3. believes that he or she is 'special' and can only be understood by, or should associate with, other special or high status people (or institutions)

---

[d] As Fred Alford (1988) has emphasized, "There is a presumption shared by most psychoanalytic theorists that there is a continuum between pathological and normal narcissism, and that even the most extreme manifestations of pathological narcissism are not entirely alien to normal narcissists, ... [and that] pathological narcissism illuminates normal narcissism" (p. 70). Kernberg (1975) has observed that he, too, sees a continuity between normal and pathological narcissism.

4. requires excessive admiration
5. has a sense of entitlement, i.e. unreasonable expectations of especially favorable treatment or automatic compliance with his or her expectations
6. is interpersonally exploitative, i.e. takes advantage of others to achieve his or her own ends
7. lacks empathy, is unwilling to recognize or identify with the feelings and needs of others
8. is often envious of others, or believes that others are envious of him or her
9. shows arrogant, haughty behaviors or attitudes."

(American Psychiatric Association, DSM IV, 1994, p. 661)

At the extremity of the personality disorder here summarized, it would be difficult for an individual to provide sustained leadership to an organization or a democratic society.

But to be narcissistic is not necessarily to be ill. Some of the traits described here, in moderate degree, can be quite appealing. To a public looking for leadership, self-confidence and optimism is quite appealing, but not when this is conveyed as arrogance.[e]

There is a spectrum of narcissistic personality features. Many of the qualities summarized in the DSM-IV would seem to lend themselves to the political arena. Or, to put it differently, the political arena provides a magnetic attraction to individuals who seek to be in the limelight, to be admired, and to be considered special.

Is the wish to be special and the object of admiration necessarily pathological, or can it not be considered as combining extreme self-confidence and ambition? Vamik Volkan (1976; 1980; 1981; 1982; Volkan and Itkowitz, 1984)[25] has made major contributions to the psychoanalytic literature on narcissism and is a pioneer in applying psychoanalytic concepts of narcissism to the study of leadership. He has emphasized some of the apparent paradoxes in the manner in which the narcissist presents him- or herself to the world. Volkan describes the individual with narcissistic personality organization as

regarding himself as endowed with great power, physical appeal, and the right to assert his will. He gives the impression of ambitiously striving for brilliance in all he does. He seems to regard others – especially those not among his worshippers – as beneath notice. Although he views his supporters as adjuncts to himself, he is quick to deny their existence if they withdraw their awestruck allegiance. Behaving as though self-sufficient in a superior way, he feels that he exists for others to admire. Nevertheless, close scrutiny of the behavior of such a person will reveal that, although he lives a glorious albeit lonely life in such isolation that he could be said to dwell within a "plastic or glass bubble," he is, paradoxically, constantly engaged with others on another level because he

---

[e] Kohut makes a particular point of emphasizing a distinct and separate narcissistic course of personality development that can lead to psychologically healthy narcissistic individuals (Kohut, 1971; 1977). This represents one of the central differences between the theoretical foundations of Kohut's self-psychology and the theoretical foundation of the work of Otto Kernberg, another major scholar of narcissism, who considers all narcissism pathological.

is object-hungry. He actually has feelings of inferiority and thus is overdependent on the approving attention of other people.[26]

In reflecting on the ubiquity of narcissism, Christopher Lasch, in his important 1979 social commentary *The Culture of Narcissism*, described the essence of narcissism as characterized by vanity, exhibitionism, arrogance, grandiosity, and self-absorption. But under that surface of arrogance and grandiosity lies profound self-doubt. Betraying his inner uncertainty, the narcissist looks to others for confirmation of his worth: "The other person tends to be used to make the narcissist feel good, and well-being depends upon receiving a continuously adequate quantity of positive regard."[27] This need for constant reassurance is an insatiable demand for the narcissistic person.[f]

This disturbance of interpersonal relations is central to Heinz Kohut's self-psychology. The primary function of individuals in the narcissist's personal surround is to shore up his or her self-esteem, to provide reassurance for the fragile self. The significant other serves, in Kohut's terms, as a *selfobject*. The *selfobject* completes the famished self of the narcissist.

But this is a one-way street, and the narcissist, in turn, does not see those around him as human beings with their own needs and feelings. They are there to reassure the narcissist of his worth, and when they no longer serve that function, they can be dropped precipitously, no matter how many years they loyally served, a reflection of the failure of empathy of the narcissist.[g]

---

[f] In his discussion of the interpersonal problems associated with narcissism, Fiscalini (1993, pp. 62–64) observes that this was anticipated by Karen Horney in her 1939 book *New Ways in Psychoanalysis*: "Narcissistic trends are frequent in our culture. More often than not people are incapable of true friendship and love; they are egocentric ... they feel insecure and tend to overrate their personal significance; *they lack judgment of their own value because they have relegated it to others*" (p. 98; emphasis added). Harry Stack Sullivan comments on the manner in which grandiosity serves as a defense against underlying insecurity, guarding against "invidious comparison" with others who are contented and successful. He particularly emphasizes the hostility toward the interpersonal surround: "The hostile performance is in essence an accelerating spiral of desperate attempts to prop up a steadily undermined security with the result that the patient is more and more detested and avoided ... he hates himself so much, being unable to be what he claims to be" (Mullahy, 1952, pp. 138–139).

   Thus, the grandiosity is an illusion, fragile and easily pierced to reveal the underlying insecurity. Fromm, too, emphasizes the threat posed by interpersonal relationships, in a manner that presages the *selfobject* concept of Kohut: "For the narcissistic person, the partner is never a person in his own right or in his full reality; he exists only as a shadow of the partner's narcissistically inflated ego" (1964, p. 107).

[g] Since Freud's seminal 1914 article, psychoanalysis and its treatment of narcissism has evolved along multiple paths. Attention to the self and its disorders were addressed as early as the 1920s by Harry Stack Sullivan, Karen Horney, and Eric Fromm. Building on the pioneering explorations of Melanie Klein in the 1930s, the British Object Relations School, with leading exponents D. W. Winnicott and H. Guntrip, was centrally concerned with the self, as was the American Object Relations School, with Otto Kernberg a leading figure. The Self-Psychology School, whose central figure was Heinz Kohut, elaborated the importance of the *selfobject*. An important

Hundreds of books and thousands of articles on the arcane, nuanced differences among these schools of thought and their implications for psychoanalytic theory and treatment have been published. This book will not conduct a Talmudic examination of these differences: if narcissism is a jewel, then each of these theoretical approaches is a related but different facet through which to view it. This book understands narcissism in the broadest sense of the concept: to be concerned with high ambition and self-confidence, to possess high self-estimates to the point of dreams of glory, a need to be considered special, a tendency to be so self-absorbed as to have difficulty sustaining mutual relationships, and to also possess the fragility underlying this grandiose façade, so that when the grandiose internal dreams of glory are shattered, overwhelming shame results. The political figures examined herein are characterized by one or more of these qualities.

In surveying contemporary politics, one cannot help but be impressed with the ubiquity of narcissism in political life, which led to the observation that introduced this book: it is perhaps not too much of an exaggeration to say that if one were to strip from the ranks of political leaders those with significant narcissistic personality traits, the ranks would be perilously impoverished. Moreover, understanding what leads followers to follow also rests centrally on an understanding of narcissism and its vicissitudes. This book reviews the spectrum of linked traits that make up narcissism and examines how these traits affect political leadership, followership, and decision making, employing examples from contemporary national and international affairs.

distinction between the Self-Psychology School and the Object Relations School, emphasized here, is that for Object Relations theorists, narcissism (the schizoid position) is always considered pathological, whereas Kohut and his followers describe a healthy but separate narcissistic developmental pathway.

The Interpersonal Relations School, which emphasizes the social context in which personality develops and changes, is an important contemporary development. It stresses that the self is inevitably embedded in relational contexts. Citing the reflection of Sass (1988, p. 552) that "according to many historians, concern about the self is *the* central theme of the last several centuries of Western culture," Stephen Mitchell, a leading proponent of the Interpersonal Relations School, makes the commonsense observation that "there is no experience that is not interpersonally mediated. The meanings generated by the self are all interactive products" (1993, p. 125). Mitchell and his colleagues emphasize that one of the shortfalls of Freud's drive theory that it insufficiently called attention to the importance of the role of actual interpersonal experiences in shaping mental life; they in effect replace Freud's one-person psychology with an interpersonal psychology. Mitchell, in "The Wings of Icarus," treated narcissism as a learned pattern of integrating relationships (1986). This change of emphasis permits an integration of two apparently irreconcilable approaches, that of the Object Relations School, in which narcissism is defensive and pathological and an illusion, versus the Self-Psychology School, in which narcissism is the very basis of creativity and growth and is the growing edge of the self (Mitchell and Aron, 1999).

Notes

 1. Arthur Feiner, "The Relation of Monologue and Dialogue to Narcissistic States and Its Implications for Psychoanalytic Therapy," in John Fiscalini and Alan Grey (eds.), *Narcissism and the Interpersonal Self* (New York: Columbia University Press, 1993).
 2. Feiner, "The Relation of Monologue and Dialogue," 153.
 3. Theodore Kaczynski, "Industrial Society and Its Future," *The Washington Post*, September 19, 1995, www.washingtonpost.com/wp-srv/national/longterm/unabomber/manifesto.text.htm.
 4. Jerrold Post, "Publish or Perish: The Unabomber Papers," *Psychiatric Times*, November, 1995.
 5. "Bombing in Sacramento: The Letter; Excerpts from Letter by 'Terrorist Group,' FC, Which Says It Sent Bombs," *New York Times*, April 26, 1995.
 6. "'Breivik Manifesto' Details Chilling Attack Preparation," *BBC News*, July 24, 2011, www.bbc.co.uk/news/world-europe-14267007.
 7. Kristen Wyatt, "Suspect Anders Behring Breivik's Manifesto Plagiarized from the Unabomber," *The Huffington Post*, June 24, 2011, www.huffingtonpost.com/2011/07/25/suspect-anders-behring-br_n_909022.html.
 8. "'Breivik Manifesto' Details Chilling Attack Preparation."
 9. Beau Friedlander, "An Interview with a Madman: Breivik Asks and Answers His Own Questions," *TIME*, July 24, 2011, www.time.com/time/world/article/0,8599,2084895,00.html.
10. Ann Simmons, "Norway Suspect Modeled His Writings after Unabomber Manifesto," *Los Angeles Times*, July 24, 2011, http://articles.latimes.com/2011/jul/24/world/la-fgw-norway-suspect-20110725.
11. "'Breivik Manifesto' Details Chilling Attack Preparation."
12. "Anders Behring Breivik: Oslo, Norway Bombing 'Necessary,'" *Huffington Post*, July 23, 2011, www.huffingtonpost.com/2011/07/23/anders-behring-breivik-oslo-bombing_n_907880.html.
13. Valeria Criscione, "Norwegian Terror Suspect Breivik Tells Court Today He Deserves a Medal," *Christian Science Monitor*, February 6, 2012, www.csmonitor.com/World/Europe/2012/0206/Norwegian-terror-suspect-Breivik-tells-court-today-he-deserves-a-medal.
14. "Norway Massacre: Breivik Disputes Psychiatric Report," *BBC News*, April 4, 2012, www.bbc.co.uk/news/world-europe-17613822.
15. James Knoll, "The 'Pseudocommando' Mass Murderer: A Blaze of Vainglory," *Psychiatric Times*, January 4, 2012, www.psychiatrictimes.com/display/article/10168/2013318.
16. P. E. Mullen, "The Autogenic (Self-Generated) Massacre," *Behavioral Sciences and the Law*, 22 (2004), 311–323.
17. Knoll, "The 'Pseudocommando' Mass Murderer: A Blaze of Vainglory."
18. David Morgan, "Breivik's Father: I Wish My Son Killed Himself," *CBS News*, July 25, 2011, www.cbsnews.com/8301-503543_162-20082948-503543.html.
19. Sigmund Freud, "On Narcissism," in *The Standard Edition of the Complete Psychological Works of Sigmund Freud, Volume XIV (1914–1916): On the History of the Psycho-Analytic Movement, Papers on Metapsychology and Other Works* (London: Hogarth Press, 1958), 67–102.
20. Freud, "On Narcissism," 74–75.

21. Sigmund Freud, "Psychoanalytic Notes on an Autobiographical Account of a Case of Paranoia," in *The Standard Edition of the Complete Psychological Works of Sigmund Freud, Volume XII: The Case of Schreber, Papers on Technique, and Other Works* (London: Hogarth Press, 1958), 9–82.

22. Robert Robins and Jerrold Post, *Political Paranoia: The Psychopolitics of Hatred* (New Haven: Yale University Press, 1993).

23. Cited in Joan Lachkar, *The Narcissistic/Borderline Couple: A Psychoanalytic Perspective on Marital Treatment* (New York: Brunnel Mazel 1992), 28–29.

24. Robbins and Post, *Political Paranoia.*

25. Vamik Volkan, *Primitive Internalized Object Relations: A Clinical Study of Schizophrenic, Borderline, and Narcissistic Patients* (New York: International Universities Press, 1976); Vamik Volkan, "Narcissistic Personality Organization and Reparative Leadership," *International Journal of Group Psychotherapy*, 30, 131–152 (1980); Vamik Volkan, "Object and Self: A Developmental Approach," in *Object Relations and Self: A Developmental Approach* (New York: International Universities Press, 1981), 429–451; Vamik Volkan, "Narcissistic Personality Disorder," in Jessie Cavenar and Keith Brodie (eds.), *Critical Problems in Psychiatry* (Philadelphia: J. B. Lippincott, 1982), 332–350; Vamik Volkan and Norman Itzkowitz, *The Immortal Ataturk* (Chicago: University of Chicago Press, 1984).

26. Volkan, "Narcissistic Personality Organization and Reparative Leadership," 135.

27. Irwin Hirsch, "The Ubiquity and Relativity of Narcissism: Therapeutic Implications," in John Fiscalini and Alan Grey (eds.), *Narcissism and the Interpersonal Self* (New York: Columbia University Press, 1993), 301.

2

Dreams of Glory and Narcissistic Rage

What background experiences give rise to narcissistic personalities? Are there characteristic developmental features?

The reaction of parents to the miracle of the birth of their newborn, their adoration of their creation, is the very basis of a child's self-esteem. That reveling in the perceived beauty, brilliance, and talents of their new baby and communicating it to the object of their affection, this "mirroring" of the infant by its parents, especially the mother, is the foundation of the growing child's optimism, the basis of the child's positive self-regard and good feelings about himself. The growing child takes the admiration of the parents into himself, and it becomes part of the child's positive self-concept.

Major trauma and loss during this crucial period damages the very foundation of the child's subsequent personality development, leading to the wounded self, craving the mirroring and adulation of which he was deprived. One way of compensating for this major wound is to create a grandiose self-concept, which externally is often conveyed as arrogance and certainty.

NARCISSISTIC WOUNDS AND NARCISSISTIC RAGE

The grandiose narcissistic self, with its unlimited dreams of glory, always rests on a sea of insecurity and doubt. And when reality dashes those dreams, it produces strong reactions. For some, like the recently fired dishwasher (mentioned in Chapter 1) who attempted to drive his pickup truck through the White House gates so that he could occupy his throne as king of the world, reality is so painful that there is a break with reality, and compensatory delusions of grandiosity result.

For still others, the painful reality, the narcissistic wound, produces rage at the person or organization seen as responsible for dashing those dreams, as the inflictor of the narcissistic wound. In Herman Melville's *Moby Dick*, Captain

Ahab is consumed by his quest for revenge against the great white whale that destroyed his ship and bit off one of his legs. His total obsession with revenge against the great white whale that caused him such profound injury is mono-maniacal. He cannot rest until he exacts revenge.[a]

Shame is an affect of central importance to the lashing out that occurs when the outside world does not reward the fragile grandiose image. But more impor-tant than the plaudits of the outside world is the intolerable internal affect that results when one's dreams of glory are shattered, when one's grandiose self is confronted with failure. As with the Unabomber, it was when Ted Kaczynski was confronted with the undeniable evidence that his internal image as the world's most famous and powerful serial bomber was shattered that he experi-enced passive humiliation and was driven to take restorative action to regain his sense of power and mastery.[b]

Shame can also result from the failure of a strong supporter to respond sufficiently to the narcissist's need for idealization, leading to an overwhelming demanding grandiosity that, in turn, can produce shame and then rage at the inadequately responding object. The stalker infatuated with a woman who does not reciprocate his love can be driven to strike out violently at the unresponsive object of his love. Or, as with John Hinckley's assassination attempt against President Reagan, to carry out an act of violent rage to attract attention and impress the object of his unrequited love.

The characteristic contempt of the narcissist represents exporting the shame-ful place within to the outside world, leading to the superiority and arrogance

---

[a] Kohut (1985) uses this as a metaphor for the relentless quest for revenge that occurs when a grandiose narcissist has been dealt a humiliating blow. Freud, he observes, "regarded untamable aggression as the primary cause of human destructiveness" (p. 12). And that untamable aggression is the consequence of unalloyed narcissistic wounds. When the environment does not live up to the grandiose expectations of the narcissist, shame and humiliation result. This is intolerable and begets a need for redemptive action, for revenge.

It is that individual who has a readiness to experience setbacks as narcissistic wounds and respond with insatiable rage with whom we are concerned (Kohut, 1985). In response to passive humiliation and submission, the wounded narcissist is now taking action and lashing out. The passive victim whose sense of control has been violated has regained a sense of control. From feeling defeated, striking out produces the illusion of mastery and control. His rage is a response to *unmirrored* grandiosity.

[b] Morrison (1989) takes this a step beyond the transformation from passive humiliation to powerful redemptive action observed by Kohut in suggesting that "shame is an affect central to Tragic Man, the narcissistic personality of self-depletion, suffering the empty depression of unmirrored ambi-tions and unrecognized ideals" (p. 102). This represents an important elaboration of narcissistic theory. Morrison is not addressing shame that results from having one's flaws and insufficiencies exposed to the outside world, an expression of the shame-oriented society, as depicted in 1946 by social anthropologist Ruth Benedict in *The Chrysanthemum and The Sword*, her pioneering study of Japanese cultural mores developed during World War II. Rather, Morrison conceptualizes shame as the intolerable internal affect that occurs when one's dreams of glory are shattered, when one's grandiose self is confronted with failure.

that the narcissist radiates. But this is a fragile superiority, one that, when breached by criticism or undeniable failure, can lead to enraged lashing out.

Now, it is one thing to be publically criticized by an opponent. It is quite another for a national leader consumed by dreams of glory who embarks on a military adventure as an expression of his grandiose self-concept and his feelings of invulnerability and omnipotence, to be forced to retreat and capitulate in public, with the eyes of the world on him – an intolerable public humiliation and shaming.

In this chapter, after first considering the origins of Saddam Hussein's wounded self and compensatory grandiose dreams of glory, his narcissistic rage when those dreams were thwarted is described.

THE TRAUMATIC ORIGINS OF SADDAM HUSSEIN'S WOUNDED SELF

The early years of Saddam Hussein are probably the most traumatic of any leader I have profiled. The foundations of Saddam Hussein's wounded self-concept can be traced back to the womb. During the fourth month of Saddam's mother's pregnancy with him, her husband, Saddam's father, died of cancer. During the eighth month of the pregnancy, her firstborn son died under the surgeon's knife. Not surprisingly, the mother became seriously depressed and first tried to abort the pregnancy and then to commit suicide. She was prevented from doing so by the intervention of a neighboring Jewish couple.[c]

When Saddam was born in a mud hut in the village of Tikrit, rather than joyously embracing her newborn son, she turned away from him and would not take him to breast. Her brother, Khairallah, took the infant Saddam and raised him with his family for the next two and a half years. Thus, from the very beginnings of his life, the bond between mother and newborn that is the very foundation of self-esteem was wounded. When Saddam was two and a half, his mother married Saddam's father's brother, according to custom, and, for the first time, Saddam joined his mother and new stepfather, a man who was both physically and psychologically abusive to the young Saddam.

This was not a good beginning to this life. It was guaranteed to produce a seriously wounded self. Most individuals so profoundly wounded would grow up to be ineffectual, hesitant, self-doubting adults. But when Saddam was ten, impressed during a visit by his cousin, Khairallah's son, who was in school, Saddam asked his parents if he, too, could go to school. They refused, but Saddam would not take no for an answer. Demonstrating the determination that characterized him throughout his life, he fled in the middle of the night and went back to the home of his Uncle Khairallah. In vivid contrast to what

---

[c] This information was unearthed by the remarkable investigative scholarship of Amazia Baram (1991), a leading Israeli scholar of Iraqi history. He interviewed the couple, whom he had traced to a suburb of Tel Aviv.

Saddam experienced with his mother and stepfather, Khairallah filled his young charge with dreams of glory. He told him that someday, like his grand-uncle and grandfather, he would play a major role in the history of Iraq and that he would go down in history as a great hero, following the pathways of Nebuchadnezzar and Saladin who had rescued Jerusalem from its conquerors.

For his high school years, Saddam was moved to Baghdad. There, the streets were alive with the excitement of Gamal Abdel Nasser's 1952 Free Officers Movement revolution in Egypt, which overthrew the Egyptian monarchy. Nasser became a hero figure for Saddam who aspired to inherit Nasser's mantle as champion of pan-Arab nationalism.

When he came to power, Saddam, consumed with these dreams of glory, came to see himself as belonging to the elite stratum of world-class socialist leaders – Mao Zedong, Ho Chi Min, Fidel Castro, Josip Tito – but the world did not reciprocate this elevated vision. In 1980, sensing that Iran was at a moment of vulnerability, he initiated war with Iran over the disputed Shatt al-Arab waterway, a grievance that had long consumed Saddam. The conflict was a disastrous drain on Iraq, especially when Khomeini mounted "human wave" attacks against Iraq, and the conflict was not settled until 1988.

It was only in July 1990, with Iraq's invasion of Kuwait, that Saddam seized the world's attention. He gave a guttural grunt, oil prices jumped $20 a barrel, and the Dow-Jones stock average plummeted 200 points. He was the very cynosure of international attention. At last, he was seen as a powerful world leader. Even more importantly, the Palestinian people, disappointed in Yasser Arafat's leadership, came to see him as their new hero. When he wrapped himself in the Palestinian flag and declared that the UN resolutions requiring his withdrawal from Kuwait would only be heeded after the previous UN resolutions concerning the future of Palestine were followed, it changed his act of naked aggression in invading Kuwait into the transformative moment of his life.

Saddam defiantly and courageously standing up to the United States to force a just settlement of their cause caught the imagination of the Arab masses, and their shouts of approval fed Saddam's already swollen ego as he went on a defiant roll. Intoxicated by the elixir of power and the acclaim of the Palestinian people and the radical Arab masses, Saddam may well have been on a euphoric high and optimistically overestimated his chances for success because his heroic self-image was engaged as never before. He was fulfilling the messianic goal that had obsessed – but eluded him – throughout his life. He was actualizing his self-concept as leader of all the Arab peoples, the legitimate heir of Nebuchadnezzar, Saladin, and Nasser. He would rescue Jerusalem from its captors, thus fulfilling his uncle's prophecy. It was dreams of glory achieved; an explosion, so to speak, of narcissistic nourishment.

So, the notion was inconceivable that he would meekly withdraw from Kuwait in the face of the massive military buildup of the U.S.-led coalition. How could he conceivably withdraw from this long-coveted but only recently achieved position as powerful world leader? It would have been an unthinkable capitulation, shattering his only recently fulfilled dreams of glory.

When his uncle filled him with these dreams of glory, it provided a heady message for this lad so starved for parental love, for mirroring. But, however grand the future his uncle prophesied, it could not fill the painful void of the underlying wounded self. To employ an architectural motif, the mud hut in which Saddam was born represented the emotional deprivation and economic poverty into which he was born. When he came to power, Saddam dotted the landscape with splendid palaces featuring inlaid wood, fine marble, superb carpets, and gold fixtures in the bathrooms. This was the architectural representation of the dreams of glory with which his Uncle Khairallah had filled him. This was the glittering, grandiose, messianic façade that Saddam presented to the world. But what was concealed beneath the palaces? Underground bunkers, bristling with weapons, communications equipment, even a helicopter with an escape pathway. This was an architectural motif for the siege state that underlay Saddam's grandiose façade, the default position in his political psychology. Always ready to be attacked, ready to strike out and defend.

But always, underneath, at his very core, was the painful void of the wounded self represented by the mud hut in which he was born. And how ironic that when he was finally captured, he was found in a spider hole beneath a mud hut near his birthplace of Tikrit. Temporarily, his wounded self was in full view as he meekly bowed his head to be examined for lice and submitted to a dental examination – to all appearances a shattered man. But, all too soon, his defensive grandiosity manifested itself as he arrogantly declared, "I am the president of Iraq. Who is here to negotiate with me?"

He maintained this surface posture of contempt and arrogance throughout the trial, stating that he was the president of Iraq and that the proceedings were illegitimate; he attacked the credentials of the judge and prosecutor, making a mockery of the proceedings. In so doing, he was following the model of Milosevic during his four-year trial at the International Criminal Court in the Hague from 2002–2006.[1] And he maintained this arrogant posture to the end, including at his hanging on December 30, 2006, after his conviction of crimes against humanity by the Iraqi Special Tribunal.

VANITY OF VANITIES

Insufficiently nourished emotionally at the very beginnings of life, Saddam was left with an insatiable craving for mirroring and adoration. Cults of personality abound among world leaders with significant narcissistic personality features as a consequence of their insatiable appetites for praise and their need for continuing reassurance of their specialness.

Travelers to Baghdad have remarked that it was easy to get lost in the confusion of Saddam Avenue, Saddam Parkway, Saddam Road, and the like. There was a Saddam School of Art, where artists specialized in portraying the many magnificent roles of Saddam Hussein: Saddam the military hero, Saddam the statesman, Saddam the sportsman, Saddam the benevolent father, and more. Large pictures and statues of Saddam were seen throughout the city, dressed appropriately for his many roles. Asked if he didn't find these displays excessive, he shrugged his shoulders as if helpless and replied, "How can I stop them? If that's what they want to do, why should I interfere?"

SADDAM HUSSEIN'S RETALIATORY NARCISSISTIC RAGE

When the massive military buildup assembled in the fall of 1990 under the impressive leadership of U.S. President George H. Bush forced Saddam Hussein to retreat from Kuwait, he was faced with the failure of his dreams of glory. Temporarily, his fragile grandiose self was breached by undeniable reality. He had reasoned himself into a righteous entitlement to Kuwait's petroleum fields, convinced that the Kuwaitis were stealing oil that was rightfully Iraq's (his). Forced to retreat, he would be damned if he would let the Kuwaitis escape unscathed. The passive humiliation and shame was unbearable. And so, as he was exiting Kuwait, he set the oil fields afire, causing massive economic and environmental damage. Indeed, as revealed in the recently released first tranche of documents from the Saddam archive, Saddam was so enraged that he told his senior officers "If we have to leave, burn everything."[2]

This was white-hot narcissistic rage, taking retaliatory action against the adversary that had so humiliated him. If he could not have Kuwait's oil, then neither would the United States. To passively bend the knee and submit to superior force was impossible for Saddam; he was compelled to take action to restore his sense of efficacy and power, defending against passive powerlessness with redemptive and powerful action.

THE GREAT TURKMENBASHI

Saddam Hussein's cult of personality paled by comparison to that of the first president of Turkmenistan after the collapse of the Soviet Union. Saparmurat Atayevich Niyazov, self-designated as Serdar Turkmenbashi, was characteristically referred to as the Great Turkmenbashi, which means "Great Leader of all Turkmen." The title referred expansively to his position as the founder and president of the Association of Turkmens of the World.

In the center of the country's capital, Ashgabat, is the 200-foot Neutrality Arch, which features a huge gold-plated statue of Turkmenbashi that rotates to always face the sun. Other statues and posters of Turkmenbashi abound and are found in every public place. Commenting on this in an interview with *60 Minutes*, he modestly allowed that "If I was a worker and my president gave me all the things they have here in Turkmenistan, I would not only paint his picture, I would have his picture on my shoulder, or on my clothing."[3] Sounding eerily like Saddam Hussein, he went on to say, "I'm personally against seeing my pictures and statues in the streets – but it's what the people want." The extent to which Turkmenbashi identified himself with his new nation was striking. His picture is on the currency, on the national airplane, and even on the national vodka. He authored a giant tome, the *Ruhnama*, which is required reading for schoolchildren, and he decreed that no other books are necessary; it is the president's spiritual guide for the people of Turkmenistan. In the same *60 Minutes* interview, in response to a question concerning why all children must read it, he stated, "Please read the *Ruhnama* and you will find the answers to all your questions. The *Ruhnama* is not a book to replace the Ku'ran. It simply explains how the Turkmen nation has been reborn." As Laura Kennedy, the former ambassador to Turkmenistan, observed, "It's being taught almost as theology."[4] Among other innovations, he renamed several months in the calendar: January after himself, April after his mother. As he has explained, "There's no harm done. You can't have a great country without great ancestors – and we had none before."

IDI AMIN DADA OF UGANDA

Although it is difficult to top a mammoth gilded statue that rotates to always face the sun, in terms of his grandiose self-designated title, Idi Amin Dada is assuredly a worthy contender for grandiose vanity to compensate for underlying insecurity. His remarkable title was "His Excellency, President for Life, Field Marshall Al Hadj, Dr. Idi Amin Dada, VC, DSO, MC, Lord of All of the Beasts of the Earth and Fishes of the Sea, and Conqueror of the British Empire in Africa in General and Uganda in Particular."

So brief as to easily be ignored in this grandiloquent title is "Dr.," notable because Idi Amin probably had no more than two years of primary schooling and was extremely sensitive about his lack of education and his limited intelligence. Amin's violence was sweeping, but it was focused particularly on intellectuals and the educated elite. While he initially courted this class, sensing that he needed their expertise to manage his nation, each encounter with a competent, well-educated individual was for Idi Amin a painful reminder of his inadequacy. His purge of intellectuals was motivated in part by his wish to eliminate those threats to his self-esteem. The extent of the purges stripped Uganda of its managerial elite, by whom he felt shamed and humiliated.

Patrick Marnham,[5] a journalist who spent time in Amin's Uganda six years after the tyrant's fall, wrote "Looking back on the Amin days, it was his fear and hatred of educated peoples that were the most characteristic and unpredictable aspects of his tyranny."[6] He was clearly inadequate for the tasks of nurturing a national economy, carrying on international relations, and developing social institutions. One of his ministers reported that Amin could not sit in an office for very long and could not concentrate on a single topic for half a morning, noting "It is impossible for him ... to comprehend what is going on from the point of view of policy."[7] Yet, at the same time, he was clearly taken with his role as chief of state. He criticized his fellow chief of state, President Richard Nixon, for his conduct during the Vietnam War, and, when the Watergate scandal broke, Amin wrote letters of advice to him.[8]

IDI AMIN'S RETALIATORY NARCISSISTIC RAGE AGAINST INTELLECTUALS

In the earlier description of Idi Amin Dada's grandiosity, reference was made to his purge of the intellectual class. This can be seen as narcissistic rage in retaliation for the narcissistic shame and humiliation Idi Amin experienced when his intellectual inadequacy to the tasks of national leadership was challenged by his clearly being out of his depth, in over his head. Again, it is this shame of having one's grandiose self confronted, this revealing of the underlying inadequacy, that produces a painful narcissistic wound that then leads to narcissistic rage. In Amin's case, this led to a purge of the intellectual class.

MUAMMAR QADDAFI: NARCISSIST IN EXTREMIS

The rambling statements of Muammar al-Qaddafi[d] following the uprising in Libya began on February 17, 2011, and led many to characterize the idiosyncratic Libyan leader as a madman, a psychotic, out of touch with reality. Among statements made by Qaddafi that led observers to question his sanity were his characterization of the rebels as "drug-crazed youth" whose Nescafé the United States laced with hallucinogenic drugs. He also accused al-Qaeda of being behind the rebellion, only to again accuse the United States. On February 28, in his first media interview with the BBC, ABC, and the *Sunday Times* after the uprising began, when asked about his countrymen rising against him, Qaddafi denied it: "There are no demonstrations at all in the streets. Did you see the demonstrations? Where? They are supporting us. They are not against us. There is no one against us. Against me for what? Because I am not president. They love me. All my people are with me. They love me all. They will die to protect me, my people."

When he was asked in the interview whether he would step down, Qaddafi again denied that he had any authority: "If they want me to step down, what do I step down from? I'm not a monarch or a king. It's honorary. It has nothing to do with exercising power or authority. In Britain, who has the power? Is it Queen Elizabeth or David Cameron?"

Later, Qaddafi indicated that the rebellion was the result of a conspiracy by the West to recolonize Libya in order to gain control of its oil.

Characterizations of being psychotic have been leveled at Qaddafi since he took over the reins of Libya in a bloodless coup in 1969 at the age of 27. A *Time*

---

[d] This assessment is based on Jerrold Post (2011), "Qaddafi Under Siege: A Political Psychologist Assesses Libya's Mercurial Leader," *Foreign Policy (online)*, March 15.

Magazine article quoted U.S. President Ronald Reagan as calling him "the mad dog of the Middle East."[9] But, for the most part, during his 42 years at the helm of Libya, he has been crazy like a fox.

Although this is not a definitive clinical diagnosis, Qaddafi can best be characterized as having a borderline narcissistic personality. The "borderline" often swings from intense anger to euphoria. Under his often "normal" façade, he was quite insecure and sensitive to slight. His reality testing was episodically faulty. While most of the time Qaddafi was "above the border" and in touch with reality, when under stress he could dip below it, and his perceptions could be distorted and his judgment faulty. And, as his regime came under stress, he was under the greatest stress since taking over the leadership of Libya. Thus, his quotes probably accurately reflected his true beliefs. He did sincerely cling to the idea that his people all loved him.

Qaddafi's strong anti-authority bent and his tendency to identify with the underdog can be traced back to his childhood. He was born in a tent in the desert to a Bedouin family in 1942. When Qaddafi was 10 years old, Gamal Abdel Nasser took over the reins of Egypt at the head of the Free Officers Movement, which made a deep and lasting impression on the young Qaddafi. He initially attended a Muslim school, where he was recognized as being very bright, and he was sent to Tripoli to continue his education. There, he was teased by the children of the cosmopolitan elite for his coarse manners, leaving him with a bitter resentment against the establishment.

In Libya at that time, a military career provided an opportunity for upward mobility, and Qaddafi entered the Libyan military academy in Benghazi in 1961. Nasser and his revolutionary nationalism assumed heroic stature in the minds of Qaddafi and his fellow students. He first began to think of organizing a military coup against the corrupt regime of King Idris while in military college, and, on September 1, 1969, with a small group of junior military officers, he formed Libya's own Free Officers Movement and successfully led a bloodless coup to depose the king.

From the very beginnings of his leadership of the junta known as the Revolutionary Command Council, the deeply antiestablishment Qaddafi actively supported groups that he considered underdogs, those who represented themselves as attacking imperialism. He became one of the world's most notorious supporters of terrorist groups around the world, even if this policy resulted in no particular benefit to Libya. His support of terrorism was both wide and deep. He sent arms to the Irish Republican Army and provided financial support to the social revolutionary group FARC in Colombia and to the Red Army Faction in Germany and the Red Brigades in Italy. He reportedly provided major financial support to the Black September organization responsible for the massacre of the Israeli Olympic team at the Munich Olympics in 1972. He praised the terrorist attack by the Japanese Red Army on the Lod Airport in Tel Aviv, urged Palestinian terrorist groups to carry out attacks on Israel, and offered to provide financial support and training.

Following Nasser's lead, he attempted to create a pan-Arab nation, merging first with Egypt and Syria, and then later attempting to merge with Tunisia, but his would-be partners were quick to discover that to merge with Libya was to be taken over by Qaddafi, leading to the swift failure of these proposed unions. In Qaddafi's modest view, Libya was at the very center of three overlapping circles: the Arab world, the Muslim world, and the Third World, particularly Africa. And in this Venn diagram, Qaddafi was at the very center.

Reflecting his deep antipathy to formal authority, Qaddafi not only disclaimed any formal title, but he also institutionalized this as a governing philosophy in what he called a "popular democracy," and later "Islamic socialism." Dismantling parties and institutions, he formed "people's committees" across the country to establish a direct democracy. This principle was codified in the three slim volumes of his *Green Book*, the quixotic tome on political philosophy he published in 1976. Then, in 1977, at Qaddafi's bidding, the General People's Congress, which was in effect a committee of committees, conferred on him the honorific title of permanent "Brotherly Leader and Guide of the First of September Great Revolution of the Socialist People's Libyan Arab Jamahiriya" (*jamahiriya* is loosely translated as "democracy of the masses" or "state of the masses," having no formal organizations other than the "people's committees"). In this democracy of the masses, Qaddafi would have no formal leadership role. This was the basis for Qaddafi's explanation in his February 28 press conference that he couldn't resign because he had no official position.

After the revolution, Libya nationalized some 70 percent of the oil companies operating in the country, including British Petroleum and Continental Oil, and joined the Organization of Petroleum Exporting Countries (OPEC), with a resultant large increase in oil revenues for Libya. Using Libya's petroleum wealth, Qaddafi not only bankrolled terrorists but almost indiscriminately funded rogue leaders around the world, including Idi Amin Dada of Uganda, Emperor Bokassa of the Central African Empire, Haile Mengistu of Ethiopia, and Daniel Ortega, leader of the Sandinistas in Nicaragua.

In reviewing Qaddafi's career, two things stand out. A consistent theme is his identification with the underdog standing up against authority. And while he eschewed the titles of power, he was, in fact, quite ruthless in eliminating any threats to his own power. It is estimated that 10–20 percent of the Libyan population worked for the people's committees, identifying threats to his power, dissidents, and regime critics and eliminating them, thus forming a network of secret informers rivaling that of Saddam Hussein, Josef Stalin, and the East German Stasi. So sensitive to plots was his regime that even to engage in a discussion with a foreigner was a crime punishable by three years in prison. The fear of dissidents included those living abroad who sought the sanctuary of exile, and he dispatched assassination teams abroad to silence outspoken anti-Libyan dissidents, for example, shooting at 10 anti-Qaddafi protesters in Britain in 1984. And his reach extended to the United States: in 1980, he launched an attempted assassination against a Libyan graduate student at the University of Colorado, seriously wounding him, and he had a Libyan exile killed just before his U.S. citizenship ceremony in 1990. Amnesty International once estimated that Libya carried out at least 25 assassinations abroad in the 1980s.

In Qaddafi's constellation of enemies, the United States was to occupy a special role. To have the courage to stand up to the world's only superpower would surely magnify his stature. And stand up he did. Reagan recalled in his diaries that Qaddafi mounted an assassination plot against him in November 1981. In early 1986, when Qaddafi declared the Gulf of Sidra as Libya's territory, an area extending some 200 miles beyond its coastline, and threatened attacks against anyone who dared to cross "the line of death," the U.S. Navy carried out a long-standing planned exercise that indeed crossed that line. Qaddafi sent two sorties of jets against the American fleet, which were promptly shot down. Qaddafi then thanked the United States for making him "a hero to the Third World."

Later that year, Libyan agents bombed the La Belle disco in West Berlin, a favorite hangout for the U.S. military, killing three and wounding 229. Intercepts revealed that this was a Libyan plot, providing Reagan the long-sought "smoking gun" to fulfill his inaugural commitment to make attacking terrorism his number-one priority. In reprisal, the United States mounted a bombing raid against Tripoli, the Libyan capital. Qaddafi claimed that his adopted daughter was killed in the raid. Now, Qaddafi was fully engaged with his archenemy. A year later, a Japanese Red Army terrorist hired by Qaddafi was apprehended at a rest stop on the New Jersey turnpike with three pipe bombs discovered in his car. According to a February 1989 article in the *New York Times*, he intended to set them off in a Navy recruiting station in New York City on the first anniversary of the U.S. bombing raid on Tripoli.[10] In 1988, the bombing of Pan Am Flight 103 occurred over Lockerbie, Scotland, a flight filled with American students returning home after study abroad, killing all 259 people on board and 11 on the ground. Meticulous forensic examination traced the bomb back to Libya, leading to UN economic and political sanctions in 1992, sanctions that bit deeply and led to Libya's economic and political isolation. The Libyan associate minister of justice, who defected, confirmed that it was Qaddafi himself who gave the orders.

In 2003, the UN Security Council made the lifting of the sanctions contingent on Libya's accepting responsibility for the actions of its officials and payment of up to $2.7 billion in compensation for the victims of the 1988 attack. Libya watchers believed that Qaddafi's son and designated successor Saif al-Islam Qaddafi, who had a Ph.D. from the London School of Economics and was considered more worldly than his father, persuaded the colonel to agree to the compensation and to abandon Libya's weapons of mass destruction program. (The question of whether the Ph.D. dissertation was ghostwritten and partially plagiarized was investigated, but Saif was permitted to retain the doctorate.) This decision led to the lifting of the sanctions, thus ending Libya's diplomatic isolation. It represented a rare example of Qaddafi being able to exercise wisdom in pursuit of Libya's international position.

Saif's experience in London led to the wistful hope that, with his international experience, he would be a force for reform and moderation, perhaps leading Libya back into the community of nations from which it was so long been isolated. Indeed, the decisions to pay compensation to the victims of the Pan Am 103 bombing and to abandon Libya's weapons of mass destruction program may well have been influenced by Saif's broader international perspective. Recognizing that his father was nearing the time when he would hand over the reins of power to him, Saif did not want to succeed to the leadership of a nation economically and diplomatically isolated.

But these decisions did not exhaust Qaddafi's fondness for the United States as adversary. In 2009, Qaddafi found common cause with Venezuela's Hugo Chávez to propose a South Atlantic Treaty Organization to counter NATO.

The violence against unarmed civilians disaffected many within Qaddafi's diplomatic corps and the military. What began as a small stream became a virtual river of resignations and defections, as many attempted to dissociate themselves from a regime accused by UN Secretary-General Ban Ki-moon of "serious transgressions of international human rights and humanitarian law." Several senior military officers defected and assumed leadership roles within the rebel forces, and the former ambassador to India, Ali Assawi, became the foreign minister for the new rebel shadow government, the Libyan National Council, headed by Qaddafi's former justice minister.

Throughout his life and career, Qaddafi lived out his core psychological value, that of the outsider standing up against superior authority, the Muslim warrior courageously confronting insurmountable odds. A man does not mellow with age, especially a highly narcissistic leader consumed by dreams of glory. Indeed, as a man grows older, he becomes more like himself. But as the stress mounted, Qaddafi seemed increasingly to lose touch with reality. Having dedicated his life to Libya, his creation, he found it inconceivable that his people were not all grateful to him, and when he said that his people all loved him, he believed it. Therefore, anyone contesting his authority must be responding to foreign agents from the United States or al-Qaeda. When he said he would fight to the "last drop of his blood," he meant it: Qaddafi would not commit suicide or slink away to a lush exile.

When he spoke of "my country," he meant it literally. In his view, Qaddafi was Libya, and a Libya without him at the helm was unimaginable to him. In an article in *The Economist* of February 2011, he is quoted as having declared that "I was the one who created Libya ... and I will be the one to destroy it." Qaddafi was indeed prepared to go down in flames, and the question was how many of his supporters were prepared to fight to "the last drop of (their) blood."

Qaddafi could lose touch with reality in two circumstances: when he was failing and when he was succeeding. When he was succeeding, he could get heady with success, feel invulnerable, and get carried away. Qaddafi was almost certainly feeling that way after his forces turned the tide and were overwhelming the rebels. He had stood up against the West, the UN, NATO, and those rebel forces sent in by outside agitators, and he was winning. He threatened to go on a house-to-house search and "show no mercy" toward his enemies, whom he wished to punish and wipe out. But the UN resolution and intervention again changed the dynamic, and, once again, he was the courageous Muslim warrior, standing up against the superior enemy. And, despite wishes that his son Saif would moderate his father's extremities, apart from his brief period in London, Saif stood loyally by his father's side throughout. Just as Qaddafi vowed that he "would go down to the last drop of his blood," so, too, Saif vowed that he "would go down to the last bullet."

Hoping to escape the war crimes tribunal, a flood of senior officials defected, leaving Qaddafi increasingly isolated. Having fled from Tripoli, he was found hiding in a pipe and was shot to death – an inglorious end to his 40-year leadership of Libya, a leadership dominated by his narcissistic self-absorbed dreams of glory.

After his father was killed while attempting to escape from Tripoli, Saif was captured and is now awaiting resumption of his trial for crimes against humanity. The trial was temporarily adjourned to resolve questions concerning the degree of involvement of the International Criminal Court.

THE NARCISSISTIC QADDAFI DENYING HIS PEOPLE'S PROTESTS: RETALIATORY NARCISSISTIC RAGE

The firing by Muammar Qaddafi on unarmed peaceful protestors during the Arab Spring in 2011, which led to widespread condemnation, can be seen as his striking out in retaliatory narcissistic rage against those whose actions had shattered the illusion of the grandiose leader who was firmly in control and beloved by his people. This was especially true for Colonel Muammar Qaddafi. Denying inescapable reality, the intensely narcissistic Qaddafi kept protesting, "My people, they all love me. They will protect me,"[11] approaching delusional denial. Those he shot at were not his people, but drug-crazed youth who had been provoked by the West or al-Qaeda:

It is Qaeda, it is Qaeda, it is Qaeda, not my people. It is Qaeda, Qaeda, Qaeda, yes. They came from outside. It's al Qaeda. They went into military bases and seized arms and they're terrorizing the people. The people who had had the weapons were the youngsters. They're starting to lay down their weapons now as the drugs that al Qaeda gave them are wearing off.

After devoting his entire career to creating the state of Libya, the intensely narcissistic Qaddafi could not accept that his people were not grateful and did not give him their total loyalty and adoration. His grandiose self-concept simply could not accept this. He could not tolerate the humiliation of widespread protests against his leadership, and so, to restore his grandiose self against this profound narcissistic wound, he took a twofold approach: he denied that those who were protesting were "his people," and, in a spasm of narcissistic rage, he retaliated against them, brutally firing on unarmed protestors and thus leading to an indictment against himself and his son Saif for war crimes and crimes against humanity by the International Criminal Court in the Hague.

TREASON AS A PRODUCT OF NARCISSISTIC RAGE

If the retaliatory violence just described was a product of white-hot narcissistic rage, studies of traitors both East and West have shown that treason is often the end point of a cold, bitter, building resentment against a system that has insufficiently recognized and rewarded them. The Soviets were adroit at homing in on vulnerabilities that could be exploited in their Western targets when they recruited them as spies. They would address four psychological qualities: money, ideology, sex, and ego (MISE). Money, ideology, sex, and ego, but the greatest of these was ego. In particular, they would seek to fulfill narcissistic dreams of glory. Even where financial greed was the apparent motivation, as with the Walker family, who for 18 years committed espionage against the United States by providing top secret code word intelligence and earning more than a million dollars, the money was confirmation of their importance. It was as if they were saying, "And you thought we were only mediocrities. The Soviets recognized our true value and richly compensated us because of the value of the information we were bringing to them. They considered us their most important agents."

The Soviets played skillfully to the ego of Klaus Fuchs, a German theoretical physicist, who, in 1950, was convicted of espionage for supplying information from the Manhattan Project's work on developing the atomic bomb. Fuchs made major contributions to the first fission weapons and later to the early versions of the hydrogen bomb. After the Soviet Union invaded Germany near the end of World War II, Fuchs became convinced that the Soviets had the right to know what Great Britain and the United States were secretly working on, and he contacted the GRU, the military intelligence arm of the Soviet Union. A message dated August 10, 1941, indicated that the GRU had established contact with Fuchs. He passed information on nuclear secrets first in Great Britain, and later, after he was transferred to Columbia University and began working on the Manhattan Project.

Fuchs became persuaded, with the skillful manipulation of his GRU handlers, that he had a critical role to play in preventing a nuclear holocaust. Because of the imbalance in nuclear technology, there was a danger that the West, so far in the lead, could initiate a nuclear conflict against the Soviet Union. By providing Western nuclear secrets to the Soviet Union, Fuchs could rectify this imbalance, and the resultant stability would lead to a nuclear standoff and guarantee mankind's survival. Whatever national laws and security oaths were violated – and Fuchs had signed the Official Secrets Act – could not compare with the importance of avoiding a nuclear war that would destroy mankind. A heady responsibility!

Stig Wennerstrom was a lieutenant colonel in the Swedish air force, assigned to NATO. Recognizing his frustration over his lack of career progress, the Soviets played to his wounded ego, promoting him to the rank of general in the Soviet secret service and awarding him a medal in a secret ceremony. In return for this recognition, Wennerstrom provided information of the highest quality concerning NATO strategy, intentions, and capabilities to his Soviet spymasters. During the 1950s, he leaked Swedish air defense plans and information on the Saab Draken fighter jet project. He also worked as air attaché in Washington, D.C., where he worked closely with the Soviet military intelligence service (the GRU) and in the same role in Moscow. He was convicted of espionage in 1964.

These are universal motives for treason, West and East. The 55-year-old Lieutenant Colonel Oleg Penkovsky, a major Soviet traitor, is widely acknowledged as one of the West's most successful espionage agents. Relying on the detailed information he provided on Soviet plans and the description and state of preparedness of the rocket launchers on Cuba during the Cuban Missile Crisis, the United States was able to identify the missile sites from the grainy, low-resolution photos taken by U.S. U2 spy planes. Former GRU Colonel Viktor Suverov, a major Soviet defector, wrote: "And historians will remember with gratitude the name of the GRU Colonel Oleg Penkovsky. Thanks to his priceless information the Cuban conflict was not transformed into World War III."[12]

Penkovsky's father died fighting as an officer in the White Army in the Russian civil war. Because of questions concerning his family background, the highly competent Penkovsky was blocked from further advancement. His resentment against the system that refused to reward him mounted. At age 41, the embittered Penkovsky, after several failed attempts, made contact with British intelligence and provided valuable classified documents to demonstrate his bona fides. Both British and American intelligence systematically and exhaustively debriefed him. He insisted on wearing the uniform of a full colonel of both the British and American armies during his debriefings, thus demonstrating his bitterness against the system that had blocked his career at the rank of lieutenant colonel. It was after this narcissistic wound that he came to see the danger of the reckless Soviet regime and began to provide intelligence information of the highest quality to the West. Indeed, Penkovsky's intelligence information on Soviet intentions was of crucial importance during the Cuban Missile Crisis. The West was lavish in its praise for the importance of the information he was providing, which acted as balm to his wounded ego.

THE GAP BETWEEN DREAMS AND REALITY

What the skilled case officers, East and West, manipulated in their targets was the gap between narcissistic dreams of glory and reality. The issue, it should be emphasized, was not the degree of success measured by external standards but by internal standards. An official may be quite successful by external criteria, but if only being president of the universe will do, then he can feel like a failure. If, in fact, others are clearly on a faster career path while their own careers are blocked, as were Oleg Penkovsky and Stig Wennerstrom, this only adds to the narcissistic wounds they experience as they painfully recognize that the die is cast and that the high ambitions that drove them are never to be achieved.

So it is not external reality, but the perceived internal gap between where he is and where he should be that is the measure of vulnerability in the narcissist. Thus, the individual may well have had a successful career by external criteria, but if, to his searching eye, he has not been sufficiently recognized by the system and promoted appropriately, then, according to his internal perceptions, he has been treated badly, and his inner rancor can fester as he broods over the system that has treated him so badly. This narcissistic wound promotes a cold, bitter narcissistic rage, producing a need to exact revenge on a system that is so blind and so corrupt. So this is a cold rage that takes root and grows in contrast to the white-hot rage that characterized Saddam Hussein's destructively setting afire the Kuwaiti oil fields when he was forced to exit in humiliation.

These feelings of brooding resentment are particularly apt to peak during the midlife period, the period of the so-called midlife crisis, roughly the late 30s to mid-40s. Marking the end of youth, it is a time of taking stock, of asking, "What have I accomplished? What does the future hold for me?" For many, it is a period of painful reckoning, of confronting the hopes, ambitions, and dreams that were not achieved. It is a time of extramarital affairs and divorce. In the Catholic Church, recognizing that doubts about their religious commitment seemed to peak during this period, with a statistical peak of the laicization of nuns and seminarians, enlightened dioceses have instituted age-related counseling programs to help members get through this age-related crisis of faith.[13]

Penkovsky was not recruited but was a "walk-in" who, as his resentment mounted against the system that had betrayed him, determined to take revenge against the Soviet system. He was 41 years old, at the very peak of the "midlife crisis." After several failed attempts to make contact with U.S. intelligence, he successfully made contact with British intelligence who, in turn, shared this valuable asset with their American colleagues.

A senior agency colleague included Penkovsky in his study of "great spies of history," a project he undertook in the six-month period prior to his retirement. He asked me to review his studies to ensure that he had the right psychological take. Noting Penkovsky's insistence that he be debriefed while wearing the uniforms of a full colonel in both the British and U.S. armies, I wryly observed that his subtitle, "A Quest for Honor," was off by one letter, that "A Quest for Honors" would be better. "Given the crucial importance of Penkovsky's intelligence information," I went on, "what a shame we could not have done for Penkovsky what the Soviets did for Wennerstrom," referring to the earlier description of how adroitly the Soviets played to Wennerstrom's narcissism, promoting him to general in the Soviet secret service and awarding him a medal in an *in camera* ceremony. "Oh, we couldn't have done that," the colleague exclaimed. "Why not?," I asked. "To promote someone to general requires Congressional approval," he explained. In exasperation, I went on, "Well, at least we could have given him a medal. This is a guy who would have taken great pride in having a laminated plaque with the Herbert Hoover Medal of Freedom on his wall."

With that, my colleague's face reddened as he moved his head upward, calling my attention to the only decoration in his pre-retirement office, which I must have recognized subconsciously. Seven – count them – seven laminated plaques: CIA Distinguished Intelligence Medal, CIA Career Intelligence Medal, CIA Medal of Merit, CIA Intelligence Star, and more. Now, this is not to say that my colleague, who had an extremely distinguished career, suffered from a narcissistic personality disorder or had distorted narcissistic dreams of glory. To the contrary. Rather he had great self-confidence – which can be considered "healthy" narcissism – high ambition, and extraordinary ability, which the system recognized. These traits in concert were indeed the ingredients of his success. A major gap between dreams and reality, between high self-estimates and the system's lack of recognition – this is the vulnerable wound that drove Penkovsky and Wennerstrom to their acts of treason as revenge against the systems that had inflicted such painful narcissistic wounds and led to cold, brooding narcissistic rage.

HUMILIATION OF THE GERMAN PEOPLE IN THE WAKE OF WORLD WAR I

Within the welter of geopolitical facts contributing to the onset of World War II, psychohistorians such as Peter Loewenberg[14] have reflected on the humiliation visited on the German people in the wake of World War I by the harsh provisions of the Versailles Treaty. With hyperinflation marked by wheelbarrows full of devalued marks, Germany became an economic basket case, a country where fathers could no longer provide for their families. The requirement to bend the knee in submission to the victorious Western powers was a profound national shame and humiliation.

It was this narcissistic wound to the German national psyche that Hitler's powerful externalizing rhetoric addressed, promising to restore German greatness, justifying striking out in what can be considered narcissistic rage on a national scale. As Kohut (1985)[15] observes, the revenge motif, very important in German literature, "is a theme that plays an important role in the national destiny of the German nation, whose thirst for revenge after the defeat of 1918 came close to destroying all of Western civilization" (p. 125).

Especially for the Hitler Youth Movement, which was at the forefront of Hitler's support, Hitler's externalizing hate-mongering rhetoric was a comforting and inspiring message, and Hitler provided the strong inspiring father figure that these children could not find within their own families. But, in rebelling against their own families, they submitted uncritically to Hitler's authoritarian leadership. Importantly, Adolf Hitler's unleashing of the demons of war was turning the passive humiliation of defeat into the active experience of redemptive action.[16]

A cautionary note: by no means was German psychology uniform, and, assuredly, there were many within Germany who did not uncritically yield to Hitler's hate-mongering rhetoric. But, especially for the German youth, this rhetoric was restorative, replacing humiliation and shame with pride, an exemplar of the destructive charismatic leader–follower relationship.

Waite, in *The Psychopathic God*,[17] provides persuasive evidence that Hitler believed he was one-quarter Jewish. Indeed, uncertainty concerning his genealogy on his father's side plagued him throughout his life. In 1930, an alarmed Adolf Hitler called in his attorney, Hans Frank. A relative had threatened blackmail, claiming he had documentary evidence that Hitler's paternal grandfather was Jewish. Frank investigated and reported that he found corroborating evidence that Hitler's grandmother, Maria Ann Schickelgruber, had worked in the home of a Jewish family named Frankenberger. In 1837, at age 41, she gave birth to Alois Schickelgruber, Hitler's father. No father was recorded on the baptismal registry. Frank found records indicating that Frankenberger had paid financial support to Maria Ann Schickelgruber for Alois for 14 years. An obvious conclusion was that Frankenberger had fathered Alois. A compelling indication that Hitler believed that his grandmother had been impregnated by a Jew and that he carried Jewish blood can be found in the Nuremberg Racial Laws of 1935, which Hitler called *Blutschutzgesetz* ("law for the protection of the blood"). Paragraph 3, which was written by Hitler, declared "Jews cannot employ household servants of German or related blood who are under 45 years of age."[18] At the time, 45 was the presumptive age of menopause and the cessation of fertility. Had this law been in place when his 41-year-old grandmother was working as a domestic, she could not have become pregnant by her Jewish employer, as Hitler feared she had.

In his belief that the Jews had invaded and weakened the German body politic and therefore had to be eradicated, Hitler was projecting his own fears onto the German nation, and the final solution of the Holocaust and his relentless quest to eliminate the contaminating influence of Jews from society was a projection of Hitler's own internal fears.

It is easy to understand how the type of emotional deprivation to which Adolf Hitler, Saddam Hussein, and Idi Amin were exposed at the very beginnings of life could lead to deep and lasting wounds to their self-esteem. What is more difficult to understand is how great expectations of the newborn, continued through early childhood, could be profoundly wounding to the self-concept and self-esteem as well, which is the subject of the next chapter.

Notes

1. Jerrold Post, "Tyranny on Trial: Political Personality Profiles and Conduct at Trial of Slobodan Milosevic and Saddam Hussein" (paper presented *at International Conference on the Trials of the Century*, Cornell University Law School, Ithaca, New York, 2005).

2. Amazia Baram, "Saddam Hussein as Wartime Decision Maker" (paper presented at the conference *The Iran-Iraq War: The View from Baghdad*, Woodrow Wilson International Center for Scholars, Washington, D.C., October 25–27, 2011).

3. Mary-Jayne McKay, "Turkmenbashi Everywhere," *CBS News 60 Minutes*, February 11, 2009, www.cbsnews.com/2100-18560_162-590913.html.

4. McKay, "Turkmenbashi Everywhere."

5. Patrick Marnham, "In Search of Amin," *Granta Magazine* 17 (1985): 69–82.

6. Marnham, "In Search of Amin," 80.

7. George Ivan Smith, *Ghosts of Kampala: The Rise and Fall of Idi Amin* (London: Weidenfeld and Nicolson, 1980), 101.

8. Robert Robins and Jerrold Post, *Political Paranoia: The Psychopolitics of Hatred* (New Haven: Yale University Press, 1993).

9. George Church, "Targeting Gaddafi," *Time Magazine*, April 21, 1986, www.time.com/time/magazine/article/0,9171,961140,00.html.

10. Robert Hanley, "US Links Man with 3 Bombs to Terror Plot," *The New York Times*, February 4, 1989, www.nytimes.com/1989/02/04/nyregion/us-links-man-with-3-bombs-to-a-terror-plot.html.

11. "Libya's Gaddafi: 'My People Love Me,'" *BBC News*, February 28, 2011, www.bbc.co.uk/news/world-africa-12603086.

12. Viktor Suvorov, *Soviet Military Intelligence* (London: Grafton Books, 1986), 155.

13. Jerrold Post, *Leaders and Their Followers in a Dangerous World: The Psychology of Political Behavior* (Ithaca: Cornell University Press, 2004).

14. Peter Loewenberg, "The Psychohistorical Origins of the Nazi Youth Cohort," in *Decoding the Past: The Psychohistorical Approach,*. Peter Loewenberg (New York: Alfred A. Knopf, 1983).

15. Heinz Kohut, *Self-Psychology and the Humanities: Reflections on a New Psychoanalytic Approach* (New York: W.W. Norton & Company, 1985).

16. Loewenberg, "The Psychohistorical Origins of the Nazi Youth Cohort."

17. Robert Waite, *The Psychopathic God: Adolf Hitler* (New York: Basic Books, 1977).

18. Waite, *The Psychopathic God: Adolf Hitler*, 128.

3

Great Expectations

Besotted with love, each member of the young couple consumed with blinding infatuation for each other finds the partner flawless. Surely, a more beautiful woman never graced the earth, nor a more handsome man. He (she) is so brilliant, so witty, so sensitive, warm, and nurturing. Each waking thought is consumed with the other. They feel expanded by the power of their love.

But if love is blind, it does not always remain so. Scholars of love and marriage have estimated that the duration of that blinding infatuation lasts between as little as six hours and as long as two years. The illusion of perfection gradually evolves: for many, it becomes a mature realistic love; for others, it precipitates the termination of the relationship. The flaws so blissfully ignored in that first flowering intoxication now may loom large.

OVERVALUATION OF THE CHILD

In likening the blinding infatuation of the lover to the doting adulation of the parents for their newborn, Freud[1] found the element in common to be "over-valuation." Whether in oneself or another, the element being considered is "magnified in importance, is overvalued, its unique perfection extolled."[2]

In examining the centrality of the quest for perfection, Rothstein[3] particularly emphasizes the attitude of *entitlement*. The entitled individual says, in effect, "I want what I want when I want it, and I want it now," the imperious demanding quality referred to by Freud as "His Majesty, the Baby."[4] In understanding the developmental pathways of narcissism, he observes: "If we look at the attitude of affectionate parents towards their children, we have to recognize that it is a revival and reproduction of their own narcissism, which they have long since abandoned."

The reaction of parents to the miracle of the birth of the newborn, their adoration of their own child, who is perfect in every way and has a future without limits in its potential, is palpable. The dreams of parents for their newborn children soar. "The child shall fulfill those wishful dreams of the parents which they never carried out – the boy shall become a great man and a hero in his father's place, and the girl shall marry a prince as a tardy compensation for her mother. ... Parental love, which is so moving, and at bottom so childish, is nothing but the parents' narcissism born again."

The excessive and overinflated praise such parents bestow on their proud creations leads inevitably to an unconscious awareness that "the lady doth protest too much," producing an insatiable appetite for praise lest the underlying inadequacy be revealed. As a consequence, in the narcissistic individual, there comes to be an idealized self-concept or "good self" and an inadequate, devalued "bad self."

Healthy parents progressively guide their children through the shoals of reality, helping them to cope with its frustrations and learn how to delay their quest for immediate gratification. They learn to integrate the "good self" and "bad self" into a realistic self-concept. It is important to emphasize that we are speaking of a continuum. After all, it is the mother's praise and love, communicated in the context of reality with an appreciation of the child's individuality and limitations, that leads to a healthy self-concept and healthy self-esteem. But some parents, reflecting their own unfulfilled narcissistic dreams of glory, are so consumed by their need for their children to be special that they fail to help their children develop a realistic self-concept.

MY SON, THE PRIME MINISTER

In the world of politics, Robert J. Hawke, the longest serving Australian Labor Prime Minister (1983–1991), provides a vivid example. His mother indicated that she looked into the crib at her newborn son and knew that someday he would be prime minister.[5] Indeed, she was later to acknowledge that, nine months earlier, she knew something very special had happened.

A colleague spent a summer semester in Oxford where he became friendly with Valery Giscard d'Estaing, the future president of France. After the summer semester ended, he visited with his new friend in the family estate on the outskirts of Paris. On first meeting, Giscard's mother said in a matter-of-fact manner to my colleague, "I'm so glad to meet you. I suppose you know that someday he will be president of France."[6] She advised him accordingly on the wisdom of sustaining their friendship.

Were Hawke's and Giscard's mothers prescient, gifted with eerie prognostic powers? No. They raised their sons to be special, and that special sense of self with which they endowed them, combined with intellectual gifts and opportunity, led to their glittering, predicted success.

WOODROW WILSON: INCULCATED EARLY WITH A SPECIAL SENSE OF SELF

In *Woodrow Wilson and Colonel House*, the exemplary 1964 psychobiography of Woodrow Wilson by Alexander and Juliette George,[7] the authors provide powerful evidence that the perfectionistic, demanding qualities of Wilson's father played a seminal role in shaping his son's perfectionistic bent and unwillingness to compromise. The authors suggest that this personality characteristic played a central role in the two major defeats at the end of Wilson's career, defeats that weakened his historical legacy: his failure to win Senate approval for the United States to enter the League of Nations and his failure to obtain agreement to moderate conditions of the Versailles Treaty. Minor cosmetic compromises with Senate Majority Leader Henry Cabot Lodge would have led to Senate approval, but Wilson would not compromise, would not yield a whit, would not change a word, and the measures went down to defeat.

At the time that the Georges were conducting research with the Wilson papers at Princeton University, material on Wilson's mother was not available. But, in fact, Woodrow Wilson's mother's letters to her son, the future president, are a remarkable record of the origins of his dreams of glory.[8] Consider the following example:

My darling Boy, I am so anxious about that cold of yours. How did you take it? Surely you have not laid aside your winter clothing? Another danger is sitting without fire these cool nights. Do be careful, my dear boy, for my sake. You seem depressed, but that is because you are not well. You need not imagine that you are not a favorite. Everybody here likes and admires you. I could not begin to tell you the kind and flattering things that are said about you, by everybody that knows you. Yes, you will have no lack of friends in Wilmington – of the warmest sort. There seem to be an unusual number of young people about your age there – and of a superior kind – and they are prepared to take an unusual interest in you particularly. Why, my darling boy, nobody could help loving you, if they were to try. I have a bad headache this morning, dear – won't attempt to write you a letter. My chief object in writing is to tell you that I love my absent boy – oh so dearly ... (Link, 1968, p. 50)

Heady yeast, that! This is the stuff of which narcissistic personalities are brewed. In this brief missive, Mrs. Wilson communicates to her son – who is away, not at summer camp for the first time, as the tone of the letter suggests, but at college – that she and he are one and inseparable and that her well-being depends on him. She conveys to him that among superior people, he is especially admired. The perceptions and urgings of such mothers are not designed to produce sons and daughters of modest ambitions. Indeed, these early perceptions and the continual psychological shaping undoubtedly play a major role in leading their "beneficiaries" to reach for – and achieve – the stars.

GENERAL MACARTHUR'S MOTHER'S TOWERING AMBITIONS FOR HER SON

But if the letter by Mrs. Wilson conveys her special view of her special son, consider this poem by the mother of General Douglas MacArthur. In his own 1964 autobiographic memoir, *Reminiscences*, MacArthur included a poem his mother wrote to him, with an excerpt that read:

> Like mother, like son, is saying so true
> The world will judge largely of mother by you.
> Be this then your task, if task it shall be
> To force this proud world to do homage to me.
> Be sure it will say, when its verdict you've won
> She reaps as she sowed: "this man is her son!"

(p. 32)

This excerpt is evidence in and of itself that Mrs. MacArthur viewed much of her own worth and importance as dependent on how her son presented himself to the world. And she explicitly told him this: that her success in the world depended on his! To further this goal, so nakedly stated, his mother, concerned for the welfare of her oh-so-special son, took an apartment in the nearby Craney Hotel, within easy viewing distance of the West Point campus, to always be there for young Douglas. She advised him on a daily basis of the lessons she deemed important in life. The pressure to succeed and carry the family honor must have been immense, especially given the line of military heroes in the MacArthur lineage that preceded him.

General MacArthur came from a long tradition of military leaders. He was the youngest of three sons born to Mary Pinkney Hardy (or "Pinkie" as she was widely known) and Lieutenant General Arthur MacArthur, Jr., a Medal of Honor recipient for his heroic service during the American Civil War. It is said that the MacArthur clan can trace its lineage back through a long line of warriors to Robert the Bruce of Scotland, who guided Scotland in gaining its independence from England and took over its leadership. There is an old Scottish proverb that says "Nothing has stood longer than MacArthur, the hills, and the devil."[9]

Apart from her determination to ensure that her son pursue and succeed in a military career, his mother also oversaw his personal relationships. When he became simultaneously engaged to eight young women, his mother apparently intervened to ensure that her young son would not meet the vengeance of the eight young women and their families for his disinterest in following through with any of the engagements. Asked about this episode later, MacArthur laughed coyly and responded, "I have never been so hotly engaged by the enemy."[10]

Douglas's brother Malcolm died suddenly at the age of five from measles. "This was a terrible blow to my mother, but it seemed only to increase her devotion to Arthur and myself ... the tie was to become one of the dominant factors in my life."[11] Douglas recalls his mother discussing his duties to his family, his country, and to God from an early age and of his dreaming of one day becoming a soldier and entering the family line of military heroes. To him, his mother spoke about moral principles and a sense of obligation. Douglas reported that "We were to do what was right no matter what the personal sacrifice might be. Our country was always to come first."[12]

And when his socialite wife and recent divorcee Louise Cromwell, to whom MacArthur proposed in 1922 when his mother was out of town, persisted in complaining about the army lifestyle in the Philippines and urged her husband to resign from the Army, it was duty to country and the family's military tradition, emphasized by his mother, that won the day: the couple divorced in 1929.

His mother was instrumental in finding a suitable choice for his second marriage. Jean Faircloth, the granddaughter of a Confederate captain as well as a Daughter of the Confederacy and Daughter of the American Revolution, turned out to be an ideal match.[13] Mrs. MacArthur met her on a cruise and was immediately captivated by her Southern roots, her lively personality, and her love of the Army. She introduced her son to her immediately on her return, hoping for love to blossom. MacArthur showed little interest at first because he was concerned about the health of his mother, who had been sick for some time.[14] But his mother persisted, pressing the young Jean Faircloth to accompany her and her son to Manila, where he ultimately yielded. They were married in a low-key civil ceremony in 1937. On her deathbed, MacArthur's mother turned to Jean and said, "He is going to love you very much."[15]

Thus MacArthur's mother played a determining role both in his military career and in his marital choice. But the manner in which she, in effect, commanded his career choice was to emphasize the length and distinction of his military provenance, which from early in life was played and replayed for him, powerfully contributing to his emerging identity. He was helpless to refuse. It represented a remarkable case of the telescoping of generations.[16]

Indeed, his father's Medal of Honor was awarded when he was but 18, after he flouted his order to retreat, seized the regimental flag, and planted it on the crest of Missionary Ridge in Tennessee, thus inspiring his regiment to a heroic victory.[17] That Douglas MacArthur, who made no secret of his disdain for civilian authority, flouted President Truman's order to restrict interaction with the media when he publicly called on China to admit that it had been defeated in the Korean War – an act that led Truman to recall MacArthur from his position as UN commander – reflected his identification with his father.

Dreams die hard, and MacArthur continued to aspire to dreams of glory and the ultimate prize, the presidency of the United States. But he was thwarted at the 1952 Republican convention by Dwight D. Eisenhower. MacArthur would not endorse the Eisenhower candidacy, and he withdrew from public view for several weeks. The failure to achieve his dreams of glory to which, at his mother's urging, he had devoted his life and believed he was destined to achieve was a bitter blow, one from which he would never recover.

THE DOMINATING INFLUENCE OF FRANKLIN DELANO ROOSEVELT'S MOTHER

Franklin Delano Roosevelt's mother Sara was strongly invested in her son's success and indeed interfered with Franklin's marriage to Eleanor. When Franklin, at age 22, proposed to Eleanor Roosevelt, Theodore Roosevelt's 19-year-old niece, who accepted the proposal, it seemed entirely natural to them, but Sara Roosevelt was stunned. As James MacGregor Burns relates in his 1956 biography of Roosevelt, having lost her husband only three years earlier, she had looked forward to her son's companionship at Hyde Park, the family estate, and told her son that the couple was much too young to get married. Young Roosevelt was firm but diplomatic. He wrote her that "I know my mind" and then attempted to ease her worries about this threat to their closeness. "And for you, dear Mummy, you know that nothing can ever change what we have always been & always will be to each other – only now you have two children to love and to love you." Eleanor made an overture to her powerful future mother-in-law: "I do so want you to learn to love me a little. You must know that I will always try to do what you wish, for I have grown to love you very dearly during the past summer."[18] Franklin's mother was not persuaded by these notes and did her best to deter her son from what she deemed his headlong course, taking him on a Caribbean cruise, but to no avail. Franklin remained determined to wed on his return, and Sara ultimately yielded. But this did not end her overly close relationship with her newly married son. On the couple's return from an extended European honeymoon in 1905, they moved into an apartment on East 36th Street in New York, which had been rented and furnished by Sara in their absence. They lived there for two years while Sara built two adjoining houses on 65th Street – one for the new couple and one for herself, with a passage between the two. Sara continued to be a dominating presence in their marriage.

For Prime Minister Hawke of Australia, President Giscard d'Estaing of France, and President Woodrow Wilson, General Douglas MacArthur, and President Franklin Delano Roosevelt of the United States, the historical record suggests the importance of their mothers in shaping the dreams of glory of these oh-so-special sons.

KING HUSSEIN OF JORDAN: LIVING UP TO HIS GRANDFATHER'S DREAMS

For King Hussein of Jordan, it was his grandfather Abdullah, a man of towering charismatic stature, who very early conveyed to his grandson the special role and responsibilities he would someday bear as King of Jordan.

In 1962, at the relatively tender age of 27, Hussein wrote an autobiographical memoir entitled *Uneasy Lies the Head*. To write an autobiography at so young an age suggests a special sense of self (the same observation has been made of U.S. President Barack Obama who wrote *Dreams from My Father* when he was 25). Hussein begins his memoir on June 20, 1951, in Jerusalem, when he, a boy of 16, was by his grandfather's side on the steps of the al-Aqsa mosque when King Abdullah was struck and killed by an assassin's bullet. His grandfather's aides vanished in the turmoil. Hussein pursued the assassin into the mosque, and the assassin fired at young Hussein, striking him in the chest. As Hussein writes, a medal he was wearing at his grandfather's insistence deflected the bullet and saved his life. This imbued Hussein with a sense of destiny, a belief that his life had been spared so that he could lead his country.

Hussein wrote of the special place he held in his grandfather's eyes: "I have decided to start these memoirs with the murder of my grandfather since he, above all men, had the most profound influence on my life. So, too, had the manner of his death ... To me he was more than a grandfather, and to him I think I was a son."[19] Three days before the trip to Jerusalem, his grandfather had spoken to him about his future responsibilities: "I hope you realize, my son, that one day you will have to assume responsibility. I look to you to do your very best to see that my work is not lost. I look to you to continue in the service of our people."[20]

That Abdullah, the founder of the modern state of Jordan, had invested so much in his grandson, whom he indeed called "my son," was a consequence of the fact that his own son, Talal, suffered from serious mental illness, paranoid schizophrenia, that would render him incapable of ruling. At the time of the assassination, Talal was in Switzerland receiving psychiatric treatment. King Abdullah, who prided himself on being tough, did not understand his son's ailment and treated him with contempt. While in his memoir, Hussein dutifully praised his father for his courage in dealing with his illness, the net result was that Hussein did not have a stable father figure to identify with, and his grandfather early on fastened on Hussein as his successor: "We watched our father with loving care, but my grandfather, who lived partly in the heroic past, saw him from outside. He had wanted a brave, intrepid Bedouin son to carry on the great tradition of the Arab Revolt. He was incapable of accepting an invalid in place of his dream. It was the bitterest disappointment of his life. ... Looking back now, I can see how and why toward the end of his life, my grandfather had lavished such affection on me as he grew older. I had possibly become the son he had always wanted."[21]

Hussein accompanied Abdullah everywhere and often acted as Abdullah's English translator: "he taught me how to come to terms with adversity as well as with success. And he taught me above all else that a leader's greatest duty is to serve."[22] He went on to write that "it was his death which taught me the ultimate lesson ... his murder was the first time that violence had touched me personally and on that terrible day I learned much, even if I did not realize it. ... I learned the unimportance of death ... it behooves a man to give of his utmost in the brief span which can end as swiftly as my grandfather's. ... Without doubt, it was the death of my grandfather that brought me face to face with myself and made me clarify my philosophy of life for the first time. ... I had no wish then to reign as King of Jordan and it was with relief that I learned that my father, who was being treated in Switzerland, appeared to be recovering."[23] Talal indeed ascended to the throne, but it was swiftly apparent that his illness would not permit him to rule. Hussein was sent to school in England (Sandhurst), which he enjoyed and where he did very well. But occasional warnings of his father's declining health reached him, and "I knew that if anything happened I would have to return. I hated the idea. ... I loved my country, but I felt the responsibility of leading Jordan and serving it was far too much for me to undertake. At this time, I did not want to be King."[24]

Hussein went on to indicate that he was disillusioned by the way he had seen Abdullah's aides scatter at the time of the assassination but also that he wanted to lead an ordinary life. "But it was a dream I never realized."[25]

On August 12, 1952, he received a cable addressed to "His Majesty, King Hussein," informing him that his father had abdicated. Hussein knew that his days as a schoolboy were over. A regency council ruled until Hussein was 18. He was to rule for nearly 43 years.

His grandfather had impressed on young Hussein their family responsibility for the holy places in Jerusalem, the al-Aqsa Mosque and the Dome of the Rock. When King Hussein, at Nasser's request, belatedly entered the 1967 Arab-Israeli war started by Egyptian President Nasser, despite warnings to the contrary by Israel, Israel swiftly captured the West Bank, including Jerusalem and the Temple Mount. Although it was a day of great joy and prophetic significance for the Jewish people, restoring their access to the Wailing Wall, it would forever stain King Hussein's reputation. He had lost custody of his holy responsibility. (The manner in which, at the end of his life, he acted to redress this failing will be discussed in the chapter on the impact of terminal illness on leadership behavior.)

THE TELESCOPING OF GENERATIONS

For some, it is as if their destiny is preordained, as if they were programmed to assume the role of political leader. But at what psychological cost? Can individuals who are specially designated in this fashion early in life ever achieve enough to feel fulfilled? Can they ever be truly satisfied? It is a heavy burden to be the vehicle of the parents' success. The unique hopes and dreams of the individual have been eclipsed by the parents' dreams of glory. It is not the individual who is valued for himself or herself, but rather his or her accomplishments that are valued. To be cabinet minister at an early age may be perceived as failure by the narcissistic leader; if programmed for the highest glory, only the prime ministership will do.

What has been described in this chapter is another pathway to the wounded self, the individual who becomes an extension of the parents' dreams of glory and the vehicle for the parents' success. There is a constant imperative to succeed because parental love and approval is contingent on that success. Designated at birth to follow a path selected by the parents, there has been a premature foreclosure of identity; the child so burdened cannot individuate, cannot choose his or her own path. A role has been ascribed, and the child so designated is choiceless but to fulfill that role. King Hussein would have liked to have lived an ordinary life, but he was choiceless.

South Asia has provided us with the examples of two women who followed in the paths of their fathers, and, in the case of Indira Gandhi, the pathway of her grandfather as well. Indira Gandhi and Benazir Bhutto, and the great expectations into which they were born, are the subjects of the next two chapters. They were truly "Daughters of Destiny," with an emphasis on the generational transmission of their roles as leaders.

Notes

1. Sigmund Freud, "On Narcissism," in *The Standard Edition of the Complete Psychological Works of Sigmund Freud*, Vol. XIV (1914–1916): *On the History of the Psycho-Analytic Movement, Papers on Metapsychology and Other Works* (London: Hogarth Press, 1958), 67–102.

2. Stephen Mitchell, "The Wings of Icarus: Illusion and the Problem of Narcissism," *Contemporary Psychoanalysis*, 22, 107–132 (1986), 1456.

3. Arnold Rothstein, *The Narcissistic Pursuit of Perfection* (New York: International Universities Press, 1980).

4. Freud, "On Narcissism," 91.

5. Blanche D'Alpuget, *Robert J. Hawke: A Biography* (East Melbourne: Schwarts, in conjunction with Landsdowne Press, 1982).

6. George Carver, 1975, Personal Interview.

7. Alexander L. George and Juliette L. George, *Woodrow Wilson and Colonel House: A Personality Study* (New York: John Day, 1964).

8. Jerrold Post, "Woodrow Wilson Reexamined: The Mind-Body Controversy Redux and Other Disputations," *Political Psychology* 4(2) (1983): 289–306.

9. Frank Kelley and Cornelius Ryan, *MacArthur: Man of Action* (Garden City, N.Y.: Doubleday, 1959), 30.

10. Kelley and Ryan, *MacArthur: Man of Action*, 43.

11. D. Clayton James, *The Years of MacArthur* (Boston: Houghton Mifflin, 1985), 54.

12. James, *The Years of MacArthur*, 54.

13. Kelley and Ryan, *MacArthur: Man of Action*, 52.

14. Ibid., 53.

15. Ibid., 51.

16. Haydée Faimberg, *The Telescoping of Generations: Listening to the Narcissistic Links between Generations* (London: Routledge, 2005).

17. James, *The Years of MacArthur*, 14.

18. James MacGregor Burns, *Roosevelt: The Lion and the Fox* (New York: Harcourt, Brace & World, 1956), 26.
19. Hussein, King of Jordan, *Uneasy Lies the Head: The Autobiography of His Majesty King Hussein I of the Hashemite Kingdom of Jordan* (New York: B. Geis Associates, 1962), 13–14.
20. Hussein, *Uneasy Lies the Head*, 6.
21. Ibid., 19–20.
22. Ibid., 21–22.
23. Ibid., 24–25.
24. Ibid., 36.
25. Ibid.

4

Daughters of Destiny I: Indira Gandhi

Jessica Chaudhary, M. D. and Jerrold M. Post, M. D.

POLITICAL PEDIGREE

In reviewing Indira Gandhi's rise to power, one first needs to search her family's past and consider her rise from within a generational framework. It is useful to consider this from the perspective of a "telescoping of generations," which Faimberg[1] describes as the unconscious narcissistic link between generations, in which the identity of the individual can be influenced to incorporate the hopes, wishes, and traumas of prior generations.

The Nehru-Gandhi dynasty has been the predominant political family in India since 1958. Indira was born to Jawaharlal and Kamala Nehru in the home of her paternal grandfather, Motilal Nehru, in Allahabad, a city known to be a prominent cultural hub in northern India. The Nehru clan belonged to an exclusive community of high-caste Hindus. Motilal's father was a respected police chief in Delhi who died three months before Motilal was born.

Motilal was a natural leader, and the admiration he received from others ultimately led him to become a member of the Indian National Congress.[2] It was said that he had "the exquisiteness of attire which symbolized the clean fighter and the great gentleman and that impressive face, deeply lined and careworn, on which character and intellect were so deeply imprinted ... Eminent as a lawyer, eminent as a speaker, and in the first rank as a political leader, he could not but take the foremost place wherever he might be."[3] At the age of 26, Motilal was thrust into the position of family caretaker after the sudden death of his brother.[4] He rapidly became more prominent in Indian society, and he was truly looked on as a secular and worldly individual in Allahabad.

This chapter was presented as a paper to the annual scientific meeting of the International Society of Political Psychology, July 9–12, 2011, in Istanbul, Turkey, by Dr. Jessica Chaudhary at a symposium organized and chaired by Dr. Jerrold Post entitled "Dreams of Glory: Narcissism and Politics."

As a former moderate in nationalist politics, Motilal was voted president of the Indian National Congress in the wake of the Amritsar massacre in 1919, and again in Calcutta in 1920, when he backed Mohandas (who later came to be known as Mahatma, meaning "great soul") Gandhi's call for withdrawal of British influence in the country. Politics was the family business and, indeed, a core aspect of the family's social identity.

Indira's father, Jawaharlal Nehru, was born into a wealthy and prominent lifestyle, surrounded by the family's tennis courts, rich furnishings, swimming pools, and servants. As the only son, he was held in high regard by his parents. Mohandas Gandhi was once asked what he thought Motilal's greatest quality was, to which he responded "love of his son," stating that his love of India was derived from his unwavering admiration and hope for his child.[5] As Jawaharlal grew, his father made sure that he was educated in Western ways, just as he had been. Jawaharlal was sent to England for his education at Harrow, Trinity College, Cambridge, and the Inner Temple, a prominent society mostly reserved for individuals seeking a career in law. In many ways, Jawaharlal grew up much like his father, and he later wrote that spending so much time away from India to receive his education made him "a queer mixture of East and West, out of place everywhere, at home nowhere."[6] This conveys Jawaharlal's sense of loneliness and feelings of isolation. Perhaps this is why he found a home within the independence movement after meeting Mohandas Gandhi in 1916; he finally connected to something that felt important to him.

The sense of isolation that Jawaharlal felt was later experienced by his daughter Indira, who often lived alone when her parents were jailed. Indira, as an only child, grew up fiercely independent but often lonely and longing for her parents' attention.

At the time of Indira's birth in 1917, it was customary for women to return to their parents' house to deliver a child, but Motilal was excited by the prospect of his first grandchild and convinced his young daughter-in-law, Kamala, to stay. It was said that Indira's grandmother remarked that Indira should have been a son, seemingly in line with the sentiment of a male-dominated society in India at the time. Motilal, in turn, remarked that "This daughter of Jawaharlal, for all we know, may prove to be better than a thousand sons."[7] Perhaps he felt a special connection with Indira and had great aspirations for her from the start. Motilal's love for his son was passed on to his granddaughter. His love was blind to her gender.

Motilal's prediction of Indira's greatness was a prelude to her family's desire for her success. After her birth, letters and telegrams were sent from around the country to congratulate the Nehru family on their blessing. One such telegram from politician and poet Sarojini Naidu said that young Indira was a "new soul of India."[8]

THE YOUNG INDIRA

Indira grew up as an only child, largely alone and isolated, witnessing the constant intrusion into her home of police who would take both of her parents to jail on numerous occasions. Several times, in fact, Indira would tell a visitor to the house "I'm sorry, but my grandfather, father and mummy are all in prison."[9] This led her to anticipate being left alone, but also to idealize her parents and grandfather because family members largely wore their imprisonment as a badge of honor. Indira strived to be included within the family's beliefs and ideals, and this can be seen throughout many instances in her childhood. As part of the close friendship the Nehrus formed with Mohandas Gandhi, they gave up their luxurious lifestyle to join in his protest against the British; in a revolt against foreign fabrics, the Nehrus burned their clothes in a ceremonial bonfire and took to wearing handspun clothing.[10]

Once, a foreign relative visiting from France brought Indira a frock, but Kamala refused to give it to her. The relative's protest prompted Kamala to call her daughter to either accept or reject the garment by her own accord. Indira returned the frock to the visitor, only to be asked why she had a foreign doll. Despite her love for the doll, Indira set fire to the doll later that evening, showing how deeply she introjected her family's ideals and values. Furthermore, when Indira was 12 years old and unable to actively join her family in their protests (and jail sentences), she formed her own children's group of freedom fighters, the Monkey Brigade.[11]

Indira seemed to cherish the idea of becoming a martyr and was eager to join the ranks of those seeking India's independence, along with her other family members. Her actions throughout her childhood revealed how she viewed herself and the person she wanted to become. Indira would often stand on a table and gather the servants in her household so that she could give speeches, often reciting slogans and terms that she heard from the elder members of her family.[12] Krishna, Indira's aunt, caught her one day with her arms outstretched, muttering words while standing on the verandah. When asked what she was doing, Indira responded that she was practicing being Joan of Arc and that someday she would lead her people to freedom as Joan did.[13] She would also split her dolls into rival teams of freedom fighters and baton-wielding police.[14] When her parents were away in prison, as they often were during her politically tumultuous childhood while the country struggled toward independence, Indira said that she did not play with dolls but rather with toy metal soldiers. At the head of the column of soldiers was one with a white shield bearing a red cross, suggesting her identification with Joan of Arc. She marched the soldiers into a fire again and again, perhaps indicating the early foundation of her career-long bent for conflict and presaging her ultimate martyr's death in her assassination by Sikh bodyguards after her attack on the Golden Temple in 1984. It is instructive to observe that she was characterized as "the goddess of destruction" by her political opponents and was seen as a leader who regularly promoted political conflict, lacking her parents conciliatory skills.[15]

These acts, along with her patterns of repeating the actions and words of her elders, help paint a picture of Indira longing to play an important role in India's development and history. In fact, Gandhi did ultimately destroy thousands of

Sikhs; she also suffered the ultimate consequence for her actions and came to be seen as a martyr. She had been warned against entering the Golden Temple, that it would be considered provocative and dangerous, and yet she proceeded despite (or because of) these warnings, in self-fulfillment of her martyr's destiny.

As a young child, Indira was never considered an intellectual, unlike her father. In fact, Indira failed her Latin exam twice and was asked to leave Oxford University.[16] Jawaharlal controlled many aspects of Indira's life, including what books she read and how she exercised, but he always stressed the importance of her education. Indira grew up to adore her mother, who was neither wealthy nor politically connected. Because her mother was never fully accepted by her father's family because of her presumed naïveté and inferior social class, Indira became critical of her father and his family for allowing her mother to be treated with a lack of respect. Indira later cared for her mother, who died from complications of tuberculosis in 1936, leaving Indira filled with grief.[17] This would be the first of several family deaths for Indira, but her mother's memory and the close relationship Indira had with her may have contributed to her desire to ascend to the top ranks of government as a woman.

Indira seemed to connect with women, as Jawaharlal observed in a letter to his sister:

> When voting finished today, large numbers of our Congress workers turned up at Anand Bhawan, including many women. Indu [Indira] has specially shaken up the women, and even Muslim women came out. Indu has indeed grown and matured very greatly during the last year, and especially during these elections ... she is quite a heroine in Allahabad now and particularly with the women.[18]

Research on women's identity development in India has contributed to understanding Indira's role within her own family. Looking at the inherent patriarchal structure of society and the roles women play in the family, Kakar and Seymour[19] describe the importance of interpersonal relationships that define a woman in India, both in the context of her parents and later also with her husband and children. Seymour, in an intergenerational study of females in India, found that women created an identity and personal development that were linked primarily to their jobs and duties within their families and that were passed down through female generations.

Indira most certainly pushed the boundaries of societal norms for females in India at the time, arguably coming from a family that was more encouraging in her efforts to break societal norms, given the education and status of her grandfather and father. When looking at accounts of Indira's life as she grew up, we are aware that her paternal grandfather did not believe in the worth of a male as superior to that of a female, as evidenced by his comment upon hearing that Kamala had given birth to a daughter. However, Indira grew up watching her mother play the role of dutiful wife and daughter-in-law, despite the reported cruelty she faced from the other Nehru women.[20] Kamala, however, also played an active role in the movement against British rule with her husband. This dual role as both a traditional and activist woman in society undoubtedly had an effect on the way Indira viewed her own role at the time and may have created inner conflict.

FATHER AND HUSBAND

It was Indira's relationship with her father that largely shaped her identity. As mentioned, Indira strongly identified with her parents becoming champions for their political causes. Indira's father, Jawaharlal Nehru, was the first and longest serving prime minister of India. Her birth into a wealthy and prominent political family, the "ultimate political pedigree ... was an enormous asset in a country where heredity still commanded reverence."[21]

In fact, when Gandhi put Jawaharlal's name forward for the presidency of the 1929 Congress at Lahore, Motilal was overjoyed and referred to the occasion with the Persian adage "What the father is unable to accomplish, the son achieves."[22] Perhaps Indira, being an only child, internalized a belief that the child was destined to perform greater deeds than its parents. Without intending to, Motilal and Jawaharlal's relationship and own rise to power instilled in young Indira similar aspirations, which Indira later passed to her son Sanjay, her second-born.

Indira went through numerous transitions and stages in her life with respect to her relationship with her father, first as a rebellious young woman who didn't respond to her father's letters, then as a "small mouse" next to her father,[23] and ultimately as a hostess, personal assistant, and one of her father's closest confidantes. Indira was not overtly groomed for the role of prime minister. In fact, her father never encouraged political ambitions, being an opponent of nepotism. But having grown up in this intensely political household must have inevitably stimulated Indira's desire for a career in politics, as reflected in her fantasized association as a young girl with Joan of Arc, who was martyred in the service of her people.

Although Indira was largely self-sufficient, she was internally insecure and lacked a sense of stability. She developed a defiance toward authority, leaving against medical advice during treatment for tuberculosis, having two children when she was strongly advised against this by her doctors, and marrying in 1942 the man she loved, Feroze Gandhi, despite her father's disapproval.[24]

Nehru's objections to Feroze were myriad. Feroze had courted the young Indira since she was 16 years old and had helped to care for Indira's ailing mother. It was perhaps this devotion to Kamala that initially won Indira's affection. But Feroze was not a Hindu but a Parsi,[25] and he was Indira's first suitor. He studied at the London School of Economics, but left to join the independence movement. Feroze served in parliament and was also a journalist, becoming publisher of the *National Herald*.

Jawaharlal felt Indira should wait to explore other prospects, but the young Indira's mind was decided and could not be changed.

Several years later, Indira was forced to choose between her husband and her widowed father. In 1946, amid the turmoil of the "Calcutta killings" prior to independence, Jawaharlal needed his daughter's help more than ever. Indira moved from Lucknow, where she was living with Feroze, to Delhi (several hundred miles away) to help her father manage the growing political unrest. Indira likely felt conflicted in her roles as wife and daughter. Now the dutiful daughter, she moved away from her husband and devoted herself to her father's causes.

The physical distance between her and Feroze only served to widen the growing psychological distance between the couple. The killing of Mahatma Gandhi in 1948 created a further rift between Indira and Feroze. Since Motilal's death, Mahatma Gandhi served as a father to Jawaharlal and a spiritual guiding light. When Mahatma was killed, Jawaharlal lost a father figure – again. Mahatma's death was heartbreaking to Nehru, who spoke spontaneously to a grieving nation: "The light has gone out of our lives and there is darkness everywhere."[26]

Jawaharlal looked to Indira to fill the emotional void created by Mahatma Gandhi's death. Indeed, in Indira, Jawaharlal saw his own greatness and the narcissistic extension of himself, and he unconsciously shaped her to fulfill his political ambitions throughout her childhood and adolescence. This could have only been done by guiding her sole focus to be on politics, even at the expense of her personal family life, and resulting in a narcissistic transference of ambition from himself to Indira. From generation to generation, the foundation for this narcissistic ambition was originally laid by Motilal. Jawaharlal had been a great moral support to Indira, and, throughout her life, she relied on strong men: her grandfather, her father, and her son Sanjay.

After Mahatma Gandhi's death, Indira knew that her father needed her even more, and her father's needs at this point clearly overshadowed those of her husband, although she may have still felt internally conflicted in the loyalty owed to her father versus that owed to her husband. She moved into Teen Murti House, the prime minister's official residence, to serve as her father's hostess and confidante. Rumors swirled about Indira's distance from Feroze. Media blamed Feroze's roving eye and stated that Indira wanted to be at the seat of power.[27]

Indira became her father's confidante as she grew estranged from her husband. This was a critical time in laying the foundation for Indira's political aspirations. While Jawaharlal may not have been conscious of his actions, by separating Indira from Feroze and keeping her by his side through political turmoil, Jawaharlal was grooming his daughter for her later prime ministership.

In 1958, Feroze suffered his first heart attack at the age of 45. Indira was away on official travel with her father at the time but returned to Kashmir to nurse him back to health. He had a second and fatal heart attack in 1960, dying at age 47. Her father died in 1964 at the age of 74. Thus, by the age of 47, she had lost all of the important men in her life, her grandfather Motilal, Mahatma Gandhi, her husband Feroze, and her father Jawaharlal Nehru.

When Indira became prime minister in 1966 after the unexpected death of Prime Minister Lal Bahadur Shastri, she was largely seen as living in her father's shadow. Congress Party seniors thought that she would be submissive and easily controlled, and while she "was lampooned as the 'dumb doll' (goongi gudiya)," she would soon become one of India's most powerful prime ministers.[28] Indira transitioned in her relationship with her father from a rebellious youth to her father's docile companion.

As prime minister, she emerged from the shadow of her father to become a near-dictator, especially during the 21-month National Emergency. Her son Sanjay is largely seen as the impetus behind the Emergency and as author of some of the most extreme actions taken during this period, including the jailing of her opponents and forcing men and women to undergo sterilizations under the family planning initiative.

SONS

Although Rajiv was the elder son, he was not the chosen son; he was always reluctant to enter the family business, enjoying instead a career as a pilot and even identifying himself as "Captain Rajiv" instead of as a Gandhi.[29] Although the first son is often prized and seen as natural successor, it was felt that Rajiv did not have the interest or temperament for leadership, and he stayed away from politics. "He looked like a weakling compared to his younger brother."[30]

After her father died, it was Sanjay, the more aggressive of her two sons, who replaced him as Indira's tower of strength, emboldened by his mother's vulnerable state –she had lost both father and husband within a few years of each other – to assert strong leadership. Sanjay became a close advisor to his mother. It was widely speculated that he had strong influence over her. The prime ministership was run from the home, not the office, with "Sanjay behaving more and more as if he was prime minister."[31]

Sanjay represented one of Indira's conflicted identities, playing to her aggressive, dark, and dictatorial side. After losing Jawaharlal and Feroze, Indira lost much of the male support network in her life, and she turned to Sanjay for help as the closest male figure. Sanjay, in some ways, became Indira's voice and her *selfobject*, becoming more aggressive and exerting control.

"Indira Gandhi had [indulged], one should say over[indulged], her sons, particularly Sanjay, with love and care. She was blind to his shortcomings. Her concern for Sanjay's future well-being was not an inconsiderable factor in her fateful decision [to declare the Emergency]."[32] In 1975, immediately prior to the declaration of Emergency Rule, Indira was in the midst of her worst political crisis, with leaders of the opposition parties calling for her resignation amid increasing violence in the country, marked by the assassination of a railway minister and an assassination attempt on the chief justice of India. The economy was in shambles. Indira believed that "there was a conspiracy against her and the government"[33] as violence increased during this period of political unrest.

Sanjay convinced his mother to declare Emergency Rule for the sake of her political future and to hold on to the power of the office. He also knew "he would get into serious trouble if his mother were not around to protect him"[34] because a number of Indira's colleagues disliked Sanjay. Sanjay had an influence on Indira unlike any other. Indira eventually lost power in 1977, but she was reelected three years later, the same year that Sanjay was killed in an airplane crash.

Unlike her father, who did not consciously groom his daughter to succeed him, Indira was consciously grooming Sanjay to become prime minister, and it was just a day before his tragic death that Indira declared Sanjay Party General Secretary, "the first step in her grand design for him."[35] When Sanjay died, all of Indira's dreams for him died as well. Sanjay's death was a great blow to Indira, but she then focused her hopes to continue the Nehru-Gandhi legacy on her older son, Rajiv, who later became prime minister, a move signifying a shift in the telescoping of generations.

Although Sanjay has been largely blamed for the imposition of the Emergency, he has also been credited with engineering his mother's return to power in 1980.[36] In some ways, it was Sanjay who replaced Nehru, helping his mother hold her office. When Sanjay was killed in an air crash, Indira lost nearly every male figure around her: Mahatma Gandhi, Jawaharlal, Feroze, and Sanjay. The only person she now had left was Rajiv, the default but reluctant choice to succeed her.

Indira was killed by her own Sikh bodyguard in 1984, to avenge the attack she ordered on the Sikh's holiest shrine, the Golden Temple, during Operation Blue Star. Prior to Operation Blue Star, Indira was warned not to enter the gates of the sacred temple for fear that such inflammatory action would incite retaliation. However, she defied the warnings and ordered the attack on a Sikh religious day honoring the martyrdom of the Sikh guru and founder of the Temple, arguing that a militant was held inside who had a cache of weapons that could lead to a terrorist attack or the secession of the state of Punjab from India. However, "nothing particularly new had occurred in the preceding months: incidents of violence had continued as before, Bhindranwale had continued to make provocative statements against the Hindu Government and the Delhi Darbar from the sanctuary of the newly fortified Akal Takht (Golden Temple)."[37] "The most disturbing aspect of the entire operation was that a whole mass of men, women, and children were ordered to be killed merely on the suspicion that some terrorists were operating from the Golden Temple and other Gurdwaras."[38] It is interesting to note that the attack began on a day of martyrdom. It was, perhaps, Gandhi unconsciously seeking the martyrdom that had preoccupied her as a young child, when she identified herself with Joan of Arc. Looking to incite inflammatory action, she was fulfilling the martyr's legacy, and, indeed, it was this attack that ultimately led to her own demise. The attack was seen as confrontational and highly aggressive, carried out on innocent people while they worshipped. This action was in sharp contrast to her father's fine-tuned political abilities and conciliatory nature; she was living up to her reputation as "the goddess of destruction."

Indira's own transformation in ordering both Emergency Rule and the attack on the Golden Temple is noteworthy. While initially Indira was seen as a weak woman who could be easily manipulated, only chosen by party elders after her father died because she was seen to be easily malleable, she in fact later revealed a more aggressive side. While Emergency Rule may have been at the behest of Sanjay, Operation Blue Star was solely Indira's decision.

Indira, the daughter of a political dynasty, underwent numerous transformations during her lifetime. A lonely child, Indira grew to become a powerful political figure. Although both she and her father served as prime minister, their approach to leadership was quite different: "Nehru could perhaps take a broader view of things and consider a longer historical perspective ... but Mrs. Gandhi was not subject to these considerations to the same extent."[39] She also ruled with an iron fist toward the end of her term, acting in a manner both aggressive and decisive, influenced by her son Sanjay. When Sanjay was killed, the telescoping of generations shifted to her eldest son, Rajiv.

It took Rajiv nearly one year to agree to run for office, and he was encouraged by Indira "in part to thwart Sanjay's glamorous and ambitious widow, Maneka."[40] Rajiv was killed in 1991 by an assassin from the Liberation Tigers of Tamil Ealam. Rajiv's wife, Sonia Gandhi, served as the president of the Indian National Congress.

Notes

1. Haydee Faimberg, *Telescoping of Generations* (New York: Routledge Press, 2005), 5.
2. Nayantara Sahgal, *Indira Gandhi: Her Road to Power* (New York: F. Ungar, 1982), 15.
3. Uma Vasudev, *Indira Gandhi: Revolution in Restraint* (Delhi: Vikas Publishing House, 1974), 4.
4. Inder Malhotra, *Indira Gandhi: A Personal and Political Biography* (Sevenoaks: Coronet Books, 1991), 28.
5. Vasudev, *Indira Gandhi*, 8.
6. Ibid., 9.
7. Malhotra, *Indira Gandhi*, 26.
8. Ibid.
9. Jad Adams and Phillip Whitehead, *The Dynasty: The Nehru-Gandhi Story* (London: Penguin Books, 1997), 80.
10. Malhotra, *Indira Gandhi*, 35.
11. Blema Steinberg, *Women in Power* (Montreal: McGill-Queen's University Press, 2008), 49.
12. Malhotra, *Indira Gandhi*, 37.
13. Ibid.
14. Steinberg, *Women in Power*, 18.
15. Jerrold Post, ed., *Psychological Assessment of Political Leaders* (Ann Arbor: University of Michigan Press, 2003), 73–74.
16. Steinberg, *Women in Power*, 19.

17. Ibid.
18. Sahgal, *Indira Gandhi*, 2.
19. Sudhir Kakar, "Feminine Identity in India," in *Women in Indian Society: A Reader*, ed. Rehana Ghadially (New Delhi: Sage, 1988); Susan Seymour, *Women, Family and Child Care in India: A World in Transition* (Cambridge: Cambridge University Press, 1999).
20. Malhotra, *Indira Gandhi*, 26.
21. Steinberg, *Women in Power*, 25.
22. Adams and Whitehead, *The Dynasty*, 2.
23. Steinberg, *Women in Power*, 21.
24. Ibid., 49–50.
25. Malhotra, *Indira Gandhi*, 48.
26. Ibid., 59.
27. Ibid., 60.
28. Inder Malhotra, "Remembering Indira Gandhi," *The Hindu*, October 31, 2001, accessed June 20, 2011, www.hindu.com/2001/10/31/stories/0531134c.htm.
29. Tariq Ali, *An Indian Dynasty: The Story of the Nehru-Gandhi Family* (New York: G. P. Putnam's Sons, 1985), 271. Angus Deming, Edward Behr, Sudip Mazumdar, Patricia J. Sethi, and Anne Underwood. "The Gandhi Legacy." *Newsweek*, 46, November 12, 1984, p. 59.
30. Deming, "The Gandhi Legacy."
31. Ali, *An Indian Dynasty*, 281.
32. P. N. Dhar, *Indira Gandhi, The "Emergency," and Indian Democracy* (Oxford: Oxford University Press, 2000), 261.
33. Dhar, *Indira Gandhi*, 257.
34. Ibid., 261.
35. Malhotra, *Indira Gandhi*, 222.
36. Deming, "The Gandhi Legacy."
37. Khushwant Singh, *A History of the Sikhs Volume II* (Oxford: Oxford University Press, 1999), 352.
38. C. K. C. Reddy et al., *Army Action in Punjab: Prelude & Aftermath* (New Delhi: Samata Era Publication, 1984), 46.
39. A. K. Damodaran and U. S. Bajpai eds., *Indian Foreign Policy: The Indira Gandhi Years* (New Delhi: Radiant Publishers, 1990), 95.
40. Deming, "The Gandhi Legacy."

5

Daughters of Destiny II: Benazir Bhutto

Kristen Moody, Psy.D. and Jerrold M. Post, M.D.

As with Indira Gandhi, to understand Benazir Bhutto requires accurately locating her in the context of her family history. In Pakistan, apart from the family, a child is born into clan or tribal affiliations that act as a critical network for identity development. The honor of the clan is sacred and enmeshed with one's own self-worth, and interdependence is the basis for social organization and self-perception. In Benazir's case, the Bhutto clan's fortune and prestige were well established in the country in the early 19th century by the legendary Dodo Khan Bhutto who warred ruthlessly with other tribes in order to acquire land.

Subsequent generations acquired more land, and their prestige increased, with Benazir's great-great-great-grandfather regarded as the virtual Nawab (ruler) of the Pakistani province of Sindh after an alliance was made with the ruling Talpur family.[1] This alliance established the Bhuttos among the elite families in the area, and this position was the foundation both for Benazir's father, Zulfiqar, and Benazir herself to move into political leadership roles.

A LEGACY OF CORRUPTION AND POLITICAL CHARGES

In a foretaste of the accusations that would later be made against both Zulfiqar and Benazir, Zulfiqar's grandfather, Ghulman Murtaza Bhutto, was arraigned on the charge of murder.[2] Just as Zulfiqar's and Benazir's close friends and allies were to claim they were framed by political foes seeking to oust them from power, so family tradition says that Murtaza was the victim of a politically inspired plot hatched by local British authorities. Murtaza was acquitted on his

This chapter was prepared for the annual scientific meeting of the International Society of Political Psychology, July 9–12, 2011, Istanbul, Turkey, by Dr. Kristen Moody and Dr. Jerrold Post at a symposium organized and chaired by Dr. Post entitled "Dreams of Glory: Narcissism and Politics."

charges, but his enemies instituted a series of new murder cases against him, sending Murtaza fleeing into hiding for several years.[3]

During this time, his young son Shahnawaz (Zulfiqar's father) was brought up in the custody of his uncle and educated first in the Madrasa-e Tulf Islam, Larkana, and then at the prestigious preparatory school of St. Patrick's School, in Karachi. After his father's premature death at the age of 31, reportedly by poisoning, the teenaged Shahnawaz was forced to interrupt his education to take a role in managing the family estates. He was never able to continue his formal education, but he was able to acquire enough revenue from his estates to live a comfortable lifestyle and enter the political arena at a young age.[4]

From these early historical accounts, an image emerges of the Bhutto family's struggle, one that continues today. Generations of the family would find their name associated with various corruption charges, murder scandals, and mysterious conspiracies that, at times, could never be connected to anything more than pure speculation. The perseverance to overcome these associations seems to have become an internalized drive for members of the Bhutto clan to restore honor to the disgraced members of their family who came before them.

In Shahnawaz's case, this meant to rise steadily in prominence and prestige by winning elections within Sindh. He married a young woman who was largely disliked by the larger Bhutto clan due to her humble origins and roots in the Hindu religion. She later abandoned her religion and converted to Islam at the time of their marriage in 1924, which was Shahnawaz's second. Because of family disapproval, the wedding took place in secret. Their son Zulfiqar, the future president of Pakistan, recalls his family's opposition to the marriage, as well as the mistreatment and humiliation his mother faced for years (eerily similar to that suffered by Indira's mother, as noted in Chapter 4).

Shahnawaz continued to obtain titles and recognition from the British. He earned a lasting place in the history of the subcontinent by fighting for the separation of Sindh from the old Bombay Presidency. This happened as a result of the Round Table Conference in 1931 and 1932, where he directly confronted British Prime Minister Ramsay MacDonald and argued that the rights of Sindh were being brushed aside. A procession was taken out through the village to celebrate the arrival of their leader, and although only an infant at the time, Zulfiqar would say that he remembered the scene: "I was taken up on the roof to watch the people and the procession. I can recall all the excitement."[5] Given that Zulfiqar was an infant, it is highly unlikely that he actually remembered this experience. However, it does point to the idea that memories are often implanted in an individual's mind as part of family tradition. This implanted memory became a myth for young Zulfiqar as he grew up, and he would hold on to the feeling of excitement and pride that came with admiration from the populace. Thus, we see generational shifts of power in the Bhutto clan that were well established before Benazir herself would later take office years after the untimely death of her father.

ZULFIQAR BHUTTO: THE IDEALIZED FATHER

Shahnawaz showered attention on his son Zulfiqar. When Zulfiqar was born, it was Shahnawaz who chose the name Zulfiqar Ali – the name that Hazrat Ali, one of four Caliphs of Islam and a great warrior, gave to his sword.[6] The sword of Ali was regarded as a symbol of struggle against oppression – something that could be seen later in Zulfiqar's politics and in the creation of Pakistan's People's Party.

Shahnawaz took Zulfiqar everywhere and ensured that this son would excel in ways that differed from those of himself or of Zulfiqar's older stepbrothers, Sikandar and Imdad. Zulfiqar was sent to the best educational institutions, and it was said that Shahnawaz envied his younger son's gifts.[7] Shahnawaz may have suffered a sense of shame for having married Zulfiqar's mother, who was from a class beneath his own, and he was unconsciously attempting to alleviate that shame by making sure that Zulfiqar, the product of that marriage, excelled.[8]

This also highlights the beginning of a narcissistic extension from Shahnawaz to Zulfiqar, with Shahnawaz feeling inadequate because of his own limited education after being pulled from school after his father's death. He vicariously reveled in his son's intellectual achievements, with the son's successes compensating for his disappointment not only in his own interrupted education, but also in the interrupted lives of his two elder sons: Sikandar died of pneumonia at the age of 7 in 1914, and Imdad passed away in 1953 at the age of 39 from cirrhosis. Shahnawaz hoped to fulfill his own frustrated dreams through the achievements of his third son.

Interestingly, several prominent members of the Bhutto clan, including Zulfiqar's grandfather and two brothers, all died long before they were 50. Sensitive to this, Zulfiqar privately told those around him that he had a premonition of an early death and therefore must accomplish whatever he could before the age of 50.[9] He was overthrown from power by the army at the age of 49, tried for murder, and hanged on April 4, 1979, when he was 51 years old.

Despite his earlier eminence, when Shahnawaz was defeated in the Sindh elections in 1937, he suffered a major and lasting narcissistic wound. He retired from politics and left for Bombay. As a child, Zulfiqar did not have the capacity to understand or rationalize what was happening to his parents, including the vicious attacks against his father that eventually led to his political defeat and the criticism of his mother by his father's family.[10] It was now up to Zulfiqar to restore the family's reputation and stature. Zulfiqar was said to have never forgotten what his father had suffered in his defeat, feeling that it was an insult to the family honor, which he took upon himself to restore.[11] His father had groomed him for a political career and frequently impressed on him the necessity of developing links and alliances with the politically well-connected and powerful; Zulfiqar was Shahnawaz's political heir and was expected to bring compensatory honor to the Bhutto name.

Zulfiqar had a tendency to idealize those in power. With great expectations placed on him at an early age, Bhutto would join the elders in his father's house as an adolescent, participating in the discussions surrounding the separation of Pakistan and "vociferously" taking the same position as his father did.[12]

Zulfiqar held an uncritical admiration for Napoleon Bonaparte and Metternich, and, in fact, many of the books in his personal library were about "great men." As a child, Zulfiqar believed that he was destined for greatness, and he continued to crave power and admiration as an adult. For example, he was so sure that he would win the election and assume office as the fourth president of Pakistan that he held a mock ceremony in his own house, calling on 100 of his employees to come to his house, where bugles were played and flags were hoisted in honor of Zulfiqar Bhutto's "win." He "appointed" his cousin Mumtaz Bhutto as governor of Sindh.[13]

This is reminiscent of the young Indira Gandhi, who often stood on a table in her house and gathered servants to listen to her give speeches and recite slogans that she had heard spoken by older members of her family.[14]

Zulfiqar's rise to power came fairly quickly and unexpectedly. It commenced in 1958, when he was selected to the cabinet of Iskander Mirza, the president of Pakistan and a good friend of his father Shahnawaz. In 1958, Mirza declared martial law in Pakistan and named Muhammad Ayub Khan the chief martial law administrator. Zulfiqar was able to retain his position even after Khan removed Mirza from power in a bloodless coup just weeks later and took over the position of president of Pakistan. Zulfiqar won praise and trust within the cabinet, exemplified by his being named the leader of the Pakistani delegation to the UN, and, over the next few years, he obtained high positions within the government and won Ayub Khan's continued trust. This friendship secured him a position as foreign minister in 1963, when his help paved the way for Ayub Khan to be declared overall head of the Convention Muslim League, a faction of the Pakistan Muslim League that split off to help support Khan's military regime (in the years to come, many other factions of the Pakistan Muslim League served as political platforms and opposition parties).

However, fallout between Bhutto and Khan began in 1965 over the war with India. Bhutto felt strongly that constant confrontation was the best way to deal with India, whereas Ayub Khan disliked the idea of prolonging a war and instead accepted a cease-fire. During the consequent negotiations, Bhutto was described as ill-mannered, quick-tempered, and openly disdainful of Khan for having been duped by the Indians and the Soviets.[15] In Pakistan, Bhutto publically denounced the treaty with India and the USSR over Kashmir, undermining Khan's quick acceptance of this treaty. Thus, Bhutto first idolized Ayub Khan for six years and then rebelled and turned against the very man who helped bring him to power.[16]

Based on Zulfiqar Bhutto's childhood and his subsequent relations with Ayub Khan, a picture emerges that underlines Bhutto's own difficulties with authority and authority figures. He was narcissistically attracted to figures he could idolize as a way of sharing their greatness, but he also had a great need for others to admire him. Both his mother and father treated him as a narcissistic *selfobject*, showering him with special attention in childhood and leaving with him an unquenchable thirst for praise and admiration. They used him as a means of vicariously fulfilling their own desire for admiration, and, because of this, he was likely instilled with a sense of entitlement. One instance that highlights this sense of entitlement was when Zulfiqar met with President John F. Kennedy in 1963, and Kennedy stated that if Bhutto were an American citizen, he would be in the president's cabinet. To this, Bhutto modestly responded, "Mr. President, if I were in America, I would be in *your* place."[17]

This need to be idealized caused Bhutto to turn a blind eye to the real motives of those initially singing his praises. An example was the elevation of General Zia-ul-Haq to the position of Chief of Army, the highest military position in the country, skipping over several others who had served longer and displayed better credentials. Zia, it would seem, knew how to manipulate Bhutto through fulsome praise. He subsequently used his position to remove Bhutto from power in July 1977. This unquestioned trust placed in those around him was a fault that both Zulfiqar and later his daughter, Benazir, shared. Indeed, their narcissistic rage at those who betrayed them and their shame at their own naïveté may well have contributed to their inexorable march toward martyrdom.

Bhutto's approach continued to be confrontational and combative throughout his career. He was cunning, ruthless, and determined to succeed.[18] He displayed narcissistic vengefulness and would humiliate people for petty wrongs or minor slights that he interpreted as challenging, humiliating, or insulting. He was viewed as a charismatic individual who vowed to restore the identity of the people of Pakistan after the war with India, but, under this charismatic façade, he needed to be recognized for his accomplishments and actively sought approval and acceptance from others.

He rose to power and popularity quickly in the country, and his attitude became increasingly bold and defiant. In an interview with Akbar Ahmed, the Ibn Khaldun Chair of Islamic Studies at American University and former Ambassador to Pakistan, Ahmed stated that Bhutto enjoyed almost a cult-like following in the country.[19] His promise of "Rotti, Kapra aur Makan" (food, clothing and shelter) helped create a massive following for his politics.

In response to the loss of Dacca, which was once part of East Pakistan but then became the capital of an independent Bangladesh in December 1971, Bhutto gave a fiery, theatrical speech to the UN Security Council, claiming that "The Security Council has acted short sightedly. We have come to a point to say 'do what you like.' It is a disgrace to my person and my country to be here."[20] He then tore up his papers and stormed off the floor.

When Bhutto first came to power, he had little competition from civilian opposition parties because his personal appeal and powerful leadership style dominated the domestic political scene. Despite this popular acceptance, an underlying insecurity made him act in a controlling fashion at times. Displaying a narcissistic sensitivity to slight, he used coercive methods such as manipulating newspaper advertising, arresting dissenting journalists, and using member of his People's Party of Pakistan (PPP) to break up public meetings of opposition parties.[21] The opposition, particularly that of Asghar Khan, the political leader who most strongly opposed Bhutto's PPP, was given no access to the media, and newspapers and broadcasters could only express pro-government stands.

The National Awami Party was particularly opposed to Bhutto's PPP, even though it had a broadly similar platform: it was secular in outlook, with a left of center economic program.[22] The formation of a coalition would have been a rational step, providing a way to smooth out provincial discord and bring much needed stability to the country. However, this would have required Bhutto to accept the National Awami Party leaders as co-equals and to share power, something that his egotistic narcissism and dominating style would not allow him to do. Psychologically, he was unable to share power, and he seemed afraid of those who would try to take it from him. This very fear became a reality after political unrest and a series of conflicts led to a successful military coup by the very man Zulfiqar had promoted, General Zia-al-Haq, who arrested him and ousted him from office. Ultimately, Zulfiqar was executed in 1979, after the Supreme Court of Pakistan sentenced him to death for authorizing the murder of a political opponent. The swift execution, which was widely believed to have been politically motivated, caused international outrage.[23]

Zulfiqar's charismatic personality and unwavering pursuit of political power, as well as his worldview, had a strong influence on the people of his country. His larger-than-life persona powerfully affected his own family, particularly his firstborn daughter and later leader of the country, Benazir. As with Jawarhalal to Indira, we can highlight the telescoping of generations with Zulfiqar to Benazir, who showed the same blind adoration of her father, Zulfiqar, that Zulfiqar had shown for his own father, Shahnawaz. An examination of Benazir's behavior in the political arena highlights the transgenerational shifts of personality and power from the men in her family who served before her.

BENAZIR BHUTTO: A WORTHY SUCCESSOR IS BORN

Benazir Bhutto was the eldest of four children born to Zulfiqar Ali Bhutto and his wife, Iranian-Kurdish beauty Begum Nusrat Ispahani. Much like Zulfiqar's mother's rejection by the Bhutto clan, Benazir's mother recalled her own feelings of rejection, claiming that no one visited her for three days after Benazir's birth because the entire family was in mourning that she had been born a girl, not a boy.[24] Reminiscent of Indira's grandfather's words prophesying her impending greatness, it was Zulfiqar who embraced his daughter and named her Benazir, literally "one without equal."[25]

Zulfiqar emphasized his children's education and politics in the same manner that his own father had with him, sending Benazir first to a private nursery school and then, at age five, to one of the top schools in Karachi, the Convent of Jesus and Mary.

Benazir went on to be educated at Harvard and Oxford. At Harvard, she roomed with Kathleen Kennedy, the eldest daughter of Senator Robert Kennedy. She recalled that period of her life as shaping much of her political ideology. There, she watched her fellow classmates protest the Vietnam War and participate in rallies for equal rights for women. Bhutto would later attempt to make strides for the equality of women in her own country, including such acts as building schools for girls and establishing all-female police departments.[26]

Benazir was, in many ways, like Indira Gandhi; both seemed groomed for political leadership position from a young age. However, the difference lies in how each of their fathers interacted with his daughter. The widowed Nehru treated Indira like his companion, apprentice, and confidante. Nehru stated that he never intended to have his daughter follow in his footsteps but only to understand the functions of his role and be there as an educated support system, although his actions belied his words. On the other hand, Zulfiqar actively encouraged his young daughter to learn politics early on, taking her on international trips and having her sit in on various international meetings.

As the eldest child, Benazir was the ultimate loyal daughter, nearly sycophantic in her adoration of her father and crediting him with her outstanding education. She recalls a time when her mother asked her father "Why do you want to educate her? No man will want to marry her," to which her father responded, "Boys and girls are equal. I want my daughter to have the same opportunities."[27] This is reminiscent of Indira's grandfather's comment upon her birth that she "may prove to be better than a thousand sons."[28] Knowing the emphasis her father put on her education, Benazir excelled in her studies, noting "I found that he would always be so pleased when I did well." She also remembers her father saying, "my daughter is going to make me more proud than Indira Gandhi made her father."[29] Interestingly, while at times Indira Gandhi rebelled against her father, Benazir never questioned her father's goals for her and always followed his wishes. Benazir recalled meeting Indira Gandhi when her father was negotiating the Simla Agreement in 1972, and she remarked on the similarity between herself and the daughter of India's leader: "Was she seeing herself in me, a daughter of another statesman? Was she remembering the love of a daughter for her father, a father for his daughter?"[30] This wouldn't be the first time Bhutto compared herself to Indira. When asked if she enjoyed doing things that other girls didn't, Benazir responded "To me, these weren't things girls didn't do. I saw Indira Gandhi in India and Mrs. Bandaranaike in Sri Lanka and Mrs. Fatima Jenna in Pakistan … a female member of a family can become a symbol of a male's message. Indira was seen as the symbol of Nehru's concept of India."[31]

Not only was Benazir's identity shaped by Zulfiqar, but Benazir in significant ways became an extension of her father, going on to promote the ideals of democracy that he advocated, although his ideals and his controlling actions were often at variance.

During the political unrest in Pakistan in 1977, in the early hours of the coup d'etat, Zulfiqar was advised to leave Pakistan to avoid the fate he ultimately suffered. The coup was initiated by General Zia-ul-Huq, who had been appointed by Bhutto as the Army Chief of Staff 13 months earlier.[32] Bhutto began facing criticism and increasing unpopularity as his term progressed, and, after the murder of a leading dissident's father led to public outrage, Zulfiqar was accused of masterminding the crime.[33] Although Zulfiqar called for fresh elections in 1977, and his party won, the Pakistan National Alliance (the main opposition) called the newly elected Bhutto government a farce because of low voter turnout due to the opposition's boycott in the provincial elections. When political and civil unrest continued, Bhutto imposed martial law in major cities,[34] but, in July, he and his cabinet members were arrested by troops under the order of General Zia.

It seems that he knew that he might be killed, saying to Benazir, "My life is in God's hands. If the army is going to kill me, they'll kill me. There's no point in hiding. Nor in any of you resisting. Let them come."[35] (This language foreshadowed Benazir's own attitude when, as she was later planning to return from an eight-year self-imposed exile after her government's dismissal in 1996, she rejected the warnings of the dangers facing her if she returned to Pakistan.)

Benazir Bhutto was the only person in contact with her father during his incarceration, where he would hand off notes and discuss what duties he wanted her to fulfill for the PPP.[36] During his imprisonment, while awaiting execution, Benazir described waking up during the night "feeling my father's noose around my neck."[37] Benazir claimed that, in her last visit to him in his death cell, her father said, "You have suffered so much. You are so young. You just finished your university. You came back. You had your whole life and look at the terror under which we have lived. I set you free. Why don't you go and live in London or Paris? ... [You should be] well taken care of, and have some happiness because you have seen too much suffering." Bhutto's response was to grasp his hands and say, "No papa, I will continue the struggle that you began for democracy."[38]

Zulfiqar's execution by public hanging and the subsequent seven years that Benazir spent either under house arrest, in detention, or in prison, months of which were in solitary confinement, allowed Benazir to consider her father's politics and her developing mission to restore glory to his name and democracy to Pakistan. Upon visiting her father's grave, Benazir pledged to herself that "I would not rest until democracy returned to Pakistan ... [I] felt the strength and conviction of his soul replenishing me."[39] Quite literally, Benazir here is describing a narcissistic telescoping of generations, as she not only embraces her father's cause, but also makes his life and the continuation of his policies her central focus. While she states that a part of her died with her father, her father's death gave meaning to Benazir's own political life, identity, and death.

Zulfiqar's premonition of his early death became a self-fulfilling prophecy, and Benazir may have been unconsciously emulating him, ignoring the security warnings and being assassinated at the age of 54.

Much like her father, it appears that Benazir evoked intense reactions from those around her, creating polarized views of either extreme hatred or extreme admiration. Akbar Ahmed recalled one visit Bhutto made to Washington, D.C., where he was sitting on the couch with her in a room with fellow "movers and shakers of the Muslim world in DC."[40] Ahmed remembered a woman, the host's mother, standing at the room's doorway looking at Benazir with "love in her eyes" when suddenly a cat came into the room and jumped onto Bhutto's lap. The woman shook her head, raised her hands, and exclaimed: "Oh Allah! This cat is so fortunate. Does it realize it is sitting on the lap of Benazir Bhutto?" This story reflects the way in which the Bhutto family became idealized in Pakistan. While at times she spoke with words of humility, of the destiny thrust upon her which she must selflessly fulfill, it was clear she had internalized a grand self-concept, manifest in her public appearances in such international forums as Davos. A lifetime of praise and great expectations created a narcissistic grandiose self.

Benazir's choice of husband in many ways highlighted her political agenda. Despite her mother's concerns that her daughter would never find a man, in 1987, Benazir agreed to marry Asif Ali Zardari, a wealthy businessman and known playboy. This was partly a political move because she recognized that having a husband would help her public image and subsequent interactions with other political leaders in the region and around the world. The marriage was arranged by her mother, and Bhutto did not meet her future husband until five days before their engagement. She opted to keep her name, saying "Benazir Bhutto doesn't cease to exist the moment she gets married. I am not giving myself away. I belong to myself and I always shall."[41] By no means was she going to be the subservient Muslim wife that tradition dictated.

FROM GENERATION UNTO GENERATION

Thus, while Benazir accepted her mother's choice to marry Zardari, it was not the acceptance of a docile daughter but very much a decision made on her own terms. Although not initially engaged in the political arena, Zardari exhibited many traits similar to those of Benazir's father. Zardari and Zulfiqar were both known playboys; they were charismatic, outgoing, and quick-tempered. Given Bhutto's intense idealization of her father, we can speculate that her acceptance of her mother's choice of Zardari as her mate was a manifestation of the continuity of generations.

Moreover, Benazir appears, to some degree, to have been in competition with her mother. When she was asked why her mother was backing her brother, Murtaza, Benazir responded: "Because all my life I was such a dutiful daughter. And perhaps my mother found it difficult to accept that when the time came for a decision between political responsibility and obedience as a daughter, I chose political responsibility. She's basically angry with me because she was removed as chairperson of the party. She blames me for it. But that was a party decision endorsed by a party convention of several hundred people."[42] Her language indicates some underlying pride – that her father had raised her as his successor and not designated her mother as his successor. Revenge is sweet.

There was another resemblance, other than the temperamental ones just noted, between Zulfiqar and Zardari that may have influenced Benazir and her mother's choice of Zardari, for both Zulfiqar and Zardari were known for engaging in backdoor deals. In fact, Zardari was known as Mr. Ten Percent because of the kickbacks he took while holding office. Although there has been some speculation that this was purely an attempt by Pakistan's Inter-Services Intelligence (ISI) to smear his and Benazir's name, there are also reports that these claims have a legitimate foundation.[43] Ultimately, Benazir's husband was not the only one accused of corruption charges. Indeed, Benazir herself was dismissed from government in 1990 on charges of corruption, but she was never tried in Pakistan.[44] A Swiss judge found both her and her husband guilty of money laundering and sentenced both of them to jail and a fine. They never went to Switzerland again. A *New York Times* investigative report of their corruption left no doubt as to their deep immersion in kickbacks, bribes, and theft. By no means was there a firewall between Benazir and her husband: investigative reporting confirms that she was an active participant in and beneficiary of the long-standing family tradition of corruption.[45]

THE ROAD TO BENAZIR'S DEATH: A CHOSEN PATH TO MARTYRDOM

Whatever drive there was to stay in power, there seems also to have been a strong desire for Benazir to die as her father did, with a sense of purpose and martyrdom. Ahmed provided insight into Islamic culture and its emphasis on martyrdom by stating that "Dying for a higher cause is preferable to sitting at home waiting to die of old age."[46] Benazir was drawing on her own family lineage, as well as her on culture, in making the decisions that ultimately led to her death. Ahmed points out that on her final return to Pakistan, where it is tradition to visit the gravestone of one's father, Benazir instead chose to visit the tomb of the founder of Pakistan.[47] This choice shows a symbolism in Benazir's understanding of her role in the formation of her country. Whatever the actual case may have been, both Benazir and her father came to be seen as saint-like and martyrs by the people of Pakistan.

Before Benazir left for Harvard, her father took her to the family grave and told her that no matter where in the world she might go, she would ultimately return home to Pakistan and would be buried in that grave.[48] Benazir was buried next to her father. Her father's words undoubtedly aided her decision to return to Pakistan despite the danger posed, but she was also manifesting the sense of invulnerability and grandiosity so characteristic of narcissists, a sense that reflects her exceptional view of herself that, as destiny's child, she would survive and transcend the dangers facing her. But we can also see the powerful influence that her family and culture had in her decision-making process. Reflecting her grandiose self-concept, Benazir compared her family's tragedies to those of the Prophet Mohammed: "In every generation, Shiite Muslims believe there is a Karbala, a reenactment of the tragedy that befell the family of the Prophet Mohammed, after his death is 640 AD. Many in Pakistan have come to believe that the victimization of the Bhutto family and our supporters was the Karbala of our generation."[49]

In her mind's eye, it appeared that the Bhutto clan was destined to reenact this ancient tragedy. Benazir had opted for self-exile for corruption charges, and she returned to Pakistan to prepare for the 2008 national elections and a possible power-sharing deal with then-president Pervez Musharraf. She survived an assassination attempt by a suicide bomber almost immediately after getting off the plane in Karachi.[50] After the bombing, her family asked for greater security, including tinted windows, jammers for bombs, private guards, and four police vehicles. Although some of these were offered, Bhutto was still an accessible target. After leaving a rally in the city of Rawalpindi, she was attacked by one or more assassins who fired at her bulletproof car. A suicide bomber then detonated a bomb next to her vehicle. The exact cause of her death remains somewhat of a controversy even today, with President Pervez Musharraf's government being criticized for not providing Bhutto with adequate protection.[51]

Perhaps it was a feeling of invulnerability that brought Benazir back to Pakistan only to be killed two months after her return. More likely, though, it was her desire for martyrdom, to be remembered as a great leader, one who gave her life for her country just as her father had. It is interesting to consider her active role in playing out the "family tragedy." Her father, Zulfiqar, was executed in the city of Rawalpindi, in which Benazir was assassinated, thus emphasizing the manner in which Benazir followed in her father's footsteps even in death.

This idea of Benazir's death as a martyr also parallels that of Indira Gandhi, who also idealized the role of martyr-hero. In her case, Indira ignored the warnings of her own government and sons and kept her Sikh bodyguards close to her – despite the knowledge that attacks were being planned against her after she ordered an attack on the Sikh's holiest shrine, the Golden Temple. Both of these women ignored the pleas of those around them for safety and chose paths that ultimately ended their lives.

Just as Benazir took over for her father, the telescoping of generations continues: Bilawal Bhutto Zardari, Benazir's eldest son, was named chairman of the Pakistan People's Party after his mother's death. Bilawal resumed his university career at Oxford. During an interview, he stated "I do not claim to have any aspiration. I was called and I stepped up to what I was asked to do."[52] His father named himself interim co-chair and claimed that Bilawal would learn the ropes of politics upon his return from the United Kingdom after completing his studies. True to the plan, Bilawal returned to Pakistan in 2011 and officially began his political career by making a major public speech on December, 27, 2012, the fifth anniversary of Benazir's death.[53] Again, just as the lineage of power was passed down to Benazir, it appears that her son feels the need to uphold the wishes of his family and honor the names of those coming before him.

The telescoping of generations is an interesting concept when looking at political dynasties. For both the Nehru-Gandhi family in India and the Bhuttos in Pakistan, there is almost a predetermined fate that comes with each generation born, a desire to take up the family cause in politics, to uphold the name, and to carry on a tradition. A look at the life of each leader in Benazir's family who came before her shows a steady increase in the generational transmission of the leader's role. In many ways, both Zulfiqar and Benazir subordinated their individuality and were impelled to act as an extension of the family name, which became intertwined with the fate of their nation. As we watch Bilawal in the years to come, it will be of interest to see what he has internalized from the years of Bhutto rule and rhetoric before him, particularly since both his mother and grandfather are held in such idealized high esteem in Pakistan. He already appears to be placing his life within a predetermined fate, carrying on in the footsteps of his mother and his grandfather.

One of the remarkable aspects of the leadership of Benazir Bhutto was the powerful charismatic force of her relationship with the people of Pakistan. The psychology of the charismatic leader–follower relationship is the subject of the next chapter.

Notes

1. Salmaan Taseer, *Bhutto: A Political Biography* (New Delhi: Vikas Publishing House, 1980).
2. Ibid.
3. Ibid.
4. Ibid.
5. Ibid., 18.
6. Taseer, *Bhutto: A Political Biography*.
7. Zulfiqar S. Gilani, "Z. A. Bhutto's Leadership: A Psycho-Social View," *Contemporary South Asia*, 94, no. 3 (1994).
8. Gilani, "Z. A. Bhutto's Leadership."
9. Taseer, *Bhutto: A Political Biography*.
10. Gilani, "Z. A. Bhutto's Leadership."
11. Taseer, *Bhutto: A Political Biography*.
12. Ibid.
13. Hasan Mujtaba, "Bhutto: Man and Myth," *Newsline*, January, 1993.
14. Inder Malhotra, *Indira Gandhi: A Personal and Political Biography* (Sevenoaks: Coronet Books, 1991) 37.
15. Taseer, *Bhutto: A Political Biography*.
16. Gilani, "Z. A. Bhutto's Leadership."
17. *Bhutto*, directed by Duane Baughman (2010; United States: First Run Features), documentary.

18. Taseer, *Bhutto: A Political Biography.*
19. Akbar Ahmed, Personal Interview, December 21, 2010.
20. Benazir Bhutto, "Bhutto," 2010, accessed December 13, 2010, www.bhutto.org/1970-71.php.
21. Taseer, *Bhutto: A Political Biography.*
22. Shahid J. Burki, *Pakistan under Bhutto, 1971–1977* (New York: St. Martin's Press, 1980).
23. BBC News On This Day, "Deposed Pakistani PM Is Executed," *BBC News*, April 4, 1979, accessed April 3, 2011, http://news.bbc.co.uk/onthisday/hi/dates/stories/april/4/newsid_2459000/2459507.stm
24. Baughman, *Bhutto.*
25. Ibid.
26. Ibid.
27. "Benazir Bhutto Interview," *Academy of Achievement*, October 27, 2000, accessed December 10, 2010, www.achievement.org/autodoc/page/bhuoint-1.
28. Malhotra, *Indira Gandhi*, 26.
29. "Benazir Bhutto Interview."
30. Benazir Bhutto, *Daughter of the East: An Autobiography* (London: Simon & Schuster, 2007), 63.
31. Claudia Dreifus, "Real-Life Dynasty: Benazir Bhutto," May 15, 1994, accessed April 13, 2011, www.nytimes.com/1994/05/15/magazine/real-life-dynasty-benazir-bhutto.html.
32. Taseer, *Bhutto: A Political Biography.*
33. S. J. Burki, *Pakistan under Bhutto*; Taseer, *Bhutto: A Political Biography.*
34. Burki, *Pakistan under Bhutto.*
35. Benazir Bhutto, *Daughter of Destiny: An Autobiography* (New York: Simon and Schuster, 1989), 92.
36. Akbar, Personal Interview.
37. Bhutto, *Daughter of the East*, 11.
38. "Benazir Bhutto Interview."
39. Bhutto, *Daughter of Destiny*, 18.
40. Ahmed, Akba Personal Interview.
41. Stephanie Salmon, "10 Things You Didn't Know About Benazir Bhutto," *US News & World Report*, December 27, 2007, accessed December 5, 2010, www.usnews.com/news/world/articles/2007/12/27/10-things-you-didnt-know-about-benazir-bhutto.
42. Dreifus, "Real-Life Dynasty."
43. "BBC News – Profile: Asif Ali Zardari," *BBC News*, 2007, accessed January 20, 2011, http://news.bbc.co.uk/2/hi/4032.
44. John F. Burns, "House of Graft: Tracing the Bhutto Millions – A Special Report; Bhutto Clan Leaves Trail of Corruption," *New York Times*, January 9, 1998, accessed June 16, 2011, www.nytimes.com/1998/01/09/world/house-graft-tracing-bhutto-millions-special-report-bhutto-clan-leaves-trail.html.
45. Burns, John F. "House of Graft: Tracing the Bhutto Millions," *New York Times*, January 9, 1998.
46. Ahmed, Personal Interview.
47. Ahmed, Personal Interview.
48. Fatima Bhutto, *Songs of Blood and Sword: A Daughter's Memoir* (New York: Nation Books, 2010).

49. Bhutto, *Daughter of the East*, 299.
50. Griff Witte, "Bhutto Assassination Sparks Chaos," *The Washington Post*, December 28, 2007, accessed February 3, 2011, www.washingtonpost.com/wp-dyn/content/article/2007/12/27/A.
51. Salman Masood, "Bhutto Assassination Ignites Disarray," *The New York Times*, December 28, 2007, accessed June 16, 2011. www.nytimes.com/2007/12/28/world/asia/28pakistan.html?pagewant.
52. "Bhutto's Son Seeks Media Privacy," BBC News, January 8, 2008, accessed June 6, 2011, http://news.bbc.co.uk/2/hi/7176743.stm.
53. *Al Jazeera*, "Bhutto's Son Makes Debut in Pakistan Politics," December 27, 2012, www.aljazeera.com/news/americas/2012/12/20121227145629622237.html.

6

Narcissism and the Charismatic Leader–Follower Relationship

The victory of the Islamic Revolution in Iran did not fulfill Ayatollah Khomeini's messianic aspirations. Still driven by dreams of glory, the aged Ayatollah continued relentlessly to pursue his greater goal of one "united Islamic Nation" under his guidance.[1] The fundamental political, economic, and social changes, as well as the violence and havoc that his revolution unleashed, are vivid testimony to the powerful forces that can be mobilized by charismatic leader-follower relationships. Osama bin Laden similarly forged a powerful bond with his alienated followers, resulting in the explosive events of September 11, 2001. Indeed, Khomeini can be considered an intellectual mentor and model for bin Laden. The Islamic Revolution in Iran and the radical Islamic terrorism of al-Qaeda are pointed reminders that such relationships are not merely interesting relics of a bygone era – the era of "great men" – but continue to play an important and often determining role in world affairs.

I write not of charismatic leaders but rather of charismatic leader–follower relationships. In this chapter, I elaborate on the political psychology of this powerful tie between leaders and followers and attempt to identify crucial aspects of the psychology of the leader that, like a key, fit and unlock crucial aspects of the psychology of their followers. In delineating this lock-and-key relationship, I draw on emerging understandings of the psychology of narcissism.

When Weber[2] first introduced the concept of charismatic authority, he addressed the psychology of the followers but only in cursory fashion. He made it clear that he considered that the predominant determinant of the relationship between the charismatic leader and his followers was the compelling forcefulness of the leader's personality, in the face of which followers were

This chapter is drawn from Jerrold Post (1986), "Narcissism and the Charismatic Leader-Follower Relationship," *Political Psychology*, vol. 7, no. 4, pp. 675–688.

essentially left choiceless and felt compelled to follow. Schiffer[3] has observed that later commentators on the phenomenon of charismatic authority have also focused disproportionately on the magnetism of the leader, failing to make the fundamental observations that all leaders – especially charismatic leaders – are at heart the creation of their followers.

A notable exception to this criticism is the corpus of work by Abse and Ulman.[4] They give important attention to those psychological qualities of the followers that render them susceptible to the force of the charismatic leader and lead to collective regression, drawing on the remarkable case history of the collective "Kool-Aid suicide" at the People's Temple in Guyana. In so doing, they draw attention to the relationship between the psychological qualities of narcissistically wounded individuals and charismatic leader–follower relationships.

In *Spellbinders*, her review of the subject of charisma, Ruth Ann Wilner[5] observed that the concept of charisma has been much abused and watered down since Weber[6] first introduced it. Indeed, the media often use "charisma" as synonymous with "popular appeal," whereas Weber defined charismatic authority as a personal authority deriving from "devotion to the specific sanctity, heroism or exemplary character of an individual person and of the normative patterns or order revealed or ordained by him." To operationalize the concept, Wilner surveyed the vast (and often contradictory) literature bearing on charismatic leadership. She emerges with this definition: Charismatic leadership is a relationship between a leader and a group of followers that has the following properties:

1. The leader is perceived by the followers as somehow superhuman.
2. The followers blindly believe the leader's statements.
3. The followers unconditionally comply with the leader's directives for action.
4. The followers give the leader unqualified emotional support.

In fact, each of these properties relates to a perception, belief, or response of the followers! But Wilner nevertheless devotes the majority of her scholarly energies to analyzing the leaders who elicit these responses, paying scant attention to the psychology of their followers. Thus, Wilner has committed the same sin of omission as the authors of the earlier reviews criticized by Schiffer.[7] Indeed, she relegated Schiffer's path-breaking psychoanalytic exploration of charisma and mass society to an extended footnote, where he shares the distinguished company of Erik Erikson and Sigmund Freud.

In particular, Wilner dismisses as interesting – but unproven – hypotheses that "in times of crisis, individuals regress to a state of delegated omnipotence and demand a leader [who will rescue them, take care of them]" and that "individuals susceptible to [the hypnotic attraction of] charismatic leadership have themselves fragmented or weak ego structures."

In my judgment, there is indeed powerful support for these hypotheses. Clinical work with individuals with narcissistic personality disorders, the detailed studies of individuals who join charismatic religious groups, and psychodynamic observations of group phenomena all provide persuasive support for these hypotheses concerning the psychological makeup and responses of individuals susceptible to charismatic leadership – the lock of the follower for the key of the leader. In particular, these individuals emerge from the earliest developmental period narcissistically scarred, feeling incomplete within themselves and searching for a powerful nurturing figure to whom to attach themselves.

The central features of the development and phenomenology of the narcissistic personality have significant implications for understanding the nature of charismatic leader–follower relationships. They have been described in the first three chapters of this book, which especially delineate pathways to "the wounded self." Here, I wish to describe the consequences of the wounded self for adult personality development and emphasize how narcissistically wounded individuals are attracted to charismatic leader–follower relationships, both as leaders and as followers.

A brief word about the psychoanalytic concept of transference is in order. As originally conceptualized by Freud, transference refers to the feelings that develop between the client and psychoanalyst during psychoanalytic treatment, in which the client transfers feelings that originated in his childhood to the psychoanalyst. Thus, the client with a highly authoritarian father is apt to relate to the psychoanalyst as if he is authoritarian. But the term has been broadened in its contemporary applications so that it now refers to any distortion of a relationship wherein the individual relates to individuals in his current interpersonal surround as if they are ghosts from the past. Thus, the individual referred to earlier who had been raised by a highly authoritarian father may relate to authority figures – bosses, teachers – with anxiety. Indeed, the reason for seeking psychoanalytic treatment may well be because of recognition of this long-standing anxiety concerning authority. Interpreting and resolving the transference is at the very heart of psychoanalytic therapy.

In the earliest stage of development – the stage of primary narcissism – the infant does not distinguish between himself and others. He experiences the external world – his mother – as part of himself. He is not just the center of the universe – he is the universe. As the young child experiences the frustrating reality of the external world's less than perfect response to his needs, he begins to differentiate himself from it. He is demoted from being the universe to becoming merely its center. Two psychological constellations develop as ways of restoring a sense of completeness.

The first is the ideal or grandiose self. The "mirroring" responses of the mother – her admiration and attention – allow the child to feel special and highly valued. This treasured position is maintained by an important psychological mechanism – splitting. The very young child is unable to tolerate the bad aspects of himself and his environment and to integrate them with the good ones into a realistic whole. He splits the good and the bad into the "me" and the "not me." Thus, by rejecting all aspects of himself and his situation that do not fit his ideal or grandiose self, the child attempts to maintain it.

The child's second mechanism for remedying frustration and incompleteness is to attach himself to an ideal object (as proposed by Kernberg) or idealized parental image (as proposed by Kohut), which derives particularly from the father. This is the fantasized image of the all-powerful, all-knowing, all-giving, all-loving parent. The child gains his own sense of being complete and worthwhile by experiencing himself as connected to, united with, his idealized object. In Crayton's (1983) formulation, "If I am not perfect, I will at least be in a relationship with something perfect."

If the child is traumatized during this critical period of development, his emerging self-concept is damaged, leading to the formation of what Kohut calls "the injured self." Such damage can occur in several ways. Children rejected by cold and ungiving mothers may be left emotionally hungry, with an exaggerated need for love and admiration. A special form of rejection is overprotection by the intrusive narcissistic mother. She cannot let her child individuate because she sees him as an extension of herself. Her own sense of perfection seems to depend on her child's perfection. (This mechanism has been discussed in Chapter 3, "Great Expectations," with the examples of the mothers of General Douglas MacArthur, Woodrow Wilson, and Australian Prime Minister Hawke, among others, who groomed their sons to be the vehicle of their own success in this world.)

Kohut's formulations of the mirroring and idealizing transferences are particularly elegant, and an elaboration of narcissistic transference is essential to this examination of charismatic leader–follower relationships. Formation of the "injured self" results in two personality patterns that have particular implications for our study of charismatic relationships: the "mirror-hungry" personality and the "ideal-hungry" personality:

In other words, we are dealing with either (a.) the wish of a self which feels enfeebled . . . to retain its cohesion by expanding temporarily into the psychic structure of others, by finding itself in others, or to be confirmed by the admiration of others (resembling one of the varieties of mirror transference) or (b.) the need to obtain strength from an idealized other (resembling an idealizing transference).[8]

The Mirror-Hungry Personality

The first personality pattern resulting from "the injured self" is the *mirror-hungry personality*. These individuals, whose basic psychological constellation is the grandiose self, hunger for confirming and admiring responses to counteract their inner sense of worthlessness and lack of self-esteem. To nourish their famished self, they are compelled to display themselves to evoke the attention of others. No matter how positive the response, they cannot be satisfied but continue seeking new audiences from whom to elicit the attention and recognition they crave.

The Ideal-Hungry Personality

The second personality type resulting from "the wounded self" is the *ideal-hungry personality*. These individuals can experience themselves as worthwhile only so long as they can relate to individuals whom they can admire for their prestige, power, beauty, intelligence, or moral stature. They forever search for such idealized figures. Again, the inner void cannot be filled. Inevitably, the ideal-hungry individual finds that his god is merely human, that his hero has feet of clay. Disappointed by the discovery of defects in his previously idealized object, he casts him aside and searches for a new hero to whom he attaches himself in the hope that he will not be disappointed again.

Narcissistic Transferences and the Charismatic Leader–Follower Relationship

The phenomenon of the charismatic leader–follower relationship is surely too complex to lend itself to a single overarching psychodynamic personality model. In addition to features of the leader, the followers, and their relationships, one must take into account complex sociocultural, political, and historical factors. Nevertheless, I believe that elements of the narcissistic transferences just described are present in all charismatic leader–follower relationships, and, in some charismatic leader–follower relationships, they are critical determinants.

In certain of these cases, the complementarity between the two transference postures is so striking that it is extremely tempting to relate the two principal actors in this relationship – leaders and followers – to these postures. In the balance of this chapter, I yield to that temptation and relate charismatic leaders to the narcissistically wounded mirror-hungry personality and charismatic followers to the narcissistically wounded ideal-hungry personality. In so doing, I wish to emphasize that this is in the service of illuminating certain elements of the psychology of charismatic leaders and their followers and is not intended as an all-encompassing explanation of all charismatic leader–follower relationships.

The Charismatic Leader as Mirror-Hungry Personality

The "mirror-hungry" leader requires a continuing flow of admiration from his audience in order to nourish his famished self. Central to his ability to elicit that admiration is his ability to convey a sense of grandeur, omnipotence, and strength. These individuals, who have had feelings of grandiose omnipotence awakened within them, are particularly attractive to individuals seeking idealized sources of strength. They convey a sense of conviction and certainty to those who are consumed by doubt and uncertainty. This mask of certainty is no mere pose. In truth, so profound is their inner doubt that a wall of dogmatic certainty is necessary to ward it off. For them, preserving grandiose feelings of strength and omniscience does not allow acknowledgment of weakness and doubt.

For the "mirror-hungry" charismatic leader, the roar of the admiring crowd is music to his ears, a heady elixir. Especially early in his career, Fidel Castro would deliver eight-hour perorations and would seem to gain strength during these remarkable performances. There was an almost chemical connection between Castro and his adoring followers, and their energy seemed to flow into him. On these broiling days, they would be wilting while he apparently grew stronger. He required their shouts of approval.

The mechanism of splitting, to which we referred earlier, is of central importance in maintaining their illusion.

The Language of Splitting Is the Rhetoric of Absolutism

There is the "me" and the "not me," good versus evil, strength versus weakness. Analysis of the speeches of charismatic leaders repeatedly reveals such all-or-nothing polar absolutism.

Either-or categorization, with the charismatic leaders on the side of the angels, is a regular characteristic of their evocative rhetoric. Consider these words of Robespierre: "There are but two kinds of men, the kind that is corrupt and the kind that is virtuous." By the virtuous, as Bychowski[9] notes in *Dictators and Disciples*, Robespierre means those who thought as he did; his main criterion for judging the morals of others became the extent to which they agreed with his ideas. Bychowski has observed the predominance of the theme of strength and weakness in Hitler's speeches: the emphasis on the strength of the German people, the reviling of weakness, the need to purify the race of any contamination or sign of weakness. But what could be the barrier to the German people achieving its full measure of greatness? "If we Germans are the chosen of God, then they [the Jews] are the people of Satan." This is very similar to the rhetoric of Osama bin Laden. Here, the polarity is between good and evil, between children of God and the people of Satan.

"Look at our splendid youth ... I do not want anything weak or tender in them;" Hitler invokes the cult of strength and reviles weakness. "One must defend the strong who are menaced by their inferiors," he asserts, and he then indicates that "A state which, in a period of race pollution, devotes itself to caring for its best racial elements must someday become the lord of the earth." The fear of appearing weak is projected onto the nation with which he identifies.

Being on the side of God and identifying the enemy with Satan is a rhetorical device found regularly in the speeches of charismatic leaders. Ayatollah Khomeini continued to identify the United States as "the great Satan," as did Saddam Hussein. Wilner[10] sees this as an identifying feature of the speeches of the charismatic leader, one that heightens his identity as a leader with supernatural force.

In another example, Wilner has observed the frequency of biblical references in the speeches of Franklin Delano Roosevelt. In his second inaugural address, for example: "We of the Republic pledged ourselves to drive from the temple of our ancient faith those who had profaned it . . . our Covenant with ourselves did not stop there." And, in the stirring conclusion, "I shall do my utmost to speak their purpose and do their will, seeking Divine guidance to help us and every one to give light to them that sit in darkness and to guide our feet into the way of peace." As Wilner points out, not only is the authority of the Bible invoked, but also there are suggestions of God speaking through the mouth of the prophet Franklin. He identified himself with Moses as well, asking, "Shall we pause now and turn our back upon the road that lies ahead? Shall we call this the promised land?"

The invocation of divine guidance and use of biblical references are surely the currency of American political rhetoric, and no politician worth his salt would ignore them. What is the difference between the politician whose use of such rhetoric rings false, as hollow posturing, and the politician whose religious words inspire? Is this related to Wildenmann's[11] distinction between charisma and pseudo-charisma? I would suggest that the narcissistic individual who does indeed consciously believe that he has special leadership gifts and, accordingly, a special role to play may utilize religious rhetoric much more convincingly. Most convincing of all is its use by leaders like Ayatollah Khomeini and Osama bin Laden, who were indeed genuinely convinced they had a religious mission to perform.

Although the ability to convey belief is an important asset, real belief is most convincing. This is also true of the polarization of good and evil, *we* versus *them*. Again, although it is a common political tactic to attempt to unify the populace against the outside enemy, the rhetoric of polarization is most effective when, as in the case of Hitler, *they* are absolutely believed to be the source of the problem, *they* are evil, and to eliminate *them* is to eliminate *our* problems. Greenacre[12] observed that, in order to be effectively charismatic, it is a great asset to possess paranoid conviction. Although there is no necessary relation between charisma and paranoia, when the two are linked, some of the most fearful excesses of human violence in history have occurred.[13]

As will be observed later in discussing the ideal-hungry follower, the posture of total certainty, of total conviction on the part of the leader, is very attractive to one besieged by doubt. Indeed, this posture is necessary to ward off the inner doubt of the leader, too. In one of his last essays, Kohut considered the implications of self-psychology for group psychology and historical phenomena. He summarized the characteristics of the individual who is especially suitable to become the admired omnipotent model, observing that

certain types of narcissistically fixated persons (even bordering on the paranoid) ... display an apparently unshakeable self-confidence and voice their opinions with absolute certainty ... Such individuals' maintenance of their self-esteem depends on the incessant use of certain mental functions ... they are continually judging others – usually pointing up the moral flaws in other people's personality and behavior – and, without shame or hesitation, they set themselves up as the guides and leaders and gods of those who are in need of guidance, of leadership, and of a target for their reverence.[14]

Indeed, the degree of moral righteousness is often quite extraordinary. Kohut goes on to observe that the psychological equilibrium of such charismatic leaders is of "an all or nothing type: there are no survival potentialities between the extremes of utter firmness and strength on the one hand, and utter destruction on the other."[15]

It is important to re-emphasize that such individuals have disowned and projected on the environment all of the unacceptable weakness and imperfection within themselves. Psychologically, they cannot permit themselves to recognize that the source of their feared destruction is not from without but from within. The "mirror-hungry" personality is held together by this rigid shell of apparently total self-confidence to keep profound inner doubt from breaking through. For the charismatic leader with paranoid characteristics who is projecting his inner aggression, the rhetoric becomes the basis for justifying attacks on the outside enemy: "We are (I am) not weak. The problem is out there, with them. By destroying them, by expelling them (the weakness within me) from our midst, we (I) will be the strong people (person) we (I) want to be." And each time the admiring crowd shouts its approval in response to his externalizing rhetoric, the leader's façade of certainty is strengthened and his inner doubts assuaged.

Charismatic Leader–Follower Relationships as a Form of Mass Hypnosis

There is a quality of mutual intoxication in the leader's reassuring his followers, who in turn reassure him. One is reminded of the relationship between hypnotist and subject. Manifesting total confidence, the hypnotist instructs his subject to yield control to him and to suspend volition and judgment. To watch the films of Hitler's rallies – his hypnotic use of language, the repetition of simple phrases building to a crescendo, the crowd echoing his phrases – is to watch hypnosis on a large scale. Observers of the powerfully mesmerizing effect of Hitler on his followers at mass rallies likened him to a hypnotist who placed his entire audience into a trance. Even those who did not understand a word of German described themselves as coming under his hypnotic sway; most striking of all, this was autohypnosis because Hitler himself apparently entered a trance state, mesmerized by the enraptured responses of his mesmerized followers.[a]

The power of the hypnotist ultimately depends on the eagerness of his subjects to yield to his authority, to cede control of their autonomy, to surrender their will to the hypnotist's authority.

Followers as "Ideal-Hungry" Personalities as Well as Temporarily Overwhelmed Individuals

Let us turn now to an examination of the psychology of the admiring crowd of hypnotic subjects – the ideal-hungry followers without whose uncritical response the charismatic leader would be but an empty shell, "full of sound and fury, signifying nothing." I should like first to make a distinction between those who, by virtue of external circumstances, are rendered temporarily susceptible to entering into a charismatic leader–follower relationship and those narcissistically injured personalities who are permanently prone to entering such relationships.

SOCIETAL CRISIS PRODUCES TEMPORARILY OVERWHELMED FOLLOWERS

At moments of societal crisis, otherwise mature and psychologically healthy individuals may temporarily come to feel overwhelmed and in need of a strong and self-assured leader. But when the historical moment passes, so, too, does this need. Few would omit Winston Churchill from the pantheon of charismatic leaders. The sense of conviction and assuredness he conveyed provided a rallying point to Great Britain and the Western Alliance during their darkest hours. During the crisis of World War II, Churchill's virtues were exalted and idealized. But when the war passed and the need for a strong leader abated, the British people quickly demystified the previously revered Churchill, focused on his leadership faults, and cast him out of office.

Indeed, the process of idealization carries within it the seeds of disillusion. And the intensity of disengagement from the charismatic leader can be every bit as powerful as the attraction, a reflection of the cyclic course of history and the changing needs of the populace.

This demonstrates that charismatic leader–follower relationships require not only the congruence of a particular leader with a particular followership, but

---

[a] I had a colleague whose father was a diplomat in Germany in the 1930s, during Hitler's rise. As a boy of eight, he accompanied his father to a Hitler Youth Rally and was transfixed by the experience. He described the theatrical spectacle, the solitary figure walking alone, the spotlight on him, the stadium in darkness. At times, Hitler's voice dropped to a whisper, the stadium was so quiet one could hear a pin drop as the adoring crowd strained to hear his every word. At other times, his voice was an exultant roar. "I didn't understand a word of German, but I would have followed him anywhere."

also a special historical moment. Weber[16] characterized a time of societal readiness for revolutionary change and a charismatic revolutionary leader. Through
the years of exile in Iraq and France, Ayatollah Khomeini retained a loyal
following. His basic personality, leadership style, and rhetoric remained consistent over the years. But it was only when the Shah hastened the pace of societal
change in hopes of achieving his White Revolution before he died,[17] thereby
creating massive societal dislocation and disrupting the social order, that the
ideal-hungry followers and the special historical moment were also present, and
the charismatic leader–follower relationship blossomed and grew.

I do not mean to imply that charismatic leader–follower relationships only
develop at such historical moments. Rather, I am suggesting that they are
particularly apt to occur at those times when the ranks of dependent followers
are swollen by normally self-sufficient individuals who have temporarily been
rendered psychologically vulnerable by external events.

THE NARCISSISTICALLY WOUNDED "IDEAL HUNGRY" FOLLOWERS

But, even in the quietest of times, charismatic leader–follower relationships
develop. What are the characteristics of the *ideal-hungry* followers? As has
been suggested earlier, one of the possible vicissitudes of damage to the self-
concept during early childhood development is to leave the individual permanently psychologically scarred, with an enduring need to attach himself to a
powerful, caring other. Incomplete unto themselves, such individuals can only
feel whole when in relationship with, attached to, or merged with this idealized
other. The charismatic leader comes to the psychological rescue of these ideal-
hungry followers. Taking on heroic proportions and representing what the
followers wish to be, he protects them from confronting themselves and their
fundamental inadequacy and alienation. The leader's success becomes the follower's success, a succor to his self-esteem.

Charismatic Religious Cults

Marc Galenter's[b] studies of charismatic religious groups provide confirmation
for the hypothesis that narcissistically wounded individuals are especially
attracted to charismatic leader–follower relationships. He found that the more
lonely and isolated the individual was before joining, the more apt he was to
affiliate himself strongly with the Unification Church and stay through the entire
recruitment process. There was a tendency to suspend individual judgment
and follow unquestioningly the dictates of the leader. Moreover, the more

---

[b] Using carefully designed questionnaires together with structured interviews, Dr. Mark Galanter
then with the department of psychiatry, Albert Einstein Medical School, has systematically
studied the social psychology of the members of charismatic religious cults (1978, 1979, 1980,
1983, 1986).

psychological relief that was experienced on joining, the less likely the individual was to question the leader's requirement for actions and behavior that ran counter to his socialization.

Repetitive Patterns of Group Behavior

Cult members seek the comfort of the group and seem to develop a "group mind," and this is also true of psychologically scarred individuals and individuals under stress who are particularly prone to act as if they have a group mind, as if they are acting under the same psychological assumptions – a situation that social psychiatrist Wilfred Bion has described as a "basic assumption state."[c] For alienated and marginal individuals who tend to externalize the source of their own failures – for the narcissistically wounded "ideal-hungry" individuals described by Kohut[18] – I believe the psychological attractiveness of these states is overwhelming.

I would go so far as to suggest that these basic assumption states regularly characterize the followers in charismatic leader–follower relationships and that the skillful charismatic leader intuitively shapes and induces these states in his followers. Some may be attracted to the charismatic religious cults described by Galanter, others to the path of terrorism, as I have noted elsewhere,[19] and, especially in times of societal stress, some may be attracted to the banner of charismatic political leaders.

When one is feeling overwhelmed, besieged by fear and doubt, it is extremely attractive to be able to suspend individual judgment and repose one's faith in the

[c] The observations of Wilfred Bion (1961) concerning repetitive patterns of group behavior add further to our understanding of the forces mobilized in followers by charismatic leaders. Bion's work has been elaborated by the Tavistock Institute in Great Britain and the A. K. Rice Institute in the United States through their Human Relations Conferences on the role of Leadership, Authority, and Responsibility in Organizations. Working with psychologically healthy executives, educators, and health care professionals, the staffs of these organizations continue to reconfirm the observations Bion first made with psychiatric inpatients in military hospitals in Great Britain. He noted that no matter how healthy the individual, when people come together in a group, they behave as if they are acting on the basis of shared basic assumptions. He described three psychological states that regularly come into play – three emotional states by which group members act as if they are dominated. He calls these three "basic assumption" groups the dependency group, the pairing group, and the fight–flight group. The dependency group turns to an omnipotent leader for security. Acting as if they do not have independent minds of their own, the members blindly seek directions and follow orders unquestioningly. They tend to idealize and place the leader on a pedestal, but when the leader fails to meet the standards of omnipotence and omniscience, after a period of denial, anger and disappointment result. In the pairing group, the members act as if the goal of the group is to bring forth a Messiah, someone who will save them. There is an air of optimism and hope that a new world is around the corner. The fight–flight group organizes itself in relationship to a perceived outside threat. The group itself is idealized as part of a polarizing mechanism, whereas the outside group is regularly seen as malevolent in motivation. The threatening outside world is at once a threat to the existence of the group and the justification for its existence.

leadership of someone who conveys conviction and certainty, someone who has the answers, who knows the way, be it Reverend Moon or Reverend Jim Jones, Adolf Hitler or Ayatollah Khomeini. Particularly through skillful use of rhetoric, the leader persuades his needy audience: "Follow me and I will take care of you. Together we can make a new beginning and create a new society. The fault is not within us but out there, and the only barrier to the happiness, peace, and prosperity we deserve is the outside enemy out to destroy us."

There is an additional bonus for the potential follower lured by the siren song of the leader's strength and conviction. Promised "Join my followers and you will no longer be alone," the follower then draws additional strength from sharing his allegiance with others. The identity of follower becomes a badge of honor, a statement of membership in a collective self. And, in having merged his self with the collective other, the success of the followers becomes his own personal success.

For isolated individuals with damaged self-esteem and weak ego boundaries, this sense of "we" creates and imparts a coherent sense of identity. For such individuals, the self and the "we" are fused so that the self is experienced *as* the relationship. This leads to a tendency for such individuals to merge themselves with the group. In a figurative manner, as I have noted, we can speak of the development of a group mind or group ego. The group becomes idealized, and the standards of the group, as articulated by the leader and his disciples, take over and become the norm. This helps explain the startling degree to which individuals can suspend their own standards and judgment and participate in the most violent of actions when under the sway of the psychology of the group, if persuaded that the cause of the group is served by their actions. Even that most basic of human needs – the drive for self-preservation – can be suspended in the service of the group, as was horrifyingly evidenced by the phenomenon of collective suicide using cyanide-laced Kool-Aid at the Peoples Temple in Jonestown, Guyana. The Branch Davidians is another example of a closed religious cult that ended tragically, in this case with a fiery conflagration that ended the 51-day siege at Ranch Apocalypse in Waco, Texas.

David Koresh and the Branch Davidian Charismatic Cult at Waco

A ninth-grade dropout, David Koresh[d] began life as Vernon Howell. His early years were marked by instability and abuse. He moved back and forth between his grandmother's home and his mother's. He suffered from dyslexia, which made school very difficult for young Vernon. He was placed in special education classes but ultimately dropped out in the ninth grade. Howell's grandparents

---

[d] This discussion is drawn from a detailed study of David Koresh and the Branch Davidians in the chapter "David Koresh: The Messiah of Ranch Apocalypse," in Robert Robins and Jerrold Post (1997) *Political Paranoia*, pp. 121–130.

were practicing Seventh Day Adventists, and his years with them were steeped in Bible study. He built a shed in their backyard, took up the electric guitar, and became consumed with the ambition to become a rock star. Writing his own lyrics and already demonstrating the charismatic appeal that was to characterize his leadership at Ranch Apocalypse, he was idolized by young teenagers. Many of his lyrics had a satanic theme. Given what was to eventuate, the lyrics to the song "The Mad Man from Waco" are striking:

> There's a mad man living in Waco
> Pray to the Prince of Hell
> Please, please won't you listen?
> It's not what it appears to be
> We didn't want to hurt anybody.
> Just set our people free.

His behavioral difficulties ultimately led his grandparents to reject him and send him back to his mother. Thus, Howell's early years were marked by rejection from his mother, two abusive stepfathers, his grandparents, and school authorities, and he had no stable male role model.

Howell was very active sexually. After a teenage girl he was seeing became pregnant and her father refused to let Howell marry her, he began attending a Seventh Day Adventist Church. Seeking atonement for the impure sexual thoughts with which he was preoccupied, he prayed a great deal. This intense involvement with the church proved to be transformational for young Howell. Coming from a background of instability, he found a home in the church. Absorbing its strict doctrine, he began to piously lecture about sexual immorality. After hearing a series of "fire-and-brimstone" seminars from an evangelical preacher conducting Revelation Seminars and predicting the approaching apocalypse, Howell was mesmerized. He told his sister that what was missing was the Great Seal for the next great prophet, and he indicated that he quite possibly could unlock that Seventh Seal. He became progressively convinced that he was destined to be "a new prophet and a new light" in the Seventh Day Adventist church, a quite splendid, grandiose compensation for his shambles of a life.

Unable to persuade the church leadership of his divine role, the 23-year-old Howell was disfellowshipped by the Tyler, Texas, Seventh Day Adventist congregation in 1983. He found his way to the Davidian branch of the Seventh Day Adventists, which had as a central tenet of its doctrine that a prophet was in their midst, a fact that definitely appealed to young Howell. The Branch Davidians were the diehard true believers who had clung to their faith after selling all of their possessions and waiting for the final days in 1959, in what came to be known as the Great Disappointment. After founder Victor Houteff died in 1955, there was a period of leadership instability, during which Howell cleverly maneuvered to become the exalted leader of the Branch Davidians.

What a distance he had traveled! From uncertainty to total command; from dyslexic to Master of the Word, especially the inspired words of the Book of

Revelations; from school dropout to leader of a devoted congregation and eloquent preacher whose sermons emphasized religious freedom, the right to bear arms, and the right to be free of government interference. He took control of the Waco section of the Branch Davidians, systematically transforming the grounds into an armed compound. In 1990, he legally changed his name to David Koresh (*Koresh* is Hebrew for Cyrus, the Persian king who allowed the Jews to return to Palestine). His divine role was now established in his own mind, and his sermons were eloquent and inspiring, especially for those who had lost their moorings, thus reflecting the fit between a mirror-hungry leader and his ideal-hungry followers. He traveled widely in pursuit of recruits, being especially successful in Australia, Israel, Great Britain, and Jamaica. To others like himself, whose world had been shattered, he offered a shared vision: "These feelings you have, which you thought reflected personal weakness, reflect a transcendent reality. So you are not alone. And I, who am divinely inspired, possess knowledge of that awful reality, and I have the keys to paradise." From hopelessness and despair, he offered to the weak and dispossessed a message of hope and redemption.

Gradually, he began to reshape the church ideology to reflect his own grandiose vision. He was the seventh and final angel, destined to be the angel of God who brings about the end of the world. The triggering event would occur at their compound in Waco, and he urged his followers to prepare for the final battle between the forces of good and the forces of evil. Eerily predictive, in the final battle, the world would be consumed and purified by flames to receive Christ the Messiah. David Koresh would return as Christ, and those who believed in him would find paradise in the New Jerusalem.

But his new-found status as prophet did not end his sexual preoccupations, and he reconfigured the Branch Dravidian ideology to provide a sacred rational for his sexual proclivities. Koresh systematically developed a closed and totally controlled social system that required total devotion to his divine personage and enshrined him as "the chosen one" while totally subordinating his followers to his whims. Prolonged Bible study sessions – as long as 15 hours – had a hypnotic effect on his followers. By 1987, he was living in what detectives described as a harem of young girls, some as young as 12. They believed he was Jesus Christ, and he had persuaded their parents and themselves of their duty to serve him sexually, indicating that it was his divine right to "plant his seed" in order to "fill the house of David." Abstinence was required between the member couples, but husbands were joyfully to offer their wives to the chosen one, and parents were joyfully and proudly to offer their adolescent daughters to him. It is estimated that he fathered as many as 17 children. He justified this sexual entitlement by a rather unique interpretation of the 45th Psalm, in which it is written that the king is anointed with "the oil of gladness." Koresh interpreted "the oil of gladness" as vaginal secretions, and held that it was his penis that was to be anointed.

In sanctifying his sexual proclivities, he was following the lead of Mormon leader Joseph Smith, who indulged his sexual appetites and those of his close colleagues by enshrining polygamy as religiously sanctified. The manner in which Koresh became the sexual hub of the Branch Davidians is also reminiscent of the People's Temple Reverend Jim Jones, who required husbands to watch as he had sex with their wives and wives to watch as he had sex with their husbands. Family unity was a threat to his totalitarian system and, through this enforced humiliation and degradation, Koresh, like Jones, ensured his control.

It is striking that Koresh was able to persuade his followers to embrace this sexually licentious lifestyle, as required by a reformulated and quite harsh morality and justified theologically by Koresh as being required by God, who told him to build a new House of David by having many wives and spreading his seed as King David had done. Like many narcissistic leaders discussed earlier in this volume, David Koresh made an exception of himself and wrapped this exception in theological justification.

As he gathered his flock to him, Koresh preached constantly about the approaching end of the world and of his followers' need to protect themselves against the coming attack. And so it was that, when the Bureau of Alcohol, Tobacco, and Firearms attacked the compound, it seemed to be the fulfillment of Koresh's prophecy. During the 51-day siege that followed, the FBI profoundly misread the nature of the social system within the compound and the nature of David Koresh's grandiose narcissistic personality. They defined the circumstances as a hostage-and-barricade situation, and hostage-rescue doctrine prescribed a two-track strategy of negotiation while increasing pressure. They applied this pressure through what they termed "psychological operations," an array of tactics including flashing lights and high-intensity sound bombardment. They misdiagnosed Koresh as a psychopath, a con man who would ultimately fold under pressure and surrender to save his life.

Koresh's followers, however, were by no means hostages; they were committed followers of a closed, apocalyptic religious cult. In addition to being manipulative, the intensely narcissistic Koresh was paranoid, grandiose, and delusional, moving in and out of reality – traits consistent with the diagnosis of borderline disorder. Individuals with this disorder can function quite normally but, when under pressure, can slip into psychosis. When such an individual is hanging from the edge of the cliff of sanity by the skin of his teeth, you do not subject his teeth to merciless pounding with a high-frequency dental drill for dental prophylaxis.[e] That was the equivalent of the FBI's unremitting and escalating pressure on David Koresh and his followers. Moreover, the government and media attention on Koresh, the failed rock star who yearned for prominence, must have rewarded his grandiose narcissism. He was the very center, the cynosure, of America's attention.

---

[e] This remarkable mixed metaphor was employed by Christopher Standish, Professor of Psychiatry at Harvard Medical School, in supervision with the author to caution against putting pressure on a disintegrating psychotic.

If Koresh's followers had doubt about the "truth" Koresh was conveying to them, the spectacle of armor-plated vehicles and the experience of sound and light bombardment during the FBI's campaign of psychological warfare were not designed to magnify those doubts. To the contrary, they seemed to confirm Koresh's apocalyptic visions: in prophesying the final battle, Koresh quoted from the Book of Revelations, which spoke of dragons and the sound of trumpets. When an armor-plated vehicle began to punch holes in the compound and pump in tear gas, one did not have to be a paranoid psychotic to disbelieve the government's message, transmitted through bullhorns, that this was *not* an attack. For the Branch Davidians, the nature of the government's actions confirmed their belief that this was the prophesied final battle.

Under this pressure, the narcissistic borderline David Koresh was inexorably pushed across the border of reality, confirming his grandiose delusions. Like many paranoid movements, this messianic, grandiose, and paranoid leader and his followers interacted with the surrounding environment in a tragically self-fulfilling prophecy, producing the very reactions they both feared and anticipated. Along with Koresh, 75 died in the fire that consumed the appropriately named Ranch Apocalypse.

Differentiating the Destructive Charismatic from the Reparative Charismatic

In citing the phenomena of Jonestown, Waco, and Germany under Hitler, I may falsely convey the impression that charismatic leader–follower relationships are only a force for human destructiveness. This is true if the narcissistically wounded leader rages at the world for depriving him of "mirroring" and enlists his followers in attacking it. This is the destructive charismatic, as exemplified by Hitler.

By contrast, charismatic leader–follower relationships can also catalyze a reshaping of society in a highly positive and creative fashion, what Volkan and Itzkowitz[20] have termed *reparative leadership*. They have persuasively demonstrated in their study of Ataturk of Turkey that the narcissistically wounded "mirror-hungry" leader, in projecting his intrapsychic splits on society, may be a force for healing. The reparative charismatic leader seeks a sense of wholeness through establishing a special relationship with his "ideal-hungry" followers. As he tries to heal his own narcissistic wounds through the vehicle of his leadership, he may indeed be resolving splits in a wounded society. Other examples of reparative charismatic leadership are Mohandas Gandhi and Martin Luther King, who modeled his nonviolent resistance on that of Gandhi.

Just as the temporarily needy person may attach himself to an idealized object at trying moments in his personal psychological development, so, too, a temporarily needy nation may require the leadership of an idealized object at trying moments in its historical development. And, just as the object of individual veneration is inevitably dethroned as the overwhelming stress on his followers is relieved and they no longer require rescuing, so, too, the idealized leader will be discarded when a nation's moment of historical need passes, as evidenced by the rise and fall of Winston Churchill.

But whatever the fluctuations in the external circumstances of whole populations, within them there will always be individuals whose internal needs lead them to seek out idealized leaders. And when these "ideal-hungry" followers find a "mirror-hungry" leader, we have the elements of a charismatic leader-follower relationship. These relationships can be looked on as peculiar aberrations – cults – during times of relative societal repose. Microscopic in scale at first, in times of social crisis, these powerful relationships can become the nuclei for powerful transforming social movements, as was the case with the reparative charismatic leadership of Mustafa Kemal Ataturk, Mohandas Gandhi, Martin Luther King, and Nelson Mandela, and the destructive charismatic leadership of Adolf Hitler, Ayatollah Khomeini, and Osama bin Laden.

The adoration of the crowd sustains the "mirror-hungry" leader. He is incomplete without it. Similarly, he turns to those in his immediate surroundings for psychological stability, reassurance, and a sense of completeness; these include both his wife and his inner circle. These special, albeit distorted, relationships that are psychologically required by the narcissistic leader are called *self-object relationships*, the subject of the next chapter.

Notes

1. Marvin Zonis, "Shi'ite Political Activism in the Arab World," draft manuscript, available from the author (Middle East Institute, University of Chicago, 1985).
2. Max Weber, *The Sociology of Religion* (Boston: Beacon Press, 1922).
3. Irvine Schiffer, *Charisma: A Psychoanalytic Look at Mass Society* (Toronto: University of Toronto Press, 1973).
4. D. W. Abse and Richard B. Ulman, "Charismatic Political Leadership and Collective Regression," in *Psychopathology and Political Leadership*, ed. Robert S. Robins (New Orleans: Tulane University, 1977).
5. Ann Ruth Wilner, *The Spellbinders: Charismatic Political Leadership* (New Haven: Yale University Press, 1984).
6. Weber, *The Sociology of Religion*.
7. Schiffer, *Charisma*.
8. Heinz Kohut, "Creativeness, Charisma, Group Psychology," in *Self Psychology and the Humanities*, ed. Charles Strozier (New York: W. W. Norton & Co., 1985), 192.
9. Gustav Bychowski, *Dictators and Disciples: From Caesar to Stalin* (New York: International Universities Press, 1948).
10. Wilner, *The Spellbinders*.
11. W. Wildenmann, Personal Communication, 1984.
12. Phyllis Greenacre, Personal Communication, 1971.
13. Robert Robins, "Paranoia and Charisma" (paper presented at the annual meeting of the International Society of Political Psychology, Toronto, Canada, 1984).
14. Kohut, "Creativeness, Charisma, Group Psychology," 197.

15. Ibid.
16. Weber, *The Sociology of Religion.*
17. Jerrold Post, "Dreams of Glory and the Life Cycle: Reflections on the Life Course of Narcissistic Leaders," *Journal of Political and Military Sociology* 12, No. 1 (1984).
18. Heinz Kohut, *The Restoration of the Self* (New York: International Universities Press, 1977); Heinz Kohut, *The Search for the Self* (New York: International Universities Press, 1978).
19. Jerrold Post, "It's Us Against Them: The Basic Assumptions of Political Terrorists," in *Irrationality in Organizational Life*, ed. James Kranz (Washington, D.C.: A. K. Rice Institute Press, 1987), pp. 68–75.
20. Vamik Volkan and Norman Itzkowitz, *The Immortal Ataturk* (Chicago: University of Chicago Press, 1984).

7

Selfobjects: The Special Role of Wives and the Inner Circle

Jerrold M. Post, M.D. and Kristen Moody, Psy.D.

In trying to understand how some leaders can so grievously miscalculate their positions, it is important to understand the influence of those around the leader, both wives and the inner circle. No leader rules a country by himself. He has a circle of people around him who provide him with information and counsel and who execute his decisions. Leaders with healthy self-esteem insist on having "the best and the brightest" around them. They want advisers who challenge them and constructively criticize their decisions. But for others who are insecure under their grand façades, criticism is experienced as wounding, and the subordinate soon learns to watch his words. In addition, some leaders have wives who actively influence their husband's decision making "for better or for worse."

In characterizing the narcissistic personality, the gap between the grandiose façade and the underlying self-doubt and low self-esteem has been emphasized. This, in turn, is regularly associated with disturbances in interpersonal relationships. The deeply uncertain narcissist turns to those closest to him to provide reassurance and a sense of equilibrium.[a]

---

[a] In conceptualizing the use the narcissist makes of his relationships to provide self-cohesion, Heinz Kohut developed the concept of the *selfobject*, with an emphasis on the self, as the way the narcissist maintains self-esteem. This leads to a major imbalance in the relationships of narcissists, which are not mutual. Rather, the narcissist experiences his wife or close adviser as almost a part of himself whose reassuring presence helps him feel whole; hence, the apt term *selfobject*. As Kohut observes, "the care-taking adult, with a radar of empathy for the child, is continuously in tune with his need to be narcissistically put into equilibrium" (cited in Elson, 1987, p. 52). When he is hungry, he needs to be fed; when he is wet, he needs to be changed. "It is the failures of this equilibrium, if they are appropriately frustrating – in tune with the child's maturation and progress in taking over – which enable the child to grow." This is an essential aspect of healthy parenting. It is traumatic failures in equilibrium and empathy that produces "fragmentation," associated with disruption or failure of self-esteem regulation. The adult narcissist is not able to regulate his own self-esteem and continues to need selfobjects to help him maintain a coherent sense of self.

"FOR BETTER OR FOR WORSE": NARCISSISTIC LEADERS AND THEIR WIVES

If narcissists are unable to see others in any way beyond how those others fulfill the narcissist's own needs, it represents a shallow attachment.[b] Thus, narcissistically organized political leaders may choose partners who idealize them or have attributes that help bolster the leader's image, as was the case with Arnold Schwarzenegger and Maria Shriver. As will be seen in Chapter 10, Schwarzenegger's marriage to Shriver checked off three boxes in his life strategy: to be invited to the White House, to marry a glamorous and intelligent woman, and to enter politics. She completed him. She was an active political partner, helping him craft policies that would appeal to both Democrats and Republicans in the complex arena of California politics.

Narcissistic leaders use their partners to create a fuller sense of self because they feel incomplete without the structure that the relationship provides. Moreover, the partners they choose may themselves be narcissistically organized. In Chapter 6, on Narcissism and Charisma, the fit between the "mirror-hungry" leader and the "ideal-hungry" follower was described. This can also be seen in some marriages of narcissistic leaders. Those individuals who are organized as "ideal-hungry" are forever in search of another whom they can admire for their prestige, power, beauty, or intelligence. Individuals like this experience themselves as worthwhile only so long as they can relate to their *selfobject* in this manner. But how these partners relate to their counterparts, the narcissistic leaders, can be "for better or for worse." Different partners can have different effects on how a narcissistically organized person behaves in office. A look at three leaders – Robert Mugabe, Slobodan Milosevic, and Nicolae Ceausescu – and their wives highlights these concepts.

People with narcissistic personalities lack an inner sense of self-worth. Their lives are organized around maintaining their self-esteem by getting affirmation from outside of themselves, and this strongly influences whom they choose for partners. For individuals with narcissistic personalities, there is a disproportionate degree of self-concern and an unusual response to approval and sensitivity to criticism. Narcissistically organized people will be preoccupied with how they appear to others but privately feel fraudulent and unlovable, leaving them with an insatiable need for reassurance. This, of course, seriously distorts the person the narcissistic leader chooses as a partner.

[b] Different patterns of narcissistic personality characteristics influence the type of partner the narcissist chooses: "mirror-hungry" narcissists who thirst for individuals whose confirming and admiring response will nourish their famished self, thus counteracting their inner sense of worthlessness and lack of self-esteem; "alter-ego" narcissists need relationships with others that possess the opinions, appearance, and values that they have, thus confirming the existence of their own sense of self; "merger-hungry" narcissists need to control others, so much so that the boundaries between themselves and the other are fluid, and this interferes with their ability to discriminate between their individual thoughts, wishes, and intentions and those of their partners; and "contact-shunning" narcissists avoid social contact completely and become isolated, not because they are disinterested in others, but because their need for them is so intense that it leads to an oversensitivity to rejection and annihilation anxiety (McWilliams, 1994).

ROBERT MUGABE: FROM FATHER OF HIS COUNTRY TO DESTROYER OF THE NATION

He was my hero at independence. I admired his eloquence, what I saw as his vision. He made us believe we could be different (from) other African countries yet instead he destroyed it all.   – Trevor Ncube, editor of the *Zimbabwe Independent*,
March 2000

Robert Mugabe is a striking example of how different partners can bring out different qualities in the narcissistic leader. While his early political achievements may now be overshadowed by the later brutality of his regime, early in his career, Mugabe was an inspirational leader among the ranks of the fledgling Zimbabwe nationalist movement in the 1960s.

As leader of the Zimbabwe liberation struggle, Mugabe was seen as the savior of the Zimbabwean people, leading them out of the bonds of a repressive government marked by racism and discrimination into a new era of prosperity, education, equality, and advancement. His first wife, Sally, the "Mother of the Nation," provided a humanizing and stabilizing influence and acted as a constraint against the more florid expressions of his self-aggrandizing personality that were increasingly to flower after her death in 1992. In contrast, his second wife, 40 years his junior and known as "Grasping Grace," has encouraged flamboyant personal excesses while neglecting the nation's disintegration.

BACKGROUND AND EARLY YEARS

Robert Gabriel Mugabe was born on February 21, 1924, at the Katama Jesuit Mission in Zvimba District, about 80 miles from then Salisbury, Southern Rhodesia, today Harare, Zimbabwe. Robert, his two brothers, and one sister grew up in a devoutly Catholic family; his father, Gabriel Mugabe, was the carpenter at the Catholic mission, and his mother, Bona Mugabe, was considered a deeply religious woman. Mugabe has maintained his relationship with the Catholic Church throughout his life. Mugabe's father abandoned his family when Robert was aged 10, the same year Robert's eldest brother Michael died. This double loss no doubt had a profound impact on Mugabe throughout his life – scarred by the absence of a father figure, he overcompensated by striving to become father of his nation.

Mugabe was educated in a strict Jesuit mission school and was remembered as the youngest and smallest of his classmates. A former teacher remembers him as a serious student who pushed himself to excel at his studies. His mother, who never remarried, was an ardent supporter of Robert continuing his education. After six years of elementary education, he accepted an offer, at great expense to his family, to attend a teacher training school. He graduated from this training school in 1941 and immediately embarked on a series of mission school teaching jobs until he entered Fort Hare University in 1945 to pursue a bachelor's degree in history and English. He spent the 1950s at a series of mission teaching jobs in Ghana during a self-imposed exile in response to the minority rule of Southern Rhodesia, at that time a member of the British Commonwealth.

In the 1950s, black nationalists in Southern Rhodesia, despite internal fractures among the various tribal groups, began a struggle against colonial rule, a movement that Mugabe returned to join in 1960 and in which he played a crucial leadership role during the armed insurrection. The situation intensified when Ian Smith, committed to white minority rule, unilaterally declared the independence of the state of Rhodesia in 1965. The Smith government was highly criticized for its racist policies and treatment of the majority black population as second-class citizens. As early as 1962, Mugabe gave voice to his belief that it was only through the exercise of raw power that the unjust situation of blacks in Rhodesia could be rectified: "It may be necessary to use methods other than constitutional ones."[1]

FOR BETTER: SALLY HEYFRON

Mugabe met his first wife, Sally Heyfron, while both were teaching at a college in Ghana.[2] They came from very different worlds. Sally, in contrast to the bookish and lonely Mugabe, was described as exuberant and beautiful, and she was brought up in a political family that was part of the nationalist movement in colonial Ghana. Her family had strong links to Ghana's then Prime Minister Kwame Nkrumah.[3] It is easy to see why Mugabe was so drawn to Sally; she was a strong, independent, and intelligent woman, and she was to have a great deal of influence in his life. They married in 1961, after Sally converted to Catholicism.

Sally was very active in Zimbabwe's political arena before and after her husband took power as the country's president in 1980. Mugabe once said, "I married a Ghanaian because Ghanaian women don't leave the men to do all the work." Both shared political goals for a free Zimbabwe, and both played key roles in Rhodesia's burgeoning independence movement. While Mugabe rose up through the ranks of Joshua Nkomo's Zimbabwe African People's Union (ZAPU), Sally helped enfranchise and mobilize women. She spoke at rallies, visited guerrilla camps, and was an active advocate for her husband. It was a strong political partnership. She became known as "Comrade Sally" for her visits to the guerrilla camps in Mozambique and Tanzania during the struggle for the country's independence.

Sally played an important psychological role for her husband as well; wise and mature, she served as a constraint on his impetuous and more negative impulses, and she brought out the best in her husband as they devoted their energies first toward liberating Rhodesia and later to nation building in Zimbabwe.

She faced her own challenges during the struggle for liberation. In 1961, after delivering a speech that the watching Rhodesian police considered inflammatory, she was arrested and served six weeks in jail. In 1963, Sally gave birth to the couple's son, Nhamodzenyika ("our country's troubles"), the same year that Robert left the ZAPU to help establish the rival Zimbabwe African National Union (ZANU). In 1964, the now prominent insurgent leader was arrested and sentenced to 10 years imprisonment in the country's notorious Salisbury Prison, being forced to leave Sally and their infant son. Two years later, while Mugabe was still imprisoned, Nhamodzenyika died of cerebral malaria at the age of three. Mugabe was denied permission to attend the child's funeral. In her autobiography, Sally writes of this time,

I am a mother, I could have gone out and grabbed Ian Smith by the throat when I had to write and tell my husband that our child had died. ... But he taught me to realize that if you spend all your time wanting revenge you stay always in the position that you were before you gained your freedom.[4]

Overall, Sally and her husband spent only 6 of their 19 married years together.

Mugabe's 10 years of imprisonment were significant. He devoted himself to his education and obtained multiple degrees, including a law degree. It was during this time in prison that Mugabe developed his Marxist-Leninist ideology (he continues to this day to prefer to be called Comrade Mugabe). Mugabe believed in the power of an education, and he has, in his later years, become convinced of his superiority as a result of his education. He once described himself as "the only man in Africa who really understands Marxism-Leninism."

Mugabe is known to have told people that he continued his studies for himself and for his country, suggesting that he had already begun to identify himself as playing a central role in creating a new nation. Sally spent the years of her husband's imprisonment in London, working and studying in a variety of positions. As a remarkable testament to her belief in her husband and his future leadership role in Zimbabwe, she spent long hours copying in longhand from texts borrowed from the local library to provide materials for her husband's own studies while in prison. She brought out the best in her husband and actively encouraged him to constantly strive to better himself in order to fight for their nation's independence.

After his release from prison in 1974, already an active member of the ZANU and representing the Shona majority, Robert Mugabe joined the armed struggle against the Ian Smith regime. The highly educated Mugabe quickly emerged as a leader, vocally denouncing the Smith regime. His fiery and impassioned speeches criticizing the Smith regime spoke of racial equality, freedom of speech, freedom of the press, and of education. He articulated a hopeful vision for the future of Zimbabwe. Interestingly, the very issues that were the cornerstone of his political agenda as Rhodesia became Zimbabwe remain central in Zimbabwe today. Today, though, it is Mugabe who is the focus of criticism. It is ironic that, in a 1979 speech,[5] Robert Mugabe referred to the imminent collapse of the decadent

Ian Smith regime, which he characterized as trying every possible ploy and maneuver to survive. He also called the elections a farce. Opposition parties level these very same accusations against Mugabe and his government today.

In 1980, Robert Mugabe was sworn in as the first president of the new African nation of Zimbabwe. When her husband became president, in recognition of her important role, Sally became known as First Lady Amai, or Mother of the Nation. When Mugabe came to power, he was viewed as a beacon of hope, justice, and equality in a country trying to recover from decades of civil discord and war. Despite his Marxist rhetoric, "Mugabe, when he became president, was hailed as a new African hero, respected as an intellectual and sincere Catholic, and admired as a non-racist who, on coming to power, assured the former white Rhodesians that they were welcome to stay in the new Zimbabwe."[6] Following his ascension to power, Mugabe gave a Mandela-style speech about the need for reconciliation between whites and blacks. He even included white ministers in his government. Sally, his full political partner, was seen as playing a major role in his positive leadership.

If yesterday I fought you as an enemy, today you have become friend and ally with the same national interest, loyalty, rights and duties as myself . . . The wrongs of the past must now stand forgiven and forgotten. If ever we look to the past, let us do so for the lesson the past has taught us, namely that oppression and racism are inequalities that must never find scope in our political and social system. It could never be a correct justification that because the whites oppressed us yesterday when they had power, the blacks must oppress them today because they have power. An evil remains an evil whether it is practiced by white against black or black against white.

I personally recognize and accept that the collective will of the people is the most powerful force in the land and for this reason must be the main influence on governments and their policies. It follows, therefore, that it is by letting the people exercise their power on those aspects affecting their daily lives that the best basis for formulating change emerges.[7]

Despite ferocious ethnic conflict in the early 1980s, Zimbabwe became a symbol of African progress and achievement. By the end of the 1980s, Zimbabwe had achieved one of the best educational systems in Africa, with a literacy rate that ranged between 41 and 64 percent; its per capita income was at the highest level ever, and the future looked bright. After a bitter struggle with the white Ian Smith government, Zimbabwe under the leadership of Robert Mugabe made concerted efforts to develop an inclusive government and consciously worked to eliminate racial barriers. The mid- to late-1980s were the boom years.

Although Robert Mugabe began his career with an apparent commitment to the people of Zimbabwe and popular participation in government, he increasingly came to see himself as the country's savior. As Zimbabwe continued to succeed and be heralded as an example of African progressiveness, Mugabe began to personalize this success, internalizing it as a direct reflection of his personal leadership, thus enhancing his narcissistic view of his singular importance to what he increasingly came to see as *his* nation.

In the early years of Mugabe's rule, it was Sally who was credited for helping to temper his excesses. She could lighten his mood, said one of his former colleagues, just by entering the room.[8] It was Sally who encouraged her husband to be a father to the country, just as she took on the role of the nurturing mother. She acted as a wise counsel to inhibit him from carrying out acts that would reflect poorly on him and endanger the country. With Sally by his side, the narcissistically organized Mugabe could be influenced by a strong, secure attachment to an individual who used her ideas of reform to influence the country for the better. Richard Dowden of the Royal African Society characterized her as being "a really soothing sensible influence on him, and many people trace his going completely over the top to after she died. Up until then, she was the one that restrained him."[9]

It is no coincidence, then, that at about same the time that Sally, a major source of psychological stability for her husband, began to suffer from the serious kidney illness that would ultimately claim her life, Mugabe's Zimbabwe also began to deteriorate. Her illness increasingly interfered with her ability to constrain her husband's excesses. Sally provided a counterbalance against the more florid expressions of his narcissistic, self-aggrandizing personality that were increasingly to flower after her death. As she became increasingly ill and unable to devote all of her faltering energy to supporting her husband, Mugabe responded to her threatened loss by starting an affair with his married secretary, Grace Marufu, 40 years his junior. After Sally's death in 1992, Mugabe began making increasingly radical decisions that adversely affected Zimbabwe's already failing economy and quality of life. He grew into a tyrant, without Sally there to caution him against extreme politics, something that Grace was not vocal in doing. The perception was widespread that, with Mugabe's marriage to Grace, everything changed.

AND FOR WORSE: "GRASPING GRACE"

In 1994, when journalists began publicly reporting about his relationship with Grace, who had by this time acquired the sobriquet "Grasping Grace," Mugabe verbally lashed out at the press. Subsequently, two journalists were taken into government custody and tortured. This attempt to intimidate and eliminate the free press in Zimbabwe continued, and it has become a hallmark of the current Mugabe regime. In 1996, Mugabe, at the age of 74, married the 31-year-old Grace, with whom he already had two children. The wedding itself, attended by 6,000 guests, was an ostentatious and much criticized public event – its extravagance standing in sharp contrast to the deteriorating standard of living of the majority of the Zimbabwean people.[10]

The extravagant wedding itself, though, was only a shadow of what was to come. Among many other things, Mugabe has spent exorbitant amounts of money building multiple estates for Grace, and they routinely "hijack" commercial airliners for their personal shopping and pleasure trips. Grace has become universally despised for her greed and extravagant living, with accusations that she is a gold-digger more interested in her personal stature than in the country of Zimbabwe or in Mugabe himself. One well-documented story occurred in 2002 when Grace was photographed spending approximately $120,000 during a short spree in Paris. The widely publicized shopping excursion was clear evidence that she was violating the 2002 European Union sanctions, an element of which was a ban to "stop Grace Mugabe going on her shopping trips in the face of catastrophic poverty blighting the people of Zimbabwe."[11]

Despite the near-absolute financial collapse of Zimbabwe, the Mugabes continued to live a flamboyant lifestyle, apparently oblivious to the reality of the Zimbabwean situation. In contrast to the moderating influence of Sally, Grace seemed to have fueled the very elements of Mugabe's narcissistic personality that Sally helped to constrain. Grace is not thought to have political influence on her husband, except to the extent that she lacked the restraining influence that Sally had, and insofar as she encourages massive corruption to feed her insatiable appetite for riches.

As the Mugabe government has continued to face increasing pressure and reports of corruption, failures, and discontent, a concerted effort has been made to muzzle the press. In ironic contrast to his inaugural address, Mugabe dismissed criticism of his regime as coming from "white men":

The only white man you can trust is a dead white man ... Our party must continue to strike fear in the heart of the white man, our real enemy![12]

Attempts to severely restrict the freedom of the press have met with outrage. In addition to the international community and internal opposition groups, the Zimbabwe parliamentary legal committee, responsible for evaluating all bills from a constitutional perspective, declared the recent bill introduced by Information Minister Jonathan Moyo as "manifestly unconstitutional" and "obscure, vague, ill-conceived and dangerous."[13] Judges were harassed, and those whose rulings displeased Mugabe were deposed. These antidemocratic actions would not have occurred were Sally still the first lady and acting to moderate Mugabe's excesses.

As discontent grew, genuine political opposition grew apace, and, to Mugabe's consternation, in 2000, his constitutional referendum that would allow seizure of white-owned land without compensation was defeated. From that point onward, Mugabe manipulated the electoral process to maintain his firm grip on power, which in turn led to a more determined opposition.

By 2002, the government of Zimbabwe had, for all intents and purposes, become a parody of the Ian Smith regime, which many current insiders fought so hard to dethrone. It became the antithesis of the ideals that Mugabe, with Sally and his inner circle, rode to power – namely, freedom, democracy, and equality. Mugabe himself had been transformed from a heroic figure to a malevolent tragic figure obsessed with his own survival and lifestyle at the expense of his nation.

In 2003, Mugabe caused further uproar by comparing himself to Adolf Hitler. At the state funeral of one of his cabinet ministers, not recognizing how odious the comparison was, Mr. Mugabe said,

I am still the Hitler of the time. This Hitler has only one objective, justice for his people, sovereignty for his people, recognition of the independence of his people and their right to resources.[14]

In 2008, Grace joined the ranks of human rights violators. She was accused of human rights violations and crimes of extreme corruption related to the violence-plagued diamond fields in eastern Zimbabwe. It was alleged that Grace, along with other high-ranking officials, was generating millions of dollars in personal income by hiring teams of diggers to hand-extract diamonds from the Chiadzwa mine.[15] In a counteraction against these claims, Grace sued, stating that the story damaged her reputation as "mother of the nation,"[16] a rather remarkable claim given the extent of her self-indulgent behavior, which has displayed no regard for the people of Zimbabwe.

In 2008, Mugabe launched his election campaign on his birthday, perhaps showing further evidence of the enmeshment of his identity with that of the country. After the Zimbabwe Election Commission confirmed that Mugabe and his party had lost control to the Movement of Democratic Change (MDC) under the leadership of Morgan Tsvangirai, Mugabe ordered his forces to crack down on the MDC. At least two foreign journalists who were covering the disputed presidential election were arrested, including a correspondent for the *New York Times*.[17]

The brutality of the crackdown led Tsvangirai to drop out of the contest and take refuge in the Dutch Embassy, citing violence targeted against his campaign. He complained that the elections were pointless because Mugabe himself would determine the outcome: "We have resolved that we will no longer participate in this violent, illegitimate sham of an election process."[18] In September 2009, however, after more than a month of negotiations mediated by South African President Thabo Mbeki, a power-sharing deal was struck. Mugabe retained presidential power and said he was committed to national unity and would do "his best." But Mugabe's words were soon belied by his deeds. For the consummate narcissist, words are instrumental, and he will say anything to accomplish his goals – which for Mugabe was to retain his power. Despite the accord, Mugabe's army proceeded to grab nearly all the key ministries and appoint provincial leaders, leaving little authority to Tsvangirai. Mugabe maintained his grip on the security forces, which provide crucial elements of power. As Mugabe earlier stated, the constitution was what he, the president, said it was, and he was boss.

There is a stark difference in how Mugabe acted with each of his wives. Sally, his *selfobject* "for better," helped modulate his self-esteem and keep his impulses in check. His narcissistic self-aggrandizing features were calmed by Sally's stabilizing influence. The threat of losing her was too overwhelming for him, perhaps because he had relied on her so much to bolster his own image as a politician. In essence, Sally was his other half, and she created a fuller sense of self for Mugabe. When this was challenged by her illness, he turned to another for comfort.

This time, however, his choice was "for worse." Rather than stabilize his behavior and counter his politically unwise and destructive impulses, as Sally had done, Grace has become a negative *selfobject* that has fed his narcissistic desires, encouraged his darker side, and brought out the worst in him. The fusion of self and country – *L'état c'est moi!*, as Louis the XIV of France famously declared – has become a critical element of Mugabe's psychological makeup, taking on greater importance as he has aged. The now 88-year-old Mugabe has become so psychologically fused with his state that he truly believes that Zimbabwe could not survive without him at the helm and, by extension, that he cannot survive without Zimbabwe. This belief has strengthened over the past decade. It would be psychologically extremely difficult for Mugabe to leave his position as leader of Zimbabwe because to do so would be to give up his identity.

Accordingly, the Arab Spring that swept the Middle East in 2011, with its overthrow of long-standing dictators, was particularly threatening to Mugabe. In response to these events, Mugabe denounced what he called "revolts" against the "legitimate governments" of Egypt, Tunisia, and Libya: "Revolts are not democratic, and they must be opposed," he said.[19] This is a far cry from the liberating and transformational leadership of the first three decades of Mugabe's political career when Sally was by his side, but it is emblematic of Mugabe's intolerant and destructive leadership that has emerged since her death. Grace has clearly not provided him the much-needed restraint and realistic reasoning ability that Sally had. Had he stepped down when he, with his political partner Sally, had successfully brought his independent nation to power, Mugabe would have been recorded as a nation builder and achieved heroic status in his country's history. Instead, he will go down in history for his sorry, self-absorbed role in destroying the very nation he had created.

PARTNERS IN CRIME: LADY MACBETH ET AL.

In a memorable soliloquy in Act I, Scene 5 of *Macbeth*, Lady Macbeth reflects with concern on the weakness of her "dearest partner of greatness," which she fears will inhibit his pursuit of power:

Yet do I fear thy nature, it is too full o' the milk of human kindness to catch the nearest way ... thus thou must do if thou have it ... hie thee hither that I may pour my spirits in thine ear, and chastise with the valor of my tongue all that impedes thee from the golden round.

In this section, three wives are characterized who, liked Lady Macbeth, were even tougher than their husbands and were believed to have put the steel in their husband's spine: Mira Markovic, wife of Slobodan Milosevic, president of Yugoslavia; Elena Petrescu, the wife of Nicolae Ceausescu, president of Romania; and Simone Gbagbo, wife of President Laurent Gbagbo of the Ivory Coast.

SLOBODAN MILOSEVIC AND MIRJANA MARKOVIC

Slobodan Milosevic was the president of Serbia from 1989 to 1997 and the president of Yugoslavia from 1997 to 2000. He also led the Socialist Party of Serbia from its foundation in 1990. Quite the resume for any leader, yet Milosevic will be known more for his crimes against humanity, corruption, abuse of power, and embezzlement charges than for his leadership qualities.

Looking at the woman Milosevic chose to be his partner in life is key to understanding his political decisions. Born in wartime Serbia, in 1941, Milosevic was the son of a Montenegrin theologian and a Serbian communist school-teacher, both of whom committed suicide during his young adulthood. He grew up in Pozaravac, where he met his wife Mirjana Markovic, who later became a sociologist, columnist, university professor, and head of her political party, the Union of the Yugoslav Left. The two were inseparable from adolescence, when it is likely that she was the only consistent source of comfort for Milosevic, functioning as a *selfobject* to her husband. But he, too, functioned as a *selfobject* for Mira; indeed, they were partners in crime. They each provided the other with love and support, but also with consistency in the relationship.

Mirjana, who had her own tragic childhood, was all too ready to fill that role. Her mother, a partisan fighter, reportedly paused for a day in the forest to give birth to Mira and then resumed her wartime duties. According to Mirjana, her mother Vera was captured by the Nazis and tortured, later dying in a concentration camp. Less heroic accounts have been published, including that her mother was executed by the partisans for betraying her comrades to the Nazis under torture.

Not only did she not have a mother, but her father also refused to acknowledge her existence until the age of 15. All documents pertaining to her mother's death mysteriously vanished when Milosevic took office, and Mirjana took up her mother's name, Mira. Without the care of her mother and feeling rejected by her father, Mirjana developed a defense pattern of intellectualization and projected power to cover up her own feelings of worthlessness. Her attempts to erase the history of her mother's death and make her own story the "true" version of events indicates a certain level of shame and narcissistic wounding. Her taking on of her mother's name further suggests a certain level of enmeshment that is important to keep in mind when thinking about the man she chose as a partner in life.

When young Mira met Milosevic, he was a lonely boy who shunned company, sports, and the usual pursuits of small-town adolescents in favor of buttering up local party elites. He was looking for someone to idealize, someone he could admire for prestige, power, and intellect so that he could feel a connection to status. Mira, on the other hand, was what McWilliams[20] would describe as "merger hungry," someone who needed to control her *selfobject* (in this case Milosevic) in an enactment of the need for structure. Taking her mother's name and subsequently choosing a husband who was looking for someone to idealize seems to indicate that Mira was trying to create an almost corrective experience from her childhood. She wanted to become the heroine that she believed her mother to be and to have a partner act as a vessel in which she could have structure and control.

Mira harbored exhausting self-expectations of herself, once weeping because she only got four, not five, top grades in exams.[21] She immersed herself in Greek tragedy, her favorite story being that of Antigone, the young woman who seeks to avenge the memory of her beloved brother, a rebel against the tyrant Creon, which again points to her enmeshment with her mother's identity.

Once Milosevic found his way to power, he and Mira set out to establish their dream of an ethnically pure Greater Serbia, one cleansed of Croats and "mongrel" races such as Bosnia's Muslims and Kosovo's Albanians. However, Mira was the driving force in the relationship, and it was said that Milosevic "utters her thoughts as his own, unaware of where she ends and he begins."[22] Mira's diaries and interviews are notable for their surreal quality, where it is apparent that she serves the role not only as Milosevic's intimate confidante but political and social critic as well. Reportedly, she wrote the majority of Milosevic's most electrifying speeches that led to his rise to power, including the 1987 speech delivered in Kosovo that catapulted him into prominence as a heroic champion and leader of Serbian nationalism. Sent to Kosovo by his mentor Ivan Stambolic to quell ethnic unrest, Milosevic, defying Stambolic's instructions, inflamed the nationalist passions of the Kosovar Serbs. He spoke eloquently, in words believed to have been crafted by Mira, "this is your country" – of Serb land, homes, fields, gardens, and memories. To not fight for what belongs to Serbs, he told his enthralled listeners, would be to "disgrace your ancestors and disappoint your descendants." He evoked the spirit of Prince Lazar, enshrined in Serbian history for his heroic leadership in the 1389 battle of Kosovo Polje, who refused to yield to the overpowering might of the Ottoman invaders, vowing it was better to die in glory than to live in shame. In identifying Milosevic with the mythologized Prince Lazar, Mira's words played a crucial role in transforming her husband from an *apparatchik* to a heroic nationalist leader.

Her writings also indicate a unique vanity and self-absorption, which has led to her being reviled for her insincerity and being characterized as Serbia's Lady Macbeth. The Lady Macbeth analogy is an interesting one because she in many ways was considered tougher than her husband, the steel in his spine. Most observers agree that without Mira's guidance and sleight of hand, there would have been no Slobodan Milosevic as we came to know him.

Mira wrote books on politics, with titles like *The Answer* and *Between East and West*, as well as a column for the magazine *Duga*, where she states: a "New World Order" is plotting to crush the defiant Serbs in general and her family in particular. Despite her Marxist roots, she also harbored a penchant for New Age ideology, often consulting fortunetellers, collecting crystals, and wearing a moonstone to receive protection from the cosmic energy of the moon. She cannot live without mirrors, often spending hours combing her hair each day, and she had a plastic surgeon regularly flown in from Italy.[23]

NICOLAE AND ELENA CEAUSESCU: SPIRALING GRANDIOSITY

One Eastern European leader not in lock step with the Stalinist rulers was Nicolae Ceausescu of Romania, secretary general of the Romanian Communist Party from 1965 to 1989 and president of Romania from 1974 to 1989, until the 71-year-old dictator and his wife Elena were executed after the December 1989 revolution.

The radio announcement that cold winter day in 1989 was dramatic. The announcer declared: "The anti-Christ has been executed on Christmas Day!" The antichrist or the "Idi Amin of Communism" referred to Romanian President Nicolae Ceausescu, who ruled the country from 1965 to 1989. By his side in death, as throughout their lives together, was his wife Elena.

Ceausescu was born in 1918, in the small village of Scornicesti, Olt County, before he moved to the larger capital of Bucharest at the age of 11 to begin working in factories. He was the son of two peasants: his father, a descendant of a family of shepherds and his mother, the descendent of an officer in Tudor Vladimirescu's army. His father was rumored to be an alcoholic who physically abused both his wife and children. His mother was allegedly a very religious woman, and although Nicolae himself was an atheist, he ordered a church built in her honor after she passed away in their home village.

Ceausescu joined the then-illegal Communist Party of Romania in 1932, when he was 13 years old. His communist career was marked early by his arrest at age 14 in 1933 for street fighting during a strike, and again in 1934, for collecting signatures for a petition to protest the trial of railroad workers. His time in prison only served to confirm his budding identity as a communist revolutionary. He went underground after release from prison, only to be arrested again in 1936 at age 17 for antifascist activities. In particular, as a member of the Communist Youth Movement, he was a leader in the fight against the virulently anti-Semitic and anticommunist "Iron Guard," the paramilitary wing of the ultra-nationalistic Romanian fascist group the Legion of the Archangel Michael, funded by Nazi Germany.

In 1940, he was released from prison, all the more committed to his revolutionary path. Before he was again arrested for revolutionary activities, he met Elena Petrescu, his future wife. She, too, was a member of the Communist Youth Movement.

Elena was the daughter of an innkeeper in the town of Petresti, and she joined the Communist Party in 1937, at the age of 18. She met Nicolae two years later, when she was elected queen of the May Day parade and celebration. They married in 1946, and, sharing narcissistic dreams of glory, began their spiraling dance of grandiosity. She was to become his strong political partner.

Because he was arrested several times, Nicolae earned the description of "dangerous communist agitator" and "active distributor of communist and antifascist propaganda" on his police records. He was imprisoned in 1936 for two years at Doftana Prison for his antifascist activities; his years in and out of jail would prove useful for his political career. When he was transferred to Targu Kiu internment camp in 1943, he shared a cell with Gheorghe Gheorghiu-Dej and became his protégé. Gheorghiu-Dej would later become the communist leader of the country in 1948, making young Ceausescu his deputy minister of the Armed Forces. Ceausescu quickly rose through the ranks to occupy the second-highest position in the party hierarchy.[24]

Three days after the death of Gheorghiu-Dej, in March 1965, Ceausescu became first secretary of the Romanian Worker's Party, the name of which he immediately changed to the Romanian Communist Party, and he declared the country the Socialist Republic of Romania rather than a People's Republic. In 1967, he consolidated power by becoming president of the State Council.

Shortly after he became first secretary, Elena was held up as a model for Romanian women and was officially given the title "The Best Mother Romania Could Have."

In his first decade in office, Ceausescu established an open policy toward the West, in contrast to the other Warsaw Pact leaders, and, in the 1960s, he increasingly distanced Romania from Soviet influence and ended Romania's participation in the Warsaw Pact. Very popular with the Romanian people, Ceausescu had a special sense of himself, abetted by his wife, and where he wanted to lead his country. While the Soviet Union for the most part tolerated his not complying with directives from Moscow, he attained a reputation as an increasingly go-it-alone maverick, further magnifying his popularity, which in turn further confirmed his confidence in his own judgment. It was narcissism rewarded.

Indeed, Ceausescu created a personality cult reflecting his judgment about his stature. He gave himself the title "Conducator," which means "leader," and, modestly, "Geniui din Carpati" (Genius of the Carpathians). As a symbol of his imperial self-concept, he even had a king-like scepter made for himself.

Romania was the first communist country to recognize West Germany, the first Eastern European country to join the International Monetary Fund, the first Eastern Bloc country to receive a U.S. president (Richard Nixon), and, with Yugoslavia, under the leadership of his fellow maverick Marshal Josip Broz Tito, the two became the only Eastern European countries to enter into trade agreements with the European Economic Community.

Ceausescu's friendship with Tito lasted into the 1980s. Ceausescu was impressed by Tito's doctrine of "independent socialist development," which was in line with his own refusing to bend the knee to Moscow. By proclaiming itself a socialist republic, not a "people's republic," Romania under Ceausescu further emphasized that it was following a Marxist path but one not under the central control of Moscow.

But, as a presentiment of his later authoritarian bent, in 1966, the Ceausescu regime, in an attempt to boost Romania's population, issued a decree that made abortion illegal and provided benefits to mothers with at least five children, as well as declaring mothers with at least 10 children *heroine mothers* of Romania. Elena is believed to have been the author of these authoritarian policies.

Initially, Ceausescu was a popular figure both in Romania and in the West due to his independent foreign policy and his defiance of the Soviet Union. Ceausescu was briefly enamored of Czechoslovakia's Alexander Dubcek's doctrine of "socialism with a human face," but the increasingly unilateral nationalistic role pursued by Ceausescu was not consonant with the more liberal philosophy articulated by Dubcek. After the first liberal decade of leadership free of Soviet control, which made Ceausescu quite popular, he became increasingly imperious and controlling.

An apparent transformational turning point for Ceausescu was his 1971 visit to China, North Korea, and North Vietnam. He greatly admired the societal transformation these countries' hardline communist leaders had effected. The ideology of *juche* (self-reliance) promulgated by President Kim Il-sung of North Korea particularly impressed Ceausescu, and he had Kim's books about *juche* translated into Romanian and distributed throughout the country. Mao's powerful autocratic leadership was very impressive to Ceausescu, as was the magnitude of the changes in the Peoples' Republic Mao had brought about. On his return, Ceausescu delivered a speech patterned after Mao, which came to be known as the "July Theses." In this speech, he decried the liberalism of the 1960s and called for mass political action, for involving youth in large construction projects to be a part of their "patriotic work," and for greatly expanded political propaganda. Moreover, he established an index of banned books and authors.

However, despite his attempts and a more open relationship with the United States and Western Europe, things began to change. A program he initiated in the first years of his rule called "20 Years of Light" plunged the country into an economic darkness.[25] He and Elena, intoxicated by their power, squandered billions of dollars on grandiose public works that didn't work and left many of their people hungry and freezing.[26] His 20-year rule turned Romania into a land of legendary deprivation. He tore down acres of ancient houses and churches in the once elegant capital of Bucharest and made the area into a parade ground, and he pushed for a program to destroy half the nation's villages and move their inhabitants into new "agro-industrial" centers.[27]

His second decade of power was characterized by an increasingly erratic personality cult, nationalism, and deterioration in foreign relations with both the Western powers and the Soviet Union. The liberal leader who resisted the dictatorial control of Moscow was now becoming a dictator himself. He purged the leadership circles of those not loyal to him and, in 1974, became president of Romania, further consolidating his control. In all of these actions, his wife Elena was a strong partner, encouraging him in his pursuit of increasing authority and power. When the Ceausescus were received by Queen Elizabeth II at

Buckingham Palace in 1978, it seemed to be confirmation of their own royal status.

Forty of his relatives were in powerful jobs within his government. His brothers were army generals, deputy defense ministers, police generally, deputy interior ministers, diplomats, and editors for the party newspaper, among other positions. However, his wife, Elena, was the second most powerful figure in both the party and the state hierarchy.[28] As her husband climbed the political ladder, Elena rose as well. She was elected director of the Bucharest Central Institute of Chemical Research and chairman of National Council for Science and Technology, despite not having an academic background in the field. When her husband assumed the presidency, Elena played an increasingly active role in meetings with foreign leaders.

The First Lady of Romania was increasingly known as the power behind the throne. It was said that she saw herself as Nicolae's successor, no doubt due to the amount of power he gave her in dictating terms and social reforms in the country. It was speculated that she was "infinitely more hated than the President ... she is much crueler and her decisions are more dictatorial."[29] She was the object of a personality cult that rivaled that of her husband. Her birthday, like his, was a national holiday, said to be "a crucial date in Romanian history, by which the nation, glorifying its chosen ones, is glorifying itself."[30] Elena was also said to be the "perfect personification of the traditional values of the Romanian people" and to have a place reserved for her in "the golden gallery of the great personalities of national history."[31]

Elena's portrait was carried in street parades, and the media frequently referred to her as the "woman hero," the "party's torch," the "guiding spirit behind science and culture," and even "mother of the fatherland."[32]

Her rise was extraordinary, and she became part of the country's top decision-making body: the Permanent Bureau of the Political Executive Committee. She supervised the secret police as their first deputy premier, determined promotions in the party, and launched numerous social reform programs.[33]

Elena is believed to have been the force behind many oppressive government decisions. She launched a determined campaign against religion; more than 60 Orthodox churches were demolished since 1977 as part of her drive to renovate urban and religious centers with monumental government buildings. Elena also launched an aggressive drive to boost Romania's population by giving new mothers $125 dollars for each child after their first.[34] Families were also urged to follow her and her husband's example by having three children, and abortion was made illegal, with those performing the operation being swiftly incarcerated. To enforce the law, gynecological wards were watched by police representatives who needed to approve obstetric operations.[35]

As her husband moved in his political career, so did his partner Elena. Speeches she made were published in book form, and she showed herself more prominently in Ceausescu's meetings with foreign leaders. In fact, during a visit to Yugoslavia with her husband in December 1985, published photographs showed a rather placid looking Nicolae seated alongside his energetic wife.

When Ceausescu protested the Soviet invasion of Czechoslovakia in 1968, which crushed the Prague Spring, once so bright with promise, it endeared Ceausescu to the West, which, hoping to create a rift in the Eastern bloc, loaned Romania some $13 billion, which Ceausescu invested in economic development programs. The foreign debt became a painful burden to Romania, devastating its economy and leading Ceausescu to amend the constitution to bar Romania from incurring foreign debt, an extremely popular move.

But, in the 1980s, in order to pay down their crushing financial obligations, Emperor and Empress Ceausescu – for this increasingly was how they seemed and acted – ordered the export of much of Romania's agricultural and industrial production. This in turn created an internal nightmare, with the people suffering food shortages, food rationing, and rotating brown-outs because of the unavailability of heating oil, gas, and electricity. The privations were explained as a temporary necessity to correct the economy.

But as the people were asked to make this collective sacrifice and bear this burden, the former peasant and his wife continued to live in royal splendor, apparently oblivious to their people's misery. The most striking example of this discontinuity was the House of the Republic (Ceausescu's title) built to house both Houses of the Romanian Parliament, as well as to serve as the Ceausescus' residency, reportedly the world's largest and most expensive civilian administrative building, as well as the heaviest, built at an estimated cost of $10 billion.

Preparing the site for the massive building required razing much of central historic Bucharest, including 19 Orthodox Christian churches, 6 Jewish synagogues, 3 Protestant churches, and some 30,000 private residences. Measuring 890 by 790 feet, 282 feet high, and 302 feet underground, the building has 1,100 rooms, 2 underground garages, and is 12 stories high. Beyond its massive size, the lavishness of its furnishings was, by any standard, extraordinary. Designed in Neoclassical style by a team of 700 architects, the building was constructed almost entirely of Romanian materials. It contains an estimated 1 million cubic meters of Transylvanian marble; 3,500 tons of crystal, with 480 chandeliers, 1,409 ceiling lights, and mirrors manufactured on site; 700,000 tons of steel and bronze used for the monumental doors, windows, chandeliers, and capitals; 9,700,00 square feet of wood used for parquet floors, including walnut, oak, sweet cherry, elm, sycamore, and maple; and 2,200,000 square feet of woolen carpets, the largest of which were woven on site and adorned with embroidery and silver and gold ornamentation. That this lavish building was being constructed as the country was in a period of austerity and widespread deprivation was a remarkable, and not unnoticed, affront to the Romanian people.

In the run-up to the 14th Congress of the Romanian Communist Party in November 1989, in which Ceausescu was elected to another five-year term, the couple seemed oblivious to the dire straits of their country. Reminiscent of Potemkin village, large stocks of food would be shipped to a particular store that would then be shown on national television so that the Ceausescus could boast of its well-stocked shelves – this while the people elsewhere faced empty shelves and long lines.

During the last months of his time in power, Ceausescu made it clear that as long as he was in charge, Romania would not follow other East European countries along the paths toward democracy or capitalism. "Some socialist countries have adopted measures with a view to increasing the wealth of some people and increasing the number of poor, the focus is not socialist, and we cannot admit it in any way."[36] In the same speech, he said that capitalism was characterized by unemployment, homelessness, and growing illiteracy, as well as by increased crime and drug use. His disillusioned view of the rest of the world in comparison with his own country no doubt came from the influence of his wife.

The virus of democracy that was racing through Eastern Europe in the fall of 1989, precipitated by the fall of the Berlin Wall, spread to Romania. There was a series of violent actions in December 1989, beginning with a revolt in Timisoara, in which state security forces fired on unarmed demonstrators, wounding and killing many in a mass demonstration on December 17. The Ceausescus left for a state visit to Iran the next day, leaving instructions to subordinates to crush the uprising. On his return, Ceausescu delivered a televised speech blaming outside agitators. This was not merely scapegoating: until the violent end, the Ceausescus apparently had no idea how unpopular and reviled they were, how much resentment was building in Romania, instead believing that they were the objects of veneration.

A mass meeting to demonstrate popular support for Ceausescu was arranged for December 21 and shown on state television. Instead, chaos ensued, with an open unarmed revolt of the population of Bucharest calling for freedom. This was brutally suppressed by Romanian security forces firing on the unarmed protestors. Hundreds were arrested. By the next day, the revolution had spread to cities across Romania. It was reported that 64,000 Romanians were killed in Securitate attempts to quell the rebellion, which further inflamed the populace.

It was only then that Ceausescu, astonished by the magnitude of the out-pouring of rage, said to his wife, "They are going to kill us," a rather belated recognition of the murderous rage their self-adoration had caused. The desperate Ceausescu assumed control of the Army on December 22, but when he attempted to address a crowd in front of the Central Committee building, the frenzied crowd opened the doors, swept in, and the Ceausescus were barely able to escape with their lives by helicopter.

They fled from city to city and were finally arrested by police while watching the revolution on television and turned over to the Army. On December 25, a show trial was held. The two were tried in a military tribunal on charges of genocide, damage to the national economy, and abuse of power by executing military actions against the Romanian people. They were found guilty on all charges following a hastily organized two-hour court session and executed by firing squad within hours.

When the crowd swept into the Palace of Parliament, they were astounded to find the opulence in which the Ceausescus planned to live, and this confirmed their righteous rage. The Palace was at once a monument to the scope of the Ceausescus' grandiosity as well as to their lack of empathy for the impoverished Romanian people. To highlight the stark contrast between this extravagant luxury in which the Ceausescu's would have lived and the stark poverty and squalor of many of the surrounding neighborhoods, the new leaders of Romania called it "The House of Ceausescu."

The gap between the poverty of Romania and the manner in which Ceausescu and his wife Elena surrounded themselves with luxuries, seemingly oblivious to the suffering of their people, was demonstrated once again in the January 2012 sale by a leading Romanian auction house of luxury items from the Ceausescu era, which the auction house ArtMark called the country's "Golden Age." The offerings including a leopard skin, which fetched 2,750 Euros at auction; a bronze yak, the gift of Mao Zedong, which fetched 12,000 Euros; and two silver doves, a gift of the Shah of Iran.[37]

It was as if Nicolae and Elena – mutually intoxicated with their grandeur, consumed by their own splendor (most vividly exemplified by the "House of Ceausescu"), and oblivious to the poverty and growing resentment of the Romanian people – continued, to a nearly delusional extent, to see themselves as beloved Emperor and Empress until the end. Their names will undoubtedly be linked to one of the largest government-inflicted massacres since World War II.

LAURENT AND SIMONE GBAGBO OF THE IVORY COAST

Unlike "Grasping Grace" Mugabe who lacked political influence except insofar as her avarice stimulated her husband's corruption, Simone Gbagbo, wife of Laurent Gbagbo, former president of the Ivory Coast, acquired the sobriquet of "the Ivory Coast's Iron Lady." After refusing to step down after losing the October 2011 election, following a bloody nearly five-month-long struggle for the presidency, Laurent Gbagbo's rule ended ignominiously on April 11, 2011, when he and his wife Simone were dragged out of a bunker. They were initially taken to the headquarters of Laurent's rival, Alassane Ouatara, a man Simone derisively referred to as "the head bandit," who had won the presidency. Laurent Gbagbo is now awaiting trial at the International Criminal Court in The Hague. According to Richard Dowden of the Royal African Society, "Simone Gbagbo was a more militant version of him. As a politician he was a bit shifty, but she was really hardline and used language that Gbagbo would not have used." In addition to being the first lady, she had a formal political role. "She was always in the newspapers and a really rabid anti-foreigner."[38]

Simone Gbagbo, 62, became First Lady of the Ivory Coast, the world's largest cocoa producer, in October 2000, when the man she married a decade earlier became president.[39] When they married in 1989, they were "comrades-in-arms," co-founders of the Ivorian Popular Front. Often regarded as the power behind the president, she was known as "Simone" or "mother." Although respected for her political activism, she was feared for her alleged involvement in death squads that targeted her husband's rivals for power. She fought tenaciously for her husband in the 2002 uprising and attempted coup, condemning sedition. She was vociferous in condemning the 2003 peace accord that split the country into a Muslim north and a Christian south, and she rejected the unity government proposal that her husband accepted, demonstrating that she was more hardline than he. The outspoken Iron Lady called the rebel leader Ouatarra, her husband's opponent in the 2010 election that Laurent had managed to postpone for five years, the "scourge." "If you put a fighter at the head of your country, it is because you want violence."[40] A vociferous critic of neo-colonialism, she referred to French President Nicolas Sarkozy as "the devil." She was jailed several times for her public criticism of the first president of the newly Independent Ivory Coast, Felix Houphouet-Boigny. Given her outspoken extremity and the widely recognized fact that she was the power behind her husband's presidency, in many ways functioning as co-president, the only wonder is that she is not sharing a prison cell with her husband in The Hague.

THE SYCOPHANTIC CIRCLE OF ADVISERS SURROUNDING THE NARCISSISTIC LEADER

Just as the wife can serve as *selfobject* to her narcissistic husband, so, too, does the inner circle serve as *selfobjects* to their narcissistic leader, telling him what he wants to hear, not what he needs to hear. Because of the narcissistic leader's sensitivity to criticism, his advisers soon learn that to criticize their leader's ideas or plans is to risk losing their jobs or, in some cases, their lives. Thus, a leader can be psychologically in touch with reality but politically out of touch with reality if his only interest is in being praised and having his own ideas mirrored back to him from those around him. The inner circle, in this case, is all too eager to please their great leader from fear of the wrath they will receive if they proffer constructive criticism.

Saddam Hussein is an exemplar of this distorted relationship between the leader and his inner circle. In 1982, the war he initiated with Iran in 1980, undertaken at a perceived vulnerable moment for the new Khomeini regime, was going badly; missiles were raining down on Baghdad, and Saddam proffered a cease-fire to the Ayatollah. But Khomeini, who by now was obsessed with Saddam, rejected his proffer, indicating that there would be no peace between Iran and Iraq until Saddam was no longer president. Saddam presented this dilemma to his cabinet and asked their advice. Loyal to a fault, they unanimously declared that Saddam must stay on as president, that Saddam was Iraq, Iraq was Saddam. Showing his pleasure, he then asked them for their frank, candid, and creative suggestions. His Oxford-educated minister of health, Dr. Ibrahim, suggested that Saddam temporarily step down and then

assume the presidency again after peace was established. A very clever sugges-
tion. But Dr. Ibrahim soon found that his candor had caused narcissistic injury.
Saddam reportedly gravely thanked him for his candor and had him arrested on
the spot. The minister's wife begged Saddam for her husband's return. He
promised her he would return her husband to her the next day, which he did;
his dismembered body arrived in a black canvas body bag.[41] This powerfully
concentrated the attention of his remaining ministers who, to a man, were
agreed that Saddam must remain in power. The war went on for another
bloody six years. Saddam's advisers had learned that to criticize Saddam in
any way could have fatal consequences. This sensitivity to criticism deprived
Saddam of wise counsel, leaving him surrounded by a group who told him what
he wanted to hear rather than what he needed to hear.

They had learned this lesson well at the first meeting Saddam held with his
senior advisers, when he took full control over the leadership in 1979. One of his
first acts was to meet with his senior officials, some 200 in number, of which
there were 21 whose loyalty he questioned. This dramatic meeting was captured
on film. While Saddam watched, smiling, smoking luxuriantly on a Cuban cigar,
the 21 "traitors" were identified. After the "forced confession" by a "plotter"
whose family had been arrested, the "conspirators" in the audience were identified, seized by security officials, and dragged off. As the remaining officials,
relieved that they had not also been identified as plotters, shouted their approval
for Saddam, he praised them for their loyalty and rewarded them by indicating
that they would carry out their colleagues' executions the next morning.
A powerful lesson had been learned.

Basking in the adoration of the crowd, the narcissistic leader comes to see
himself as special, entitled to special privileges, not burdened by the constraints
that inhibit mere mortals. Similarly, the *selfobject* relationships just described
enhance the leader's special view of himself. In recent years, it seems like scarcely
a day goes by without the revelation of another politician whose private life
belies the public morals that he espouses. The next chapter presents a sweeping
overview of this cascade of "exceptional" leaders, followed by two in-depth
studies of exceptional exceptions.

Notes

1. David Mutori, "The President's Office ... the Albatross in Our Midst!" September 8, 2011,
   http://zimbabweinsights.blogspot.com/2011/09/presidentsoffice-albatross-in-our.html.
2. Robert Verkaik, "The Love That Made Robert Mugabe a Monster," *The Independent
   (UK)*, April 6, 2008, www.independent.co.uk/news/world/africa/exclusive-the-love-
   that-made-robert-mugabe-a-monster-804287.html.
3. Verkaik, "The Love that Made Robert Mugabe a Monster."
4. "Sally Mugabe," *The Times*, January 30, 1992.
5. Glen Frankel, "Zimbabwe Shifts Strategy to Tough Austerity Plan," *The Washington
   Post*, September 14, 1983, pp. A23–24; David Winder, "Zimbabwe's Mugabe: Labels
   Like Marxist Don't Stick to him," *Christian Science Monitor*, October 11, p. 183.

6. Colin Legum, "The New Statesman Profile – Robert Mugabe: Once Hailed as a New African Hero and a Non-racist, His Behaviour Is Now That of the Paranoid Pers," *New Statesman*, August 27, 2001, www.newstatesman.com/node/141018.

7. Grant H. Cornwell and Eve Walsh Stoddard, *Global Multiculturalism Comparative Perspectives on Ethnicity, Race, and Nation* (Lanham: Rowman & Littlefield Publishers, 2000).

8. Verkaik, "The Love That Made Robert Mugabe a Monster."

9. Tom Geoghegan, "Asma al-Assad and the Tricky Role of the Autocrat's Wife," *BBC News Magazine*, February 8, 2012, www.bbc.co.uk/news/magazine-16930738.

10. "Mugabe Marriage Splits Nation," *The Daily Telegraph*, August 16, 1996.

11. "Mugabe's Wife on EU Sanctions List," *BBC News*, July 22, 2002, news.bbc.co.uk/2/hi/africa/2143442.stm.

12. J. T. Young, "Zimbabwean Double Standard," *Washington Times*, January 14, 2003.

13. Peta Thornycroft, "Attack on Mugabe's Media Laws," *The Telegraph*, January 30, 2002, www.telegraph.co.uk/news/worldnews/africaandindianocean/zimbabwe/1383222/Attack-on-Mugabes-media-laws.html.

14. Peta Thornycroft, "'Hitler' Mugabe Launches Revenge Terror Attacks," *The Telegraph*, March 26, 2003, www.telegraph.co.uk/news/worldnews/africaandindianocean/zimbabwe/1425727/Hitler-Mugabe-launches-revenge-terror-attacks.html.

15. Antony Squazzin and Brian Latham, "Zimbabwe's Political Elite Profited from Gems, Wikileaks Says," *Bloomberg*, December 10, 2010, www.bloomberg.com/news/2010-12-10/zimbabwe-s-political-elite-profited-from-illicit-diamonds-wikileaks-says.html.

16. Angus Shaw, "Grace Mugabe Sues Paper over Wikileaks Diamond Story," *The Christian Science Monitor*, December 17, 2010, www.csmonitor.com/World/Latest-News-Wires/2010/1217/Grace-Mugabe-sues-paper-over-WikiLeaks-diamonds-story.

17. "Raids Target Zimbabwe Opposition," *CNN*, April 4, 2008, www.cnn.com/2008/WORLD/africa/04/03/zimbabwe.election/index.html?eref=rss_topstories.

18. "Mugabe Rival Quits Election Race," *BBC News*, June 22, 2008, http://news.bbc.co.uk/2/hi/africa/7467990.stm.

19. Celia Dugger, "Health in Doubt, Mugabe, 87, Vows to Stay in Power," *The New York Times*, May 20, 2011, www.nytimes.com/2011/05/21/world/africa/21zimbabwe.html?_r=1&pagewanted=all.

20. Nancy McWilliams, *Psychoanalytic Diagnosis: Understanding Personality Structure in the Clinical Process* (New York: Guilford Press, 1994).

21. Ed Vulliamy, "Mira Cracked," *The Guardian*, July 7, 2001, www.guardian.co.uk/world/2001/jul/08/warcrimes.balkans?INTCMP=SRCH.

22. Steven Erlanger, "Crisis in the Balkans: The Power Couple; The First Lady of Serbia Often Has the Last Word," *The New York Times*, May 31, 1999, www.nytimes.com/1999/05/31/world/crisis-balkans-power-couple-first-lady-serbia-often-has-last-word.html?pagewanted=all&src=pm.

23. Vulliamy, "Mira Cracked."

24. "Ceausescu, Nicolae," 2005, www.ceausescu.org.

25. John Greenwald et al., "Rumania Mother of the Fatherland," *TIME Magazine*, July 14, 1986, www.time.com/time/magazine/article/0,9171,961751,00.html.

26. "'The Genius of the Carpathians,'" *The New York Times*, March 15, 1989, www
.nytimes.com/1989/03/15/opinion/the-genius-of-the-carpathians.html?n=Top%2f
Reference%2fTimes%20Topics%2fPeople%2fC%2fCeausescu%2c%20Nicolae.

27. Craig Whitney, "Bucharest Journal; To Rumanians, It Just Feels Like the Third
World," *The New York Times*, July 20, 1989(a), www.nytimes.com/1989/07/20/
world/bucharest-journal-to-rumanians-it-just-feels-like-the-third-world.html?
pagewanted=all&src=pm.

28. Craig Whitney, "Upheaval in the East: The Old Order, the Collapse of Stalinism,"
The New York Times, December 24, 1989(b), www.nytimes.com/1989/12/24/world/
upheaval-in-the-east-the-old-order-the-collapse-of-stalinism.html?pagewanted=all&
src=pm.

29. Greenwald et al., "Rumania Mother of the Fatherland."

30. Minton Goldman, *Revolution and Change in Central and Eastern Europe: Political,
Economic, and Social Changes* (Armonk, N.Y.: M. E. Sharpe, 1997), 271.

31. Anneli Maier, "Enhanced Personality Cult for Elena Ceausescu," *Open Society
Archives*, January 8, 1986, www.osaarchivum.org/files/holdings/300/8/3/text/53-8-
63.shtml.

32. Greenwald et al., "Rumania Mother of the Fatherland."

33. Ibid.

34. Ibid.

35. Ibid.

36. Alan Riding, "Clamor in the East; Rumanian Leader Refuses Changes," *The New
York Times*, November 21, 1989, www.nytimes.com/1989/11/21/world/clamor-in-
the-east-rumanian-leader-refuses-changes.html.

37. "Romania Sells Ceausescu Luxuries from Communist Era," *BBC News*, January 27,
2012, www.bbc.co.uk/news/world-europe-16756590.

38. Geoghegan, "Asma al-Assad and the Tricky Role of the Autocrat's Wife."

39. "Simone Gbagbo: Profile of Ivory Coast's One-Time 'Iron Lady,'" *Newstime Africa*,
April 12, 2011, www.newstimeafrica.com/archives/19278.

40. "Simone Gbagbo."

41. Jerrold Post, *Leaders and Their Followers in a Dangerous World: The Psychology of
Political Behavior* (Ithaca: Cornell University Press, 2004).

8

Narcissism, Entitlement, Sex, and Power

Kristen Moody, Psy.D. and Jerrold M. Post, M.D.

In his brilliant and eerily prescient novel of social commentary, *Bonfire of the Vanities*, Thomas Wolfe[1] characterizes financial superstars as "masters of the universe." Wolfe pungently describes their sense of entitlement, their feeling that they have special rights and privileges allowing them to act as if they are above the laws and moral sensibilities that govern the rest of us. The world of the protagonist, an arrogant investment banker, unravels while he is on a clandestine liaison with his mistress: he accidentally takes a wrong exit off a New York City parkway and ends up in a dangerous Bronx neighborhood where his car accidently hits and seriously injures a black pedestrian, and, in their panicked state, he and his mistress leave the scene of the accident.

Just before the financial crisis that began in 2008, with its arcane financial instruments – derivatives, collateralized debt obligations, and credit default swaps – the "masters of the universe" were riding high. It was not until the economy began to falter that their intimate connection to the political system became clear. And just as these economic superstars showed a remarkable sense of entitlement, so, too, did their political confreres. This was not a failing confined to one side of the political aisle either: it was very much a bipartisan endeavor.

For a while, it seemed as if scarcely a week went by that another political figure, another champion of strong family values, did not hold a press conference – with his long-suffering wife standing dutifully by her husband's side as he acknowledged that he had been involved in a sordid affair.

It was as if the wives had all been inspired by country singer's Tammy Wynette's hit "Stand By Your Man":

> Sometimes it's hard to be a woman
> Giving all your love to just one man
> You'll have bad times
> And he'll have good times

> Doin' things that you don't understand
> But if you love him
> You'll forgive him
> Even though he's hard to understand
> And if you love him
> Oh, be proud of him
> Cause after all he's just a man
> Stand by your man
> And show the world you love him
> Keep giving all the love you can
> Stand by your man
>
> (Tammy Wynette and Billy Sherrill, 1968)

It was not always this way. There once was an informal social contract between the media and politicians that placed their personal lives out of bounds. Consider the now well-known womanizing of JFK or the long-standing affair of FDR with Lucy Mercer, which, when discovered by his wife Eleanor almost precipitated a divorce and materially changed their relationship. But these affairs did not become the subjects of media stories.

SENATOR GARY HART: CATCH ME IF YOU CAN!

In many ways, one must credit Senator Gary Hart with breaking this comfortable arrangement with the press. When Hart officially declared his candidacy for presidency in 1987, rumors began circulating that he was having an extramarital affair. In an interview, Hart taunted reporters saying: "Follow me around. I don't care. I'm serious. If anybody wants to put a tail on me, go ahead. They'll be very bored."[2] Little did Hart know that journalists at the *Miami Herald* had been investigating him for weeks and had observed him in the company of a young woman later identified as 29-year-old model Donna Rice. Photos began surfacing of Hart with Rice on a yacht ironically named "Monkey Business."[3] Furthermore, photographers snapped shots of Hart leaving his D.C. townhouse with Rice on several occasions. His taunts at the media prompted a firestorm of activity, and Hart could no longer avoid the incessant questioning about his extramarital activities. He finally came clean. His statement in the earlier *New York Times* interview can be looked at as almost a challenge to the media, reflecting a sense of narcissistic entitlement, as though he towered above ordinary people and thought he couldn't be caught.

Hart dropped out of the presidential race on May 8, 1987, lashing out at the media saying, "I said that I bend, but I don't break, and believe me, I'm not broken." After a few months, Hart returned to the race declaring, "let's let the people decide."[4] He competed in the New Hampshire primary and received only 4 percent of the votes, prompting him to again withdraw from the campaign on March 8, 1988, after Super Tuesday. Since then, Hart resumed his law practice, remained moderately active in politics, and became a blogger for the *Huffington Post* in 2005.

Although he has certainly not slinked away into a life of quiet misery, we have to wonder what would possess a man so close to capturing the presidential nomination in the late 1980s to invite such a thorough and relentless investigation of his personal life by the press, knowing what such a relentless investigation might uncover. Although this may have been only a sense of narcissistic entitlement, there is another possibility to consider.

Some individuals, on the very threshold of success, seemingly take actions designed to destroy their success. This has been termed "the success neurosis," defined by Freud as an "intrapsychically determined aberration in which one is wrecked by one's success, that success triggers recollections of one's 'criminal' intent from childhood, that of being the oedipal victory."[5] Holmes emphasizes particularly that when one has experienced in childhood and youth impoverished conditions related to race and social class, this can damage the self and be associated with psychological discomfort over succeeding, over traveling too far from one's roots.

Levy, Seelig, and Inderbitzin[6] go on to distinguish those who avoid success from those who may become wrecked by success:

Those wrecked by success are individuals who, on achieving some material success – for example, the consummation of a long sought after love affair or promotion to a professional position with greater responsibility, prestige, and compensation – rather than enjoying satisfaction in the success, experience some kind of psychological, professional, emotional, and personal wreckage . . . such individuals wreck their own success.[7]

These individuals experience guilt over their undeserved success and act to punish themselves before those around them discover, as surely they will, how undeserving they are and punish them.

MERELY NARCISSISTIC ENTITLEMENT OR NEEDING TO SELF-DESTRUCT ON THE VERGE OF SUCCESS?

The psychobiographic data bearing on Gary Hart, who served as a Democratic Senator for Colorado from 1975–1987, is interesting to consider in evaluating whether he suffered from a success neurosis.

Certainly, in terms of his social origins, Hart traveled a remarkable distance. Hart's roots can be traced to Ottawa, Kansas, where his father worked as a farm equipment salesman who never earned more than $5,000 a year; his mother, a railroad worker's daughter, was a dedicated housewife.[8] His parents were devout members of the revivalist Church of the Nazarene, which, among other stipulations, forbade smoking, drinking, dancing, and movies. Hart apparently abided by his religion and his mother's constraints.[9] A former philosophy professor of Hart's was quoted as saying that "His mother may have been an inhibiting, impositional factor on him and squelched his spontaneity as a person early on."[10] These, however, are just small windows into what his childhood was like, and relatively little is known about the specifics of Hart's upbringing.

When he worked as George McGovern's campaign manager in 1972, he joked that no one would really ever know him, testily labeling questions about his past as irrelevant.[11] Hart greatly admired John F. Kennedy and aspired to be like him. But the differences were palpable. In contrast to the poor, small-town boy Hart was, Kennedy had wealth, power, and fame.[12] Although Hart stated that his admiration for Kennedy was purely political, it seems that, with the fame and recognition he gained during the McGovern campaign, Hart discovered a more lavish lifestyle. While the press was kind in ignoring the womanizing and partying of his idol, they were much less forgiving of Hart, who openly challenged them to follow him around, a challenge the press accepted – with devastating results.

Hart's rapid rise to the brink of political power and the subsequent shattering of his success may be seen as a reflection of Hart's psychological discomfort with so far exceeding his father's limited success. Instead of feeling the satisfaction of his accomplishments and rise to the top, he wrecked it by inviting others to tear apart a life that, to understate it, he was not trying very hard to keep secret.

Recognizing the voracious public appetite for scandal, the media has adeptly evolved with increasing efficiency to expose politicians to the eagerly awaiting public and members of the opposing party. With escalating coverage and easy access to statements given to the press through archival searches online, more and more politicians seem to be afflicted with foot in mouth disease, as they are being caught with their pants down (literally). Over the past few decades, with the change in the media climate, especially the blogosphere, it is all too easy to seek out and publicly air the righteous politicians' dirty deeds.

With such an intense spotlight and such scrutiny focused on every move they make in life, one might ask how it is even possible for politicians in today's society to think they could hide their corrupt private lives. After all, some of the things they are doing in private are the very things they are so vocal in decrying in public. And when that veil of secrecy is pierced, it gives a devastating appearance of hypocrisy and deceit, which more often than not will be politically fatal. How can this be explained?

NARCISSISTIC ENTITLEMENT

Individuals with narcissistic personalities have feelings of grandiosity and a sense of entitlement, indulge in arrogant behavior, and engage in exploitative actions. This sense of entitlement and grandiosity produces a unique situation in which such individuals feel justified in passing judgment on others while they engage in the same acts they decry themselves. It is as if they are living in some rarefied strata, gifted with a unique and superior nature that lifts them above the moral expectations and laws that apply to mere mortals.

Some have described this as a "Swiss cheese conscience," one in which there are strict moral prohibitions, but where the individual can satisfy his own needs without moral prohibition, as if he pours through the holes and is able to justify his actions. These characteristics and behaviors are easily found in the countless news stories about politicians spouting strong family values in their speeches while secretly having affairs, righteously expressing campaign messages of disgust and outrage for other politicians caught-red handed while engaging in the exact same behaviors themselves, demanding the end of homosexuality while privately engaging in homosexual acts, and the like.

Some politicians are impelled to stray from the path of marital fidelity when their partners no longer meet the criteria of the perfect individual who they had in mind to complement themselves. These individuals may have unconsciously chosen partners who idealized them or had attributes that helped bolster their image as politicians. The qualities, career choices, or physical features of these women made idyllic matches for their husbands, who used their "other half" to create a fuller sense of self, the narcissistic *selfobject* relationship referred to earlier. When their sense of self was threatened through their partner's illness, age, or a lessening of the mirroring they were so accustomed to receiving, the narcissist's underlying vulnerability and sense of worthlessness were triggered. Instead of accommodating to the inevitable vicissitudes of the lifecycle in oneself and one's partner, such individuals may seek rejuvenation through another partner, one who possesses the capacity to mirror them in ways that their famished ego demands. In doing so, these politicians are repeating the cycle of searching for that perfect other to complete their image or to make them feel worthy or important. And insofar as their relationship with the now flawed partner only depended on the partner's ability to complement them, to mirror them – the narcissist has no genuine ability to empathize with his partner as having needs and feelings of her own – such acts of betrayal and casting off may occur with bewildering swiftness.

Behaviors such as these can quickly land an individual in an uncomfortable position. For some politicians, it means the end of their careers, their marriages, and the prestige and trust they built within their communities.

DUELING IDENTITIES: POLITICAL AGENDAS VERSUS PERSONAL LIFE

Eliot Spitzer, governor of New York, was a man grooming himself for the presidency. Son of a real estate tycoon, Harvard Law educated, a former attorney general, beloved by the citizens, in an apparently solid marriage, and the father of three daughters, Spitzer seemed to be on the path to the presidency of the United States when he was found to have been involved with prostitution rings since his days as attorney general. What would cause a successful politician with sights on the presidency to engage in such reckless behavior?

Spitzer admitted to having relationships with various call girls through services provided by the Emperor's Club VIP and repeatedly with one woman, Ashley Dupre. The same man who had been touted as the "Sheriff of Wall Street" for his reining in of corporate excess and greed and his espousal of ethics and values in the corporate world was unable to exercise restraint in his private life. Spitzer's involvement with prostitution rings began during his term as attorney general and continued as governor. During his resignation speech as governor, Spitzer said that "Over the course of my public life, I have insisted – I believe correctly – that people regardless of their position or power take responsibility for their conduct. I can and will ask no less of myself. For this reason, I am resigning from the office of governor."[13]

In 2009, Spitzer went on to deliver a speech at Harvard's ethics center regarding institutional corruption. A madam who allegedly was an escort to Spitzer for five years said of the speech: "I am greatly intrigued as to what Mr. Spitzer could contribute to an ethical discussion when as Chief Executive Law Enforcement Officer of NY he broke numerous laws for which he has yet to be punished." In a letter posted to her website, the madam, Kristin Davis, wrote "As Attorney General he went around arresting and making examples out of the same escort agencies he was frequenting."[14] During the speech, Spitzer did not make reference to his personal scandal, but did state in an article in *Newsweek*: "One of the hardest things to accept is that we are replaceable ... Intellectually, I think we all know it. But it's harder to accept it emotionally. And, to a certain extent, you feel like saying, 'But wait a minute, how can things be continued without me?'"[15] This statement is reflective of Spitzer's exceptional conscience, particularly as he was prosecuting in public the very escort agencies whose services he was privately retaining.

RIGHTEOUSLY CONDEMNING PRESIDENT CLINTON'S AFFAIR WHILE CARRYING ON THEIR OWN

The 115th governor of South Carolina, Mark Sanford, is an example of a man whose personal life contradicted his politics.[a] Sanford voted to impeach President Clinton for his extramarital affair, stating "I think what he did in this matter was reprehensible ... I feel very comfortable with my vote." Furthermore, he declared, "This is very damaging stuff. I think it would be better for the country and for him personally to resign." Toward the end of the

---

[a] The reader will observe that there are several examples of politicians who righteously criticized former president Bill Clinton's extramarital activities, especially the notorious Monica Lewinsky affair that led to calls for his impeachment, while carrying on sordid affairs of their own. But Bill Clinton's extramarital activities are not subjected to searching analysis in this chapter. To do so would overwhelm the rest of the chapter, and this topic has been treated exhaustively elsewhere; as, for example, in Renshon (1996).

Clinton impeachment proceedings, Sanford insisted that Clinton could not operate with any effectiveness because he'd been untruthful:

The issue of lying is probably the biggest harm, if you will, to the system of democratic government, representative government, because it undermines trust. And if you undermine trust in our system, you undermine everything.[16]

This was an interesting moral standard being conveyed, considering that from June 18 to June 24, 2009, the whereabouts of Governor Sanford were unknown to the public, including his wife and four sons. After lying to his staff about a hiking trip in the Appalachians and leaving his calls unanswered for six days, there was finally an answer: a reporter intercepted him arriving at an airport in a neighboring state after flying back from Argentina, where he admitted having been unfaithful to his wife.[17] In interviews over the next couple of days, Sanford stated that he had "crossed the lines" with a handful of other women during 20 years of marriage to his wife, but he had "met his soul mate."[18] She was later identified as former Argentine TV reporter María Belén Chapur.

On top of engaging in the very acts for which he had earlier condemned Clinton, a reporter using the Freedom of Information Act found that public funds had been used to pay for Sanford's trip to Argentina – this after a statement he had made in the previous year that "No public money was ever used in connection to advance my admitted unfaithfulness."[19] Sanford's wife has since divorced him, and he is engaged to his "soul mate."

In amazing contrast to his criticism of President Clinton, who he said was unfit for service because of his lying, Sanford sought to enter public service, running as a Republican for the House of Representatives and, in what must be considered a remarkable political comeback, won convincingly in the April 2013 Republican primary for the solidly Republican 1st District. This prompted a Democratic blogger to comment "you can be a puppy-kicking, baby-eating rapist; as long as you have that 'R' next to your name, you'll get elected in the South" (May 13, ChronoT). He has been remarkably candid in acknowledging his adultery but insists that he wishes to be judged by his record in public service, thus applying a strikingly different standard to himself than to President Clinton. Recently, Sanford spoke of how well his former wife had managed his earlier campaign, and he offered her a similar role, magnanimously indicating that this time she would be paid. Not surprisingly, she refused this generous offer.

Sanford was not the only person critical of President Clinton's extramarital affair who later went on to have an affair of his own. Gary Condit, former California House of Representatives member from 1989 to 2002, gained significant national attention when his affair with Bureau of Prisons intern Chandra Levy became public in May 2001 after she was reported missing. Condit, who previously based his election on "family values" and his background as the son of a Baptist preacher from Oklahoma, had his own dark secret that emerged when phone records and Internet searches on Ms. Levy's computer indicated that the two shared more than just a close friendship, as Condit had claimed.

Condit was quiet on the issue, taking a hypocritical stance after stating during the Clinton trial "The public airing of every detail is needed. Only when we strip away the cloak of secrecy and lay the facts on the table can we begin to resolve this matter."[20] This video of Condit publicly demanding Clinton to "come clean" on his relationship with a young woman was aired almost daily during the investigation of the extent of Condit's involvement with Levy.

David Vitter, the junior Republican U.S. Senator from Louisiana, made headlines when identified as a client of a prostitution service. Vitter's number appeared at least five times between 1999 and 2001 on billing records belonging to a Ms. Deborah Jeane Palfrey, aka the "D.C. Madam" who has been charged with racketeering for allegedly running a prostitution ring in the nation's capital. In a press conference in Louisiana, with his wife, Wendy, by his side, Vitter admitted that he had committed a "very serious sin."[21] A day after he acknowledged his connection in D.C., he was linked to a former madam in New Orleans, Jeanette Maier, who stated Vitter had once been her client at her Canal Street brothel in the late 1990s.[22]

Like Sanford, Vitter had railed against the sexual indiscretion of former President Bill Clinton and others. Vitter had replaced Representative Bob Livingston who abruptly resigned after disclosure of his own numerous affairs in 1998. Vitter stated "I think Livingston's stepping down makes a very powerful argument that Clinton should resign as well and move beyond this mess."[23] His opponent in 2010, Charlie Melancon, who stated that "David, you never had family values," brought up the hypocrisy in his claims. "You've sinned, you've lied, you've broken the law, and you've embarrassed the state – yet you've not hinted once that you think you should step down."[24] Yet, despite the noted and now highly public affairs, Vitter won reelection and continues to serve.

John Ensign, a Republican Nevada senator known for his conservative ideology and family values, is another politician who made headlines in recent years. Ensign admitted in 2009 to having an affair with a female staffer on his campaign, which only came to light after the woman's husband (who was also his best friend) wrote to *Fox News* anchor Megyn Kelly requesting that she investigate the senator's behavior.[25] Ensign had previously attacked President Clinton for his affair with Monica Lewinsky, stating that the president's conduct was "an embarrassing moment for the country. I think we have to feel very sad for the American people and Hillary and Chelsea." Weeks later, Ensign would call on Clinton to resign. "I came to that conclusion recently, and frankly it's because of what he put his whole Cabinet through and what he has put the country through. He has no credibility left,"[26] further stating, "I think we are dealing with a very serious problem here. With what we know and what we already knew, to me the honorable thing to do would be to resign."[27]

At the time, Ensign was in a tight Senate race with incumbent Harry Reid, an election he would ultimately end up losing. He tried to exploit the moral trip-ups in Clinton's personal life to benefit himself and the GOP, stating that "It could have a dramatic effect on Democrats like President Nixon's resignation after the

Watergate scandal had on Republicans in 1974."[28] Moreover, he actively made it an issue in his campaign against Reid. At one point during the campaign, Ensign accused his opponent of having a double standard when it came to politicians and sexual dalliances. Reid, he argued, had been much tougher on former Senator Robert Packwood – who resigned from the Senate under allegations of sexual harassment – than he was on Clinton.[29]

Ensign, however, initially continued to run for election in 2012, not applying the standards to himself that he had applied to Clinton. But ultimately, as a result of his affairs, Ensign did not seek reelection in the state for 2012. "There are consequences to sin," Ensign said in a conference. He did not want to put his family through an "exceptionally ugly" campaign.[30] However, in May 2011, Justice Department officials who had investigated Senator Ensign revealed that he not only had broken the law with his secret payoffs, lobbying, and hush money following his disastrous affair, but that he also could have been expelled from the Senate had he not made the decision in April to quit first.

REPLACING THE AILING SELFOBJECT

John Edwards, the 2004 Democratic nominee for vice president and former junior senator from North Carolina, became the subject of leading news when rumors began in 2007 that he had an extramarital affair with his one-time videographer, Reile Hunter. This affair occurred during a time when his wife, Elizabeth Edwards, was diagnosed with breast cancer. Although he adamantly denied both the affair and paternity of Hunter's baby girl for a year, he finally made a statement in an August 8, 2008, interview on *ABC News* that he indeed did have an affair with Hunter. Before this, Edwards was vocal on the importance of strong family values:

> Our nation was built on the values of hard work, equal opportunity, thrift and strong families. Americans believe in the importance of community, responsibility and most of all, family. We need to strengthen this institution that –for most of us – is the central pillar of our lives and the foundation of our own and our children's success. The first financial cushion we need is a stable family, and the first lessons we learn about responsibility are learned in our homes.[31]

He further stated that "Children who grow up without fathers are much more likely to be poor and at greater risk for a host of problems into adulthood,"[32] an interesting quote considering that he was already engaged in an extramarital affair and would wait for two years after the birth of his daughter Quinn before accepting responsibility for his actions and his role as her father. Despite her own embarrassment and pain, heeding the words of Tammy Wynette, Elizabeth Edwards stood stoically by her man during his admission to the affair. While she would later file for divorce, in the moment, she worked hard to project the image of the "stable family" that her cheating husband had previously publicly promoted. In the trial for misuse of campaign funds to cover up the affair, the magnitude and complexity of the double life Edwards was leading became all too clear, leading many to ask, "How could he think he could get away with this?" This would seem to represent another example of the "exceptional conscience" of the narcissist. Ultimately, Elizabeth's fatal breast cancer deprived Edwards of her valuable role as stabilizing *selfobject*.

Newt Gingrich, who served as the 58th Speaker of the House of Representatives from 1995 to 1999, was married to Jackie Battley, his high school geometry teacher. Battley bore two daughters, put Gingrich through graduate school, and stood by him over the course of two losing Congressional campaigns. When Battley was in the hospital recovering from uterine cancer, Gingrich had affairs and insisted on working out his divorce while she was lying in her sick bed.

A few months later, Gingrich married Marianne Ginther, a woman he had previously met at a political fundraiser. His relationship with her extended back to 1993, while he was speaking of reforming the corrupt welfare state and promoting society's moral regeneration.

In October 1998, Marianne was diagnosed with a serious neurological condition, multiple sclerosis.[33] Eight months later, Gingrich called his wife at her mother's home. After wishing his 84-year-old mother-in-law a happy birthday, he told Marianne he wanted a divorce. It has later emerged that Gingrich indicated to his ailing wife that he was having an affair with an aide in his office, Callista Bisek, and had asked her to agree to this affair, to agree to an open marriage. When she declined, divorce proceedings were carried out. For both ailing wives, their serious illnesses deprived Gingrich of their stabilizing role as *selfobjects*.

An exemplar of hypocrisy at the highest level, Gingrich was the one of the biggest advocates for the impeachment of Bill Clinton when news of the president's extramarital affair with Monica Lewinsky broke, piously speaking of the importance of the president as role model.

It is worth noting that Robert Livingston, who had been chosen to succeed Gingrich as Speaker of the House, decided to leave Congress because of revelations of his own adulterous affair, yet Gingrich remained silent with reference to his own infidelity.

Gingrich invoked comparison between Clinton's actions in office and the forces that led to the decline of the Roman Republic, stating

> They tell the story about how the Roman Republic, which had been founded under the rule of law, was corrupted by foreign money, by personal ambition, by politics so vicious that people were killed. The fabric of the republic collapsed ... the Democrats ought to be ashamed of their actions and ought to be helping us get at the truth rather than finding some flimsy excuse to avoid voting for impeachment.[34]

Gingrich continued to insist that Americans had the right to know the truth about the Lewinsky matter and that the president was not above the law:

> This is not about politics. I don't know and I don't care how this strategy polls. This has nothing to do with vendettas or witch hunts or partisan advantage. This is very simply

about the rule of law, and the survival of the American system of justice. This is what the Constitution demands.[35]

The intensity of his vehement attacks on Clinton led many to believe he over-stepped his role as Speaker of the House, eventually leading him to step down in 1999.

As a candidate for the Republic presidential nomination in 2012, it's no surprise that Gingrich's own affairs became more publicized and played out in the media. Gingrich responded to this in a remarkably creative fashion by saying,

There's no question at times of my life, partially driven by how passionately I felt about this country, that I worked far too hard and things happened in my life that were not appropriate. And what I can tell you is that when I did things that were wrong, I wasn't trapped in situation ethics. I was doing things that were wrong, and yet I was doing it. I found that I felt compelled to seek God's forgiveness.[36]

Furthermore, Gingrich denied the hypocrisy of his involvement as a leader in pushing for the impeachment of former President Clinton, saying that he was focusing on the law, not on Clinton's private life.

It's not about personal behavior . . . it's not about what he did in the Oval Office. You can condemn that. You can say it's totally inappropriate, but it was about a much deeper and more profound thing, which is: Does the president of the United States have to obey the law?[37]

When asked if he was in a position to be throwing stones, considering his own adultery, Gingrich responded "No. I thought to myself if I cannot do what I have to do as a public leader, I would have resigned."

Perhaps Al Kamen of *The Washington Post* put it best in his wry commentary:

His [Gingrich's] passion for America, not another woman, eventually led him on a path that was not appropriate. It's not easy to wrap yourself in the flag while you're naked and it's not particularly comfortable. But it's certainly a lot more creative than the usual lame old excuses.[38]

Comedy aside, it certainly begs the question of how someone can cheat on his spouse and leave her when she is ill but still attack a man for his own affairs and then go on to claim that he was not a hypocrite; that he had, in fact, engaged in his behaviors, in part, because of love for his country.

A review of Gingrich's past may prove useful in thinking about how he came to be the man he is today. In a 1995 interview with *Vanity Fair's* Gail Sheehy, Gingrich stated "I think you can write a psychological profile of me that says I found a way to immerse my insecurities in a cause large enough to justify whatever I wanted to do." He further stated, "I'm a mythical person . . . I had a period of thinking that I would have been called 'Newt the McPherson' [McPherson is his biological father's name] as in Robert the Bruce . . . . [he] is the guy who would not, could not, avoid fighting . . . He carried the burden of being Scotland."[39] Like Bruce, Gingrich feels he must carry the burden of his nation, which seems as true today as it did in 1995.

Gingrich's biological father was described as a "very angry" person, one who frightened his wife Kit so much that she divorced him and married Bob Gingrich, Newt's stepfather. Gingrich was reportedly upset about having his biological father's name taken from him when he was officially adopted by Gingrich Senior, "I was furious because I figured out that my real father had agreed to allow me to be adopted."[40]

Although Gingrich's biological father had a famed temper, it appears that his new stepfather had one as well. Bob Gingrich was a colonel in U.S. Army and was described as a "typical military father," reportedly responding to his son by withholding endearing statements of love or affection by stating "If I tell you once, that's all that's necessary. If it ever changes, I'll let you know."[41]

You know the John Wayne movie *Hondo*, where I think it's a six year old boy who can't swim well? Wayne picks him up, throws him in the lake and watches him thrashing around? The mother comes over crying. And Wayne says, "He had to learn." In my childhood, that made sense.[42]

Gingrich reportedly endured his stepfather's disapproval and criticism stating "I don't think I ever impressed him ... He and I fought from the time he adopted me until I was 19. It wasn't tough. It was just a fact." His mother agreed, stating "Bob was a tyrant, no question about it."[43] Not only did Gingrich endure an authoritarian stepfather and a rejecting biological father, but he also had a mother who was described as having a "manic-depressive" illness for which she took medications. His life was unpredictable, and he seemed unable to measure up in anyone's eyes.

The grandiosity of Gingrich's thoughts and actions fit well with his description of how he views himself as "a psychodrama living out a fantasy"[44] and that he found an escape in the movies. Gingrich himself points to movies featuring John Wayne or other epic heroes as being where he discovered that "you can draw inspiration from heroes ... you can create a story for yourself to star in."[45] It was easier for him to battle against his inner feelings by creating roles for himself as a leader, perhaps even choosing a career in politics because his stepfather disapproved.

He continued to reach for ever-higher positions; in this case, the Office of the presidency. Consider the following stark example of dreams of glory personified:

It's not altruism! It's not altruism! I have an enormous personal ambition. I want to shift the entire planet. And I'm doing it ... Oh, this is just the beginning of a 20- or 30-year movement. I'll get credit for it ... As a historian, I understand how histories are written. My enemies will write histories that dismiss me and prove I was unimportant. My friends will write histories that glorify me and prove I was more important than I was. And two generations or three from now, some serious, sober historian will write a history that sort of implies I was whoever I was.[46]

Although John McCain's first wife, Carol, did not have cancer, she was in a terrible car accident while McCain was a prisoner of war in a North Vietnamese prison. Doctors had to cut away at her leg bones, making her both shorter and heavier than the swimsuit model she had once been. She was no longer the ideal *selfobject* McCain needed. Upon his return, McCain had an affair with Cindy Lou Hensley, his current wife, and left Carol.

GENERAL DAVID PETRAEUS: RANK HATH ITS PRIVILEGES

From a decorated cadet at West Point to director of the Central Intelligence Agency, David Petraeus certainly climbed the ladder of success quickly and efficiently. He remains one of the most well-known generals from the wars in Iraq and Afghanistan, having commanded the 101st Airborne Division at the beginning of Operation Iraq Freedom, the Multinational Security Transition Command in Iraq, U.S. Central Command in Florida, and NATO's International Security Assistance Force in Afghanistan. In fact, Petraeus was so well regarded by his peers and in the media that the chairman of the Joint Chiefs of Staff Administration, Mike Mullen, compared him to the likes of Ulysses S. Grant, John J. Pershing, George Marshall, and Dwight D. Eisenhower.[47] And, like Eisenhower, his name was being bruited about as a potential presidential candidate.

His resume alone would indicate that Petraeus would go down in history as the type of general that every young cadet who entered the halls of West Point would strive to emulate. That is, until he was knocked from his pedestal of stardom by a scandal that rocked the media world in late 2012. The timeline of the story involved a number of different components and key figures and ultimately resulted in a public admission of an extramarital affair with his biographer, Paula Broadwell. The biography, in a marvelous double entendre, is entitled *All In.*

General David Petraeus grew up in Cornwall, New York, a mere seven miles down the road from West Point. His Dutch father, Sixtus, was the captain of a U.S. Merchant Marine ship that sailed in hostile waters during World War II. His mother, Marion, was a Brooklyn-born native who worked as a devoted librarian in town.[48]

As a boy, Petraeus apparently was a nonimposing figure who was physically immature for his age.[49] In fact, his childhood nickname, "Peaches," certainly encapsulated the image of a small-framed, innocent boy who was unable to grow facial hair.[50] Stories of Petraeus as a child begin to build a picture of a successful, diligent, hard-working individual. In fact, an early childhood friend said that she and the young David played house together: she as the stay-at-home mother, David as the father who went to work as a U.S. senator.[51]

Growing up down the road from West Point certainly had an influence on Petraeus's life. The town was home to many West Point graduates. His soccer coach was a captain at West Point, his math teacher had taught at the academy, and Petraeus delivered a daily newspaper to the director of admissions for the college, who conveniently lived just around the corner. Petraeus said that "Growing up with it [West Point] next door, and with so many graduates, I think you just sort of develop a degree of respect for them, for what the academy stands for, and all the rest of that."

David Petraeus quickly rose to the top 5 percent of his West Point class based on performance in leadership, athletics, and academics. These three areas are ranked by the peers of the cadets at West Point, and Petraeus would go on to graduate as a "Starman" (a distinguished cadet) in 1974. He married Holly Knowlton, the daughter of West Point Superintendent Lt. General William Knowlton, in 1974, an interesting choice for this ambitious young man.

Petraeus has a long and involved history in the U.S. Army. His first combat command included leading the 101st Airborne Division during the 2003 invasion of Iraq and overseeing post-combat operations in northern Iraq. After a brief return to the United States, he was soon back in the region, recruiting, training, and developing the Iraqi military. Drawing on his Ph.D. thesis in international affairs at Princeton (in 1987), he led the effort to revise counterinsurgency doctrine and to redraft the Army/Marine Corps Counterinsurgency Field Manual, and he helped overhaul numerous aspects of the Army's preparation of leaders and units for deployment. He commanded the "surge" in Iraq in 2007, when the country was on the brink of civil war.[52]

Petraeus had developed a reputation as an intensely competitive and talented officer, a man who exhibited an almost insatiable need for praise and recognition. He could be a generous mentor to junior officers, kind in his words and praise, but he often alienated his peers with his determination to win every prize.[53] His need to be beloved and admired by others, by a show of numerous medals and awards, highlights a man invested in making sure he remained untouchable by his peers.

In June 2010, President Barack Obama nominated Petraeus to succeed General Stanley McChrystal as commanding general of the International Security Assistance Force. Less than a year later, when CIA Director Leon Panetta left his post to become Secretary of Defense, President Obama nominated Petraeus to take his place. He was unanimously confirmed as the next director of the CIA by the U.S. Senate in a 94–0 vote,[54] and shortly thereafter he retired from the military.

In 2006, at Harvard's Kennedy School of Government, Petraeus met a young, vibrant mother of two, Paula Broadwell, who was also a West Point graduate.[55] Petraeus would later state that he admired Broadwell's "combination of intellect and physical prowess,"[56] referring to her ability as a runner. Broadwell expressed interest in writing about military leadership styles, and Petraeus offered to help her in any way he could. After several email exchanges, Petraeus invited Broadwell to discuss her project during a run on the Potomac River. Soon after, Broadwell became the personal biographer to Petraeus. Although well-spoken, ambitious, and intelligent, those surrounding General

Petraeus questioned how someone with minimal writing experience and education was able to obtain such high-profile access to Petraeus. The answer would soon become evident in the months following the release of the biography. On November 9, 2012, President Obama accepted David Petraeus' resignation from the CIA after his affair with Broadwell became public knowledge.[57]

The individuals who lead the nation's military services and those who oversee troops around the world enjoy a lavish lifestyle. They benefit from executive jets, beautiful homes, personal drivers, security guards, aides to carry their bags and press their uniforms, gourmet chefs, and people to track their schedules. Robert Gates may have pinpointed it best by stating "There is something about a sense of entitlement and of having great power that skews people judgment."[58] A retired three-star general who commanded U.S. troops in Afghanistan stated that the life of a commander in the Army has the potential to "become corrosive over time upon how they live their life. You can become completely disconnected from the way people live in the regular world – and even from the modest lifestyle of others in the military. When that happens, it's not necessarily healthy either for the military or the country."[59] This continued lifestyle of stardom and admiration may well have led Petraeus to believe that he was an untouchable celebrity.

He assuredly was a celebrity. No general in recent memory has been more revered than Petraeus. He managed to cultivate his fame with an understanding that the narrative of modern warfare is shaped not simply by battlefield exploits; he invited authors to accompany him to meetings, granted frequent interviews to newspapers and graduate students, fostered close relationships with Washington think tanks, and made a point to reach out to politicians on both sides of the aisle. When Present George W. Bush needed a savior for the war in Iraq, he turned to Petraeus. Petraeus was literally given the stage and made the front-man for the troop surge. In the first six months of 2007, Bush mentioned Petraeus' name *150 times* in speeches.[60] What better exposure could a narcissist ask for but for the leader of the free world to hold him up as the shining example for patriotism and leadership overseas?

Petraeus quickly became an A-list guest at Washington parties, where he maintained a position of authority and demanded to be noticed. There are stories of him and his wife, herself a role model of the senior military wife, attending a party hosted by socialite Jill Kelly by means of a 28-motorcycle police escort.[61] In 2009, Petraeus actually flew back to the United States from combat in order to flip the coin at the Superbowl.[62] Thomas Rick said "Being a 4 star commander in a combat theater is like being a combination of Bill Gates and Jay-Z with enormous firepower added."[63] Petraeus had an uncanny ability to occupy center stage in celebrity status.

There seem to be several factors that exacerbated Petraeus's narcissism. His obvious leadership style and charisma were noticed, and applauded, both by high-ranking members of the government and by appreciative followers.

His allowing journalists and media to trail him during the war gave rise to his stardom and fame through frequent articles and increased airtime. These events helped Petraeus flaunt his personality to a receptive audience in new and bolder ways.

One official who worked with Petraeus in Iraq and Afghanistan reported that "over the years I knew him, he became increasingly fixated on his image."[64] A former CIA agent who met Petraeus posted on his blog that he was left with one impression: "not so much about him [Petraeus], but about his already-well-commented-on entourage of 'Petraeus guys.' He had a reputation as a fast-moving reformer, but it was an outsized group of admirers, I thought, who showed not respect for him, but devotion – even awe."[65]

ACQUIRED SITUATIONAL NARCISSISM IN THE MILITARY

Cornell Medical School psychiatrist Robert B. Millman coined the term "acquired situational narcissism" to describe celebrities, such as movie stars and politicians, whose narcissism is magnified by believing their own press. "When a billionaire or a celebrity walks into a room, everyone looks at him. He's a prince. He has the power to change your life and everyone gets so used to everyone looking at him that he stops looking back at them."[66] This is not to say that, for Petraeus, the celebrity status caused his narcissism. Rather, his intense ambition and quest for honors demonstrated a healthy narcissism early on and contributed to his success. His star status as military hero magnified his narcissism, giving him the feeling of invulnerability.

As important as the role of CIA director is, it was not easy for Petraeus to give up his role as military celebrity for a life in the shadows. On one occasion, he showed up to speak at a dinner in Washington wearing a row of military medals on the lapel of his suit jacket soon after taking office at the CIA, suggesting an individual who still wished to be tied to the military and to the fame that accompanied it.

His naïveté in the manner in which he continued his affair with Broadwell was particularly remarkable, given that he headed an agency noted for its sophisticated counterintelligence. The revelation of his affair shattered what had been a legendary life and heroic reputation. Despite his remarkable military accomplishments, he will always be remembered as the naïve general who acted as if he was untouchable and ruined his impeccable reputation through his involvement in this tawdry affair.

What is going on here? How, in this age of opposition research and vigorous investigative journalism, when the political stage is littered with the bodies of politicians who piously preached family values while carrying on sordid affairs, do these political figures continue on their ultimately destructive paths? It is as if they believe they are enveloped in an invisible cloak of invulnerability that protects them from the consequences of the sexual peccadilloes that have laid their colleagues low. They seem to believe that they are special, that they are entitled, and that they will get away with it.[b] The entitlement of the narcissist warps the individual's judgment of the consequences of his actions; there is no insight into the destructive consequences of his acts. Narcissists apparently believe that they are exempt from the rules and standards that govern ordinary behavior.

CORRUPTION IN POLITICS

Not every person who exhibits narcissistic traits will have them manifest in sordid extramarital affairs that are replayed in the media as a form of public entertainment. One example of a prominent long-time incumbent who came to see himself as increasingly identified with his position and entitled to the perquisites of power was Republican Senator Ted Stevens of Alaska. Stevens, known to many Alaskans as "Uncle Ted," served as senator from 1968 to 2009, becoming the longest serving Republican in U.S. history.

In December 2003, the *Los Angeles Times* reported that Stevens took advantage of lax Senate rules to use his political influence to obtain a large amount of his personal wealth. He was convicted on counts of lying on financial disclosure forms about gifts, including the renovation of his Alaska home, which the FBI investigated.[67] Although a federal judge would later throw out the case, finding that the prosecutors withheld evidence at the trial, Stevens still lost his 2008 reelection bid following the accusations.

Stevens thought highly of himself and came increasingly to see himself as the very embodiment of the state that he had represented for 41 years. He made not so veiled threats of punishment to some senators who voted against oil exploration in the Arctic National Wildlife Refuge, stating: "I make this commitment: People who vote against this today are voting against me, and I will not forget it."[68] Statements like these emphasized significant narcissistic entitlement and wounding and a fusion of the political role and the self to the point where Stevens understood opposition to his cause as a personal attack.

PAY TO PLAY

Illinois is a state notable for its long history of corruption in high office; until 2009, six governors had been arrested or indicted, with three jailed since 1971.

---

[b] Kohut (1985) observes that "these persons appear to have no dynamically effective guilt feelings and never suffer any pangs of conscience about what they are doing" (pp. 200–201). On the one hand, there seems to be "a stunting of their empathic capacity: they understand neither the wishes nor the frustrations and disappointments of other people. At the same time, their sense of the legitimacy of their own wishes and their sensitivity to their own frustrations are intense." Kohut quotes Freud's reference to the entitlement of Shakespeare's Richard III as a consequence of his congenital deformity: "I have the right to be an exception, to disregard the scruples by which others let themselves be held back. I may do wrong myself, since wrong has been done to me." Freud, 1916 "Some Character Types Met with in Psychoanalytic Work," *Standard Edition*, pp. 314–315.

Governor Rod Blagojevich raised this tradition to an art form, becoming the seventh arrested and indicted, the fourth jailed, and the first Illinois governor ever to be impeached.

After serving three terms as a member of the U.S. House of Representatives, Blagojevich was elected governor in 2003 and served in that role until the impeachment that removed him from office in 2009. He took the stand to testify in his own defense at his corruption trial. The evidence was overpowering that a centerpiece of his philosophy of governing was the requirement that others "pay to play," and he saw a valuable asset in the then-vacant Obama senatorial seat. A particularly damning piece of evidence from the FBI tapes were the following earthy remarks: "I've got this thing, and it's f_____ golden and, uh, uh, I'm just not giving it up for f_____ nothing. I'm not gonna do it . . . give this "motherf___ [Obama] his Senator. F___ him. For nothing? F_____ him . . . they're not willing to give me anything except appreciation. F___them."[69]

In early 2009, the Illinois House of Representatives voted to impeach him by a 114–1 vote for corruption and misconduct in office, the first time any such action has been taken against a governor in the state.[70] His demeanor during the trial has been described as "ebullient and cocky" as well as "nervous and beaten down" minutes later.[71] When Blagojevich made the decision to testify in his own defense, federal prosecutors used their first hour of cross-examination to remind jurors that this experienced politician was well-practiced in the art of lying and that it had already resulted in at least one conviction – making a false statement to the FBI.[72] He made matters worse for himself by attempting to outduel assistant U.S. Attorney Reid Schar about what constitutes lying, as though he were in a televised political debate as opposed to a trial – one that resulted in a long prison sentence. An excerpt from this examination highlights how his own arrogance ultimately worked against him:

Schar's first question: "Mr. Blagojevich, you are a convicted liar, correct?"
Blagojevich, after the judge overruled objections by the defense: "Yes."
Schar: "Is it true that, as a politician, you not infrequently lied to the public?"
Blagojevich: "I try to be as truthful as possible. Politics is a difficult business."
Schar: "That was a lie?"
Blagojevich: "That was a misdirection play in politics."
Schar: "It was a lie."
Blagojevich: "I don't see it that way."[73]

For the most part, it seemed as if he was playing a role, preening in the limelight. And part of the benefit package that went with playing the role of governor was receiving "contributions" for access to him to garner his support for various programs. That was politics. And having the power to fill a vacant Senate was a big one for which he should be well compensated. Among the possibilities he considered was a cabinet seat or appointment as an ambassador. The idea that gratitude was all he would get from President Obama for appointing someone he preferred was ludicrous.

As noted earlier, Blagojevich rather enjoyed crossing verbal swords with assistant federal attorney Schar. Following the lively trial was quite entertaining. But if the audience was entertained, the starring actor should be compensated. And so Blagojevich entered negotiations to play himself in a televised reality show, but was blocked by the judge from profiting from his criminal acts.

Blagojevich was convicted and sentenced on December 7, 2011. He is currently serving a 14-year sentence in federal prison.

In cases such as these, narcissistic traits are highlighted by grandiose thinking and feelings of entitlement. The positions of power that these men, and sometimes women, find themselves in, complete with the plaudits of their constituents ringing in their ears, fuels their sense of entitlement and justifies their actions. Over time, their grandiose thinking and feelings of invulnerability increase as they come to see themselves as exceptions.

An exceptional exception in a democratic society is Silvio Berlusconi, former prime minister of Italy, whose womanizing and corruption were of truly monumental proportions. He is the subject of the next chapter.

Notes

1. Thomas Wolfe, *The Bonfire of the Vanities* (New York: Farrar, Straus, Giroux, 1987).
2. E. J. Dionne, Jr., "Gary Hart, the Elusive Front-Runner," *The New York Times*, May 3, 1987, www.nytimes.com/1987/05/03/magazine/garry-hart-the-elusive-front-runner.html?pagewanted=all&src=pm.
3. Photograph of Gary Hart and Donna Rice, *National Enquirer*, June 2, 1987, front cover.
4. "Hart First Withdrawal," *C-SPAN*, December 15, 1987, accessed March 30, 2011, www.c-spanvideo.org/program/Wit&showFullAbstract=1.
5. Dorothy Holmes, "The Wrecking Effects of Race and Social Class on Self and Success," *Psychoanalytic Quarterly* 75, No. 1 (2006): 223.
6. Steven T. Levy, Beth J. Seelig, and Lawrence B. Inderbitzin, "On Those Wrecked by Success: A Clinical Inquiry," *Psychoanalytic Quarterly* 64 (1995): 639–657.
7. Levy, "On Those Wrecked by Success," 641.
8. "The Enigmatic Candidate," *People Magazine*, March 26, 1984, www.people.com/people/archive/issue/0,,7566840326,00.html.
9. "The Enigmatic Candidate"; E. J. Dionne Jr., "Courting Danger: The Fall of Gary Hart," *The New York Times*, May 9, 1987(b), www.nytimes.com/1987/05/09/us/courting-danger-the-fall-of-gary-hart.html?pagewanted=all&src=pm.
10. Dionne Jr., "Courting Danger: The Fall of Gary Hart."
11. Ibid.
12. Ibid.
13. Dany Hakim and William K. Rashbaum, "Spitzer Is Linked to Prostitution Ring," *The New York Times*, April 6, 2011, www.nytimes.com/2008/03/10/nyregion/10cnd-spitzer.html?pagewanted=all.
14. Globe Staff. "Eliot Spitzer to Lecture at Harvard Ethics Center," *Boston.com*, November 12, 2009, www.boston.com/news/local/breaking_news/2009/11/eliot_spitzer_t.html.

15. Jonathan Darman, "Spitzer in Exile," *Newsweek*, 153, No. 17 (April 27, 2009).
16. Sam Stein, "Ensign Whacked Bill Clinton for His Infidelities, Called Them 'Embarrassing' for Country," *The Huffington Post*, July 17, 2009, www.huffington post.com/2009/06/16/ensign-whacked-clinton-fo_n_216508.html.
17. Alex Roth and Valeria Bauerlein, "Gov. Sanford Struggles to Hang On," *The Wall Street Journal*, June, 26, 2009, http://online.wsj.com/article/SB12459606132835 5673.html.
18. Tamara Lush and Evan Berland, "AP Newsbreak: SC Gov 'Crossed Lines' with Women," *U-T San Diego*, June 30, 2009, accessed December 16, 2013, www .utsandiego.com/news/2009/Jun/30/us-sc-governor-063009/.
19. Peter Hamby, "S. C. Attorney General to Review Sanford's Travel Records," *CNN*, July 1, 2009, http://articles.cnn.com/2009-06-30/politics/sanford_1_maria-belen-chapur-sanford-spokesman-joel-sawyer-governor-sanford?_s=PM:POLITICS.
20. "Transcript of Gary Condit Interview," *CNN*, August 23, 2001, http://edition.cnn .com/2001/US/08/23/condit.transcript/.
21. Bill Walsh and Bruce Alpert, "Senate Leader Wants 'Airing' of Vitter Scandal," *The Times Picayune*, July 17, 2007, http://blog.nola.com/times-picayune/2007/07/sen ate_leader_wants_airing_of.html.
22. Associated Press, "New Orleans' Madam Says Sen. David Vitter Used Her Brothel," *Fox News*, July 11, 2007, www.foxnews.com/story/0,2933,288868,00.html.
23. Anne Rochell Konigsmark, "A Week of Crisis Impeachment: The Speakership Livingston's Constituents Decision to Resign Jolts Home District," *The Atlanta Journal-Constitution*, December 20, 1998, D4.
24. Jan Moller, "David Vitter Sex Scandal Gets Spotlight Again in Debate with Charlie Melancon," *The Times-Picayune*, October 28, 2010, www.nola.com/politics/index .ssf/2010/10/david_vitter_sex_scandal_gets.html.
25. Associated Press, "John Ensign Affair, Apology & Drama: Timeline Leading to Senator's Resignation," The Huffington Post, March 20, 2011, www.huffington post.com/2011/04/21/john-ensign-affair-apolog_n_852346.html.
26. Stein, "Ensign Whacked Bill Clinton for His Infidelities."
27. Randy James, "Senator John Ensign: 'I Had an Affair,'" *TIME*, June 18, 2009, www .time.com/time/nation/article/0,8599,1905351,00.html.
28. Stein, "Ensign Whacked Bill Clinton for His Infidelities."
29. Ibid.
30. Chris Cillizza and Paul Kane, "Republican Sen. John Ensign of Nevada Won't Seek Reelection," *The Washington Post*, March 7, 2011, www.washingtonpost.com/wp-dyn/content/article/2011/03/07/AR2011030704306.html.
31. John Edwards, et al., *Ending Poverty in America: How to Restore the American Dream* (New York: New Press. 2007), 263.
32. Edwards, *Ending Poverty in America*, 262.
33. Mickey Porter, "Newt's a Beaut," *Akron Beacon Journal*, July 25, 2000.
34. Frank Bruni, "Gingrich Sees Echo of Ancient Rome in America Today," *The New York Times*, May 3, 1998, www.nytimes.com/1998/05/03/us/gingrich-sees-echo-of-ancient-rome-in-america-today.html?pagewanted=all&src=pm.
35. "Gingrich Attacks Clinton on Lewinsky Matter, Foreign Policy," *CNN*, May 18, 1998, http://articles.cnn.com/1998-05-18/politics/gingrich.clinton_1_gingrich-foreign-policy-missile-technology?_s=PM:ALLPOLITICS.

36. Maggie Habberman, "Newt Gingrich: 'I Was Doing Things That Were Wrong,'" *POLITICO*, March 8, 2011, www.politico.com/news/stories/031.
37. Gabriella Schwarz, "Gingrich: I'm Not a Hypocrite," *CNN*, March 27, 2011, http://politicalticker.blogs.cnn.com/2011/03/27/gingrich-i%E2%80%99m-not-a-hypocrite/.
38. Al Kamen, "Rumsfeld: The Boom Years," *The Washington Post*, March 11, 2011, A14.
39. Gail Sheehy, "The Inner Quest of Newt Gingrich," *Vanity Fair* 421 (September 1995): 147.
40. Sheehy, "The Inner Quest of Newt Gingrich."
41. Ibid.
42. Ibid.
43. Ibid.
44. Ibid.
45. Ibid.
46. Lois Romano, "Newt Gingrich, Maverick on the Hill: The New Right's Abrasive Point Man Talks of Changing His Tone and Tactics," *The Washington Post*, January 3, 1985, B01.
47. Jim Garamone, "Petraeus Garners Praise at Retirement Ceremony," *United States Department of Defense*, August 31, 2011, www.defense.gov/News/NewsArticle .aspx?ID=65213.
48. Mark Bowden, "David Petraeus's Winning Streak," *Vanity Fair*, March 30, 2010, www.vanityfair.com/politics/features/2010/05/petraeus-exclusive-201005; Paula Broadwell, "General David Petraeus's Rules for Living," *The Daily Beast*, November 5, 2012, www.thedailybeast.com/newsweek/2012/11/04/general-david-petraeus-srules-for-living.html.
49. Bowden, "David Petraeus's Winning Streak."
50. Ibid.; Broadwell, "General David Petraeus's Rules for Living."
51. Paul Vitello, "Worried Town Recalls a Young Petraeus," *The New York Times*, September 12, 2007, www.nytimes.com/2007/09/12/washington/12petraeus .html?_r=0.
52. Bowden, "David Petraeus's Winning Streak."
53. Rajiv Chandrasekaran and Greg Jaffe, "Petraeus Scandal Puts Four-Star General Lifestyle under Scrutiny," *The Washington Post*, November 17, 2012, http://articles .washingtonpost.com/2012-11-17/world/35505221_1_robert-m-gates-commanders-joint-chiefs.
54. Kathleen Hennessey, "Senate Confirms David Petraeus as CIA Director," *The Los Angeles Times*, June 30, 2011, http://articles.latimes.com/2011/jun/30/news/la-pn-petraeus-confirmed-20110630.
55. Richard Engel, "Petraeus' Biographer Paula Broadwell under FBI Investigation over Access to His Email, Law Enforcement Officials Say," *NBC News*, November 9, 2012, http://usnews.nbcnews.com/_news/2012/11/09/15056607-petraeus-biographer-paula-broadwell-under-fbi-investigation-over-access-to-his-email-law-enforcement-officials-say.
56. Chandrasekaran and Jaffe, "Petraeus Scandal Puts Four-Star General Lifestyle under Scrutiny."
57. Associated Press, "Petraeus Affair Timeline of Events," *Politico*, November 12, 2012, accessed February 23, 2013, www.politico.com/news/stories/1112/.

58. Chandrasekaran and Jaffe, "Petraeus Scandal Puts Four-Star General Lifestyle under Scrutiny."

59. Ibid.

60. Ibid.

61. Amy Scherzer, "Amy Scherzer's Diary," *Tampa Bay Times*, February 4, 2010, www .tampabay.com/news/humaninterest/amy-scherzers-diary/1070401.

62. Chandrasekaran and Jaffe, "Petraeus Scandal Puts Four-Star General Lifestyle under Scrutiny."

63. Thomas E. Ricks, *The Generals: American Military Command from World War II to Today* (New York: Penguin Press, 2012).

64. Chandrasekaran and Jaffe, "Petraeus Scandal Puts Four-Star General Lifestyle under Scrutiny."

65. Lewis Shepherd, "Petraeus as Ozymandias," *Shepherd's Pi*, November 10, 2010, http://lewisshepherd.wordpress.com/2012/11/10/petraeus-as-ozymandias/.

66. Stephen Sherrill, "The Year in Ideas: A to Z; Acquired Situational Narcissism," *The New York Times*, December 9, 2001, www.nytimes.com/2001/12/09/magazine/the-year-in-ideas-a-to-z-acquired-situational-narcissism.html.

67. Richard Cooper and Chuck Neubauer, "Senator's Way to Wealth Was Paved with Favors," *Los Angeles Times*, December 17, 2003.

68. Congress.org, March 3, 2011.

69. Massimo Calabresi, "Can Obama Escape the Taint of Blagojevich?" *TIME*, December 10, 2008, www.time.com/time/nation/article/0,8599,1865370,00.html.

70. "Governor Says Impeachment Vote Is Politically Driven," *CNN*, January 9, 2009, http://articles.cnn.com/2009-01-09/politics/blagojevich.impeachment_1_impeachment-rod-blagojevich-illinois-house?_s=PM:POLITICS.

71. Mark Brown, "Rod Blagojevich on the Stand Breathes Life into Retrial," *Chicago Sun-Times*, June 3, 2011, www.suntimes.com/news/watchdogs/6990852-452/with-rod-blagojevich-convicted-others-now-face-sentencing.html.

72. Brown, "Rod Blagojevich on the Stand Breathes Life into Retrial."

73. Ibid.

9

An Exceptional Exception: The Rise and Fall of Italy's Silvio Berlusconi

Ruthie Pertsis and Jerrold M. Post, M.D.

The preceding chapter dealt with the issues of entitlement and political affairs, but no work on these themes would be complete without considering a man who has not only become synonymous with inappropriate sexual behavior while in political power, but who has also used and thoroughly abused his country's legal and media systems to shamelessly further his own personal interests. Silvio Berlusconi dominated Italian politics for nearly two decades, making "Berlusconismo" his own unique political brand.[1] And, even though he spent much of that time actively undermining some of the most basic features of his country's democracy, it was only the tremendous outside pressure exerted in the form of the Euro crisis that eventually removed him from power in November 2011. Between changing laws at the highest levels in order to free himself from prosecution and ultimately securing control of roughly 90 percent of the Italian media, it is a wonder that he still had time to socialize with women much younger than himself, even being accused of having sex with an underage prostitute. It would not be an exaggeration to say that, for the past two decades, Italy has been more a reflection of Berlusconi than Berlusconi has been of Italy, a feat attributable to his intensely narcissistic character.

BACKGROUND

To understand how he managed for so long to run his party – and Italy – like his own personal fiefdom,[2] it is important to understand how he came to power in the first place and his appeal to the Italian public. Without delving too deeply into Italian political history, it is enough to note that postwar Italy was domi-nated by a communist ideology that appealed to the masses because of the horrors that characterized the wartime fascist system of Benito Mussolini. But when the Berlin Wall came tumbling down in 1989, leading to the dissolution of the Soviet Union in 1991 and communism lost what was left of its already severely weakened appeal, the Italian people decided that it was time for their country to reinvent itself.

This movement was also significantly encouraged by the *mani pulite* (clean hands) campaign carried out by Italy's judiciary beginning in 1992. This widespread investigation uncovered a system of mass political corruption at the highest levels of the Italian government, resulted in a complete overhaul of the country's power structure, and dramatically boosted the influence of the judiciary (this last point would later be crucial to Berlusconi's thwarted attempt to consolidate ultimate power).

Enter Silvio Berlusconi, in 1994, at the height of Italy's political turmoil. The successful self-made millionaire businessman had created a center-right political party espousing the capitalist notions of individualism, consumerism, and transparency, and he was offering a new way of life for Italians. Sealing his mass appeal and playing on Italian patriotism, he named his party *Forza Italia* (Go Italy), a popular soccer chant, and used himself as an example that anything was possible and that anyone could be successful in the new Italy. He was elected prime minister a mere three months later, and although his cabinet collapsed shortly thereafter due to internal disagreements within his coalition, he remained the preeminent figure in Italian politics for 17 years, serving as prime minister from 1994–1995, 2001–2006, and 2008–2011.

The legacy of Silvio Berlusconi is one of a leadership wrought with manipulation, corruption, and scandal. Alexander Stille, an American author and journalist of Italian descent, has eloquently summed it up in the following way:

The election of the richest man and the largest media owner, who is also a defendant in numerous criminal trials, to the highest public office has created a bizarre and anomalous situation and led to a new model of power in the heart of Europe. Imagine if Bill Gates of Microsoft were also the owner of the three largest national TV networks and then became president and took over public television as well. Imagine that he also owned Time Warner, HBO, the Los Angeles Times, the New York Yankees, Aetna insurance, Fidelity Investments and Loews theaters, and you begin to get an idea of how large a shadow Silvio Berlusconi casts over Italian life. Imagine also that dozens of members of parliament and most of the key people in government are also current or former employees of the TV-tycoon prime minister, that he has been indicted and convicted in several criminal trials, which his personal lawyers, who also sit in parliament, have legislated or tried to legislate out of existence.[3]

Taken together with his famously flamboyant sex life, we begin to see a portrait of an extremely narcissistic man who used an entire country to fulfill his own personal narcissistic dreams of glory.

CORRUPTION

Berlusconi's appeal to the Italian people in the early 1990s was based largely on his pledge to root out the corruption that had become rampant in Italian politics and that had precipitated the *mani pulite* campaign; he was a nonpolitician and a self-made man, and the hope was that he would run Italy like a respectable business. Overflowing with corruption, the Italian populace craved a rescuer, someone who could clean up the system and set the country on a fresh path.

The larger-than-life figure of Berlusconi the successful businessman seemed ideally suited to fill that role. If, as Schiffer[4] has observed, the leader is fundamentally the creation of his followers, then the Italian people had idealized Berlusconi. They saw in him what they needed to see: someone to lead them out of a welter of corruption. He was the ideal rescuer for those troubled times, and they chose to ignore evidence to the contrary.

However, information about his earlier life and the manner in which he achieved such remarkable success in the world of business later came to light to prove that such hope was illusory. First inklings of his corrupt political career can be traced to his boyhood, when young Berlusconi sold completed homework to his classmates in exchange for their mid-morning snacks or small amounts of money.[5] Questions about potentially illegal money dealings going back to the 1960s, when Berlusconi began his business career in property development, remain unanswered, and paper trails have led nowhere. It is alleged, for example, that Berlusconi received money from foreign companies for various projects, but it is still not clear what the exact sources of the money were and if the money was obtained legally. There are also questions surrounding possible financial support from the Italian Mafia for the media empire that Berlusconi began to develop in the 1970s.[6] It is not all that surprising, then, that two decades later, the man who had cast himself as Italy's savior had actually proved himself to be one of the most corrupt leaders in a modern democracy, with his own particular brand of corruption more than rivaling what he had sworn to eradicate.

One of the most salient features of the narcissistic personality is its grandiose sense of self-importance and specialness, including feelings of entitlement and exceptionalism. This was very obviously evidenced in Berlusconi by his various living quarters. In 1974, well before he officially entered politics, Berlusconi bought an extravagant 18th-century villa with 147 rooms north of Milan.[7] What was most remarkable about the villa was not its luxuriousness, however, but the mausoleum standing in the park surrounding the villa, a structure that reflected its owner's intense vanity and imperial self-concept. A BBC journalist recalled visiting the grounds:

The grandiose Berlusconi tomb has a 10-tonne abstract sculpture of white Carrara marble as a grave marker above ground. An imitation of an Etruscan chamber tomb, broad marble steps lead down to a narrow passage to a spacious burial chamber – a monumental pink granite sarcophagus which reminded me of one of the tombs of the Pharaohs in the Valley of the Kings in Egypt. Thirty-six empty burial recesses surrounded Mr. Berlusconi's future resting place on a central plinth. "Who will occupy them?" I asked. "Family and business associates," he replied.[8]

What is more, Berlusconi chose not to live in the official prime ministerial residence during his time in power, opting instead to rent a whole floor in the Palazzo

Graziole, where several noble Roman families lived over the centuries. It was from that location that he chose to officially announce his resignation on November 12, 2011,[9] again displaying his imperial self-concept and his unmistakable sense of exceptionalism.

More specifically related to Berlusconi's political personality, though, Kohut[10] has spoken of the messianic narcissistic personality in which the self and the idealized superego are fused; there is no separate superego to constrain behavior, thus leading the individual to consider himself an "exception" and above the law. Over the years, Berlusconi had been involved in dozens of judicial investigations related to corruption, including money laundering, connections with the Mafia, tax evasion, paying bribes, blackmailing judges, and committing perjury. Until his conviction in 2013 for tax fraud, he had successfully avoided prosecution for his crimes, even boasting that "I am without doubt the person who's been the most persecuted in the entire history of the world and the history of man."[11]

The judiciary's difficulty in convicting him is not at all surprising; whereas the messianic narcissist typically feels himself to be above the law, Berlusconi took this one step further by having the law completely changed. This, Italian political scientist Maurizio Viroli argues, makes the Italian people Berlusconi's servants: "In order for there to be true liberty it is necessary for everyone to be subject to the laws or, in the words of the classical precept; that laws be more powerful than men. If, in a state, instead there is a man who is more powerful than the laws then there exists no liberty for the citizens."[12] Berlusconi is known to have had the Italian parliament, populated with his own personal lawyers, make changes to laws that directly affected the outcomes of his trials, and, in 2008, he won the ultimate victory when he persuaded the parliament to approve a law giving him full immunity from prosecution, essentially discontinuing all criminal trials while he was in office.[13]

Although that law was overturned the following year, Berlusconi continued to delay prosecution by claiming that the legal proceedings were a politically motivated tactic used by the judiciary to discredit him. He even went so far as to call prosecutors the "cancer of democracy," a compelling metaphor given that Berlusconi himself had been treated for prostate cancer in 1997.[14]

Berlusconi also claimed that the judiciary's attack on him interfered with his ability to lead the country. This last point is especially noteworthy because it alludes to another basic characteristic of the narcissistic leader, namely, the tendency to rationalize private interests in terms of the public good. He once said "If I, taking care of everyone's interests, also take care of my own, you can't talk about a conflict of interest."[15] Berlusconi often argued that he was, in fact, changing outdated laws in the country in order to free the Italian people from the restrictive influence of the judicial system, and it is true that many Italians overlooked his legal troubles because they believed that Italian society in general was excessively regulated.[16] Still, Berlusconi had a major role to play in the acceptance, and even institutionalization, of impunity in Italian society, which was very beneficial to his own personal cause and also his cause as prime minister.

It seems that, with his abrupt departure after so many years in office, and with the state of affairs in their country so obviously dysfunctional, Italians are beginning to reassess and realize that he was, in fact, the cause of many of their recent problems and not the solution that he claimed to be. This would explain the celebrations that accompanied his final exit from the palace of the President of the Council of Ministers on November 12, 2011, and also the traditional burning of an effigy on New Year's Eve that bore a picture of Berlusconi's face: "On the night of 31 December we always burn what is old and belongs to the past and, with that, everything negative connected with the year that's just ended. . . . Berlusconi's politics certainly represent one of these things."[17]

Even more indicative of his narcissistic personality was Berlusconi's genuine surprise at the strong reaction against him in response to the Italian economic crisis that eventually brought him down. Much like Libya's Muammar al-Qaddafi at the end of his rule, Berlusconi could not believe that all of his people did not love him and that members of his own parliament could turn on him and vote him out of power. A photographer captured a priceless shot of a piece of paper on which Berlusconi had been scribbling during that fateful session of parliament; on it was written, among other things, "traitors."[18] Here, we see not only a narcissistic leader whose conscience is dominated by self-interest focusing primarily on his own personal loss when his country is falling apart, but also the characteristic sensitivity to defeat and humiliation that often leads to exaggerated feelings of rage, inferiority, emptiness, and shame in the narcissist.

In fact, Berlusconi is reported to have compared his sense of betrayal and isolation after the parliamentary vote to that of Benito Mussolini after his fall from power in 1943. Berlusconi quoted a letter that Mussolini had written to a lover, saying: "At a certain point he says: 'Don't you understand I don't count for anything anymore?' I have felt in the same situation."[19] Berlusconi commanded such loyalty from those close to him, as narcissistic leaders often do, that even they saw the comparison to Mussolini. Lele Mora, a talent manager who had worked and socialized with Berlusconi for 25 years, once said "Mussolini did a lot of good things for Italy, and he's seen only for certain ugly things that his people did – the traitors! . . . Like Berlusconi has a lot of traitors who speak badly about him and do ugly things to him."[20] It also does not help Berlusconi's case that he himself defended Mussolini, betraying a certain admiration for him by declaring "Mussolini never killed anyone. Mussolini used to send people on vacation in internal exile."[21] Berlusconi's special relationship with Muammar al-Qaddafi demonstrated a similar tone deafness, given the Libyan leader's problematic relationship with the West, and it reflected the inflated sense of grandiosity that led Berlusconi to conclude that he would be the one to single-handedly resolve the decades-long conflict between Libya and the West. It also confirmed his underlying insecure self that craved the adoration and acclaim of others, which surely would have overflowed if he had succeeded in that unlikely task.

MEDIA CONTROL

Berlusconi's manipulation of the Italian political system also made it possible for him to take nearly full control of the country's media. This, in turn, further increased his political influence, essentially creating a self-perpetuating cycle of growing power that continuously fed his narcissistic need for constant attention. He began buying up local television networks in the 1970s, and, because of his personal connections to Bettino Craxi, then secretary-general of the Italian Socialist Party and also prime minister of Italy (and who was also best man at his wedding),[22] Berlusconi was able to have a law overturned in 1984 that previously restricted nationwide broadcasting to RAI, the state-owned public service broadcaster.[23] This catapulted Berlusconi onto the national stage, and he used the momentum to further build up his empire, buying newspapers, publishing companies, banking and insurance institutions, and even wildly successful sports clubs.

When he became prime minister for the first time in 1994, he was already well-known throughout the country as the successful businessman who had come from nothing to prove that the American dream could be achieved in Italy, a welcome message after decades of corruption. And the corruption was widespread, engulfing the entire system. It involved not only members of the Communist Party, but also the Christian Democrats and the Socialists (under Craxi), all of whom were swept up in bribery scandals at the beginning of the 1990s. In fact, in 1994, Craxi took refuge in Tunis to escape prison time.

By the time that Berlusconi left office in November 2011, he was in control of roughly 90 percent of the Italian media, comprising both his private holdings as well as the public organizations that he indirectly controlled as the head of the government.[24]

Not only did this overwhelming control of the media ensure that Berlusconi would remain in power in a country where most of the population relies on television broadcasting for political information, but it also provided Berlusconi with an outlet for his narcissistic self-centeredness, egocentricity, and self-absorption. At the beginning of his 2006 campaign for office, he shamelessly declared "I am the Jesus Christ of politics. I am a patient victim, I put up with everyone, I sacrifice myself for everyone."[25] He also indirectly manipulated his image in the media by firing reporters, journalists, and television personalities who criticized him, and he even tried to sue the British weekly news and international affairs publication *The Economist* for libel after they ran a piece entitled "Why Silvio Berlusconi Is Unfit to Lead Italy" in April 2001; he ultimately lost and had to pay all legal expenses.[26] This anecdote, like that of his scribbling the word "traitor" on a piece of paper after the vote of no confidence in parliament, demonstrates the standard exaggerated response to criticism exhibited by narcissists who hunger for confirming and admiring responses to counteract their inner sense of worthlessness and lack of self-esteem. This would certainly explain his immense efforts to gain as much influence over Italian media as possible.

Berlusconi's near-total control of the television media (he also owned significant print media outlets) served another purpose in addition to cementing his enormous political influence in the country: namely, it satisfied a distinctive narcissistic preoccupation with appearance over substance. As someone who was constantly being followed in the media, he took great care to manage his physical appearance, perhaps reflecting the narcissist's general difficulty in dealing with aging, admitting to having had plastic surgery to improve his appearance. But, as a *New Yorker* journalist reported, it may have done more harm than good:

When I finally met Berlusconi ... I was shocked. He is tiny, no more than five feet four inches tall. He wears white eyeliner on his lower lids to make his eyes pop in photographs, and he uses heavy foundation on his face, which renders him the same orangey-brown color as the cast of the "Jersey Shore." His hair is thinning – "because I had too many girlfriends," he once said, before he got implants – and dyed a vivid burnt sienna. Despite these efforts, he is not a young seventy-four; Berlusconi, in the words of his best friend, "is a bit dilapidated."[27]

Whether or not he was able to correct the physical shortcomings that probably contributed to his low self-esteem, especially in a culture that places so much emphasis on physical appearance, what is important is that, counterintuitively, he went through the process of trying to improve his looks in order to charm the Italian public instead of ameliorating his dishonest behavior, which the largely positive response to his ultimate departure proved was unappreciated by many Italians. It seems strange, then, that he was able to remain in power for so long, but this can be explained, at least in part, by his charismatic relationship with the Italian people.

As already discussed, Berlusconi rose to power because the wounded Italian people desperately needed an antidote to decades of corruption that plagued the country since the fall of fascism in 1943. Berlusconi exploded on the scene as a rescuer, a successful businessman who would adopt a Western political system and break with the past. Considered in this way, the strength of his appeal is not all that surprising.

Berlusconi, at the same time, needed his followers. As Italian political scientist Gianfranco Pasquino notes:

The Italian word is *vanitoso*. He's a vain man. He likes to be photographed, quoted and loved, as everybody knows. The President of the Republic is the father of the country and he wants to be that. It would also secure him a place in the history books. He wants to be remembered.[28]

That Berlusconi craves positive attention from his followers and wants to be idealized is rather obvious, and it fits very well with the clear characterization of him as a narcissistic leader.

But the explanation behind the idea of his wanting to be father of the country is more complex and may have its roots in his childhood. In describing his early life, Ginsborg[29] writes about Berlusconi's father who fled to Switzerland for two years when his son was seven years old in order to escape being recruited into the

Italian army during World War II. Thus, it may be that not having a father during his formative years, when he needed one most, pushed the wounded Berlusconi to want to be a father to the Italian people when he believed that they needed one most. Similar observations have been made with other narcissistic leaders who had absent fathers, such as Mustafa Kemal Ataturk, the founder of modern-day Turkey. But despite his aspiring to be father to his nation, Berlusconi often demonstrated little empathy for his people, saying, for example, of the 17,000 homeless survivors of the April 2009 earthquake in the town of L'Aquila that "Of course, their current lodgings are a bit temporary. But they should see it like a weekend of camping."[30] Instances like these demonstrate the dichotomy between the overt and covert aspects of Berlusconi's narcissism; this typical narcissistic inability to empathize with others because of the centrality of the self in reality betrays a profound psychological need for acclaim, which Berlusconi did initially receive for his immediate handling of the crisis before his insensitive remark.

WOMANIZING

Still, the issue for which Berlusconi was always most notorious, for which he appeared frequently in the international media, was his inappropriate relationships with women. One of the clinical features of the narcissistic personality disorder deals with love and sexuality and is characterized by overt seductiveness, promiscuity, and lack of sexual inhibitions, which actually mask a covert inability to remain in love, a tendency to treat a love object as an extension of the self, and occasional sexual deviations. Over the years, Berlusconi provided ample evidence of the narcissistic foundations that underlay his distorted relationships with the opposite sex.

Just as his corrupt behavior began long before he entered politics, Berlusconi's difficulty with women goes back at least to the late 1970s, when he began an extramarital affair with Italian actress Veronica Lario, 20 years his junior. Although there were reports that he felt tremendous guilt about the secret love affair, it was only because it conflicted with "his deep-felt need to be loved, even worshipped, by all members of his family and entourage."[31] Berlusconi displayed a very flexible conscience, consistent with the narcissistic personality, finally revealing the affair and divorcing his wife only when Lario gave birth to their first child. Somewhat ironically, Lario herself was to divorce Berlusconi in 2009 because of his inappropriate female relationships, including his attendance at the 18th birthday party of an aspiring Italian model and his appointment of unqualified young women to positions within his government.[32]

Since then, "Burlesqueoni"[33] only seems to have gotten worse, perhaps because he is having a difficult time coming to terms with aging, as is characteristic of narcissists. Among other things, he is currently awaiting trial on the charge of having sex with Karima el Mahroug, a prostitute who was also a minor at the time, and he was infamous for hosting "bunga bunga" parties at his lavish estate, where he reportedly danced in the nude and participated in orgies with young women, on one occasion bringing in a group of strippers dressed as nuns.[34] This last point speaks to the perverse fantasies and sexual deviations that often characterize the emotionally disturbed narcissist and might also help to explain Berlusconi's tense relationship with the church, whose support is very important for political success in Italy.

But what lies beneath this apparent inability for Berlusconi to see women as anything more than sexual objects? Part of the answer may lie in the prostate cancer for which he was treated in 1997. It is not uncommon for men to experience sexual difficulties after such a physically and emotionally traumatic event, and this could explain Berlusconi's subsequent need to exaggerate his sexuality to prove his prowess as a man. This would be particularly salient for a narcissist like Berlusconi who is already especially hypersensitive to threats to an insecure inner self. More so, however, it would appear that he was using his asymmetrical power relationships with women to overcome deeper feelings of inadequacy and low self-esteem. Giuliano Ferrara, editor of an Italian newspaper funded by Berlusconi and briefly a cabinet minister in his government, once said of him that he "is pathologically inclined to please other people; he needs their affection."[35] It is crucial to note that Berlusconi was developing actual relationships with many of these women and not just using them for sex. For example, Berlusconi was strongly criticized for placing a 26-year-old dental hygienist and former showgirl on his party's ticket in 2010, getting her elected to the legislature for the Italian region of Lombardy.[36] Also in 2010, he was slammed, including by many of his own people, for abusing his position and personally arranging for the release of el Mahroug from jail after she was arrested for theft, claiming that she was the granddaughter of then-Egyptian President Hosni Mubarak.[37] The picture that these and many other examples paint is one of a wounded man seeking positive attention and reassurance from women, even if it had to be bought or jeopardized his status. Once again, in attempting to trace the roots of this wounded self, it is useful to bear in mind that Berlusconi's father left during the war, leaving his mother to provide for the family and with less time to nurture her son at a critical period during the young boy's development. This may have instilled in him a lifelong quest to fulfill that need for nurturance, especially by women.

It is interesting to observe that, during the war, the Berlusconi family pledged no allegiance, choosing not to be loyal to either side.[38] This would later work very well for Berlusconi, the ultimate narcissist, a man who was loyal to no one, least of all the Italian people, and whose only fundamental and stable belief was the centrality of himself. Using rampant corruption, virtually complete control of the media, and his advantageous position relative to women, he transformed an entire country into the vehicle that he hoped would carry out his dreams of glory, all the while driven by his underlying insecurity. His charismatic relationship with the majority of Italians ensured that they would stand by him during his tough times, which he, in true narcissistic fashion, blamed on his political opponents. Still, Berlusconi could not surmount the crisis in the Euro zone, and his inability to provide stable leadership to his country, which was a major casualty of Europe's declining economic situation, stopped him short of becoming the savior of Italy – a role he had long dreamed of playing. But when he had the opportunity to do so, he did not reform the distortions in Italy's archaic economic system; he did not, for example, change the popular but overgenerous work rules. He took no steps to fulfill his role as rescuer of the system, the idealized hope that brought him to power. It was as if he believed that by using the sheer force of his personality he would change the system, but without undertaking the hard work necessary to address major, necessary, but unpopular changes. Did his narcissistic sense of invulnerability lead him to deny the obvious seriousness of the situation facing the Italian economy? Or, was he simply unaware of the situation, either because he was too absorbed in his own personal matters or because his inner circle of loyal advisors failed to adequately prepare him for it, for fear of falling out of favor with him? In fact, the answer is both, with the bottom line being that Berlusconi has only himself to blame for his and his country's present misfortunes.

Only one year later, in 2013, demonstrating remarkable hubris (although not remarkable for Berlusconi) and despite being on trial for tax fraud, for making public the taped contents of a confidential phone call, and for paying for sex with an underage girl, he attempted a political comeback. Shamelessly pandering to populist sentiment, Berlusconi promised that if his party won he would eliminate the home ownership tax earlier introduced by Mario Monti, the technocrat appointed to lead Italy out of its economic crisis. He even promised to refund the tax levied the previous year, if necessary going into his personal fortune to do so. International economists widely predict that such measures would send the already teetering Italian economy into recession and would damage the entire Euro zone economy. Nevertheless, his party finished a strong second, throwing the Italian political system into a state of disarray with no clear winner. Once again, Berlusconi's narcissism triumphed over national interest.

Throughout his career, Berlusconi has adroitly managed to avoid being held accountable for his many extralegal excursions. But, in September 2013, a definitive criminal sentence for tax fraud, which is not subject to appeal, was rendered by the courts. Compounding his difficulties, the Italian senate responded by voting to have Berlusconi expelled from parliament, causing him to lose immunity from prosecution for other criminal cases in which he is involved. A less "exceptional" man might recognize this as a good time to quit, particularly at the age of 77, with a net worth of $6.2 billion.[39] But Berlusconi, the "exceptional exception," the unrelenting narcissist, is unlikely to accept defeat. In his mind, he may be down, but he is not out, and it would not be prudent to place a wager that he will finally be going to prison. Indeed, the sentence was reduced to community service, but the most important consequence of his conviction was that he was expelled from parliament.

Notes

1. Rachel Donadio and Elisabetta Povoledo, "Magnetic and Divisive, A Man Whose Politics Were Always Personal," *The New York Times*, November 13, 2011, accessed December 28, 2013, www.nytimes.com/2011/11/13/world/europe/berlusconi-both-drew-and-divided-italians.html?pagewanted=all&_r=0.
2. Paul Ginsborg, *Silvio Berlusconi: Television, Power, and Patrimony* (London: Verso, 2004).
3. Alexander Stille, *The Sack of Rome: How a Beautiful European Country with a Fabled History and a Storied Culture Was Taken Over by a Man Named Silvio Berlusconi* (New York: Penguin Press, 2006), 9–10.
4. Irvine Schiffer, *Charisma: A Psychoanalytic Look at Mass Society* (Toronto: University of Toronto Press, 1973).
5. Ginsborg, *Silvio Berlusconi: Television, Power, and Patrimony*.
6. "An Italian Story," *The Economist*. April 26, 2001.
7. Ginsborg, *Silvio Berlusconi*.
8. "The Secret of Silvio Berlusconi's Success," *BBC News Magazine*. November 12, 2011, www.bbc.co.uk/news/magazine-15629283.
9. "Silvio Berlusconi Resigns After Italian Parliament Approves Austerity Measures," *The Huffington Post*. November 12, 2011, www.huffingtonpost.co.uk/2011/11/12/silvio-berlusconi-resigns-after-italian-parliament-approves-austerity-measures_n_1090149.html.
10. Heinz Kohut, "Creativeness, Charisma, Group Psychology," in *Freud: The Fusion of Science and Humanism*, ed. John E. Gedo and George H. Pollock. Psychological Issues no. 34/35 (New York: International Universities Press, 1976), 379–425.
11. "In Quotes: Italy's Silvio Berlusconi in His Own Words," *BBC News Europe*, November 8, 2011, www.bbc.co.uk/news/world-europe-15642201.
12. Maurizio Viroli, *The Liberty of Servants: Berlusconi's Italy* (Princeton: Princeton University Press, 2012), 11.
13. Phil Stewart, "Italy's Berlusconi Wins Immunity from Prosecution," *Reuters*, July 22, 2008, www.reuters.com/article/2008/07/22/us-italy-immunity-idUSL2221007200 80722.
14. "Berlusconi: The Power of Personality," *BBC News World Europe*, May 14, 2001, http://news.bbc.co.uk/2/hi/europe/1298864.stm.
15. "In Quotes: Italy's Silvio Berlusconi in His Own Words."
16. *The Prime Minister and the Press*, first broadcast August 12, 2003 by PBS. Written and directed by Andrea Cairola and Susan Gray.
17. Dany Mitzman, "Italy Wrestles with Berlusconi Legacy," *BBC News Europe*. January 12, 2012, www.bbc.co.uk/news/world-europe-16518599.
18. Rachel Donadio and Elisabetta Povoledo, "European Debt Crisis as Berlusconi's Last Stand," *The New York Times*, November 8, 2011, www.nytimes.com/2011/11/09/world/europe/support-for-berlusconi-ebbs-before-crucial-vote.html?pagewanted=all.
19. Anthony Faiola, "Debt Finally Does in Italian Premier," *The Washington Post*, November 12, 2011.
20. Ariel Levy, "Basta Bunga Bunga: Have Italians Had Enough of Silvio Berlusconi – and the Culture He Embodies?," *The New Yorker*, June 6, 2011, www.newyorker.com/reporting/2011/06/06/110606fa_fact_levy.
21. "In Quotes: Italy's Silvio Berlusconi in His Own Words."

22. Alexander Stille, *The Sack of Rome*.
23. "An Italian Story," *The Economist*, April 26, 2001.
24. Cairola and Gray, *The Prime Minister and the Press*.
25. "In Quotes: Berlusconi in His Own Words," *BBC News*, May 2, 2006 http://news .bbc.co.uk/2/hi/3041288.stm.
26. "The Economist Wins Berlusconi Lawsuit," *The Economist*, September 5, 2008, www.economist.com/node/12076765.
27. Levy, "Busta Bunga Bunga."
28. Mitzman, "Italy Wrestles with Berlusconi Legacy."
29. Ginsborg, *Silvio Berlusconi*.
30. Courtney Subramanian, "Top 10 Worst Silvio Berlusconi Gaffes," *TIME*, December 8, 2011, www.time.com/time/specials/packages/article/0,28804,1874098_1874099_2098984,00.html.
31. Ginsborg, *Silvio Berlusconi*, 29.
32. "Berlusconi's Wife to Divorce Him," *BBC News Europe*, May 3, 2009, http://news .bbc.co.uk/2/hi/8031520.stm.
33. "Silvio Berlusconi Under Pressure: A Comedy That Has Gone on Too Long," *The Economist*, November 4, 2010, www.economist.com/node/17416756.
34. Frank Bruni, "The Agony and the Bunga Bunga," *The New York Times*, September 12, 2011a, www.nytimes.com/2011/09/13/opinion/bruni-the-agony-and-the-bunga-bun ga.html.
35. Subramanian, "The Top 10 Worst Silvio Berlusconi Gaffes."
36. Frank Bruni, "The Affliction of Comfort," *The New York Times*, September 18, 2011b, www.nytimes.com/2011/09/18/opinion/sunday/bruni-in-italy-and-america- the-affliction-of-comfort.html.
37. Levy, "Busta Bunga Bunga."
38. Ginsborg, *Silvio Berlusconi*.
39. "Silvio Berlusconi & Family," *Forbes*, March 2013, www.forbes.com/profile/silvio- berlusconi/.

10

Phallic Narcissism in the Governor's Mansion

Kristen Moody, Psy.D. and Jerrold M. Post, M.D.

It was Wilhelm Reich, initially a member of Freud's inner circle, who first conceptualized a particular form of narcissism that he called the *phallic narcissistic personality type*. These individuals are characterized by an excessively inflated self-image, are admiration seeking, self-promoting, and empowered by social success. Because a large identifying factor for this type of narcissist concerns athletic prowess and body image, it is more common to see this type of narcissism manifest in men. The characteristic traits of exhibitionism, bold recklessness, and confident arrogance are, in concert, often quite impressive. These persons also can be very effective in their manipulative behavior.[1] Individuals with this character type are generally looked on as desirable sexual objects because they reveal all the marks of obvious masculinity in their appearance and in their exaggerated hypersexuality. But their sexual prowess is not in the service of love but rather of exhibitionism, aggression, and revenge.[a]

In their everyday life, these are individuals are experienced as completely aggressive by others, and they often achieve leading positions in life where they can dominate those beneath them.[2] If their vanity is offended, they react with cold disdain, ill-humor, or aggressive acts. Their narcissism is expressed in a blatantly self-confident way, with a flagrant display of superiority and dignity.

---

[a] "The phallic narcissist is characterized not only by phallic pride, but by an erotization of the entire body. Along with pride in the real or fantasized physical form and abilities, there is a strong aggression. They are never passive and submissive, for, indeed, this is what they are defending against. Rather, they are haughty, cold, and superior in their demeanour. Thus, the phallic-narcissist character comes across as self-assured and tends to be impressive in his bearing. The greater the underlying insecurity, the more obtrusive these behaviours are, and the more blatantly they are paraded. Everyday behaviour usually shows some type of arrogance, either coldly reserved or contemptuously aggressive. Narcissistic arrogance, a haughty superiority, is characteristic of the surface posture toward women, but it overlays insecurity and a wish to be found attractive. The phallic-narcissist's relationships are always infused with sadistic characteristics and are disturbed by a typical derogatory attitude toward the female sex" (Reich, 1972).

There is no psychological inhibition against openly aggressive and sadistic behavior, in contrast to other character types, because the aggressive behavior itself serves a function of defense. Because the aggression is relatively uninhibited, albeit exaggerated, social activities in which the individual is on display are strong, energetic, to the point, and usually productive, although at times impulsive.[3]

ARNOLD SCHWARZENEGGER, EXEMPLAR OF THE PHALLIC NARCISSIST

Recently, Arnold Schwarzenegger and his longtime wife, Maria Kennedy Shriver separated, after it was discovered that he fathered a son with his housekeeper and assistant of 20 years. Birth records indicated that Schwarzenegger's son Christopher and his newly revealed child were born less than a week apart.[4] Throughout the years, it had been reported that Schwarzenegger was a womanizer and had frequent affairs, something that both Shriver and he actively denied. His aggressive and often extravagant acts, as well as the many quoted derogatory comments he made about women, highlight the phallic narcissistic type that Schwarzenegger seems to embody, literally.

BACKGROUND

Arnold Schwarzenegger was born to an attention-loving and strict disciplinarian father who served as a policeman and master sergeant in World War II and a traditional, arguably subservient mother who followed every rule that her husband enforced. His father, by all accounts, was an alcoholic prone to burst of violent temper that he would take out on his wife and children.[5]

In an interview with *Fortune* magazine in 2004, Schwarzenegger told how he suffered from abuse in his childhood:

My hair was pulled. I was hit with belts. So was the kid next door. It was just the way it was. Many of the children I've seen were broken by their parents, which was the German-Austrian mentality. They didn't want to create an individual. It was all about conforming. I was one who did not conform, and whose will could not be broken.[6]

Arnold did not endure only physical violence from his father, but also emotional hardships as well, being compared unfavorably to his older brother, Meinard. Meinard was said to be the healthy, sturdy, and favorite son of his father who encouraged his behavior and forced his sons into contests claiming "Let's see who's the best at . . ." Inevitably, Meinard would win. Furthermore, it appears that fun was not deeply encouraged in the household, and, after every family outing, the disciplinarian father would require his sons to go home and write reports on what they had just experienced.[7]

The constant pressure from both his parents and the sibling rivalry with his brother shaped young Schwarzenegger to pursue activities that would assert strength and power. He and his brother bullied younger children, with Meinard eventually being expelled from school and sent to reform school. His father, however, never punished his boys for the terror they inflicted on the other children in town and, in many ways, encouraged their behavior. As one towns-person stated in an interview "That is why the Schwarzenegger's were hated in Thal. Today everyone loves them, but forty years ago, no one wanted anything to do with them."[8] Schwarzenegger began to develop a rich fantasy life, perhaps as a form of escape from his father's oppressive standards. He loved the larger-than-life comic book muscleman hero "Sieguard," who in many ways exempli-fied the strength and admiration that he so desperately craved. As he grew, his tastes for heroes progressed to the theater, where he would sneak in and watch stars like John Wayne, champion swimmer Johnny Weissmuller as Tarzan, and Hercules films that starred Steve Reeve and South African bodybuilding star Reg Park. It was Park who became an idealized figure for Schwarzenegger: "Everything I dream of was embodied in Reg Park. I responded immediately to his rough, massive look."[9]

Largely ignored by his family during his childhood, Schwarzenegger made great efforts to prove himself in their eyes and to his most important audience, himself:

Becoming a winner supplied me with something I had been craving. I'm not sure why I had this need for special attention. Perhaps it was because I had an older brother who'd received more than his share of attention from our father.[10]

Although showing some insight into his injured self-esteem from his childhood, there were still many instances when Schwarzenegger would exhibitionistically show just how much attention and approval he needed from others. One such example from his bodybuilding days was when he cut the legs off of all his pants and appeared in public to receive stares from others for the disproportionate size of his lower limbs compared to the rest of his body. Schwarzenegger used this as motivation to work harder to develop his leg muscles, and he claimed that bodybuilding was "not narcissistic [!] because you are doing it to check progress. For me, it's about taking up space and domain."[11]

This provides an interesting insight into how Schwarzenegger's view of himself evolved. Even after his bodybuilding days, a time during which he admitted to using anabolic steroids to increase his performance and appearance, Schwarzenegger continued to place great importance on his physical activity and capacity to exercise, perhaps to the detriment of the rest of his health. (Schwarzenegger was born with a bicuspid aortic valve, which had one less leaflet than normal. He opted in 1997 for replacement heart valve surgery, using his own transplanted tissue instead of a mechanical valve – the only permanent solution available – because it would have sharply limited his capacity to exercise.)

Schwarzenegger would continue to place great importance on how others viewed him. When he visited Washington, D.C., for a governor's meeting, he alone had a separate room in the White House where he could get his hair and makeup done before meeting with the president. Clearly, his ability to do so and maintain an appearance as a strong man was important for his own sense of worth.

In an interview, Schwarzenegger said that, as a bodybuilder, "I didn't think about money. I thought about fame, about just being the greatest. I was dreaming about being some dictator of a country *or some savior like Jesus*. Just to be recognized" (emphasis added).[12] This attitude branched out not only into how he hoped the world would view him, but how he viewed relationships as well. In his autobiography, Schwarzenegger stated:

I used to feel that women were here for one reason. Sex was simply another kind of exercise, another body function. I didn't have time to take one girl out regularly and go through a normal high-school romance with all its phone calls and notes and squabbles. That took too much time. I needed to be in the gym. For me it was a simple matter of picking them up at the lake, and then never seeing them again.[13]

Promiscuous womanizing was present throughout his career as a politician. Much of his youth was spent talking about his conquests as a source of pride, and this was even the way in which he and his father would bond:

He was proud I was dating the fast girls. He bragged about them to his friends. "Jesus Christ, you should see some of the women my son's coming up with." He was showing off, of course. But still, our whole relationship had changed because I'd established myself by winning a few trophies and now had some girls. He liked the idea that I didn't get involved. "That's right, Arnold," he'd say, as though he'd had endless experience, "never be fooled by them." That continued to be an avenue of communication between us for a couple of years.[14]

His bodybuilding appeared to be a means of showing his father just how powerful he could be, and his womanizing was a way in which to form an ever closer connection with a man who had so actively ignored him throughout his life. Of course, there is an element of adolescent masculinity in wanting to assert oneself and conquer attractive women, but Schwarzenegger appears to have taken it to an extreme. In an interview with *Oui* magazine, Schwarzenegger discussed the group sex he engaged in at Gold's Gym at Venice Beach and his use of women to relieve stress before big competitions.[15] These quotes, reflecting a disparaging view toward women, were used against him politically.

In 1961, when Arnold was just 14 years old, he got the chance to meet Kurt Marnul, a fitness expert and bodybuilder who later went on to become Mr. Austria. A few years earlier, Marnul had created the Athletic Union Graz for Austria's bodybuilding elite to train. This life appealed a great deal to the tall and thin Schwarzenegger, who was envious of Marnul's ladies' man status. On the very first day of his training, Marnul recalls Schwarzenegger saying, "I will be Mr. Universe."[16]

It was during this period in his life that Schwarzenegger was introduced to anabolic steroids and began using them on a regular basis to increase his performance in training. His close friendships included those of his fellow body-builders, including Karl Gerstl, a medical student who, despite a 13-year age difference, felt an immediate connection with Arnold. It was Gerstl who taught Schwarzenegger about human anatomy and its connection to bodybuilding, as well as psychology and the importance of a positive mental state. Arnold stated that each of his bodybuilding friends "became a father image to me. I listened less to my own father."[17]

To understand Schwarzenegger as a politician, one must first consider the importance he placed on his bodybuilding and acting careers and how all the elements of his life became intertwined in his own political pursuits.

Two months after his 18th birthday, Schwarzenegger entered the army to complete his compulsory service. While his father had pulled strings to get him a position as a tank driver, Schwarzenegger lost this role after going AWOL one evening to compete in – and win – the junior Mr. Europe bodybuilding contest in Stuttgart, Germany. Although he was caught on his entry back to the base and thrown in the stockade, his commanding officer was so impressed with the win and what it could mean for the Austrian Army that Schwarzenegger was ordered to focus purely on his bodybuilding for the rest of his service.[18]

After completing his service, Schwarzenegger, who felt that Austria was too "small" for him, left for Munich to begin his "Master Plan" (an interesting term to use). The plan for Schwarzenegger was to go to America; become the greatest bodybuilder who ever lived; educate himself with necessary skills for achieving his goals; learn to speak English; make a lot of money; invest his money in real estate; work in the movies as an actor, producer, and director; become a million-aire; get rid of anything from his old life that stood in his way; get invited to the White House; marry a glamorous and intelligent woman; and become involved with politics.[19] It was as if these were all boxes to be checked off, and, in a single-minded way, he managed to check them all off – and then some.

This is really quite remarkable for a young man in his early 20s, to plan a life strategy and then systematically carry it out, so much so that it is worth repeating. Go to America, CHECK, become the greatest bodybuilder ever, CHECK, become famous and wealthy through his work in the movies, CHECK, get invited to the White House, CHECK, marry a glamorous and intelligent woman, CHECK, and enter politics, CHECK.

As Schwarzenegger won award after award for his bodybuilding competitions, eventually winning the coveted Mr. Universe title in 1967, he was also starting his acting career. In 1969, under the name Arnold Strong, Schwarzenegger starred in a movie called *Hercules in New York*. A couple of years later, Schwarzenegger won a Golden Globe for Best Acting Debut in a Motion Picture for his role in *Pumping Iron*. For the majority of the next 30 years, Schwarzenegger would become a Hollywood name for his roles in action-packed movies, including *The Terminator*. His comments during these films provide interesting insight into his pursuits: "I like the Terminator, I'd like to be as resolved as he was and have that kind of power,"[20] and "I've wished I could clone myself because there are so many ambitions and so many goals in my life, and there is not enough time to do all those things."[21]

Accounts from individuals who met Schwarzenegger early in his career indicate that he was always looking ahead to a future in politics. Reg Park, his boyhood ideal, invited Schwarzenegger to come and stay at his South African house after his Mr. Universe win. Even then, claims Park, Schwarzenegger spoke about his own interest in pursuing a political career. He studied previous videotapes of his interviews before each new interview, always trying to become better and avoid embarrassing remarks, many of which would paint him as a hyper-masculine sexist with little respect for women during his campaign.[22] He bought all the rights to the *Pumping Iron* outtakes, including anything that might be embarrassing or reflect on him negatively. While his methodical and careful manner of handling his life did not always work to his advantage, his training in acting and appeal to a wider audience in his movies served him well during his future pitches and campaigns. He always went for shock value in promoting his values, at one time even trying to have his name painted on the side of a NASA rocket.[23]

Schwarzenegger, who was deeply scarred by feelings of shame and weakness from his childhood, idealized powerful men and eventually strove to make himself a handsome and powerful male himself. In pursing this erotic masculine image, he was essentially reacting against and overcompensating for the weak and shameful self-image he carried from his childhood.

Several individuals came to serve as mentors and idols in his early political career. In the summer of 1977, while doing a New York charity tennis tournament honoring the late Robert F. Kennedy, Schwarzenegger met Kennedy's niece, Maria Shriver. She was an ideal fit for his "master plan." That same day, Maria invited him back to their Cape Cod residence where Arnold became fast friends with both Eunice and Sergeant Shriver. Although their politics were quite different, Schwarzenegger had an extremely close relationship with the Shriver family, taking advice and forming bonds that would only prove to further him in his political career. Sergeant Shriver jokingly referred to Schwarzenegger as "the sponge" for his unwavering pursuit of information on how to set programs up, get people together, and initiate change.

Arnold and Maria married in 1986, on a spring weekend in Cape Cod. In many ways, it was a pairing of opposites. Her uncle was a U.S. president; his father was an Austrian policeman. She was part of an American political dynasty and a pillar in the nation's Democratic establishment; he was a Republican. Their marriage was not without its tensions.

Schwarzenegger's "break" into politics occurred just before the 1988 U.S. presidential election, when he flew to Columbus, Ohio, and was introduced to Vice President George H. W. Bush by longtime friend, Jim Lorimer. This weekend proved to be crucial in his own political future because he introduced Bush at a rally stating "I only play the Terminator in my movies, but when it comes to America's future, Michael Dukakis will be the real Terminator."[24] Impressed by his speech and ability to rally the crowd (although slightly disappointed at the crowd dispersing after Schwarzenegger's speech), Bush asked him to accompany him to other campaign stops.

It was this connection to President George H. W. Bush that provided Schwarzenegger with an "in" to politics. Schwarzenegger would lobby for the chairman position on the President's Council on Physical Fitness and Sports, sending a congratulatory telegram to the president and meeting with Jim Pinkerton, an aide running Bush's domestic policy operation and a man who would ultimately endorse Schwarzenegger as the man for the job. Further, Eunice Shriver wrote President Bush and suggested that her son-in-law would be perfect for the job.[25] Although there was some internal debate about his past steroid use and violence in movies, he was ultimately appointed to the position in 1990.

Schwarzenegger scored his first political success on November 5, 2002, when Californian's approved his personally crafted and sponsored Proposition 49, the "After School Education and Safety Program Act of 2002," which made state grants available for after-school programs. This was a huge win for Schwarzenegger who would continue fighting for educational reform and funding in the years to come. After Gray Davis's narrow win in the 2002 gubernatorial election in California, there was already a stirring for a recall. Davis was not keeping up his end of his promises, and it was Bill Thomas, who chaired the House Ways and Means Committee on Capitol Hill, who pulled Schwarzenegger aside during a visit to D.C. and made it clear that the recall election was a once-in-a-lifetime opportunity. Thomas laid out a plan, explaining that the shorter campaign would cost half as much as it would for a primary and general election, which Schwarzenegger would have no guarantee of making it through. If he could raise the money for the recall, Thomas stated, Schwarzenegger would "own the movement and have first claim to governorship if Davis was removed."[26]

Thomas was not the only person urging Schwarzenegger to pursue the office. George Gorton, his political consultant hired in 2000, pushed for Schwarzenegger to take the office, as did former Governor Pete White and other political advisors. Schwarzenegger was very careful to keep his consultants in the dark; in fact, up until he actually announced his bid on the *Tonight Show* in August 2003, his consultants were ready to hand over a statement to the press that he would not be running. Gorton later recalled that "(Schwarzenegger) was always full of mystery and misdirection when it came to big decisions."[27]

It was said that Maria was initially upset about her husband's plan to run for governor in California. But when Schwarzenegger announced his decision on *The Tonight Show with Jay Leno* in August 2003, he said his wife stood by his decision.

Schwarzenegger used catch phrases and lines from his movies to launch one of the strangest and most effective political campaigns in U.S. history. He was going to "terminate" bad politics and politicians. He was going to say "hasta la vista" to his detractors. This would be the "total recall" of California's bad politics. It was no wonder he was quickly dubbed with the nickname "The Governator," but the theatrics of his personality and the already dramatic circumstances surrounding the recall election did nothing but help his cause. As one reporter stated, in tying the timing of *Terminator 3*'s release to the time of the election "Schwarzenegger's political experience is exactly zero ... but as an incarnation of his on-screen presence, he is unbeatable."[28]

Schwarzenegger easily won, with 49 percent of the vote in California, and he was sworn in on November 17, 2003. He used more references from his past career in his acceptance speeches, stating "What I learned from bodybuilding is that we are always stronger than we know. California is like that, too. We are stronger than we know. There's a massive weight we must lift off our state. Alone, I cannot lift it. But together we can."[29] During his first year in office, he issued an executive order rescinding the increase in the unpopular car tax, signed orders halting the hiring of new state employees and the signing of any new state contracts, repealed a law giving drivers licenses to illegal immigrants, and developed a plan to borrow $15 million to deal with the state's deficit. He enjoyed popularity with both Republicans and Democrats for his own moderate stance on many issues and his work toward implementing his campaign promises.

After Schwarzenegger took office, despite her earlier reservations, Maria left her job as an NBC News correspondent and became the quintessential political wife. As the state's first lady, Shriver ran an annual women's conference that attracted a long list of business, political, and entertainment elite. Shriver also took care of the couple's four children. When accusations of his womanizing surfaced in 2003, she defended her husband and stated that "I look at him with an open heart and I accept him with all his strengths and all his weaknesses, as he does me."[5]

Much like his earlier announcement for his campaign, Schwarzenegger made no firm commitment for the 2006 reelection campaign, often evading the question or responding ambiguously. His decision to call the 2005 special election, in which voters rejected all four of his ballot propositions, as well as his propositions dealing with teachers and nurses unions, along with other political missteps, brought his approval rating down to 39 percent in April 2006.[30] He had come under heavy criticism for his "cash register politics," and he was under fire from some conservatives for supporting several taxes on Californians and from some liberals for refusing to sign a bill allowing gay marriage. Later, Schwarzenegger's aggressive push for environmentally friendly legislation, his support for stem cell research and gay rights, and his opposition to sending the National Guard to the border made him more popular with both Republicans and Democrats and secured his reelection by a wide margin.[31]

Schwarzenegger undoubtedly chose a partner who symbolized the nation that he so desperately wanted to be a part of. As a Kennedy, Maria embodied power and progress, something that would attract a man who was so adamant in coveting positions and titles to cover up his own feelings of insecurity by being viewed as powerful and unstoppable. In a commencement speech at the University of Southern California, Schwarzenegger alluded to the powerful influence Shriver had on his life. When people asked him the secret to success, he said, "I say, number one, come to America. Number two, work your butt off. And number three, marry a Kennedy."[32]

It was his womanizing that eventually led to the break-up of the 24-year marriage, when reports of an illegitimate child with the Schwarzeneggers' long-time housekeeper became public knowledge. The woman, identified as Mildred Patricia Baena, was employed in the Schwarzenegger-Shriver household in 1991. It is unclear when the affair between Mildred and Arnold began, but they were most certainly engaging in extramarital activities in 1997, when she became pregnant with his child. Shriver gave birth to the couple's fourth son just five days prior to Baena's child being born. Schwarzenegger's "love-child" had an uncanny resemblance to his father, which fueled the aggressive investigative reporting that ultimately led to the admission by Schwarzenegger that he was the father. With the admission of this long-standing adulterous relationship to his wife and publicly, their 24-year marriage ended.

All of the boxes in his master plan had been checked, but for the narcissistic Schwarzenegger, it was not enough. Was this "merely" an expression of the exploitative attitude toward women that had been formed in his adolescence, an expression of narcissistic entitlement, or were there additional elements of being "wrecked by success," of the underlying narcissistic wounds that impelled him to act in this self-destructive fashion? What a sad ending to what had been a remarkable success story.

Maria Shriver assuredly played a major role in his political success, helping him convincingly to adopt progressive policies that appealed to Democrats and Republicans alike and securing his reelection as governor. Shriver can be seen as a positive *selfobject*, shoring up his self-esteem, helping him appeal to both sides of the political aisle, and significantly contributing to his accomplishments as governor. In fact, she was responsible for the last three boxes on his career master plan: get invited to the White House, marry a glamorous and intelligent woman, and enter politics. Given his narcissistic need for the spotlight and attention, it should come as little surprise that, just over a year following the admission of an affair with his former housekeeper, Schwarzenegger released an autobiography: *Total Recall: My Unbelievably True Life Story.* Unbelievable? Not really. Schwarzenegger outlines many of his childhood, army, and body-building stories already discussed earlier in this chapter. He highlights a secrecy and game-playing strategy that was ever present throughout his life, even discussing how he only told his wife of his planned run for the governor's office hours before making it public on national television. He admits to other affairs in which he cheated on Shriver, including a semipublic one with co-star Brigitte Nielsen from *Red Sonja.* Also unsurprising is the way that Schwarzenegger talks about these affairs with a type of emotional disconnection that we could expect from a narcissist. In fact, *60 Minutes* interviewer Lesley Stahl pointed out his apparent coldness on the subject, stating "You cheated on Maria, and you don't even write that you felt bad about it. You just write it." Schwarzenegger responded: "Actually, you know, I did feel bad about it. But all of my different things, they were mistakes and you know my failure, my screw-ups." He further went on to recreate a conversation he had with his ex-wife in couple's therapy: "You're the perfect wife. It's not because anything is wrong, or you left home for a week, or any of that. Forget that. You look fantastic, you're sexy, I'm turned on by you today as much as I was on the first date."[33]

It's interesting that Schwarzenegger chose to focus on his wife's physical appearance in therapy. It's as though he was projecting his own insecurity, his own phallic narcissism and concern for body, onto her. By putting himself in her shoes, he concluded that she would be concerned that his straying from the marriage had something to do with her appearance. Furthermore, his comments emphasize his unwillingness to take responsibility for doing something wrong, something that would truly highlight him as something less than perfect. Even when discussing mistakes or failures, Schwarzenegger appears to do it with an air of authority, as if disconnecting himself from his actions.

The release of the book, the admission of numerous affairs, and many public interviews all beg a single question: Why, after adamantly refusing to talk to the media during the past year in order to protect his family's privacy, does Schwarzenegger decide to tell all in many different public forums? The answer is a simple one: self-promotion. Ever the man to put on a show to sell himself, Schwarzenegger timed the release of his book to promote his upcoming movies. The release of his book provided just another example of Schwarzenegger displaying a single-minded approach to pursuing his own course of action with little consideration for how it would affect his wife and family.

Especially for the consummate narcissist like Schwarzenegger, whose physical strength and attractiveness was a mark of pride and a constant preoccupation, moving into the late-life transition can be particularly threatening. In the next chapter, the impact of age and illness on narcissistic leaders is explored.

Notes

1. Donald Capps, *The Depleted Self: Sin in a Narcissistic Age* (Minneapolis: Fortress Press, 1992).
2. Reich, *Character Analysis.*
3. Wilhelm Reich, *Character Analysis.*
4. Luchina Fisher, David Wright, and Kevin Dolak, "Mother of Arnold Schwarzenegger's Love Child Revealed," *ABC News*, May 18, 2011, http://abc news.go.com/US/mother-arnold-schwarzeneggers-love-child-revealed/story?id=13 626896.
5. Wendy Leigh, *Arnold: An Unauthorized Biography* (New York: Congdon & Weed, 1990).

6. Betsy Morris et al., "Arnold: Power He Accumulates It. He Wields It. He Wins Over Voters with It. But Is the Governator's Star Power Enough to Win the War of Wills with His California Opponents?" *Fortune Magazine*, August 2004, accessed October 23, 2010, http://money.cnn.com/magazines/fortune/fortune_archive/2004/08/09/37 7908/index.htm.

7. Louise Krasniewicz and Michael Blitz, *Arnold Schwarzenegger: A Biography* (London: Greenwood Press, 2006); Leigh, *Arnold*.

8. George Butler, *Arnold Schwarzenegger: A Portrait* (New York: Simon & Schuster, 1990).

9. Rick Wayne, "Reg Park ... a Hero's Hero," *Muscle Builder/Power*, August/ September 1976.

10. Krasniewicz and Blitz, *Arnold Schwarzenegger*.

11. Ibid.

12. "The Hero of Perfected Mass," *Rolling Stone Archive*, June 1976, accessed November 7, 2010, www.rollingstone.com.

13. Arnold Schwarzenegger, *Arnold: The Education of A Bodybuilder* (New York: Simon & Shuster, 1977).

14. Schwarzenegger, *Arnold*.

15. Peter Manso, "Arnold Schwarzenegger: The Man with the World's Most Perfectly Developed Physique Destroys a Few Myths about Body Building; He Smokes Dope, Stays Out Late and Forgets to Take His Vitamins," *Oui Magazine*, 1977, accessed December 18, 2009. http://daggy.name/cop/effluvia/arnold.htm.

16. Butler, *Arnold Schwarzenegger*.

17. Schwarzenegger, *Arnold*.

18. Joe Mathews, *The People's Machine* (New York: Public Affairs, 2006).

19. Butler, *Arnold Schwarzenegger*.

20. K. W. Woods, *Schwarzenegger: Muscleman to Terminator (An Unauthorized Biography)* (Lincolnwood, IL: Publications International, 1991).

21. Jeff O'Connell, "End of Days," *Muscle & Fitness*, January 2000, accessed November 9, 2010, www.highbeam.com/doc/1P3-46630579.html.

22. Mathews, *The People's Machine*.

23. Ibid.

24. Maureen Dowd, "Bush, Taking Rival's Line, Says 'Labels' Don't Matter," *The New York Times*, November 4, 1988, www.nytimes.com/1988/11/04/us/bush-taking-rival-s-line-says-labels-don-t-matter.html?sec=&spon=&pagewanted=all.

25. Mathews, *The People's Machine*.

26. Ibid.

27. Ibid.

28. Oren Rawls, "In Other Words ...," *The Forward*, August 15, 2003, http://forward .com/articles/7892/in-other-words-/.

29. "Schwarzenegger's Inauguration Speech," *CNN.com*, November 17, 2003, accessed November 7, 2010, http://edition.cnn.com/2003/ALLPOLITICS/11/17/ arnold.speech/.

30. "Schwarzenegger Approval Rating: 39 Percent," *The Orange County Register*, April 13, 2006, www.ocregister.com/news/approval-188913-schwarzenegger-rat ing.html.; Evan Halper, "Schwarzenegger Approval Rating Hits New Low," posted on December 16, 2009, LA Times Blogs, retrieved November 12, 2010,

http://latimesblogs.latimes.com/lanow/2009/12/schwarzenegger-approval-rating-hits-new-low.html.

31. Mathews, *The People's Machine.*

32. The Oprah Winfrey Show, "Project Vote Smart," September 15, 2003, http://vote smart.org/public-statement/21364/the-oprahwinfrey-showbno#.UrJRKShjNL4.

33. Lesley Stahl, "Arnold Schwarzenegger: Success and Secrets," *CBSNews*, September 30, 2012, www.cbsnews.com/8301-18560_162-57523140/arnold-schwarzenegger-success-and-secrets/.

I I

The Impact of Illness and Age on Narcissistic Leaders

Though he has watched a decent age go by,
A man will sometimes still desire the world.

– Sophocles, *Oedipus at Colonus*

THE IMPACT OF THE END OF LIFE ON THE NARCISSIST

Dreams of glory never die. They don't even fade away. And as the time horizons increasingly shrink with the ebbing of the years, there is often an increased urgency for the narcissistic leader to accomplish his goals. The consummate narcissist does not mellow with age. Nor does the consummate narcissist accept with equanimity fatal illness, which instead can serve as a spur to his ambitions.

MAO ZEDONG: RACING HEEDLESSLY TO ACCOMPLISH HIS GOALS

Thus, for Mao Zedong, the reckless pace of both the Great Leap Forward and the Cultural Revolution, which had such destructive consequences for his country, may well have been a consequence of his facing the end of his years with his revolution not yet consolidated. Mao was surely designated for a place of honor in the pantheon of history-changing charismatic leaders, but for the consummate narcissist, there is never enough. He was seriously ill, aware that there was little time left to fully accomplish his goals. Indeed, many China analysts have argued that his program to achieve a balance among the sources of power in the Peoples Republic – the military, the party, and the bureaucracy – was necessary but would require decades to accomplish, and Mao knew his time was short.

This chapter draws upon Jerrold Post and Robert Robins (1993), *When Illness Strikes the Leader: The Dilemma of the Captive King*. New Haven: Yale University Press, 1993.

The problem was the pace with which he acted. It was as if he were trying to yank his stagnant country into the 20th century by an act of will in a matter of months, leading to serious disruptions and instability. He had superimposed his personal timetable on the nation's political timetable, and the terminal urgency was destructive in its consequences.

Yet, by his side was the wise and psychologically mature Premier Chou En-lai, seeking to moderate Mao's terminal excesses. Facing a painful death himself from carcinoma of the stomach, Chou, until the end, was the very model of balance and restraint. For him, what they had accomplished was enough, and he sought to consolidate the remarkable achievements of the Peoples Republic, rather than reach ever higher in a quest for greater glory.

THE SHAH OF IRAN: TERMINAL URGENCY

In *Majestic Failure: The Fall of the Shah*, Zonis[1] persuasively describes the narcissistic personality and psychological dynamics of the Shah of Iran, emphasizing how insecure the Shah was under his arrogant, imperious façade. Reflecting his narcissism, the Shah's rather grand title was His Imperial Majesty, Shahanshah (King of Kings, Emperor), Aryamehr (Light of the Aryans), and Bozorg Arteshtārān (Head of the Warriors).

From childhood on, his father made clear to his son Mohammad Reza Pahlavi his contempt for him and how much he would have preferred his twin sister as successor to the Peacock Throne. But the Shah developed compensatory dreams of glory, and, in his 1961 book, *Mission for My Country*,[2] Mohammad Reza Pahlavi spelled out what came to be known as the White Revolution, an ambitious plan relying on science and technology, while diminishing religious authority, to make Iran a leading modern nation, a beacon of progress in the Persian Gulf. It would be a revolution from the top down, one that would require major changes in Iran's feudal structure. It was a plan that, with steady, patient application, would require decades to accomplish.

For Mohammad Reza Pahlavi to accomplish this would indeed be redemptive. In his early 40s, the Shah assumed that he would live into his 70s or 80s, with two, three, or even four decades to shepherd his country's advance into the 20th century. But, as fate would have it, he did not have decades. In the fall of 1973, his 54th year, Mohammad Reza Pahlavi became ill, suffering abdominal pain and swelling, weight loss, and showing a sallow complexion. He declined alcoholic beverages, claiming "dyspepsia." His Iranian physicians examined him and found a massively swollen liver. They were alarmed and called in French physician specialists to examine him; these experts found that he was suffering from a slow-growing disorder of the lymphatic system, Waldenström's macroglobulinemia. While the news of the Shah's serious illness was not made public until 1974, it was in 1973, according to an article in the *Washington Post* by Cohn and Okie,[3] that the Shah was first informed by his French physicians of this rare form of cancer of the lymph glands that ultimately would claim his life.

His French physicians informed the occupant of the Peacock Throne that he was stricken by a rare disease that would ultimately prove fatal. It was unlikely that he would live as long as 10 years. Clearly, his patient plan for his country's development could not be accomplished in his lifetime.

1973, the year he first became ill, was the year that the Shah broke with the Organization of Petroleum Exporting Countries (OPEC), which had imposed an oil embargo on Western markets. Mohammad Reza Pahlavi accepted no production limits, but indicated that he would sell all the oil he could at the new price, thus quadrupling oil prices and leading to a vast infusion of money pouring into Iran, which did not have the infrastructure to absorb this. This led to a revolution of rising expectations, destabilizing the country, and paving the way for Ayatollah Khomeini's triumphant entrance and the Islamic revolution.

Although the Intelligence Community has been criticized for not predicting the Islamic revolution, in fact, the Ayatollah had been preaching his extremist sermons for years. What had changed was that the Shah was dying; he was fighting for his own survival while he was fighting for the survival of his country. It was widely assumed that the Shah would again be tough in dealing with the dissidents in his country, as he had been throughout his career. But Mohammad Reza Pahlavi had his eyes on the history books and did not wish to be remembered for terminal brutality. By superimposing his personal timetable on that of his nation, he was trying to hand a fully accomplished White Revolution to his teenage son, the Crown Prince. In his terminal urgency to achieve his dreams of glory for Iran, he instead created a nightmare for his country.

PRIME MINISTER MENACHEM BEGIN OF ISRAEL: TERMINAL STRENGTH

Throughout his career, Menachem Begin, inspired by the revisionist Zionist Ze'ev Jabotinsky, devoted his efforts to establishing a secure Jewish state in Israel, one coexisting in peace with its Arab neighbors. "Never again" was the clarion call of Begin, most of whose family had been killed in the Holocaust.

But his health was fragile, and each health reversal made it increasingly clear that he would not live to see his goals achieved. But if his goal of an Israel at peace could not be achieved in his lifetime, at least he could take steps to ensure a secure Jewish state. Two of his most dramatic – and provocative – moves were made from a hospital bed.

Begin suffered a minor myocardial infarction (heart attack) in June 1980. He became obsessed during his recuperation with making a dramatic move to signal to the world his commitment to the entire biblical land of Israel, including the West Bank, which he referred to as Judaea and Samaria. Despite his doctor's order that he rest, he held daily political meetings in his hospital room. He personally drafted a statement that was blessed by his inner circle and that was read to the press on July 6:[4]

It is the national consensus and the policy of the Government of Israel that Jerusalem, which has been reunited as a result of a successful legitimate self-defense, will remain forever united, forever indivisible, and forever the capital city of the State of Israel by virtue of right.

Coming as it did during an American presidential campaign, this provocative statement heightened tension with the United States, Israel's strongest and indispensable supporter. And it played to the Arab states, which were bent on maintaining hostilities with Israel. Emphasizing his commitment to this course, on leaving the hospital on July 14, he declared:

If the Arab countries recognize the State of Israel and Jerusalem as its capital, 20 Arab flags would fly in Jerusalem, the capital of Israel, which would be recognized by all the Arab countries.[5]

The next year, after a minor fall in his bathroom on July 26, 1981, he fractured his femur, a frequent affliction of the elderly, emphasizing further to Begin that his time was short. As he was recovering in the hospital from the surgical repair that was required, Begin again became preoccupied with Israel's security. He called a meeting of his security cabinet in his hospital room, and, while wearing his hospital robe, announced the extension of Israeli law to the Golan Heights, the equivalent of annexation.[6] The Golan Heights, which had been captured from Syria in the 1967 war, had long been a source of menace to Israel, with nightly rocket bombardments of the helpless settlements below in the northern Galilee. "Never again," vowed Begin, would Israel be exposed to that mortal danger. Once again, physical weakness had precipitated a politically "strong" response, an affirmation of Begin's lifelong creed, "I fight, therefore I am!" But politically, as with the annexation of East Jerusalem, his provocative annexation policy in the Golan Heights damaged Israel's standing in the West and his ability to deal with moderate Arab governments.

Psychologically, Begin's aim was to establish an identity with an eternally secure Israel. Weak physically, he was demonstrating his strength as a leader. If he could not fully achieve his dreams of glory, if he could not cross into the Promised Land, at least, like Moses, he would go to his death knowing that he had done everything he could to ensure a safe and secure Israel.

TERMINAL RELIGIOSITY: JAFAR NIMEIRI, PRESIDENT OF SUDAN

Deathbed religious conversion is a not uncommon personal reaction to a confrontation with mortal illness. When it is a chief of state who belatedly turns to the deity and makes his terminal religiosity the basis of national policy, however, it can have painful consequences for his country. Such was the case with Jafar Nimeiri of Sudan.

In 1969, after years of an ineffective democratic government, the 39-year-old Jafar Nimeiri led a group of military officers in a successful coup d'état and

assumed the leadership of Sudan. As with all successful coups, specific circumstances determined its success. In this case, it was also relevant that it occurred
on the eve of Nimeiri's 40th birthday. The press to action is a frequent reaction
to the midlife transition (ages 38–45); a disproportionate number of leaders
who assumed power by military coup took action during this period of psychological flux.

While Nimeiri portrayed himself as a lifelong devout Muslim in his 1978
revisionist history, *The Islamic Way: Why?*,[7] he was not particularly religious.
Nimeiri describes in the book how he and his colleagues prayed to Allah before
the coup, but, in fact, Nimeiri was a hard-drinking military man, and he and his
colleagues were intoxicated on the night of the coup. (The *shari'a*, the codified
Islamic law that governs the conduct of everyday life for devout Muslims,
specifically proscribes alcohol use.)

In his initial speech on assuming power, there was no sense of mission, no
mention of Allah, no description of Sudan as an Islamic republic. Rather, he
described the new regime as neither Eastern nor Western but a democratic
socialist regime working for Sudan's interests alone.

In the early years of his leadership, Nimeiri devoted his energies to dealing
with Sudan's long-standing social, economic, and political problems. He met
with considerable success and improved Sudan's position both domestically and
internationally. His greatest accomplishment was the Addis Ababa agreement of
1972, which put to an end to 17 years of civil war between the Islamic North and
the largely Coptic Christian South. This achievement alone would have assured
Nimeiri a prominent place in Sudan's history.

By exerting his influence against Islamic fundamentalists and clerics,
Nimeiri, espousing the belief that the South could remain culturally and religiously distinct, was able to craft a constitutional formulation that gave special
recognition and protection to the South's unique status within a unified Sudan.
Article 8 specified autonomy for the South, with its own governmental and
administrative structure, but most important were the guarantees of religious
freedom. Article 16 declared Islam as the religion of the Democratic Republic of
the Sudan, but it also recognized that a large number of citizens professed belief
in Christianity. The constitution guaranteed that "heavenly religions and the
noble aspects of spiritual beliefs shall not be abused or held in contempt."[8] It
expressly forbade:

the abuse of religious and noble spiritual beliefs for political exploitation ... The State
shall treat followers of religion and noble spiritual belief without discrimination and ...
shall not impose any restrictions on citizens or communities on the grounds of religious
faith.[9]

This remarkable document won widespread international plaudits for Nimeiri,
especially its emphasis on religious freedom not only for the Islamic majority in
the north but, importantly, also for the Coptic Christian minority in the south, a
remarkably farseeing feat for this army colonel.

Yet such discrimination and restrictions were exactly what occurred when Nimeiri became religiously obsessed in the face of mortal illness. His zeal to impose his own late-found religious beliefs upon his nation was precipitated by his personal illness. In the late 1970s, while still in his mid-40s, Nimeiri began to experience serious health problems. He experienced drowsiness and episodes of confusion, described as temporary dementia, and he collapsed on several public occasions. At first, his illness was undiagnosed, but ultimately, with the facilitation of the U.S. government, Nimeiri traveled to the United States and underwent a thorough medical evaluation at Walter Reed Army Medical Center in 1979.

The comprehensive medical evaluation revealed that Nimeiri's long-standing diabetes mellitus was under poor control and that he had developed widespread arteriosclerosis that was affecting circulation to both his heart and brain. In addition to involvement of the coronary arteries, an arteriosclerotic plaque had obstructed the internal carotid artery, which provided the main blood supply to the brain; this was determined to be the cause of his mental symptoms.

Nimeiri returned to Walter Reed in 1980 for a three-week checkup to treat his heart ailment and better regulate his diabetes. He returned later in 1980 for surgery to remove the clot obstructing the carotid artery. On returning from the 1980 procedure, he informed his aides that his maintenance medication sometimes affected his mental faculties and judgment. Early in 1981, he announced that he would retire in August 1982 because of illness. Nevertheless, by January 1982, he had reconsidered, claiming to be indispensable to Sudan's future, and declared himself "president for life."

When Nimeiri's health problems began in the mid-1970s, his local physicians strongly recommended that he stop his alcohol consumption, which they felt was contributing to his medical condition. At his evaluation at Walter Reed, where widespread arteriosclerosis affecting his heart and brain was diagnosed, as well as severe liver damage, he was told that unless he stopped drinking, he would be dead within six months. Nimeiri took this very seriously.

It was this siege of serious illness that prompted Nimeiri's turn to Islam. But Nimeiri was not content to apply his personal epiphany to himself alone. Not only did Nimeiri abstain, in accordance with Sharia law, but he also sent a circular entitled "Guided Leadership" to cabinet ministers and other senior officials instructing them to swear an oath to him that they would abstain from drinking. As he explained in *The Islamic Way: Why?*, the way of Allah was the way for all of Sudan, and if some did not see it that way, they would be shown it, and made to walk it. Islamic law began to be forced on all Sudanese, regardless of their religion and regardless of the constitution.

As Nimeiri's health declined, the manifestations of his public religiosity grew more intense as he violated the Addis Ababa accord, dividing his country and destroying the greatest achievement of his presidency. His leadership became increasingly personal and less institutional, and his Machiavellian manipulation of the factions within the system led to a progressive disintegration of the fragile unity he had achieved. At the same time, Nimeiri, a deeply superstitious man, fell under the sway of Sufi mystics and, to the dismay of his cabinet officials, began to rely on witch doctors to divine the future and guide his policies. One of the holy men gave him a ring and walking stick to assure him divine protection.

Nimeiri's speeches at times demonstrated paranoia and an obsession with powerlessness:

We realize that a capable and independent Sudan will always be a target of the ambitions and conspiracies of forces that mistakenly believe that they can subjugate our will, control our resources. Great peoples must pay a price whenever the ambition to dominate and control, infiltrate and encircle seeks to impose its will on us by conspiracy and subjugation ... We know that a big power is still continuing its conspiracy against Sudan and its revolution, against Sudan and its people ... Brothers, we know that a big power has not gotten over its rage against the people of Sudan who said "No" to any subjugation of their will.[10]

To compensate for his growing physical enfeeblement, he spoke of his total power, as if he were a law unto himself: "Beware, I am empowered by the Constitution to take any measures I deem necessary for the protection of the May revolution." Pointing to a guard, he said, "According to the Constitution, I can order this guard to shoot anybody and he would have to obey me."[11]

Nimeiri's assumption of religious leadership was not confined to the boundaries of Sudan. In August 1981, he sent open letters to both Assad of Syria and Qaddafi of Libya instructing them to leave Lebanon alone, to stop burning people, and enjoining them to side with Iraq in the Iran–Iraq War. They did not respond to his advice. When earthquakes struck Syria in December 1981, he sent a message to Assad explaining the natural disasters as divine punishment:

The news of the disaster which has afflicted Damascus has been conveyed to us. God gives reprieve but does not forget. What has happened in Damascus is the result of your disregard for God's law and your attempt to extinguish the fire of the Qu'ran and the Light of Islam. Justice is the only way for establishing peace and the first principle of justice which God has decreed is the sanctity of human life and the futility of manslaughter without good cause and genocide without just trials. All these are against Islamic law. God, our destiny is in your hands.[12]

Further demonstrating both his lack of international political sensitivity and his proselytizing zeal, during a trip to the Peoples Republic of China, he tried to convert the Chinese to Islam.

But although he was increasingly religious and enjoining the Sudanese officials to share his newfound piety, he had not yet strongly institutionalized Islamic practices into law, and many of his exhortations were greeted with a wink and a nod.

This was to change abruptly in 1983, the year Nimeiri again traveled to the United States for further surgery. Before the trip, he talked to his military commanders about funeral arrangements. This forcible encounter with his mortality led to a major escalation in the pace of the Islamization of Sudan.

In September 1983, without warning, he declared the Sharia, the legal code of Islam, which prescribes conduct for all aspects of life, the law of the land, including the largely Coptic Christian south. He had been warned that he must stop drinking, and now he was insisting that all of Sudan, including the Coptic Christian south, join him in abstinence. He introduced the Sharia dramatically by pouring millions of gallons of alcohol into the Nile. The Sharia was to be rigorously enforced, including flogging for possession of alcohol, hand amputation for theft, and the stoning to death of adulterous women. Previously, adultery had rarely been punished because the Sharia requires four witnesses to the adulterous event. Nimeiri, however, invented a new offense, "attempted adultery," which did not have the same witness stipulations.

He fell increasingly under the sway of his spiritual mentors and was increasingly isolated from his secular advisors. Nimeiri's rule became increasingly more idiosyncratic, and so certain was he of the righteousness of his way that he would not tolerate criticism. Indeed, those who criticized his policies found themselves not only out of a job but liable to imprisonment.

Nimeiri became preoccupied with his own spiritual role for his nation, and his speeches increasingly evidenced that he identified himself as the spiritual leader of his country, as its Imam. Beginning all his speeches with verses from the Koran, he regularly referred to his mission for his country, making it clear that its goal was to "establish the religion [Islam] amongst your ranks."[13] He prayed for God's help in carrying out his divinely ordained mission. He spoke about his enemies and the rumors they spread that he was ill by again quoting the Koran in such a way as to make it clear that he identified himself with the Prophet.

The declaration of the Sharia and Nimeiri's divisive policies, propagated under the sway of his religious advisors, led to great civil unrest and prompted the declaration of martial law in April 1984. He indicated that those in the South who had risen against him were also enemies of God. Although he pledged to carry out the Sharia mercifully, the specifics of his policies suggested the opposite:

Although Islam is the religion of forgiveness, the religion of brotherliness and the religion of honor and integrity, we will flog people publicly, we shall publish names in papers ... because the Muslim hates to hear his name ... We shall continue to publish ... to flog ... continue to amputate hands ... until we establish a righteous Islamic community.[14]

Increasingly out of touch with his own people and obsessed with his religious mission, Nimeiri continued to struggle with his health. In March 1985, he again traveled to Walter Reed for a thorough evaluation and treatment. While in Cairo en route to Khartoum, he learned that a coup d'etat had occurred and that he had lost his pulpit. Searching for the kingdom of God, he lost his kingdom on earth, for the most part living out his days in exile although dying in Khartoum.

KING HUSSEIN OF JORDAN: A TERMINAL QUEST FOR PEACE

King Hussein's grandfather had impressed on young Hussein the family's responsibility for the holy places in Jerusalem, the al-Aqsa Mosque and the Dome of the Rock. When King Hussein belatedly entered the 1967 War at Nasser's urging, despite Israel's warning to the contrary, Israel recaptured the West Bank, including Jerusalem and the Temple Mount. Although it was a day of great joy and prophetic significance for the Jewish people, restoring access to the Wailing Wall, for King Hussein it would forever stain his reputation. He had lost custody of his holy responsibility.

King Hussein was the consummate survivor, always checking carefully with his Arab neighbors before any significant undertaking. The one exception to this occurred in August 1992. The 57-year-old Hussein underwent surgery in King Hussein Hospital in Amman for a kidney cancer that had penetrated the capsule. It was, in effect, a death sentence. A man of deep faith, Hussein accepted this verdict with equanimity. But it was after this confrontation with his mortality that Hussein entered into secret negotiations with Israel. Before he died, he wanted again to ensure Muslim access to the Dome of the Rock and the al-Aqsa Mosque and redeem the stain on his reputation. These negotiations resulted in the Treaty of Peace between Israel and Jordan signed October 26, 1994.

A final testimony to his special sense of self and his historic role occurred during the Wye Plantation summit meeting in 1998, when talks hosted by President Clinton and designed to ease tensions between Israeli Prime Minister Ariel Sharon and Yasser Arafat and to pave the way for a Middle East accord were foundering. King Hussein was undergoing chemotherapy at the Mayo Clinic for the cancer that would claim his life. He interrupted his treatment to travel to the summit meeting. There, an obviously weakened Hussein, bald from the powerful, debilitating treatment he was undergoing, addressed the participants. Moved by his personal commitment, they were able to resolve (temporarily to be sure) their difficulties and draft a joint agreement. The bald and weakened King Hussein witnessed the signing of the Wye River memorandum between Israel and Palestinians on October 23, 1998, at the conclusion of the nine-day summit. The appearance of Hussein, clearly a dying man, was startling, and stood as powerful testament to his mission to bring peace to the Holy Land. It was a remarkable final act by this courageous leader who believed he had a special mission and responsibility to help bring about peace in the Holy Land.

GERONTOCRACY IN THE SOVIET UNION

In the Soviet Union, before leadership finally passed to post-Leningrad generation leader Mikhail Gorbachev, the country endured a series of aging, ailing, sclerotic leaders – Leonid Brezhnev, Yuri Andropov, and Konstantin Chernenko. The older generation had all been scarred by the siege of

Leningrad during World War II; Gorbachev was the first Soviet leader to have been born after that transformational event. For the last several years of his life, Brezhnev was little more than a figurehead, having experienced major deterioration from arteriosclerosis of the brain, and he died just before his 76th birthday. There was a virtual paralysis of leadership during this period of incapacity.

Boris Yeltsin, in his memoir, vividly described Brezhnev's incapacity and how he dealt with it:

Here's a typical example of how the country was run in those days. We needed to get a top-level decision on the construction of a subway system. Sverdlovsk was, after all, a city of 1,200,000 inhabitants. We needed permission from the Politburo, and I decided to go to Brezhnev ... I had been told how to handle him, so I prepared a text to which he had only to add his signature for approval. I went into his office and we talked for literally five or six minutes ... He was incapable of drafting the document himself. He said to me, "Just dictate what I should write." So of course I dictated it to him: "Instruction by the Politburo to prepare a draft decree authorizing the construction of a metro in Sverdlovsk." He wrote what I had said, signed it, and gave me the piece of paper. Knowing that even with Brezhnev's signature, some documents might be misplaced or disappear altogether, I told him, "No, you should call your aide." He summoned an assistant, and I said to Brezhnev, "Give him your instructions that he must first enter the documents in the registry and then take the necessary official steps to ensure that your instructions to distribute it to the Politburo members are carried out." He did all this; the aide collected the papers; and Brezhnev and I said goodbye.

The incident was typical and revealing. In the last phase of his life, Brezhnev, in my opinion, had no idea what he was doing, signing, or saying. All the power was in the hands of his entourage. He had signed the document authorizing the construction of the Sverdlovsk metro without giving any thought to the meaning of what I was dictating. Granted, as a result of that signature a good deed was done ... But how many of the rogues and cheats, indeed plain criminals, who surrounded Brezhnev exploited him for their own dishonest purposes? How many treaties or decrees did he calmly, unthinkingly sign, bringing riches to a few and suffering to many?[15]

Reluctant to appoint a "new" Soviet leader, the politburo chose two ailing leaders as transitional leaders, not despite their illnesses but because of them, before turning to Gorbachev. Andropov was already seriously ill with kidney disease at age 68 when he succeeded Brezhnev. He died after only 15 months in office. He was succeeded by the 72-year-old Chernenko, who was seriously ill with chronic pulmonary disease when he was chosen as the successor; he lasted a mere 18 months. Neither of them had the energy and vitality to respond creatively to the needs of their stagnant nation, although Chernenko, despite, or perhaps because of, his serious illness, did seek to ease the tensions between the USSR and the United States in what has been characterized as "terminal détente."[16] Dreams of glory never die; they don't even fade away – but they can assume a greater urgency when the unmistakable signs of the approach of death appear. Knowing his time was short and that he had not yet made a mark on his nation's history as his leadership was increasingly compromised by hospitalizations, Chernenko gave increasing voice to the need for detente between the superpowers, a late dream of glory, and one he hoped would establish his historical reputation as the man who reversed the spiral of hostility between the superpowers.

AGING AILING AUTOCRATS IN EASTERN EUROPE

Dictators ride to and fro upon tigers which they dare not dismount. And the tigers are getting hungry.   – *While Eagles Slept*, Winston Churchill

Similarly for the aging ailing autocrats who occupied the seats of power in Eastern Europe as the Soviet Union imploded – they were so narcissistically identified with their nations and so entrenched in their Stalinist-style leadership that they could not respond creatively to the press for greater freedom as the virus of democracy raced through the Warsaw Pact states. And, rather than loosen the reins of Stalinist control, they tightened them, often producing violent ends. The average age of Eastern European leaders was 76 at the end of their rule, and they had been in office for an average of 27 years – not exactly the actuarial statistics of flexible, youthful leaders untethered to the past and able to respond creatively to the widespread and unprecedented press for liberalization.

Moreover, each of them had risen to power by his faithful exercise of Stalinist control. Janos Kadar of Hungary invited the Soviet military into his country to crush the nascent revolution. For the 77-year-old Erich Honecker to have responded creatively and sufficiently to the burgeoning tide of rebellious youth in East Germany would have meant tearing down the wall that was the monument of his leadership, in effect giving lie to his entire career. Instead, he responded with the rigidity of the aged, and the wall came tumbling down nevertheless. And Gustav Husak of Czechoslovakia crushed the Prague Spring of 1968, which initially seemed so bright with promise. These aging autocrats manifested a situational narcissism that rendered them increasingly deaf to the pleadings of the youthful generation. It is interesting to contrast the Prague Spring of 1968 with the remarkable events of 1989: the implosion of the Soviet Union and the collapse of one Warsaw Pact nation after another. Indeed, 1989 was a remarkable year, and the Stalinist leaders of Eastern Europe were unable to suppress the full-throated cries for freedom that spread across the continent.

THE ARAB SPRING

How similar the hope and optimism then to the revolutionary wave of the Arab Spring sweeping the Middle East, forcing arrogant aged autocrats from power. Starting in Tunisia, in 2010, with 74-year-old Zine el-Abidine Ben Ali, in power for 23 years, fleeing after 17 days of demonstrations sparked by the act of public immolation by a 26-year-old vegetable vendor after a confrontation with corrupt police who had confiscated his cart This successful revolt was called the Jasmine Revolution. Next, Egypt, with 82-year-old Hosni Mubarak, the country's fourth president and in office for 30 years, stepping down after 18 days of demonstrations. This was followed by the overthrow of Muammar al-Qaddafi, 68 years old and in office for 40 years, after his battle for survival in Libya and his indictment by the International Criminal Court in The Hague for crimes against humanity for the brutal repression of the rebels. In Yemen, 69-year-old President Ali Abdullah Saleh had been in power since 1978 and was under increasing pressure to step aside; after initially agreeing in May 2011 to step down within 30 days in return for immunity from prosecution, he reversed himself, leading to an intensification of popular protests.

A major difference between the Prague Spring of 1968 and the Arab Spring of 2011 is assuredly the communication technology revolution. So, unlike the totalitarian control of information possible during the Cold War, dictators can no longer operate in the dark. With the 24/7 cable channels such as Al Jazeera, the Internet, and social network sites such as Facebook, Twitter, and YouTube, a virtual community of repressed people seeking freedom from totalitarian control was created, and the oppressed quickly came to see that, by united action, dictators can be overthrown. And with every individual armed with a cell phone now able to become a citizen photojournalist able to post photographs on the web, no longer can dictators conceal their brutal suppression from world view. A cell phone photo of the vegetable peddler in Tunis setting himself on fire in despair after his cart and his livelihood were seized went viral, playing a significant role in the social protest in Tunisia, just as the cell phone photo of Nedda being beaten to death in Iran during the Green Revolution 18 months earlier played a galvanizing role there.

Both the Eastern European autocrats and the Arab dictators shared a common trait: with an ego fed by his immediate circle of advisors, the long-standing dictator may increasingly come to see himself as identified with his country and find it inconceivable that his people could rise against him. Until the end, the Ceausescus truly believed they were beloved by the Romanian people. Qaddafi plaintively said, again and again, "My people, they all love me" and characterized those who were rebelling against him as having been manipulated by foreign provocations, either from al-Qaeda or the United States. Indeed, he went so far as to say that hallucinogenic drugs had been slipped into their Nescafe. For Qaddafi to step down was inconceivable, as it was initially for Mubarak, who also spoke of outside conspiracies. But what a powerful effect on the region and, indeed, on oppressed people everywhere, was the image of Mubarak, on a gurney in a cage, in a Cairo courtroom, being held to account for the violent suppression of peaceful protest at the end of his reign. The prosecution had asked for the death penalty. For Qaddafi, increasingly isolated as his senior officials progressively defected, his 40-year reign came to an inglorious end as he was trapped in a pipe while fleeing Tripoli and shot to death. In Qaddafi's mind, he and Libya were one and indivisible. He found it inconceivable that his people, who all loved him, were pursuing him, enraged with his dictatorial leadership.

Similarly, Bashar al-Assad could not think of the opposition as anything but terrorists and found it inconceivable that it was his own people rising up against him. Addressing his security forces, he declared "The responsibility of the Syrian government is to protect all of our residents. You have a responsibility to annihilate terrorists in any corner of the country."[17]

PRESIDENTS FOR LIFE

For the consummate narcissist, there is never enough. And yielding the throne of power, with its perquisites of power and the apparent idolization of a nation, is extremely difficult. Moreover, despite failing health, including failing mental powers, death is a consummation devoutly to be denied. One of the inconveniences of elections is being faced periodically with the disquieting fact that a portion of the population does not approve of the incumbent and would prefer someone else. A simple solution for this disquietude is to declare oneself "president for life." With that perpetuation of power, a critical press can be muzzled and political opponents jailed. The narcissistic leader, after all, is quite sensitive to criticism, and one way of avoiding criticism is to jail the critics.

In contrast to the 82-year-old Fidel Castro, the very personification of Cuba for 56 years, who ultimately felt forced to yield the throne of power for health reasons, the health of the founding father and president for life of Tunisia Habib Bourguiba had been declining for years, but he stubbornly held on to power, leading to an increasingly paralyzed nation.

HABIB BOURGUIBA, PRESIDENT FOR LIFE OF TUNISIA

When Habib Bourguiba was born in Monastir, a village 100 miles south of Tunis in 1903, Tunisia had been under French colonial control as a protectorate since 1881. After receiving his early education and baccalaureate in Tunisia, he studied law and politics at the University of Paris, graduating in 1927. Immediately on returning to Tunisia, he became involved in politics, joining the staff of two newspapers, *l'Etendard Tunisien* (*The Tunisian Flag*) and *Sawt At-Tunisi* (*The Tunisian Voice*), in the columns of which he advocated for Tunisian independence, leading to his prosecution by French colonial authorities in 1931 for "incitement to racial hatred." This led him to found his own militant newspaper, *L'Action Tunisienne*, calling for the ouster of the occupying French colonial powers.

After splitting from the Destour political party, which also had as its goal the liberation of Tunisia from French control but which Bourguiba criticized for its inaction, he founded and became secretary general of the more radical Neo-Destour party in 1934. Totally committed to the cause of Tunisian independence, he worked prodigiously as a political organizer, creating some 400 cells in his tireless travels across Tunisia over the next several years. He was ordered by the French colonial representative to be confined to a remote area on the border of the Sahara Desert in 1934 for his political incitement; he was released in 1936, only to again be arrested in 1939. Each of these imprisonments only seemed further to steel his will.

Following the allied victory after World War II, he tried to open dialogue with French authorities but was rebuffed, leading him to conclude that he had to bring the matter to international attention. In a trip that has achieved epic status in the history of Tunisia, he made his way first on a small fisherman's boat to Libya and from there, on foot and camel, made his way to Cairo, where he established a base for his international campaign. He traveled throughout the Arab world, Europe, South Asia, and to the United States to win support for Tunisian independence.

In 1950, when the French government refused to discuss his seven-point program leading to Tunisian independence, he called for unlimited resistance and general insurrection, leading again to his arrest by French authorities in 1952. By now, the narcissistic Bourguiba was imbued with his own importance to the future of Tunisia. He wrote from prison:

If my life were taken, the people would suffer an irreparable loss in losing not so much their leader and moral counselor as the fruit of all their past sacrifices ... As the creator of Tunisia, I have renewed her human substance.[18]

But when Pierre Mendes-France became French prime minister in 1954, his government's positions on the French colonies, including the withdrawal of French forces from Vietnam, opened the door to home rule for Tunisia. In 1955, Bourguiba was released from prison and was greeted with a hero's welcome. After long and difficult negotiations, in which Bourguiba played a leading role, independence was declared on March 20, 1956, and Bourguiba was named president of the constituent assembly. On July 25, 1957, Tunisia was named a republic, and Bourguiba, now 54 years old, was declared president of the new republic of Tunisia, a fitting reward for a single-minded 30-year struggle. It was narcissistic dreams of glory achieved.

ACT II: THE PRESIDENCY

If the first act of the drama of Habib Bourguiba's life was to last 30 years, the second act, when he officially assumed the role of president, was to last another 31.[a] Most reviewers would agree that the second act was much too long.

Bourguiba's presidency was always highly personalistic. On the day the republic was founded, Bourguiba modestly declared to the National Assembly,

---

[a] This description of his presidency and his medical decline draws on an analysis of the medical coup that was required to oust the senile President for Life Bourguiba from power in Post and Robins, 1993, pp. 161–168.

"I could, if I wished, install myself as monarch and found a dynasty. I prefer the Republic."[19]

It is interesting to observe that Bourguiba recognized the importance of institutions. In planning for the future of his nation, he observed:

Revolts are not led essentially in the name of nationalism, but in the name of an over-powering desire for dignity. When the rebels can assuage this desire through institutions whose every detail has been organized by their leaders, success is bound to follow. When there are no institutions, there is chaos.[20]

But on becoming leader, Bourguiba ignored his own wise counsel concerning the importance of institutions and ruled instead in what was described as the manner of a "presidential monarch,"[21] at once highly personalistic and auto-cratic, yet relying on political institutions. Bourguiba ruled as a benign mon-arch, making his decisions with a small group of advisers and then relaying them to the ministers in his cabinet to implement. In a later interview, he shamelessly characterized his own highly personal style of leadership: "The system? I am the system."[22] Bourguiba ran roughshod over the very fragile Tunisian institutions and procedures that he had put in place; his powerful personality was determinative.

In 1962, asked if he felt a historical bond with Hannibal, the greatest military commander in history, Bourguiba instead likened himself to another heroic figure:

No, my ancestor was Jugurtha, who fought the foreign invaders ... a patriot like myself, not a conqueror. *Alive or dead, I am responsible for this nation's destiny.*[23]

On the occasion of the 10th anniversary of Tunisia's independence, Bourguiba, now 63, continued in the same self-exalting vein:

Having been the major artisan of Tunisian history for thirty-five years, I believe I should shed some light on the critical moments in our struggle ... These events ought to be recalled so that the new generation may reflect upon this long journey of ours, this exalting epic which brought Tunisia to independence, whose origin was my work.[24]

The next year, the 64-year-old Bourguiba suffered a heart attack. Within two months, he suffered another major, nearly fatal, heart attack. This led Bourguiba to take a six-month leave in France for medical treatment.

Had he stepped down then for reasons of failing health, he would have had an honored place in Tunisian history as the founder of his nation. His single-minded determination and perseverance, heedless of danger to himself, the energy of his struggle to bring his nation's cause to the attention of the world – it is a saga of heroism and dedication of almost mythic proportions.

But on his return, in June 1970, he expressed his conviction, perhaps to reassure himself that his popularity had not been diminished that, "despite what the people had gone through in my absence,"[25] he could not conceive of a Tunisia without him at the helm or of himself not leading the country he created. He then abruptly dismissed his prime minister for acting in his absence, leading to a virtual paralysis of government during Bourguiba's frequent extended absences for medical treatment.

As his health declined, Bourguiba became increasingly imperious and irritable, unwilling to listen even to mild constructive criticism. As one minister explained, "There was no room for even the most cautiously worded disagreement with the leader, as it might endanger his health."[26] Bourguiba was plagued by ill health for 22 years, from the time of his first heart attack in 1967; yet, because of weak Tunisian institutions, he maintained sole autocratic control, resulting in ineffective and paralyzed governance.

The diagnosis of advanced generalized arteriosclerosis (hardening of the arteries, affecting both the heart and the brain) became public knowledge in 1971, leading to widespread discussion concerning succession. But Bourguiba would have none of that. One of the difficulties with individuals suffering from progressive disability affecting their mental processes is that they characteristically are not aware of the degree of their disability, and narcissistic leaders, in particular, are apt to deny any impairment of their leadership. At the party congress later that year, Bourguiba took an active role, dismissing one of his most outspoken critics and cautioning against too much liberalism.

In a tribute to his leadership, Bourguiba was offered the position of president for life at this party congress, but he declined, saying he would step down at the end of his term in 1974, at which time he would be 71, naming Prime Minister Nouria as his successor. But in an interview with *Le Monde* later that year, he warned "It will not be easy to replace a man like me."[27] And despite his earlier pledge, with the expiration of his term approaching and despite continuing ill health, Bourguiba reversed himself, did not step down as promised, and in effect proclaimed himself president for life, which was dutifully endorsed by the rubber-stamp parliament.

In the winter of 1976, Bourguiba went to Switzerland for three months for a restorative cure. And in the summer of 1978, an illness required Bourguiba again to leave Tunisia to enter the American Hospital in Paris for tests and evaluation. His medical problems were sufficiently severe to require postponing the celebration of his 75th birthday by a month.

By now, canceled government meetings were more the rule than the exception. Bourguiba's health and ability to continue in office, and the issue of succession, were matters of serious concern. But in 1979, at the 10th Socialist Party Congress, while addressing his mortality, no mention was made of an intention to step down. There had been a merger of self and country that, in his increasingly addled mind, were one and the same. He had created the independent republic of Tunisia, and not being at its helm was inconceivable to the gravely disabled president. Indeed, he used the considerable powers of president for life to systematically eliminate any threats to his leadership.

Matters spun out of control when he suffered yet another heart attack in 1981. Increasingly isolated, the ailing autocrat was desperately holding on. No one who criticized him was immune from retaliation, including his own son who was dismissed from his position as adviser when he criticized the wave of arrests Bourguiba orchestrated. He then dismissed his prime minister, and, when his wife of 25 years objected to his appointment of Interior Minister Ben Ali in his stead, he divorced her. After *Le Monde* published an article discussing the issue of succession, the newspaper was banned for a month in Tunisia.

During 1987, his behavior grew increasingly erratic, compounded by severe memory problems as a consequence of his senility: he made multiple appointments to the same job (Tunisia briefly had two ambassadors to the United Nations); an official was appointed minister of culture for only 30 minutes, a record of brevity of tenure; and often he would make appointments one day and then angrily deny this the following day.

Finally, on November 6, 1987, Prime Minister Ben Ali arranged to have a group of six physicians sign a document attesting to the fact that Bourguiba's "medical health no longer permits him to perform the duties entrusted to him."[28] The solemn medical declaration was made without examining Bourguiba. It was, in effect, a medical coup d'etat.

Ironically, in assuming the presidency in 1987, Zine El Abidine Ben Ali solemnly pledged that he would govern Tunisia in accord with the constitution, that the fragile institutions of government that Bourguiba had so ruthlessly trampled would be strengthened, and that he would faithfully execute the law of the land. But it was the wave of rebellions that started in Tunisia, protesting President Ben Ali's autocratic and corrupt rule and calling out for reform and greater freedom that forced Tunisian President Zine El Abidine Bin Al to flee his country after the 17 days of protest that ushered in the Arab Spring of 2011.

FIDEL CASTRO, PRESIDENT FOR LIFE OF CUBA: CASTRO IS CUBA, CUBA IS CASTRO

The prisons of Cuba are crowded with journalists and political opponents who dared to criticize Castro. Reflecting his intention to remain at Cuba's helm despite health concerns, in 1992, the then 66-year-old Fidel stated his intention to remain Cuba's leader, emphasizing how indispensable he considered his leadership to be. A Cuba without him as leader was unimaginable:

I wish they were right that political leaders should retire at age sixty. The problem is not only retiring, but being able to retire. In these very difficult times, to resign or propose that they should look for someone else to perform my duties, they would say that I am the greatest traitor in the world ... I insist that fighting for the cause that is Cuba is to fight for something a lot greater than Cuba. It is to fight for the world's greatest cause. The obstacles we are overcoming can rightly be compared to the Red Sea that Moses crossed.[29]

A modest comparison. But, indeed, Moses never entered the Promised Land, and perhaps there are intimations in this language that, like Moses, Castro would not complete his revolutionary journey, premonitions of the serious illness that would force him, in February 2008, at the age of 82, to transfer his responsibilities to his younger brother Raul. Rumors of failing health had swirled around Castro since the late 1990s. On the occasion of his 80th birthday on July 21, 2006, Castro remarked "I'm really happy to reach 80, I never expected it, not least having a neighbor – the greatest power in the world – trying to kill me every day."[30]

But it was later that year, in December, when he did not appear at the celebration of the 50th anniversary of the beginning of the Cuban Revolution, that serious concerns about his health mounted. There were rumors that he was suffering from terminal cancer, and Cubans began to worry about a future without Castro. In a letter dated February 8, 2008, Castro stated definitively that, for health reasons, he was retiring from public life: "I will not aspire to nor accept – I repeat I will not aspire to or accept – the post of President of the Council of State and Commander in Chief."[31]

When this was printed in the official Communist newspaper *Gramma*, referring to his poor health and the consequent limitations on his ability to lead with his characteristic energy, he stated: "It would betray conscience to take up a responsibility that requires mobility and total devotion that I am not in a physical condition to offer."[32] With that, the ground was set for the transfer of most of his major responsibilities to his brother Raul, his deputy for 32 years as first vice president and his constitutionally authorized successor, which occurred at the National Assembly the next week when Raul was unanimously elected president. Fidel did not quietly disappear but continued to offer commentary on the state of Cuba. Indeed, at his inauguration, Raul declared his intention to consult Fidel on matters of great importance, such as defense, foreign policy, and the socioeconomic development of the country.

Since the revolution that overthrew the Batista dictatorship that began in December 1956, Castro had been the larger-than-life figure leading Cuba, the very personification of his island nation for 51 years. Fidel was Cuba; Cuba was Fidel. He held the supreme military rank of commander in chief and was prime minister of Cuba from February 1959 to December 1976, when he became president for life. Although he had given up his positions as commander in chief and president, it was only in April 2011 that he finally yielded his position as first secretary of the Communist Party of Cuba, which he had held since October 1965.

What underlay this powerful drive to be father of his country? It is interesting to observe that Fidel was illegitimate at birth. Fidel's father, Angel Castro, who was born in Galicia in Spain to a poor peasant family, had emigrated to Cuba. He had married a woman with whom he had two daughters, but they separated after several years. He then began a relationship with a household servant, Lina Ruz, 30 years his junior, who became his domestic partner. She had three sons and four daughters with Angel. Fidel was the third son and was given his mother's surname of Ruz. Being born out of wedlock carried a particularly shameful social stigma at the time. While his father's sugar cane business was doing very well, Angel did not provide well for his son Fidel, who grew up alongside the farm's Haitian workforce. When he was six, Fidel and two older siblings were sent to live in relative poverty with their teacher in Santiago de Cuba, where often there was not enough to eat. It was only when he was 15 that Angel dissolved his first marriage, permitting him finally to marry Castro's mother. The 17-year-old Fidel was formally acknowledged by his father, and only then was his surname legally changed from Ruz to Castro. Perhaps in this painful story lay the origins of Castro holding on so tightly and for so long to the reins of power, not wishing to abandon his children, his people.

WHEN ILLNESS STRIKES THE CAUDILLO: PRESIDENT HUGO CHÁVEZ OF VENEZUELA

It is eerie to see the degree to which Hugo Chávez has modeled his career after that of his mentor and model, Fidel Castro, including the severe but unspecified abdominal illness that required intestinal surgery. In July 2006, the 80-year-old Castro underwent abdominal surgery, and on August 2, 2006, Fidel, looking gaunt, temporarily turned over the reins of power to his brother, Raul. Rumors flew throughout Cuba that Castro was on his deathbed. Chávez reportedly flew to Havana to say goodbye to his long-term hero, model, and mentor. Chávez had long harbored ambitions to succeed Castro as the leader of the Latin American left, and his speeches and actions increasingly indicated that Chávez was acting as if the baton of power had been passed to him.

At the annual UN general assembly meeting in September 2006, Chávez could not resist the opportunity to strut upon the world stage. Referring to President George W. Bush, who had addressed the UN general assembly the day before, Chávez stated, "The devil came here yesterday," and then, ostentatiously crossing himself, he indicated, "And it smells of sulfur still today."[33]

Five years after Castro's surgery, on June 10, 2011, Chávez underwent abdominal surgery for what he termed a pelvic abscess. But Chávez was soon to acknowledge that his surgery was for a cancerous tumor, and, on July 16, he arrived in Cuba to begin chemotherapy. The nature of the cancer and the extent of spread were never specified, with suggestions ranging from prostate cancer to colon cancer. The compliant Venezuelan congress voted to permit Chávez to continue to lead Venezuela from Cuba while undergoing treatment for his cancer.

For the consummate narcissist, death is unthinkable. Just as Fidel held on to the reins of power until illness finally forced him to stand aside, so, too, Chávez would not easily yield to illness. But it was compelling that on Venezuela's Independence Day on July 5, 2011, unlike in past appearances, when he was surrounded by politicians and generals, this time, he appeared with his sisters and his brother Adan, reminiscent of Castro handing the reins of power to his brother Raul. Adan warned ominously that backers of Chávez should not rule out the necessity of armed struggle.

Facing death can sometimes accelerate the timetable of the narcissistic leader who is sitting crowned upon the grave. As observed earlier in the chapter, it was when the Shah of Iran was faced with his cancer diagnosis in 1973 that he broke with OPEC, quadrupling the oil revenues pouring into Iran. The country had an inadequate infrastructure that was incapable of absorbing the great influx of funds, leading to a revolution of rising expectations that destabilized the country and paved the way for Khomeini's Islamic Revolution. Thus, in his rush to glory, the Shah superimposed his personal timetable on the political timetable of his country, and his dreams of glory became nightmares for us all.

The work of Chávez's Bolivarian revolution was by no means accomplished, but the timetable of Hugo Chávez was foreshortened. As he simultaneously struggled with the rigors of cancer and its treatment and struggled to lead his country, the months ahead would prove to be a period of immense stress for the ailing caudillo. His decision making and political actions must have been distorted by his own confrontation with his mortality. On Friday, February 17, 2011, Venezuelan President Hugo Chávez ominously declared that the election of his opponent, Henrique Capriles Radonski, in the October 9 election would put Venezuela on a path to war and violence. Stating that "if the Venezuelan bourgeoisie [were] running the government, it would be a guarantee of war, of violence, of national uproar; the guarantee of the end of the century, and we are not going to allow that,"[34] he suggested he would resort to extraconstitutional means to maintain power.

On the following Tuesday, Chávez revealed that he would be traveling to Cuba for surgery to remove a small lesion that had been found during his medical exam by his doctors. At the initial surgery in June 2011, a baseball-size tumor in his pelvis was removed. This was the third cancer surgery in eight months for the Venezuelan president, suggesting to oncologists and gastroenterologist specialists that this was a very aggressive cancer. Considering that he had had four chemotherapy sessions and that the recurrence had developed so soon, this was a very bad prognostic indicator.

In announcing his trip to Cuba for surgery, Chávez spoke of a dream in which Jesus Christ appeared before him, urging him to live. "He told me, 'Chávez, get up. It is not time to die, it is time to live.'"[35] This was intended to bring cheer to his followers, but it also indicated how threatened Chávez was by his very serious, ultimately fatal illness.

After the surgery was carried out, during the week, the minister of health indicated that Chávez was "fully capable of continuing to exercise power,"[36] and there was no anticipation of temporarily turning over power to the vice president or of a replacement candidate.

On Sunday, the popular opposition candidate Henrique Capriles was shot at a political rally by a group of unidentified attackers on motorbikes. The son of another opposition candidate suffered a knife wound in the attack, requiring hospitalization. The game was on, and the campaign was already on the path of violence that Chávez had warned against.

Later that day, Chávez indicated the cancer had returned and that he would be undergoing radiation therapy. He also offered support to President Assad of Syria and congratulated President Putin before his election.

Ironically, on returning from Cuba to Venezuela, Chávez indicated that he had information about a planned assassination attempt against Capriles. He said the government had offered protection to the opposition leader. This offer can be characterized as the fox offering to guard the chicken coop.

That the abdominal cancer from which Hugo Chávez suffered was aggressive and spreading was increasingly evident. Chávez became increasingly desperate as he faced death. On April 6, 2012, Chávez announced that he would be returning to Cuba to undergo a third round of radiation therapy, after undergoing surgery the previous month to remove a tumor that had recurred in the area of the original surgery. In church with his family on Thursday, April 5, he burst into tears, and implored God "Do not take me yet."[37] At the Mass, he begged, "Give me your crown of thorns, Christ, I will bleed; Give me your cross, 100 crosses – and I will carry them for you. But give me life, because I still have things to do for my people and my country." Venezuela political analysts, observing that he was in an emotionally desperate state, declared that "the veil of silence and mystery about his illness is now off" and that "he has made it clear that his illness is fatal."

That Chávez made an aggressive political statement preceding his announcement of the recurrence of cancer emphasized that his Bolivarian mission was unfinished. Whether his mentor Fidel would be able to counsel him to step down was not clear. Chávez indicated that he would govern Venezuela from Cuba and would not temporarily turn over the reins of power to his vice president, suggesting he would not easily yield to the grave illness he was confronting. It was already likely that he would never step down, for he could not conceive of a Venezuela without him as its leader. In fact, in 2009, he sought to modify the Venezuelan constitution so that he could become president for life, attempting to emulate Castro. His illness made it all the more likely that he would not yield the throne of power, for to be actively leading Venezuela would be to hold death at bay. As his physical health weakened, there was a strong possibility he would feel impelled to demonstrate his political strength, as suggested by his threat that he would not allow Capriles, his opponent in the October election, to lead Venezuela on a path of violence and destruction. It seemed likely that "he will not go gentle into that good night . . . but will rage, rage against the dying of the light." It would not have been surprising for Chávez, like the Shah of Iran and Mao Zedong, to exhibit terminal urgency, to see Chávez superimpose his personal timetable on his nation's timetable and make dramatic and destabilizing moves.

Chávez did prevail in the October 7 election, winning 55 percent of the votes cast. But he then announced that his cancer had recurred despite previous surgeries, chemotherapy, and radiation therapy, and, on December 11, Chávez was operated on for a fourth time in Havana. There were respiratory complications, and Chávez was reported to be "in delicate condition." This prompted a mini-constitutional crisis when he could not be present personally to be sworn in for the inauguration on January 10. He returned to Caracas on February 18. The photograph taken then was a study in contrast, showing a beaming Hugo Chávez, confined to a hospital bed and obviously still disabled. It seemed clear he could not prevail over this mortal illness.

It soon became clear that Chávez had returned to Venezuela to die in his beloved country, for it was announced on March 5, 2013, that the 58-year-old *caudillo* had died. The last months may well have represented what my colleague Bob Robins and I have designated "the captive king syndrome."[38] This refers to the disabled leader who rules while facing terminal illness. Initially, he and his inner circle conspire to conceal the extent of the illness, which was certainly the case with Chávez's medical treatment in Cuba. But as he becomes progressively disabled, the situation progressively changes from one in which he and his inner circle are managing the public, to one in which the leader is being managed by the inner circle. The failing leader is held up as a figurehead, as was probably the case with Ayatollah Khomeini of Iran and Leonid Brezhnev of the Soviet Union in their final years. The mortally wounded king and his desperate court become locked into a mutual dependency in which neither trusts the other, but each needs the other to survive – the dilemma of the captive king and his captive court. The obedient parliament permitted Chávez to govern from Havana while he was undergoing his multiple surgeries, radiation therapy, and chemotherapy, but it is highly likely that unelected officials loyal to Chávez were actually and increasingly running Venezuela as the ravages of the very aggressive cancer with which he was struggling ultimately and inevitably defeated the *caudillo*.

Chávez had designated Nicholas Maduro as his preferred successor. Maduro won narrowly in the 2013 election. Lacking Chávez's hypnotic charismatic appeal, Maduro has not been able to provide effective leadership to Venezuela. Now, a year later, the Venezuelan economy is unraveling, with high inflation (55%), a shortage of basic goods, rising crime, and waves of political protest engulfing the struggling nation.

In the next chapter, leaders who turned to their progeny to extend their grasp on power beyond the grave is discussed.

Notes

1. Marvin Zonis, *Majestic Failure: The Fall of the Shah* (Chicago: University of Chicago Press, 1991).
2. Mohammed Reza Pahlavi, Shah of Iran, *Mission for My Country* (New York: McGraw-Hill, 1961).
3. Victor Cohn and Susan Okie, "Doctors Say Shah Could Leave U.S. in Four Weeks," *Washington Post*, November 15, 1979.

4. Foreign Broadcast Information Service, *Arab Africa Report*, November 9, 1987.

5. *The Jerusalem Post*, July 15, 1980.

6. *The Jerusalem Post*, December 15, 1981.

7. Jaafar Nimeiri, *The Islamic Way: Why?* (Khartoum: Government Press, 1978).

8. Mansour Khalid, *Nimeiri and the Revolution of Dis-May* (London: KPI, 1985), 47.

9. Khalid, *Nimeiri and the Revolution of Dis-May*, 47.

10. Foreign Broadcast Information Service, *North Africa Report*, January 4, 1978.

11. Khalid, *Nimeiri and the Revolution of Dis-May*, 12.

12. Ibid., 212.

13. Ibid., 262.

14. Ibid., 269.

15. Boris Yeltsin, *Against the Grain: An Autobiography*, trans. Michael Glenny (New York: Summit Books, 1990), 69–70.

16. Jerrold Post and Robert Robins, *When Illness Strikes the Leader: The Dilemma of the Captive King* (New Haven: Yale University Press, 1993), 141–144.

17. "Assad: Duty to 'Annihilate Terrorists,'" *Reuters*, June 30, 2012, www.thehindu.com/todays-paper/tp-in-school/assad-duty-to-annihilate-terrorists/article3586545.ece.

18. Jean LaCouture, *The Demigods: Charismatic Leadership in the Third World* (New York: Alfred A. Knopf, Inc., 1970).

19. LaCouture, *The Demigods*, 171.

20. Ibid., 150.

21. Clement Henry Moore, *Tunisia since Independence: The Dynamics of One-Party Government* (Westport: Greenwood Press, 1965), 71.

22. LaCouture, *The Demigods*.

23. Ibid. Emphasis in the original.

24. Ibid.

25. "Bourguiba Returns; in Paris 6 Months," *New York Times*, June 2, 1970.

26. LaCouture, *The Demigods*, 168.

27. W. M. Habeeb, "Zine el Abidine Ben Ali," quoted from an interview in *Le Monde*, November 8, 1987, in *Political Leaders of the Contemporary Middle East and North Africa: A Biographical Dictionary*, edited by B. Reich (New York: Greenwood, 1990), 82.

28. FBIS, *Arab Africa Report*, 1987.

29. Borge, Tomas, "Part Six of Interview with Fidel Castro," *Excelsior*, June 4, 1992, http://lanic.utexas.edu/la/cb/cuba/castro/1992/19920607.

30. Anthony Boadle, "Fidel Castro, 20th Century Revolutionary," *Reuters*, February 19, 2008, www.reuters.com/article/2008/02/19/us-cuba-castro-profileidUSN19225042 20080219.

31. Cited in Lisa Abend, "Will Castro's Exit Change Cuba?" *Time*, February 19, 2008, http://content.time.com/time/world/article/0,8599,1714323,00.html.

32. GlobalSecurity.org, "Political Change in Cuba," last modified May 7, 2011, www.globalsecurity.org/military/ops/cuba-intro.htm.

33. David Stout, "Chávez Calls Bush 'the Devil' in UN Speech," *The New York Times*, September 20, 2006, www.nytimes.com/2006/09/20/world/americas/20cnd-Chavez.html.

34. "Chávez Says Opposition Would Create 'War,'" *Agence France Presse*, February 17, 2012(a), www.google.com/hostednews/afp/article/ALeqM5htBi9ZLgzNmFllywREt3 uVrpZ7bw?docId=CNG.b012575559d3dcf7e161312a2cd69fb9.2f1.

35. Juan Forero, "Hugo Chávez May Have Aggressive Tumor, Cancer Experts Say," *The Washington Post*, February 15, 2012, www.washingtonpost.com/world/hugo-Chavez-may-have-aggressive-tumor-cancer-experts-say/2012/02/25/gIQAgGuKaR_story.html.

36. "Ailing Chávez has no Plans for Replacement Candidate," *Agence France Presse*, March 2, 2012(b), http://www.google.com/hostednews/afp/article/ALeqM5jcUTgI GLZ7onk5y6cQCHxymf7jLg?docId=CNG.7dd23791b5739f8ecbd3acbo51c4 1676.2d1.

37. Natalia Ramos, "'Don't Take Me Yet,' Ailing Chávez Begs God at Mass," *Agence France Presse*, 2012, http://news.yahoo.com/dont-yet-ailing-Chavez-begs-god-mass-204022078.html.

38. Jerrold Post and Robert Robins, *When Illness Strikes the Leader*, xv–xvi.

12

Seeking Immortality: Dictators and Their Progeny

In this chapter, the manner in which narcissistic dictators seek to continue their legacy and secure their place in history by passing on the baton of power to the next generation is considered. Two examples will be reviewed: Saddam Hussein and his sons Uday and Qusay, and Kim Il-sung and his son Kim Jong-il and Kim Jong-il's son, Kim Jong-eun.

SADDAM HUSSEIN AND HIS BOYS, UDAY AND QUSAY: THE FAMILY THAT SLAYS TOGETHER STAYS TOGETHER

Saddam Hussein was not a typical soccer dad.[a] Although he considered himself a great sportsman, rather than take his sons to sports events, starting at age ten, he took his sons to witness torture sessions, apparently imbued with what I consider one of his maxims, "the family that slays together stays together." Thus, from early on, Saddam was preparing his sons to succeed him and was demonstrating the techniques for maintaining a rule of terror and total control. And he was teaching them that there were no limits to the violence they could administer, that they were special and need not fear retribution.

UDAY HUSSEIN

The temperament and unconstrained behavior of Saddam's oldest son Uday was a continuing issue. He apparently took to his father's early teaching all too well. He had a reputation as the "bad boy" of Iraq and was greatly feared among the population of Baghdad. He was involved in several widely publicized incidents,

---

[a] This material on Saddam Hussein's sons was presented in testimony to the House Armed Services Committee and the House Foreign Affairs Committee, December 1990, and was subsequently published in Post, Jerrold (ed.), *The Psychological Assessment of Political Leaders*, Ann Arbor: University of Michigan Press (2003).

but Saddam had regularly either overlooked Uday's excesses or, if the event was too public to ignore, dealt with it in the mildest manner possible. Prior to the conflict in the Gulf, there were reports of violent excesses involving Uday. In one 1988 incident, Uday, drunk at a party, used an electric carving knife to kill one of his father's aides. In a second dramatic public event that year, Uday, angry with Saddam's personal valet for his role in facilitating an affair Saddam was having with a married Iraqi woman (whose husband was rewarded for not objecting with the presidency of Iraqi Airlines), crashed a party being held in honor of Suzanne Mubarak, the wife of the Egyptian president Hosni Mubarak. Uday beat the valet to death in full view of all the guests. As a result of this, Saddam put Uday on trial for murder but, in response to the victim's family members who "pleaded for leniency," Saddam exiled Uday to Switzerland. A year later, after having been declared persona non grata by Swiss authorities, Uday returned to Iraq where he began reintegrating himself into Iraqi society.

In 1995, Uday reportedly shot one of his uncles in the leg and killed six "dancing girls" at a party – not coincidentally the night before his brother-in-law, Hussein Kamal, defected. It is believed that Uday played a major role in precipitating the defection of Kamal, whom he saw as threatening his relationship with his father.

His father appointed Uday head of the Iraqi Olympic Committee and head of the Iraqi Football Team. In that role, he tortured athletes who failed to win.

In 1996, an assassination attempt on Uday left him bedridden for at least six months with both his legs shattered. He was reportedly temporarily paralyzed following the assassination attempt. There have been some reports that he was left paraplegic from the injury, paralyzed from the waist down. There are rumors that he was left impotent, which, given the nature and location of the paralyzing spinal cord injury, may well be true. He remained in poor health. He was also the one who authorized executions of military and security officers suspected of disloyalty.

His unconstrained violence led him to fall out of favor with his father. After Uday's paralyzing spinal cord injury, Qusay was designated successor in 2000.

On July 22, 2003, during a raid on a house in Mosul, Uday and his brother Qusay, along with Qusay's 14-year-old son, were killed in a raid by the 101st Airborne Division and Taskforce 20, involving more than 200 soldiers and lasting three to four hours. Representing one of the most wanted Iraqis in hiding, Uday was designated the Ace of Hearts in the deck of cards of most wanted Iraqis; Qusay was the Ace of Clubs.

QUSAY HUSSEIN

Starting in 2000, Qusay started receiving a great deal of coverage by the Ba'th party and was referred to as "Warrior Qusay." Uday had fallen out of favor with his father because of his unconstrained violence. Supplanting Uday in the succession, Qusay was named Saddam's deputy "in the event of an emergency." Since

2001, Qusay was also a member of the Regional Leadership (RL) of the Ba'th party in Iraq and deputy secretary of its important military bureau (*al-Maktab al-'Askari*).¹ The promotion of Qusay to the RL was seen as the first step toward his inclusion in the Revolutionary Command Council (RCC) and, eventually, his promotion to the RCC Chairmanship and the office of president. After the 2003 conflict, Uday and Qusay died in a hail of bullets when they confronted invading forces, before Saddam was found in a spider hole beneath a mud hut near Tikrit.

KIM JONG-IL OF THE DEMOCRATIC PEOPLE'S REPUBLIC OF KOREA: IN THE SHADOW OF HIS FATHER

KIM IL-SUNG: FOUNDING FATHER OF THE KIM DYNASTY OF NORTH KOREA

One cannot understand the personality and political behavior of Kim Jong-il without placing it in the context of the life and charismatic leadership of his father, Kim Il-sung, North Korea's first leader.ᵇ One of the difficulties in assessing the personality and political behavior of Kim Il-sung has always been discerning the man behind the myth. The gap existing between the facts that scholars have been able to piece together and the hagiographic portrait presented to the people of North Korea is staggering. This extends to the gap between the facts of the life of Kim Jong-il and his mythic public presentation. Examining this gap is instructive because it may reflect areas of sensitivity, the ideal versus the real. Consider the following:

The great Mangyongdae family
    The Mangyongdae family is the greatest pride of our nation. From old times it is said that a great man is produced by a great family. There are many families in the world that produced great men. But there is not such a great family as Marshal Kim Jong Il's family whose all members were famous as patriots generation after generation. Marshal Kim Jong Il's family is praised as the greatest family unprecedented in all countries and in all ages ... The greatness of Marshal Kim Jong Il is related with the greatness of his family.²

Kim Il-sung was a man of larger-than-life stature. The founding father of the modern state of North Korea, he was a heroic guerilla fighter who rose to power under the patronage of Stalin and was named eternal president of his country, the Democratic People's Republic of Korea (DPRK). He conceptualized DPRK's ideology, *juche*ᶜ (independence) and its goal of reunification of the Korean peninsula. His sobriquet was "Great Leader."

ᵇ This profile of Kim Jong-Il is drawn in part from a profile published in Jerrold Post, *Leaders and Their Followers in a Dangerous World*, Ithaca: Cornell University Press, 2004.
ᶜ *Juche*, a word of Kim Il-sung's own construction, is a combination of two Korean words. The first *chu* means "lord" or "master"; the second, *ch'e*, means "the body," "the whole." The concept *chuch'e* or *juche* signifies an intense need for independence and a desire to make one's own

Kim's hold on power was absolute. Strongly influenced by Stalin and Mao, Kim Il-sung was a devoted communist who maintained a lifelong goal of uniting the Korean peninsula under his leadership. Allied with the Soviet Union and China, he established tight control over North Korea, crushing any opposition and eliminating potential rivals. Suspicious of outsiders and distraught over postmortem denunciations of Stalin and Mao's efforts to secure Chinese succession, Kim Il-sung closed the borders of his country, severely limiting not only the exit of his citizens, but also the influx of foreign visitors. Throughout the course of his life, Kim worked tirelessly to create a cult of personality that sustained him not only in life, but has continued to persist after his death. The KWP Department of Propaganda and Agitation has been devoted since its inception to furthering the image of Kim Il-sung and his family as loyal and fiercely patriotic Koreans through recreating the family history of Kim Il-sung and his family. Known as the Great Leader, the near-divine image of Kim Il-sung continued to influence North Korean policy from the grave and to materially influence the leadership decisions of his son. Indeed, Kim Il-sung was named "eternal president" in the 1972 revision of the constitution, and the slogan "The Great Leader Will Always Be with Us" is in bold yellow letters across the bottom of the DPRK website.

KIM JONG-IL, THE DEAR LEADER: UNLIKE FATHER, UNLIKE SON

But Kim Jong-il was unlike his father, who indeed in no way resembled his son. Kim Jong-il was raised to succeed his charismatic father. But he was *not* a heroic guerilla fighter, *not* the charismatic founder of his nation, *not* an ideology conceptualizer. To succeed a powerful father is always difficult, but to be the son of a god is psychologically an overwhelming challenge, and indeed, Kim Il-sung was accorded near god-like status. Instead Kim Jong-il inherited his charismatic image and national ideology of *juche* and reunification from his father. Indeed, it was he, in his role as director of the Bureau of Propaganda and Agitation, who created the cult of personality around his father and attempted to strengthen the continuity between his father and himself. So, Kim Jong-il

decisions. It often appears with the suffix *song*, forming the word *chuch'esong*, meaning to act in accord with one's own judgment. *Juche* was the most important political idea with which Kim Il-sung ruled the people. It pertains both to domestic and international policy. Internationally, it signified the end of political dependence and subservience to the Soviet Union and represented the elevation of Kim as a leader and political philosopher to the nonaligned world (Suh, 1988). Although it grew out of Kim Il-sung's personal experience, Korea as a nation had long struggled to establish its identity and independence from its surrounding great powers: Japan, China, and the Soviet Union. Internally, it meant to Kim forwarding the revolution on the basis of his own ideas, without slavishly following the precepts of Marxism. As Suh notes, *juche* became the ideological system for North Korea, encompassing the idea of *chaju* (independence) in political work, *charip* (self-sustenance) in economic endeavors, and *chawi* (self-defense) in military affairs.

knew well the gap between myth and reality, and all of his leadership was overshadowed by the halo-encircled image of his father. The myth of continuity that Kim Jong-il fostered made him captive to his father's ideology.

He created the myth of the man from Mount Baekdu (the sacred mountain in Korea from which, according to myth, the Korean peninsula emerged) when in fact he was the boy from the Soviet Union. Kim Jong-il was actually born in the Soviet Union in 1942. There is little information about his early years. There are unanswered questions about his younger brother's death in a swimming acci-dent when Kim Jong-il was six. His mother died when he was seven. His first trip out of Korea was to the Soviet Union when he was 15. There are reports that he graduated from the air force officers school in East Germany, but this is consid-ered highly unlikely. Because of his lack of military credentials and experience, he had a great deal of insecurity in dealing with military matters and military officers.

"MAJESTY SITS UNCOMFORTABLY ON HIS SHOULDERS"

Unlike his father, Kim Jong-il grew up in luxurious surroundings, pampered, raised to be special, with each grain of rice from the sacred mountain of Mount Baekdu being inspected before being included in Kim Jong-il's meal. This is the formative recipe for a narcissistic personality, with a grandiose self-concept and difficulties with empathy. Insofar as Kim Jong-il was in charge of the propa-ganda machine and directed the cult of personality around his father, as well as that stressing the continuity between his father and him, he must have been particularly conscious of the magnitude of the myths that he played a central role in creating, particularly his identity with his father, being painfully aware of the man that he was not. This disparity from his father contributed to a lifelong insecurity in Kim Jong-il, so that "majesty sits uncomfortably on his shoulders." It is always a difficult challenge to succeed a powerful father. But to succeed a father of God-like stature is psychologically impossible.

By his early 30s, he had held three positions in the Korean Workers Party (KWP) as his father systematically attempted to prepare his son to succeed him. Indeed, by the early 1970s, it was clear that Kim Il-sung was preparing his son to succeed him, and while the father remained the public face of the party, his son worked behind the scenes, progressively increasing his influence and control as the designated heir to the North Korean seat of power. By grooming his son to succeed him, Kim hoped to avoid in North Korea the aftermath of Stalin's death in the Soviet Union and of Mao's demise in the People's Republic of China. Kim Il-sung hoped to guarantee generational continuity and provide a basis not only for stability, but also for a "perpetuation of the system characteristics that tend[ed] to be unique and peculiar."[3]

It was during the 1970s that Kim Jong-il consolidated his position of power within the North Korean political system. Not tolerant of dissent during the 1970s, Kim "replaced thousands of officials at all levels of the party with younger members who would be personally loyal to him in gratitude for their promotion."[4] Kim worked assiduously to incorporate or eliminate his father's peers, depending on their support for him.

By 1973, Kim Jong-il was named Secretary of the KWP, and, in 1974, he was named a full member of the Politburo. In that year, he announced the Ten Principles, which among other things required absolute loyalty to Kim Il-sung, but also very cleverly reinforced the image of Kim Jong-il as fully aligned with his father and representative of his father's goals, stressing the continuity between Kim Il-sung and his son.

THE HEIR APPARENT, FULLY IN CHARGE

By 1980, Kim Jong-il was effectively in day-to-day control of the DPRK, including the intelligence apparatus, as manifested by three events that Kim Jong-Il is believed to have orchestrated and ordered – the 1978 kidnapping of South Korea's leading actress, Madame Choe Un-hui and her director-producer husband; the 1983 bombing in Rangoon by DPRK commandos that killed 17 senior officials only narrowly missed killing the South Korean president; and the 1987 midair bombing of KAL Flight 858 which killed 115. These bold, some would say foolhardy, missions demonstrated Kim Jong-il was fully in charge.

It was not until the 1990s that Kim Jong-Il began to assume DPRK government positions, becoming first deputy chair of the National Defense Commission and commander-in-chief of the Korean People's Army in 1990, despite having no military background himself. To cement his control of the DPRK, he became chair of the National Defense Commission in 1993. He worked hard to court the military. The issue of his lack of military experience was of concern, and thus the Propaganda and Agitation Department, where the younger Kim began his party career, began to fabricate a suitable résumé for him.[5] In addition to fabricating a military background for the younger Kim, the Department of Propaganda and Agitation aimed to further enhance Kim Jong-il's image as not only the rightful leader of North Korea, but also to portray him as an extension of his father. Further cementing his control, he became chairman of the KWP in 1997. He did not assume the presidency of North Korea, but rather maintained his control and power through chairing the National Defense Commission. Indeed, he designated his father, the charismatic founder of the nation, as, in effect, president for eternity. On the one hand, this has been characterized as an adroit political move, sparing Kim Jong-il the ultimate responsibility for policies that misfired, but it may also suggest that he was apprehensive concerning fully stepping into the giant shoes left by his father.

While reportedly a micromanager in most aspects of his leadership, he made an interesting exception in terms of economic development and devoted little or no time in his weekly schedule to economic matters. He said:

The Leader, while alive, told me that I must never get involved in economic issues. If I get involved in the economic issues, I can never take part in the party's activities or military activities. He said this to me over and over so that I do not forget the advice [passage omitted in original]. He told me I must let party officials and the administration's economic officials take charge of economic issues.[6]

This quote, from a secret speech he gave to senior officials following an inspection tour of Kim Il-sung University in December 1996, can be taken as reflecting an artful shifting of responsibility for economic problems to his subordinates.

The degree to which he was aware of the magnitude of his country's economic difficulties was not entirely clear. Was he aware that less than 10 percent of the plants in North Korea were running? He was assuredly well aware that South Korea was superior to North Korea in all aspects except in military capabilities, although he criticized South Korea, saying all that South Korean industry was doing was assembling products using parts imported from other countries. But, on the other hand, he frankly admitted that 60 percent of North Korean factories were not operating. It was on August 4, 1984, that Kim Jong-il made his statement (in the conversation with Sin) that only 40 percent of plants in North Korea were in operation.

KIM JONG-IL, INSECURE ABOUT PERSONAL APPEARANCE AND STATURE

Kim Jong-il, reportedly taking after his mother, was described as a short, overweight man who was very self-conscious about his appearance. Standing roughly 5 feet 2 inches tall, Kim reportedly had platform shoes custom built for him to reach his publicized 5-foot-6-inch height, weighed in around 175 pounds, and wore his hair in a flamboyant pompadour style to add additional height. Clearly, his short stature was a long-standing issue for him. Kang Myong-to, a son-in-law of (former) Premier Kang Song-san, in a book he wrote after defecting to South Korea, recalled: "The elders of the village [Ch'ilgol, the hometown of Kim Jong-il's mother] called Kim Jong-il 'shorty.'"[7] After eight years of house arrest, Madam Choe Un-hui, the South Korean actress he kidnapped, escaped. In her memoir, she recalled Kim's first words on meeting her. He reportedly asked, "Well, Madame Choe, you must be surprised to see I resemble the droppings of a midget."[8] He wore only custom tailored clothing made in Korea and was rarely seen without his dark glasses. He was traditionally seen in custom-made gray or tan factory foreman's slacks and a short jacket, and, for formal occasions, he most often was seen wearing a gray "Mao-style" jacket. Although he chose to wear styles in keeping with North Korean society, it was hard to miss the professionally tailored element of his wardrobe. The reason that Kim Jong-il never appeared wearing a military uniform in public places is thought to be because he had a complex about never having served in the military. He was reported to be extremely emotional, volatile, and unpredictable.

HEDONISTIC LIFE STYLE: A VIVID CONTRAST WITH THE SUFFERING OF HIS OWN POPULATION

Kim Jong-il lived an extremely hedonistic life style. Both Kim's lack of empathy and sense of entitlement were revealed in his indulgent lifestyle, which contrasts with the struggle of most North Koreans to simply feed themselves. Kim lived in a lavish seven-story pleasure palace in P'yong-yang, and defector reporting indicates that Kim maintained lavish villas in each of North Korea's provinces and had them furnished with imported luxury goods. He is reported to have secreted upward of $10 billion in Swiss bank accounts. According to the Hennessey Fine Spirits Corporation, for the decade 1989–1999, his annual expenditure for their most expensive cognac, Paradis, which sells for about $630 a bottle, was between $650,000 and $800,000, this with the annual income of the North Korean peasant at $900–$1,000 a year.

He entertained frequently at his residences, in what has been described as wild parties. These parties reportedly included entertainment provided by strippers and his "Joy Brigades." The Joy Brigades were composed of beautiful young women trained to entertain him and his cronies. Members reportedly were recruited from junior high schools every July, had to be virgins, and have pale, unblemished skin.[9] At these lavish parties, he drank heavily and expected those around him to do so as well.

According to the memoirs of the South Korean actress Choe Un-hui, Kim Jong-il was a heavy drinker. A Japanese hostess remembers having seen him drink heavily. He drank as if he were a man who believed "the amount of liquor a man drinks shows how big a man he is."[10]

When in a benevolent mood, Kim Jong-il was known to lavish his guests and friends with expensive gifts ranging from TVs and stereos, to bananas, pineapples, and mandarin oranges, all rare luxuries in North Korea. Kim appeared to maintain power both through such special perquisites and through domination and fear. Defectors reported that Kim's manipulative style included combinations of providing special privileges with humiliation and threat of punishment, including execution. Stories abound concerning executions ordered by Kim, although there is no direct evidence. There are even stories that he carried out some of these executions himself – again, whether true or not, the persistence of these stories serves to further his image. Regardless of the accuracy of these reports, the simple fact that they are so widespread adds to the cult of personality surrounding Kim, reinforcing his image as a strongman.

The gap between the self-indulgent hedonistic lifestyle of Kim and his inner circle in P'yong-yang and the privation of his people, and, for that matter, that of the lower level military, was extreme. Kim regularly called for sacrifices from the Korean people in pursuit of the mission of reunification. But the lack of sacrifice in the life of Dear Leader and his inner circle was striking, especially as he sought to create a public psychology that would maintain the nation on continuing war footage.

He was apparently very concerned with appearances and preferred to stay out of the public eye as much as possible, sometimes even being described as a recluse. In contrast to his father, who seemed at ease with large crowds and comfortable with people, Kim has been likened to the Wizard of Oz, "remaining out of sight, pulling levers from behind a screen."[11] He rarely spoke in public; in fact, his "Glory to the heroic Korean People's Army" spoken at the end of a two-hour military display in 1992 was the first time that Kim is known to have spoken in public. Even his speeches on TV and radio were read by narrators.[12]

He was fascinated by Western movies and was reported to have a DVD collection of some 10,000–20,000 titles. It may be that they informed his image of heroic leadership. Reported to be among his favorite movies was *The Godfather*, which was also said to have been a favorite of Saddam Hussein.

MALIGNANT NARCISSISM

Indeed, the characteristics Kim Jong-Il displayed indicate that he had the core features of the most dangerous personality disorder, *malignant narcissism*, the personality that characterized Saddam Hussein as well. *This personality is characterized by such extreme grandiosity and self-absorption that there is no capacity to empathize with others.* This is reflected in his lack of empathy with his own people, as well as in his difficulties in understanding his principal adversaries, the United States, South Korea, and Japan, and it can be associated with major political/military miscalculation.

No constraint of conscience. Kim's only loyalty was to himself and his own survival. But he also recognized the need to sustain his inner circle's perquisites and indulgent lifestyle because he required their support; he combined this lavish indulgence with humiliation to maintain his control over his leadership circle.

Paranoid orientation. Not paranoid in the sense of being psychotic or out of touch with reality, but rather always on guard, ready to be betrayed, seeing himself as surrounded by enemies.

Unconstrained aggression. Such a person will use whatever aggression is necessary, without qualm of conscience, be it to eliminate an individual or to strike out at a particular group.

Other characteristics of the narcissistic personality also contribute to flawed leadership performance and distortions in decision making. They include:

Great insecurity, preoccupation with one's own brilliance, appearance. Because of the need to be perfect, it is difficult to impart new information to him, and he reacts negatively to criticism.

Extreme sensitivity to slight. Accordingly, a tendency to surround oneself with sycophants who tell the leader what he wants to hear, rather than what he needs to hear, leading to an individual out of touch with political reality.

Over-optimism about one's own chances and a tendency to devaluate the adversary.

Will say or promise whatever is useful at the moment, but words are strictly instrumental to accomplish what is necessary, and apparently sincere committed agreements are easily changed or disregarded. Kim Jong-il's violation of the Agreed Framework is an excellent example.

Flawed interpersonal relationships. A tendency to see others as an extension of the self, with little capacity to appreciate the needs of others. Loyalty is accordingly a one-way street. Moreover, individuals who are seen to be powerful in their own right are perceived as a threat and are eliminated.

Because narcissistic individuals must be seen as perfect, when one of Kim's plans misfired, the problem was not the concept but the execution. Thus, Kim was ready to scapegoat when his plans didn't work out.

IMPLICATIONS FOR DECISION MAKING

Decision making in the DPRK was not by committee; Kim Jong-il held ultimate power. Although the exact decision-making structure in the military was and is unclear, it is believed that no military decision of any consequence was made without Kim Jong-il's approval. The only area he was not directly involved with was economic policy. It is unlikely that there was a free exchange of ideas with his advisers. And it was unlikely that he asked for advice or criticism or expressed uncertainty. Nevertheless, shrewd advisers were able to get information to Dear Leader and influence his opinions, as long as they did not contradict his worldview.

Kim had only limited empathy with his own people. Events testify to his comfort with tolerating high levels of deaths in the country. In confronting North Korea's famine, saving lives was not a top priority, and early in the famine cycle Kim cut off nearly all food supplies to the four eastern provinces and denied these provinces access to international aid.[13] Large numbers of deaths also occurred when, between 1997 and 1999, on Kim's orders, several hundred thousand people displaced by the famine were herded into camps where conditions allowed few to survive. Moreover, according to the testimony of eyewitnesses, Kim ordered the systematic killing of babies born in North Korea's camps for political prisoners.[14]

A revealing incident that he quoted with pride occurred during the last years of his father's life, when his father remonstrated with him concerning the starving North Korean people. This lack of concern for the Korean people was in contrast to the image of his father, Kim Il-sung. Kim Jong-il reportedly acknowledged only one occasion on which he disobeyed the Great Leader:

Only once have I disobeyed President Kim Il Sung. The President said, "Can you shave off some defense spending and divert it for the people's livelihoods?" I responded, "I am afraid not. Given the military pressure from the U.S., the Korean people must bear the hardship a little longer." How much pain I felt at my failure to live up to the expectations of the President who is concerned about raising the living standards of the people![15]

WHAT KIM VALUED

What Kim valued was his safety and regime survival, Pyong-yang, personal wealth, elite comfort, and total domestic control.

KIM JONG-IL'S VULNERABILITIES

The official DPRK policy was that the military comes first, at the expense of the economy and the general population. The North Korean economy is terminally broken and cannot be repaired, and communist-style central control and disproportionate military spending is leading to an implosion of the DPRK. As many as 3 million North Koreans have starved to death in famines; hundreds of thousands lost their lives in subsequent relocation to government-run camps. Kim Jong-il asked the population to endure continuing hardships while elites lived in luxury.

NO CORE ORGANIZING IDEAS OR PRINCIPLES

Given that his position flowed from his identification with and succession to his father, Kim Jong-il could not appear to abandon the founding principles of the republic, both *juche* and the ultimate goal of reunification of the Korean peninsula. But if we accept the premise that his basic loyalty was to himself (and by necessity to his inner circle) and that their survival with the perquisites of power were his highest priorities, how he lived up to his father's core principles was subject to interpretation. One could pay lip service to these principles while modifying them significantly from their initial intent and not being bound by them in a doctrinaire fashion. After all, the self-reliance of *juche* is not consistent with a program of actively seeking foreign assistance. Like relationships, ideas are instrumental for the consummate narcissist, and if they are no longer useful, they can be radically modified or discarded. Although Kim Jong-il did not possess core organizing ideas or principles, he was in many ways a captive of his oft-declared public policy because he employed the twin doctrines of *juche* and reunification to call for sacrifices on the part of the North Korean people.

Under Kim Jong-il's grandiose façade there was always extreme insecurity, which in turn affected his decision making. He dared not betray ignorance or uncertainty, so, after gathering input from his advisers, he would announce decisions, never vetting a proposed action with his advisers who, in fact, were reluctant to question Dear Leader's decisions. This produced a sycophantic leadership circle whose silent acquiescence gave the illusion of consensus.

THE NEXT GENERATION

It is interesting to observe, given the careful manner in which Kim Il-sung prepared for his son's succession, how Kim Jong-il ignored this issue until he suffered a major stroke in August 2008. This confrontation with his own mortality led him hastily to designate his third son, Kim Jong-Eun, as successor. The aggressive, provocative acts by the DPRK that have occurred since were probably designed to demonstrate the regime's "toughness" and pave the way for the dynastic succession of Kim Jong-eun.

It is widely speculated that North Korea's attack on a South Korean frigate, an incident that killed 46 South Korean sailors in March 2010, and the artillery shelling of Yeonpyeong Island were indications that Kim Jong-eun had to earn his stripes with the North Korean military and that Kim Jong-il was helping to build the credentials of his son. (Seoul is within artillery range of North Korea; this prompted great anxiety, led to widespread rioting, and put pressure on South Korean President Lee to act.) Unlike Kim Jong-il, who was designated successor some 30 years before his father's death and who held significant positions in his father's government – indeed, probably running North Korea for the last 15 years of his father's life – Kim Jong-eun was only designated as successor after his father's stroke. That his father had not earlier designated Kim Jong-eun as his successor, not doing so until illness forced his hand, must have contributed to insecurity in the heir apparent.

Indeed, there had been great uncertainty as to who would succeed Kim Jong-il. Kim Jong-eun has had virtually no experience, but nevertheless he was recently named a four-star general in the People's Army, deputy chairman of the military commission of the Workers' Party, a member of the party's Central Committee, and deputy chairman of the party's military commission.

Kim Jong-il died on December 18, 2011. He had been well seasoned for his position by his Father, Kim Il-sung, and while there had been provocative actions for two decades and frequent belligerent rhetoric, he always showed restraint and pulled back from the brink. In vivid contrast, Kim Jong-eun is unseasoned and inexperienced, and we cannot be confident of his wisdom, judgment, and self-control. This is especially so considering that the climate in South Korea changed under former President Lee Myung-bak, who came to office in 2008 vowing to end the decade-long Sunshine Policy[d] of his two predecessors. This change of policy spurred widespread support in South Korea for a strong response to North Korea's provocations, so there is a significant possibility that one side or the other will go too far and precipitate conflict. North Korea carried out two major provocative acts: launching a satellite, which also demonstrated their long-range missile capability, and staging an underground nuclear test as the new South Korean president, Park Geun-hye, took office. Given that Park Geun-hye

---

[d] The Sunshine Policy had as its goal easing tensions between North and South Korea through diplomatic contact and aid from the South to the North as confidence-building measures.

backed off from the more confrontational tone of her predecessor and that she had promised a strong defense as well as establishing a constructive dialogue, for North Korea to carry out these acts at that very moment seemed designed to heighten the confrontational stance between the neighboring countries.

CONCLUDING NOTE

Generational issues affecting three dictators have been discussed: Saddam Hussein who attempted early to groom his sons Uday and Qusay to succeed him, and Kim Jong-il who was carefully prepared by his charismatic father Kim Il-sung to succeed him, only to precipitously name his ill-seasoned son Kim Jong-eun to succeed him in response to a major stroke in 2008 that confronted him with his own mortality.

In this chapter, we reviewed how narcissistic dictators groom their sons to succeed them in a quest for immortality. But what happens when a son selected to carry on the family name is killed and cannot fulfill that designated role? Bashar al-Assad was the second choice as successor for his powerful father, Hafez al-Assad, after his brother Basil was killed in a car accident. And for Bashar, trying to live up to his father's towering model is a daunting task in responding to the pressures of the Arab Spring. Assad's long-time rival, Israeli Prime Minister Bibi Netayahu also was a leader by default. Setting the standard for this phenomenon of second choice sons was the 35th president of the United States, John Fitzgerald Kennedy. The next chapter explores the psychological consequences for the "second-choice" son, the leader by default.

Notes

1. Al-Hayat, June 18, 2001, FBIS-NES GMP20010618000048, London, 2.
2. NDSFK, "The Great Mangyongdae Family," March 2001, http://ndfsk.dyndns.org/kuguk8/pym/nr3/Magdae.htm.
3. Han Park, *North Korea: The Politics of Unconventional Wisdom* (Boulder, Colo.: Lynne Rienner, 2002), 149.
4. Kong Dan Oh and Ralph Hassig, *North Korea Through the Looking Glass* (Washington D.C.: Brookings Institution Press, 2000), 88.
5. Oh and Hassig, *North Korea Through the Looking Glass*, 89.
6. *Monthly Chosun*, April 1997, originally published in Korean, www.kimsoft.com/korea/kjj-kisu.htm.
7. Elaine Sciolino, "Blurred Images of North Korea's 'Junior,'" *The New York Times*, July 17, 1994, www.nytimes.com/1994/07/17/world/blurred-images-of-north-korea-s-junior.html?pagewanted=all&src=pm.
8. Sciolino, "Blurred Images of North Korea's 'Junior.'"
9. "North Korea's Likely New Leader Seen as Bizarre," *St. Petersburg Times*, July 10, 1994.
10. Osamu Eya, *Great Illustrated Book of Kim Jong Il*, trans. in FBIS document KPP 2002 0501000062 (Tokyo: Shogakukan, 2000).

11. Jeffrey R. Smith, "N. Korean Strongman: 'Crazy' or Canny?," *The Washington Post*, September 26, 1993, www.washingtonpost.com/wpdyn/content/article/2006/10/18/AR2006101800821.html.

12. "North Korea's Likely New Leader Seen as Bizarre."

13. Andrew Natsios, *The Great North Korean Famine: Famine, Politics, and Foreign Policy* (Washington, D.C.: United States Institute of Peace, 2001).

14. James Brooke, "N. Koreans Talk of Baby Killings," *The New York Times*, June 10, 2002, www.nytimes.com/2002/06/10/world/n-koreans-talk-of-baby-killings.html?pagewanted=all&src=pm.

15. Kim Myong Chol, "Kim Jong-il's Military Strategy for Reunification," *Comparative Strategy* 20, No. 4 (2001).

13

Leaders by Default: Second-Choice Sons

Ruthie Pertsis and Jerrold M. Post, M.D.

There is a small group of important international leaders who were not their parents' first choices to occupy the seats of power. They were raised in politically oriented families, chose their own paths in life (having embraced their own unique interests and skills), but were pushed into leadership positions because their brothers, the initially designated choices to carry on the family torch, died before they were able to fulfill the parents' dreams of glory. The devastated parents then turned to the sons who were next in line, who had grown up in the shadows of their brothers, and compelled them to abandon their own career ambitions and step in, paving the way for the "second-choice sons" to become leaders by default.

It is interesting to explore how they and their leaderships were impacted by the knowledge that they were not originally selected for the important positions that they eventually came to occupy and by the accompanying pressure that they surely felt at being under the watchful eyes of overbearing parents whose narcissistic needs were suddenly and belatedly projected onto them. What does it mean to grow up in the shadow of the blinding son, the designated hero, eclipsed by his larger-than-life stature?

John F. Kennedy, Benjamin Netanyahu, Rajiv Gandhi, and Bashar al-Assad are all leaders who fit this pattern. All had brothers who were rising political stars, but who died unexpectedly: Joseph Kennedy Jr. and Jonathan Netanyahu while serving in their countries' militaries, and Sanjay Gandhi and Basil al-Assad in tragic airplane and motorcycle accidents, respectively. Jack Kennedy and Benjamin Netanyahu were then called upon to continue the quest of fulfilling their fathers' frustrated dreams of glory; Rajiv Gandhi and Bashar al-Assad were then required to step in as substitute successors to continue the family dynasties.

This chapter was presented as a paper to the annual scientific meeting of the International Society of Political Psychology, July 9–12, 2011, Istanbul, Turkey by Ruthie Pertsis at a symposium organized and chaired by Dr. Post entitled "Dreams of Glory: Narcissism and Politics."

In all four cases, the challenges for the newly designated future leaders were then to step out of their brothers' shadows, become the leaders that their parents, for their own narcissistic reasons, needed them to be, and achieve identities as leaders in their own right. As the situation spirals out of control in Syria, it is becoming increasingly clear that Bashar al-Assad will fail to meet all of those challenges.

JOHN F. KENNEDY

John F. Kennedy is extolled as one of the most popular presidents in American history, but it is impossible to understand his rise to the world's most powerful position without first understanding the generational issues that made it possible. John was the second-born son of Joseph Patrick Kennedy, Sr., prominent American businessman and political figure, who long had his eye on the White House. However, it was while serving as the Ambassador to the Court of St. James that his dreams of becoming the first Roman Catholic American president were eventually crushed under the weight of his fervent anti-Semitism, his support for the appeasement of Adolf Hitler before the outbreak of World War II, and his increasingly isolationist views. Refusing to be relegated to the dustbins of history, though, Joe turned to his first-born son and namesake, Joseph Patrick Kennedy Jr., to regain his legitimacy and achieve sweet redemption.

In fact, the grooming of Joe Jr. for a life of public success went further back than his father, with maternal grandfather John Fitzgerald declaring to a reporter upon Joe Jr.'s birth that "He *is* going to be president of the United States . . . his mother and father have already decided that he is going to Harvard, where he will play on the football and baseball teams and incidentally take all the scholastic honors. Then he's going to be a captain of industry until it's time for him to be president for two or three terms. Further than that has not been decided. He may act as mayor of Boston or governor of Massachusetts for a while on his way to the presidential chair."[1] A rather heady curriculum vitae spelled out in advance!

Partly because of this, Jack never seriously challenged the assumption that his older brother would be the preeminent political figure of the new generation of the Kennedy family. Moreover, Jack was more interested in international politics from early on, even during the particularly isolationist period in American history after World War I. He was often dismayed by the extreme isolationist views of his brother and father, which contributed to his own emerging internationalist worldview.[2] It is safe to say that Jack Kennedy would have been happy as a journalist exploring the world; he spent summers in the 1930s traveling in Europe and even wrote his 1940 undergraduate honors thesis, entitled "Why England Slept," on the topic of the country's unwillingness to prepare for war until it became inevitable.[3] Still, it is possible that precisely *because* Joe Jr. had been designated as the family's political leader, Jack became attracted to international politics as a way to assert his independence and demonstrate that he was different from his brother and father.

It was only after the bombing of Pearl Harbor that the United States could no longer ignore international developments, and the country joined the Allied forces in World War II. John F. Kennedy's life was forever changed. His attempts to enlist in the military were initially blocked for medical reasons, but, through his father's influence, he was given a commission in the navy by the director of the Office of Naval Intelligence who had served as an aide to Kennedy Sr. when he was the Ambassador to Great Britain. As a result of his heroic actions during an extremely dangerous mission in August 1943, when, despite being injured, he rescued a wounded crew member and saw his entire crew to safety, Jack was awarded the Navy and Marine Corps medal and became a national war hero.[4]

But, more importantly, just a year later, his beloved brother and lifelong competitor Lieutenant Joseph P. Kennedy Jr. was killed while flying an aerial mission over Europe. In fact, the circumstances surrounding the mission suggest that his brother had stayed out in the war zone longer than required because Jack had earlier achieved heroic status, temporarily surpassing him, and Joe Jr. wanted to claim glory for himself.[5] Having in mind the long-standing rivalry and knowing that his brother had volunteered for the mission, Jack may well have felt guilty about his death.

The Kennedy family and its dreams of an American president within its midst were shattered by this death, but only temporarily. The family patriarch, who had long equated his own success and happiness with those of his eldest son, was especially devastated by the tragedy, but he soon, very unashamedly, turned to his second-choice son, John, as the new vehicle for his hopes and dreams, the son to bring him the glory that had so long eluded him. He made no mistake about the fact that "Jack went into politics because young Joe died. Young Joe was going to be the politician in the family. When he died, Jack took his place."[6] At the same time, this was a major period of psychological crisis for Jack himself; not only had he lost his brother, but now he had to step into his shoes and engrave the Kennedy name on history, as everyone was so sure that Joe Jr. would have done. In the words that John would later make famous in his presidential inaugural speech, "the torched had been passed down."

The death of his older brother continued to have a profound impact on Jack throughout his life, especially during the time surrounding his presidency. When defending himself as a Catholic running for office, John often made reference to his and his brother's time spent in the armed forces: "Nobody asked me if I was a Catholic when I joined the United States Navy ... Nobody asked my brother if he was a Catholic or Protestant before he climbed into an American bomber plane to fly his last mission ... I'm able to serve in Congress, and my brother was able to give his life, but we can't be President?"[7] (Note the "we," suggesting Jack's identification with his brother.)

Later on, memories of Joe Jr.'s death were again revived when 114 Cubans and Americans were killed during the failed Bay of Pigs invasion. President

Kennedy was racked with guilt and ultimately took full responsibility.[8] The invasion triggered memories of war, which would always come to remind Jack of his brother and his feeling of responsibility for his death. After Joe's death, an American warship was named in his honor – the *U.S.S. Joseph P. Kennedy, Jr.* – which, ironically, was among the ships that President Kennedy later used to enforce the blockade of Cuba during the Cuban Missile Crisis,[9] an event that came to define his presidency.

In all of these ways, we can clearly see the continuing looming presence of his older brother in Jack's life, long after Joe died and Jack was required to take his place. It was precisely because Joseph P. Kennedy Jr. had been such a monumental figure in life – and an even more monumental hero in death – that Jack had to spend the rest of his life working to prove himself a worthy successor.

With the enormous pressure that his father put on Jack to take over the role as the family's torchbearer, that task became even greater. The elder Kennedy once declared: "I got Jack into politics, I was the one. I told him Joe was dead and that it was therefore his responsibility to run for Congress. He didn't want to. He felt he didn't have the ability and he still feels that way. But I told him he had to."[10] These are not exactly the words of a supportive father; but they are those of an extremely narcissistic man who quite blatantly used his children to fulfill his own frustrated dreams of glory. Such exploitation would ultimately cost him the lives of three sons, Joe Jr., Jack, and later, Robert, all of whom died as a result of their father's vision of an enduring Roman Catholic presidency in the United States that bore the Kennedy name. His inability to see beyond himself was a hallmark of his own narcissistic personality. This created a situation in which his children became, as he himself described them, "hostages to his fortune."[11]

Still, John worked hard and eventually became the man, and national leader, that his father needed him to be after Joe Jr. died. Unlike Benjamin Netanyahu's father, who will be addressed in the next section, Joseph P. Kennedy was extremely proud of his son for what he had accomplished, particularly because of what it meant for his own stature. When John F. Kennedy arrived at his inauguration, "Joe rose up out of his seat to salute his son. The Kennedy patriarch had been his children's greatest enthusiast, but no matter what honors they merited, what race they won, he had never stood up to pay tribute to their achievements."[12] Joe Sr. had been waiting for that moment since his own presidential aspirations had been crushed two decades earlier, and it was only then that "he had achieved what few men do, his transcendent dream embodied in this president bearing his name."[13]

For somebody else, making his or her father proud would have been enough to feel satisfied. But for Jack, who had always been his father's second-choice son, and who was still only a leader by default, it was not enough: "his psychological agenda was always clear: to put a thumbprint on history, and ... to achieve 'greatness,'"[14] in his own right. Given that the ongoing Cold War with the Soviet Union was standing in the way of his absolute success as president, Kennedy was unable to achieve greatness on Earth. Instead, he reached for the stars, quite literally, and launched America's space program, which, together with his leadership during the Cuban Missile Crisis, were to mark his greatest presidential accomplishments. The creation of the Kennedy Space Center, in particular, would ensure that the family name would forever be hard to forget, precisely what the Kennedy patriarch had worked his whole life to accomplish.

For 27 years, John F. Kennedy's life was defined by the fact that he was second-in-line. Finally, after taking his position as leader of the entire free world, he had become number one. So well had he proved to himself and to others that he deserved to be in the seat of power, and so confident had he become, that this led to a sense of invulnerability, and he refused the additional security measures that were strongly suggested to him by his Secret Service agents for his public appearance in Dallas, Texas, on November 22, 1963. Much like Rajiv Gandhi (and his mother, Indira, before him), Kennedy paid with his life in his quest to live up to the legacy of the family name.

BENJAMIN NETANYAHU

The story of Benjamin Netanyahu, Israel's current prime minister, is remarkably similar to that of John F. Kennedy. Netanyahu's father, like Kennedy's, had been rejected by his country because of his extremist views and thus needed to redeem himself through his first-born son. However, as in the Kennedy case, that son, Jonathan, was killed while serving in the military, and the elder Netanyahu turned to his next son, Benjamin, who was a rising star in the world of business, to carry on the family name, much as Joe Kennedy Sr. turned to John.

The Netanyahu family saga really begins with Benjamin's paternal grandfather, Nathan Mileikowsky, who moved his family from Russia to Palestine in 1920 and changed his family name to Netanyahu, translated to mean "given by God" or "God's gift."[15] While still living in Russia, Mileikowsky first had been a follower of Theodor Herzl, the founder of Zionism, and then of Ze'ev Jabotinsky, who broke with Herzl and founded Revisionist Zionism, a more right-wing and radical version of the original movement to establish a Jewish homeland in Palestine. Benzion ("son of Zion") Netanyahu, Mileikowsky's eldest son, followed in his father's footsteps, at one time even working as Jabotinsky's secretary,[16] and he developed very right-wing and radical views. His views were seen to be especially extreme given the left-wing politics of the Labor party that dominated Israeli society throughout the 1940s, '50s, and '60s,[17] when Benzion was working to establish himself as a historian and an academic.

Eventually, frustrated with the Israeli universities for not taking him and his views seriously, Benzion moved his family, including his three sons Jonathan, Benjamin, and Iddo, to the United States, where he pursued a fruitful career; over the years, he held teaching positions at Dropsie University in Philadelphia, the University of Denver, and Cornell University, teaching mainly Jewish history and literature. Still, he would never forgive the country that he claimed to have helped build, as many of the early settlers did, and that subsequently turned its back on him. Even when Benzion moved his family back to Israel, Menachem Begin, the leader of the right-wing Likud party, which was born out of the Revisionist Zionist movement and took power in Israel in 1977, did not offer him a position, further alienating him from mainstream politics.[18]

Jonathan Netanyahu, Benzion's eldest son, grew up very much admiring his father, even though the latter paid far more attention to his books and his research than to his family. In a letter to his father in July 1967, after Jonathan had returned to Israel, he wrote "When I was in the army I noticed that I could endure and persevere, both physically and emotionally, way after everyone else 'broke down.' It's quite plain to me that I inherited this marvelous gift from you, just as I inherited from you most of my traits."[19] It seems that Jonathan inherited more than just his father's traits, however; Benzion's first-born son showed a continuation of his father's beliefs. About the future of Israel, he once wrote "any compromise will simply hasten the end. As I don't want to tell my grand-children about the Jewish state in the twentieth century as . . . a transient episode in the thousands of years of wandering, I want to hold on here with all my might."[20] In this way, Jonathan demonstrated his father's tough stance toward the Arab–Israeli conflict, as well as his tendency to see everything in a historical context. Benzion's frustrated dreams of glory would surely be fulfilled by his eldest son, who had already made a name for himself in the country as a very well-respected army man, one who the family believed "would one day be Israel's chief of staff, after which he would . . . get elected prime minister."[21]

The fact that Jonathan was "the talented and beloved son who 'carried the family torch' and was earmarked from an early age to be a star, the hope of the family"[22] could have made his relationship with Benjamin, the family's second son, very difficult. However, Benjamin and Jonathan Netanyahu were extra-ordinarily close and supported each other endlessly. It is possible that Benzion's virtual absence from his children's daily lives made Jonathan something of a father figure for Benjamin. In 1967, upon being accepted to Harvard University, Jonathan wrote to Benjamin: "Bibi, Mother wrote me that you were even happier about my being admitted to Harvard than by your own acceptance to Yale. I think you could say the same for me; the part of the cable that announced that you had been accepted by Yale made me happiest."[23] It was as though they were truly a team, and the success of one translated into the success of both. Later, when Jonathan returned to the United States to attend Harvard and Benjamin returned to Israel to join the army, Jonathan wrote to his brother: "Many times, especially here in America, I miss you *terribly*. Even when I was in Israel I didn't miss anyone at home as much as I missed you. I think the reason may be that you're the only true friend I ever had."[24] Clearly, they were more than just brothers; they depended on each other in the most fundamental ways.

An anecdote from their childhood is particularly illuminating: Benzion would tell them stories about Jewish heroes in history, and they were "especially fascinated by the tale of the Maccabees, the heroic brothers who led the Jewish revolt against the Greeks and restored the Temple of Jerusalem."²⁵ Benjamin and Jonathan would later serve in Israel's most elite army unit together, and they led several operations against their country's enemies to restore the Jewish homeland, themselves becoming the modern-day Maccabee brothers.

The death of Jonathan in 1976 during a military operation to rescue Jewish passengers from a hijacked plane was a tragedy for Israel, even though the mission itself was one of the country's greatest success stories. A team of Palestinian and German terrorists had hijacked the aircraft, which began its journey in Tel Aviv and was flying to Paris, and rerouted it to the airport in Entebbe, Uganda. The terrorists held 107 Jewish hostages for seven days; their aim was to coerce Israel to release Palestinian prisoners.²⁶ The Israeli Defense Forces mounted an extremely daring surprise nighttime raid on the airport, managing to save all but a handful of the hostages, but losing the commander of the operation, Lieutenant Colonel Jonathan Netanyahu. Becoming a symbol of Israel's victory over terrorism, Jonathan was immediately elevated to the status of national hero, and the operation was renamed Operation Jonathan in his honor.

No matter how devastating the loss for the country, Jonathan's death was an utter heartbreak for the Netanyahu family, especially for his father and his brother: "[Jonathan]'s death is without a doubt the worst thing that has ever happened to Benjamin Netanyahu. It left a void in [his] heart that can never be filled."²⁷ Benjamin had lost not only a brother, but a true hero, and now he had to step into his enormous shoes and take over the task of propelling forward their father's vision of a secure Jewish state that spanned both sides of the river Jordan. This was very likely in Benjamin's mind when, shortly after his brother's death, he founded the Jonathan Institute, an organization designed to raise awareness about the dangers of international terrorism.²⁸

Thus, calling attention to international terrorism and Israel's special vulnerability to it was Benjamin's extremely successful launch into the world of politics. Indeed, throughout his eloquent oratory on the world stage, the need to defend Israel was his paramount theme. In entering the world of politics, he was faced with the continuing challenge of living up to the idealized heroic image of his brother and the impossible standards of his father.

A former senior advisor to Benjamin recently divulged that his father, Benzion, had not been supportive of him during the 1996 elections in Israel in which he was elected prime minister for the first time. During the election campaign, Benjamin declared that he would support the Oslo Accords, the secretly negotiated declaration of principles to serve as a framework for negotiations to settle outstanding "final status" issues between Israel and the Palestinians. The advisor observed a sense of disappointment on Benzion's part, as though Benjamin was not the great man who should lead the country.²⁹ Indeed, for Benzion, it was a sense of betrayal by his own son. When Benjamin attempted to explain that it was necessary to compromise for tactical reasons, the embittered Benzion countered that what begins as tactical ends in betrayal of principle.[30] Apparently, Benzion never fully recovered from the loss of Jonathan and the dreams of glory that died with him, leaving Benjamin in the shadow of his brother, never able to please his father.

Still, Benzion's intense focus on history was not lost on Benjamin. Much like Jonathan, Benjamin consistently makes historical references a central feature of his writings and speeches; coincidentally, one of those references was to John F. Kennedy and his willingness to take the world to the brink of nuclear war because of a Cuban port, to which he compared the dangers of missiles reaching Tel Aviv's port.[31] More recently, however, in a 47-minute address to the U.S. Congress, he spoke of Israel's position in the world within the context of (in chronological order) the 4,000-year-old bond between Jews and the land of their forefathers, the Holocaust, the Islamist overthrow of Iran's government in 1979, the independence movements in Eastern Europe in 1989, and Lebanon's Cedar Revolution in 2005.[32]

Most tellingly, though, he spoke of the loss of his own brother to terrorism, personalizing his concern with Israel's security, a theme that has been a hallmark throughout his political career, as summed up in his campaign slogan in the 1996 election, "Peace with Security." Still, no matter how hard he works to prove that he is protecting his country or how uncompromising he is in the face of massive international pressure to find a solution to the Palestinian question, Benjamin knows that he will never live up to his brother's idealized image or his father's extreme absolutist expectations.

The elder Netanyahu's absolutist morality and his commitment to the principles of revisionist Zionism were always a constraint on his son's ability to compromise. Benzion died on April 30, 2012, at the age of 102, and on May 8, only eight days after his father's death, Benjamin stunned the political world by announcing the formation of a broad-based coalition "unity" government. This was considered by most a brilliant political move that strengthened his position, but it is doubtful that he could have accomplished this political feat while his absolutist father was still alive. For, undoubtedly, major compromises were required to accomplish this, and compromise was equivalent to moral betrayal for his father. Indeed, perhaps this need to compromise can explain the collapse of the unity government a mere 70 days after its formation, over the issue of the mandatory draft of ultra-Orthodox men into the Israeli military. After initially agreeing to uphold a Supreme Court ruling invalidating a law that granted draft exemptions to thousands of Israeli men, Netanyahu ultimately yielded to the pressure of the right-wing and religious factions of his government,[33] suggesting that his father's characteristic aversion to political concessions would live on in the younger Netanyahu. On the other hand, some might point to Netanyahu's role in the prolonged negotiations with Hamas to release captured Israeli soldier Gilad Shalit in October 2011, which saw Shalit exchanged for more than 1,000 Palestinian prisoners, as evidence that he can, in fact, make concessions when they are popularly supported. But indeed, the overwhelming explanation for this apparent about-face is that it was Netanyahu's wife, Sara – who reportedly is very involved in his policy decisions – who made the mission to free Shalit her own and persuaded him to act.[34]

He has also found it difficult to compromise on an international level, pressing the world, and specifically U.S. President Barack Obama, on the need to stop Iran from developing nuclear capabilities. While many, especially in Israel, share his general views on a nuclear Iran, very few would go as far as he has in getting his message across. This includes indirectly interfering in American domestic politics just months before the 2012 presidential election by pushing Obama to draw a "red line," which, if crossed by Iran, would commit the United States to a military strike on Iranian nuclear sites. At the UN General Assembly in September 2012, he showed the same unyieldingness, also paying homage to his historian father by making references to the Bible's King David, Joshua, Abraham, Isaac, Jacob, and, interestingly, the Maccabees.

After months of rocket fire into Israel by Hamas, Israel's targeted assassination of Hamas military leader Ahmed Jabari in November 2012 triggered a major escalation in the conflict, with, for the first time, missiles striking Tel Aviv and Jerusalem. The Israeli government mobilized reserves and massed troops along its border with Gaza but eventually agreed to a ceasefire after eight days of deadly clashes between the two sides, with both claiming victory. Had Benzion lived to see this latest surge in violence, surely he would not have considered the outcome a victory for Israel, for he believed that "We should conquer any disputed territory in the land of Israel. Conquer and hold it, even if it brings us years of war."[35] Thus, he certainly would have been critical of his son's reluctance to send ground troops into Gaza and undoubtedly would have disapproved of his willingness to accept a ceasefire under major international pressure. But only nine days later, one day after the UN upgraded the Palestinians' status from "Observer Entity" to "Observer State," as though in an attempt to redeem himself, Netanyahu authorized the construction of 3,000 new housing units in the West Bank. With the settlements one of the biggest sources of contention in the Israeli–Palestinian negotiations, Netanyahu's highly provocative act signaled that he will "hold it, even if it brings us years of war". Although his political position was significantly weakened after the January 2013 elections, at least in part due to unrelated domestic issues, he will find it very difficult to compromise his hard-line stance.

RAJIV GANDHI

Rajiv Gandhi also fits well into the overall theme of the "second-choice" son and leader by default, although he, like Bashar al-Assad – the next and final case study in this chapter – differs in at least one major way from both John F. Kennedy and Benjamin Netanyahu: he was not fulfilling the hopes and dreams of a narcissistic parent who did not become a leader in his own right. Instead, he was fulfilling the hopes and dreams of a narcissistic parent, his mother Indira

Gandhi, the third prime minister of India, who wanted nothing more than to continue the dynastic succession that had dominated Indian politics for nearly four uninterrupted decades. The immense power that the family held even made Indian novelist Salman Rushdie quip that "when it comes to power, they make the Kennedys look like amateurs."[36]

Indira was the granddaughter of Motilal Nehru, a prominent Indian independence activist and leader of the Indian National Congress, and the only child of Jawaharlal Nehru, the first prime minister of independent India. Having succeeded her father, who had succeeded his own father, the question after she took power in 1966 soon became: who would succeed her?

The answer to that question was clear from early on. Indira had two sons with her husband, Feroze Gandhi, and one of them quickly emerged as the obvious choice. Contrary to Indian tradition, in which the eldest son is usually the family's most treasured, it was in fact Rajiv's younger brother, Sanjay, who was selected as Indira's heir apparent. This important fact distinguishes Rajiv from the rest of the leaders in this paper, men who stood in the shadows of their older brothers.

Rajiv had early on made clear his disdain for politics and the way in which his family gained and retained power. The idealistic Rajiv seems to have been psychologically driven to set himself apart from his family, whom he deemed corrupt. There were several notable manifestations of these persistent adolescent psychodynamics. To begin with, he married an Italian Catholic woman, knowing that interreligious marriage is extremely contentious in Indian culture, perhaps unconsciously attempting to guarantee that the world of Indian politics would be closed to him (Indira herself, as an assertion of her own independence, had generated much controversy when she defiantly married an Indian Parsi, and Sanjay also broke with tradition when he married an Indian Sikh, but Rajiv's wife was entirely foreign and could disrupt the Indian bloodline). He also refused to live in his mother's residence when she was prime minister after returning from his studies in the United Kingdom, which was quite unusual and demonstrated how profoundly he wanted to be seen as his own man. Finally and most importantly, he eventually chose to become an airline pilot instead of entering the "family business" of politics, even refusing to use his last name while flying, preferring to identify himself as "Captain Rajiv,"[37] presumably lest others conflate his own success with that of his family.

Thus, there emerges another important difference between the brothers Gandhi: while Sanjay had first come to power because he was his mother's son, Rajiv had become a very well-respected pilot for Indian Airlines "entirely on his own, without making use of any family advantage."[38]

Sanjay, in stark contrast to Rajiv, was tough, aggressive, and had a tendency to take risks, and he was temperamentally akin to his mother. This made him her favored son and naturally inclined her to choose him as her successor. Sanjay proved himself to be a natural-born politician, and he swiftly became Indira's closest confidante and advisor. The regime they co-created led to her legacy being described as "an admixture of the 'good, the bad and the ugly,'"[39] with no shortage of corruption charges leveled against the Gandhi leadership.

Indeed, it was the charges of corruption by the country's independent judicial system that led Sanjay to press for the State of Emergency, which his mother declared on June 25, 1975, during which thousands of political opponents were jailed and severe censorship was placed on the press.[40] During the Emergency, Sanjay proved that he took his role as one of Indira's closest advisors very seriously, not afraid to direct extreme policies without her knowledge when he thought necessary. There were reports that forced and brutal sterilizations were taking place under his direction, which Indira adamantly refused to believe, being reassured that they were unsubstantiated rumors.[41] How could her idealized son possibly do such a thing? This particular episode also speaks to the possibility that Sanjay appealed to Indira's dark and aggressive side, taking care of the "dirty work" behind the scenes and putting many of his shady associates in official positions, while Indira continued to lead the country and turn a blind eye to Sanjay's rampant corruption. The Emergency ended in 1977, but Sanjay's influence continued. Indeed, he has been credited with getting her reelected as India's prime minister in 1980.[42]

Although he chose a life far away from politics, Rajiv still held very strong views about his country and was quite critical of his brother's policies.[43] Still, he remained far removed from the prime minister's house, and "to this day, no one seems to know whether he ever talked politics with Sanjay – the favoured younger brother with whom his relations are said to have been sometimes difficult."[44] Given how different they were, and their respective positions relative to their mother, it seems to be a gross understatement that their relations were "sometimes difficult." Regardless of their relationship with each other, though, it was clear to and accepted by both that Sanjay was the better candidate for Indira's successor. Still, the fact that Indira had skipped over Rajiv, her first-born son, to identify Sanjay as the family's torchbearer must have been difficult for Rajiv on some level, even though his soft-spoken nature and tendency to keep a low profile made him an ill fit for prime minister.

But Rajiv was to be left choiceless in the matter. In July 1980, Sanjay was killed in an airplane crash attributed to his reckless flying, and Rajiv, the second-choice son, was officially anointed as Sanjay's replacement as Indira's successor. Eventually, after Indira's own death at the hands of an assassin four years later, Rajiv became a leader by default. When Rajiv stepped into the political spotlight, many throughout the country and even within his own party wondered "whether the untested Rajiv Gandhi would have enough of his mother's mettle to keep his country together."[45] They were presumably comparing him to Sanjay, who had long been their mother's closest confidant and who it was clear would have emulated her leadership very vigilantly, having helped her run the country when she was in power. Thus, even before he made his first move, the new prime minister of the world's largest democracy had the overwhelming weight of his mother, his brother, and the future of India on his shoulders.

In fact, it proved to be good for Rajiv that, a short while after he officially took power in 1984, he had not had a better relationship with Sanjay. It seems that the former's "Mr. Clean" reputation,[46] having been so separated from his family's politics all along, was exactly what the country needed after the disaster of Indira's (and Sanjay's) rule, with particular reference to the period of the Emergency. One analyst captured this sentiment particularly well in noting that "Rajiv Gandhi's most obvious handicap, his inexperience, is also a strength."[47] But that inexperience, coming from a noble place as it did, may have contributed to Rajiv's own fall several years later.

It must not be forgotten that Rajiv was the great-grandson of Motilal Nehru, the grandson of Jawaharlal Nehru, and the son of Indira Gandhi; the legacy that he had to live up to was daunting. What is more, he was "the first Indian prime minister to have come of age in independent India, without direct experience of the independence struggle or the hopes it aroused."[48] But, unlike Sanjay, who had a natural flair for politics and leadership, this terrain was by no means comfortable for Rajiv. In fact, he may well have felt that he was in "over his head."

This may have contributed to an unevenness of performance as leader, perhaps manifested in Rajiv's unwise decision to send Indian troops into Sri Lanka in the hopes of enforcing an end to the country's civil war and gaining praise for himself and his efforts. Unfortunately, however, the move fiercely antagonized Sri Lanka's Tamil Tigers, one of the parties to the war, and a member of the group blew herself up while bowing at Rajiv's feet as he was campaigning for prime minister on May 21, 1991.[49]

The assassination of Rajiv was an eerie reminder of Indira's assassination seven years earlier, especially given that both had ignored warnings against their actions; Indira was advised not to attack a Sikh holy site, the revenge for which was her killing, and Rajiv was advised to take extreme security precautions during the 1991 campaign because of his polarizing actions in Sri Lanka, although "he frequently drove in an open vehicle, and greeted the people at mass rallies."[50] Rajiv's leadership from 1984 to 1989 was not particularly distinguished, but in the actions that led to his death, he demonstrated an uncharacteristic decisiveness. What seems to emerge is essentially a generational pattern of martyrdom, through which his mother was able to live out her dream of dying for the cause and her "second choice" son was finally able to gain a stature in death that had eluded him in life.

The Indian National Congress Party, which had become synonymous with the Gandhi name, was now bereft of a leader. The party's leaders decided to name Rajiv's widow, Sonia Gandhi, as his successor, even though she was an Italian Catholic, to retain its identity as the Gandhi party; she now serves as its president. It will be interesting to see how Rajiv and Sonia's son, Rahul, who is now involved in Indian politics himself, will represent the fifth generation of the Nehru-Gandhi tradition.

BASHAR AL-ASSAD

As mentioned earlier, although Bashar al-Assad fits well into the general pattern of "second-choice son" and thus leader by default, he more closely resembles Rajiv Gandhi than either John F. Kennedy or Benjamin Netanyahu in that he was brought in after the death of his brother in order to succeed his father as president and continue the family dynasty (both Kennedy and Netanyahu, on the other hand, were fulfilling their fathers' own failed dreams of glory). What also ties Bashar al-Assad to Rajiv Gandhi specifically, however, is the sharp difference between them and their brothers, who were the initially chosen successors. While both Kennedy and Netanyahu were outgoing, aggressive, and had personalities that would eventually lend themselves to the world of politics, Bashar al-Assad and Rajiv Gandhi could not have imagined more unfitting futures for themselves, and their apparent discomfort with the world of politics and leadership contributed to an unevenness in their performance as leaders.

Bashar's father, Hafez al-Assad, ruled Syria with an iron fist for three decades, including enforcing draconian emergency laws in 1963 that helped him eliminate political opponents and pave, sometimes quite literally, the way for the family to secure long-term political control.[51] Most dramatic was the near total destruction in 1982 of the population of Hama, a center of resistance where an estimated 10,000 to 20,000 Syrians were killed; Hafez subsequently paved over the town, leaving no trace of the massacre. Tom Friedman has since characterized this tendency to totally eliminate threats to his power as "Hama Rules."[52]

Hafez had originally designated his eldest and favorite son, Basil, as his successor, and Basil, the chief of presidential security, was perfect for the job, the ideal candidate. He "often appeared in full military uniform at official functions, was a forceful character, the eldest of five children, a competitive horse rider and an aficionado of fast cars who was popular with women," as opposed to Bashar, Hafez's second son, who "grew up in [Basil's] shadow, 'weak and in his own world', ... 'calm with a soft voice.'"[53] Most expected that Basil would simply continue where Hafez had left off.

But, on January 21, 1994, while Bashar was having a routine day at the Western Eye Hospital in London, where he was completing his postgraduate training in ophthalmology, Basil was killed in a car accident in Damascus.[54] Bashar was immediately called back to Syria, and the transition of successor from Basil to Bashar began very shortly thereafter. Bashar's appointment after Basil's unexpected death was a welcome development, both domestically and internationally, for Bashar appeared to be more moderate than his father and brother. But if it was welcomed by the people of Syria and by the international community, Hafez assuredly must have been uneasy about whether Bashar could fill his shoes, as he knew that Basil would have.

It wasn't until Hafez's own death in June 2000, though, that Bashar officially took power. He was raced through the military and political ranks, and the minimum age for presidential candidates was lowered to 34, not coincidentally Bashar's age at the time.[55] Many, especially in the West, had high hopes that the young new Syrian president would be a reformer who would adopt a more open approach to leading the country than his father. But, all too soon, hopes for major change were disappointed.

In the new president's inaugural speech in July 2000, he made promises of creative thinking, constructive criticism, transparency, and democracy, leading to hopes, both domestically and internationally, that he would indeed be a reformer. If there was any doubt that Bashar al-Assad has all but abandoned his supposed initial reformist ideals, then a Human Rights Watch report published in 2010 provides ample evidence to support that unfortunate reality. The 35-page document, entitled *A Wasted Decade: Human Rights in Syria during Bashar al-Assad's First Ten Years in Power*, highlights areas in which the Syrian government, and al-Assad in particular, have failed to fulfill the promises set out in 2000.[56] Identified are issues relating to significant abuses of political and human rights, with the conclusion, quite fittingly, that "without reform ... [Bashar] al-Assad's legacy will merely extend that of his father: government by repression."[57] Given the direct influence of Hafez and the vacuum left by Basil on Bashar's political development – and the added fact that the rebellion inspired by the Arab Spring has blossomed into a frank civil war – that Bashar is having difficulty in coping with this major extended crisis should come as no surprise.

But the initial hopes that Bashar would be an open-minded and liberal leader for Syria rested on a fragile foundation. Similar to Muammar al-Qaddafi's son Saif, the thrust of the argument was based on Bashar's supposed "Westernization" during his time living and studying ophthalmology in London. He was 27 at the time, a fully formed adult, and had spent his life absorbing his father's political ideas and observing his leadership style, in particular how to deal with conflict. What is more, Bashar only spent about 18 months in London[58] and was almost certainly significantly insulated by personal security forces during that time, so that his actual exposure to "Western" ways of life was likely quite limited. Moreover, mere exposure to Western culture, even if it is direct, is by no means a guarantee that an individual will adopt and internalize its values and ideals. Contributing to the Westernized image is his elegant British-born wife, Asma, whose parents emigrated from Syria to the United Kingdom. A former investment banker with J. P. Morgan, a woman whose acute sense of style has drawn the attention of East and West alike, Asma may have indeed reflected Bashar's genuine desire to bring Syria into the modern world.

But the stormy waves of political reality were to overcome whatever hopes he may have had. Under increasing press for political reform, Bashar found his minority Alawite leadership increasingly threatened, and his inner circle pressed him to put a lid on the restive population, as his father would have done.

In fact, the earliest sign that Bashar would stay true to his father's legacy – and one that speaks volumes about his destiny of fulfilling the hopes and dreams of the highly narcissistic Hafez – is the very decision that has made some contest that he is fundamentally different from his father: the decision to become an ophthalmologist. According to Leverett,[59] it was, in fact, young Hafez's dream to study medicine, but his family lacked the financial resources and he instead chose a life in the military and then in politics. "Bashar's decision to pursue a medical career undoubtedly won him a unique sort of paternal approval,"[60] and so it was not surprising that, when duty called, the devoted son would abandon his medical career to prepare to succeed his ailing father.

Since the uprisings in the Arab world spread to Syria, hardly a day goes by without the al-Assad name in the news and reports of further violence against civilians. It seems that, now more than ever, observers are looking specifically at Bashar, questioning whether he is in full control of Syria, given speculation that his younger brother, Maher, who heads the Syrian army's elite Fourth Division and Republican Guard and holds considerable sway in the country's intelligence services, is in fact behind the brutal crackdown of protesters that began in March 2011.[61] An anonymous source close to the al-Assad family revealed to the BBC that Bashar was not actually the obvious first choice as eldest brother Basil's replacement and that Maher had been considered for the position.[62] This likely would have instilled in Bashar feelings of inadequacy and inferiority on taking power, making it all the more important for him to assert his leadership, especially in the face of opposition such as that which has emerged in the popular protests.

How Bashar feels about his leadership during the crisis, which has enveloped his country, was revealed in a remarkable interview with Barbara Walters on December 11, 2011. In it, he (1) denied the extent of violence in his beleaguered country; (2) disputed the evidence in a UN report charging him and his government with crimes against humanity, asking, "Who said that the United Nations is a credible institution?"; (3) indicated that the Syrian people supported him – otherwise he would not be in his position; and (4) claimed that the forces charged with cracking down too hard on protesters did not belong to him, but instead to the government. When asked whether he thought that his forces cracked down too hard on protesters, Bashar replied: "They are not my forces; they are military forces belonging to the government. . . . I don't own them. I am president. I don't own the country." In fact, he may have been speaking the truth, reflecting that he does not have the full authority that his father had and that he was not privy to the extent of the violent crackdown. Rather, it seems to be the handiwork of his aggressive younger brother, Maher, who was initially the lightning rod for criticism of the regime's brutality and who, according to a former Syrian diplomat, because of his control of Syria's security forces, is "first in command, not second."[63]

Perhaps, as one source put it, Hafez chose Bashar as his successor, giving him the role of "the dignified leader, and Maher, the enforcer";[64] this would have worked well, fitting with Bashar's initial image as the distinguished young doctor from London. And this would not have been a new arrangement for the al-Assad family. Hafez himself had a younger brother, Rifaat, who was the head of the security forces and who personally oversaw the 1982 Hama massacre.[65] The impetuous Rifaat, anxious for power in his own right, sealed his fate and precluded any chance of succeeding his older brother when he attempted a coup while Hafez was temporarily hospitalized with serious heart problems in 1983. In fact, it was probably only the fact that he was Hafez's younger brother that saved him from being executed; he was instead sent into exile. Still, the parallel here is unmistakable, with the more aggressive younger brothers committing the atrocities that are, however, fully supported by the older brothers officially in charge.

The Assads Fiddle while Syria Burns

In March 2011, *Vogue* magazine published a feature story on the glamorous first lady of Syria under the title "Rose in the Desert." In it, they described her as "on a mission to create a beacon of culture and secularism in a power-keg region and to put a modern face on her husband's regime," calling her "the element of light in a country full of shadow zones." She described her "central mission to change the mind-set of six million Syrians under eighteen, to encourage them to engage in moving the country forward, about empowerment in a civil society."[66] Indeed, as previously mentioned, part of the high hopes that Bashar would be a modernizing, reforming president of Syria were based on his marriage to Asma; it was anticipated that she would help him as he tried to lead Syria out from the giant controlling shadow of his father.

More than a year since the *Vogue* profile, the bloom is off the rose. Indeed, the rose is now blighted, with a trove of more than 3,000 e-mails taken from the private accounts of Bashar and his wife betraying a first couple indifferent to the suffering of their people and only concerned with expensive shoes, chandeliers, and the latest Harry Potter DVD. The e-mails convey that Bashar does not feel fully in charge. While their country is going up in flames, the e-mails reveal a Bashar uploading music from iTunes while his wife shops extravagantly, as though they are detached from the violence around them. They also show Bashar mocking the reforms that he had earlier promised, as well as the extent of the advice that he was receiving from Iran.

The detached quality of this correspondence conveys a sense that they are bemused observers, somehow not responsible for the violence unfolding around them. In one of the e-mails, Bashar is amused by a crudely fabricated YouTube simulation of the battle in Homs, made with toy tanks and cookies, mocking the Arab League's observer mission. But this is not a game, and tens of thousands have been killed.

Asma's preoccupation with extravagant spending may be to distract herself from the spiraling violence in her country, with the extremity of violence centering on Homs, where her Sunni family originated. In one of the e-mails, she wrote to her husband "If we are strong together, we will overcome this together,"[67] but, in fact, the online distractions suggest that they are in over their heads and unable to cope with the deteriorating situation.

One cannot help but be reminded of the two wives of President Mugabe of Zimbabwe discussed in Chapter 7 on *selfobjects*. Initially, there were high hopes that Asma would be a modernizing, reforming mother of her country, like Sally Heyfron, who provided a stabilizing influence for her husband and who seemed to bring out the best in him. But, increasingly, she has been revealed as more like Mugabe's second wife, "Grasping Grace," preoccupied with indulging her wealthy taste and acting as a negative *selfobject* for her husband, with whom she is fiddling while Syria burns. And together, as they fail to deal with reality around them, the couple is also increasingly reminiscent of the spiraling grandiosity of the Ceausescus as their Romanian regime collapsed. Whether they meet the same fate as the Ceausescus at the hands of the angry Syrian opposition or get out in time remains to be seen.

In the al-Assad family, we see a powerful generational transfer of narcissistic dreams of glory. Interestingly, like Netanyahu, al-Assad's family name was changed by his paternal grandfather and translates into "lion," the king of the jungle.[68] Unlike Hafez, who was unambivalent and calculated in his exercise of power, and was able to operate relatively freely in his veiled society, Bashar is operating in a very different world. He has watched the downfall of his counterparts in Tunisia, Egypt, and Libya, and in the increasingly desperate manner in which Bashar is trying to hold on, what would have been a defiant roar from Hafez is actually an out-of-touch and out-of-control whimper from his son.

Reflecting on the Arab Spring, in an e-mail to Asma, the daughter of the Emir of Qatar stated that there are really only two paths: holding on until the bloody end or going into exile, and she offered the couple asylum in Qatar. However, Bashar cannot easily leave, and he will likely hold on too long for fear of letting the family dynasty crumble on his watch.

Several similarities and differences among John F. Kennedy, Benjamin Netanyahu, Rajiv Gandhi, and Bashar al-Assad are important to highlight in understanding their psychologies as second-choice sons and leaders by default. To begin with, all four of them happened to be the youngest-ever leaders of their countries when they took power, ranging in age from 34 to 46 years. Thus, in addition to foregoing their own career ambitions and adopting lives that they were not primed to lead, there was the tremendous pressure of leading the United States, Israel, India, and Syria, respectively, with relative inexperience in life, not to mention in politics. That likely further contributed to feelings of inadequacy that were born when their brothers were chosen as the families' standard bearers and that were compounded when they were thrust by narcissistic parents into the political limelight only after their brothers were killed.

Indeed, the very manner in which their brothers were killed provide for an interesting comparison. Both Joe Kennedy Jr. and Jonathan Netanyahu died heroically for their countries, while Sanjay Gandhi and Basil al-Assad were killed in accidents that were largely attributed to their own reckless behavior. In addition to the immense pressure from their fathers, we can imagine a stronger internal push for John F. Kennedy and Benjamin Netanyahu to fulfill their obligations as dutiful sons, step into the shoes of their brothers, and honor their memories as heroes. At the same time, Joe Jr. and Jonathan's heroic statuses made those shoes infinitely bigger, thus rendering them more difficult to fill. As evidenced earlier, Kennedy and Netanyahu's older brothers remained with them throughout their political careers and acted as reminders that their ultimate sacrifices lay behind their younger brothers' successes.

Significant differences also exist in the amount of time that each of the leaders had between the death of his brother and his own taking power. Kennedy and Netanyahu had 16 and 19 years, respectively, to prepare for their leadership positions after they replaced their brothers as their fathers' vehicles for personal glory. Yet, unlike JFK, Netanyahu was never able to live up to his brother's giant stature in his father's eyes. Gandhi and al-Assad, on the other hand, had only 4 and 5 years, respectively. It is possible that, with more time to prepare for their new roles, Jack and Benjamin were better able to digest their new realities and internalize their new fates and truly make the leadership positions their own. Indeed, they were both democratically elected to lead their countries long after their brothers were killed, a public validation of their own worth. Rajiv and Bashar, however, did not have the luxury of a long period of incubation, and they were yanked precipitously from the lives they knew and thrust into the center of their countries' turmoil. It must rankle both that almost always when they are mentioned in the news, their names are paired with the "chosen ones," their first-choice brothers.

The professions that the four leaders pursued before they were slated to carry on the family name may also have impacted the ways in which they embraced their roles as leaders by default. As already outlined, Kennedy found his passion early on in journalism, Netanyahu was preparing to take the business world by storm, Gandhi was already an extremely successful airline pilot, and al-Assad had found his calling as an ophthalmologist. Not only were the first two much younger when their brothers died, and much earlier on in their careers, but their professions also lent themselves more easily to a shift to politics. It is not difficult to imagine a journalist or businessperson becoming a political leader, already having the knowledge and skills to succeed in a stressful and competitive environment, as Kennedy did and as Netanyahu is doing. Whereas both pilots and ophthalmologists must also deal in stressful situations, to be sure, the skill sets required for their professions ill-prepared Rajiv and Bashar to be thrust into the maelstrom of politics. Indeed, Rajiv's leadership was shaky throughout, and Bashar faces the greatest threat to his family's rule in more than 40 years.

This chapter is concerned with the psychological dynamics of leaders who were not their parents' first choice to occupy the seat of power. John F. Kennedy, Benjamin Netanyahu, Rajiv Gandhi, and Bashar al-Assad were all second-choice sons, whose lives were forever changed by their brothers' deaths because they were required to become leaders by default and fulfill their parents' own dreams of glory. The fathers of neither Kennedy nor Netanyahu had achieved the heights that they had desired, and thus they placed extraordinary pressures on their sons to succeed in politics. The narcissistic investment of the parents in their choice to redeem the family honor was to have major consequences for these second-choice sons, the leaders by default.

In contrast, both Indira Gandhi and Hafez al-Assad sought to continue their families' dynasties and, in fact, ripped their sons from their lives as they knew them. These beginnings would ensure that all four leaders would spend the whole of their political lives trying to live up to the greatness that was presumed of their brothers and to satisfy the hopes and demands of their overbearing parents. The need to overcompensate thus dominated their career-long quests to become leaders in their own right and escape the shadows of their brothers at last. Today, these dynamics are especially important to consider for Benjamin Netanyahu and Bashar al-Assad, two leaders at the very center of the explosive politics of the Middle East, both of whom are still haunted by ghosts from the past.

Notes

1. Robert Dallek, *An Unfinished Life: John F. Kennedy, 1917–1963* (Boston: Little, Brown and Company, 2003) 20.
2. Dallek, *An Unfinished Life*, 52.
3. Nancy Gager Clinch, *The Kennedy Neurosis* (New York: Grosset & Dunlap, 1973).
4. Robert Donovan, *PT109: John F. Kennedy in World War II* (New York: McGraw-Hill, 1961).
5. Ralph G. Martin, *Seeds of Destruction: Joe Kennedy and His Sons* (New York: G. P. Putnam Sons, 1995).
6. Clinch, *The Kennedy Neurosis*, 98.
7. Dallek, *An Unfinished Life*, 253.
8. Thomas C. Reeves, *A Question of Character: A Life of John F. Kennedy* (New York: The Free Press, 1991).
9. Walter R. Mears and Hal Buell, *The Kennedy Brothers: A Legacy in Photographs* (New York: Black Dog and Leventhal, 2009).
10. Clinch, *The Kennedy Neurosis*, 98.
11. Amanda Smith, ed., *Hostage to Fortune: The Letters of Joseph P. Kennedy* (New York: Viking, 2001).
12. Laurence Leamer, *The Kennedy Men, 1901–1963: The Laws of the Father* (New York: Wm. Morrow, 2001), 474.
13. Leamer, "The Kennedy Men," 474.
14. Peter Collier and David Horowitz, *The Kennedys: An American Drama* (New York: Summit Books, 1984), 263.
15. Lisa Beyer and Eric Silver, "Israel: The Making of Bibi Netanyahu," *TIME*, June 10, 1996, accessed January 28, 2011, www.time.com/time/magazine/article/0,9171,984667,00.html.
16. Richard Cohen, "Time for Netanyahu to Ditch His Do-Nothing Policy," *The Washington Post*, May 23, 2011, accessed May 23, 2011,

www.washingtonpost.com/opinions/time-for-netanyahu-to-ditch-his-do-nothing-policy/2011/05/23/AFHgP49G_story.html.
17. Colin Shindler, *Israel, Likud, and the Zionist Dream: Power, Politics, and Ideology from Begin to Netanyahu* (London: I. B. Tauris, 1995).
18. Ben Caspit and Ilan Kfir, *Netanyahu: The Road to Power* (Secaucus, N.J.: Carol, 1998).
19. Jonathan Netanyahu, *The Letters of Jonathan Netanyahu: The Commander of the Entebbe Rescue Force* (Jerusalem: Gefen, 2001), 143.
20. Jason Epstein, "Personal History: The Eminent Publisher on His Teacher, Friend, and Political Opposite, Benzion Netanyahu," *Tablet*, July 6, 2010, accessed June 3, 2011, www.tabletmag.com/news-and-politics/38335/personal-history/.
21. Caspit and Kfir, *Netanyahu: The Road to Power*, 72.
22. B. Goren and E. Berkowitz, "Mi ze? [Who is he?]," *Ha'ir.* June 21, 1996, in *Profiling Political Leaders: Cross-Cultural Studies of Personality and Behavior*, eds. Ofer Feldman and Linda O. Valenty (Westport, Connecticut: Praeger Publishers, 2001), 35.
23. Netanyahu, *The Letters of Jonathan Netanyahu*, 130.
24. Ibid., 152.
25. Caspit and Kfir, *Netanyahu: The Road to Power*, 32.
26. Netanyahu, *The Letters of Jonathan Netanyahu*, v.
27. Caspit and Kfir, *Netanyahu: The Road to Power*, 82.
28. Shindler, *Israel, Likud, and the Zionist Dream.*
29. Anonymous, Personal Interview, "Benjamin Netanyahu," May 30, 2011.
30. Yossi Klein Halevi, "Bibi's Political Inheritance," *Tablet*, May 1, 2012, www.tabletmag.com/jewish-news-and-politics/98279/bibis-political-inheritance.
31. Akiva Eldar, "Netanyahu's Historical Genes," *Ha'aretz.com*, August 15, 2005, accessed January 29, 2011, www.haaretz.com/print-edition/opinion/netanyahu-s-historical-genes-1.166936.
32. "Transcript: Israeli Prime Minister Binyamin Netanyahu's Address to Congress," *The Washington Post*, May 24, 2011, www.washingtonpost.com/world/israeli-prime-minister-binyamin-netanyahus-address-to-congress/2011/05/24/AFWY5bAH_story.html.
33. Jodi Rudoren, "Unity Government in Israel Disbanding Over Dispute on Draft," *The New York Times*, July 17, 2012, www.nytimes.com/2012/07/18/world/middleeast/unity-government-in-israel-disbanding-over-dispute-on-draft.html?pagewanted=all&_r=0.
34. Ofer Aderet, "German Reporter: How I Got to Know Sara Netanyahu," *Haaretz*, June 9, 2012, www.haaretz.com/news/diplomacy-defense/german-reporter-how-i-got-to-know-sara-netanyahu.premium-1.435356; David Margolick, "The Netanyahu Paradox," *Vanity Fair*, July 2012, www.vanityfair.com/politics/2012/07/benjamin-netanyahu-on-israel-mitt-romney.
35. Andrew Sullivan, "Ben Zion Netanyahu 1910–2012," *The Daily Beast*, April 30, 2012, http://andrewsullivan.thedailybeast.com/2012/04/ben-zion-netanyahu-1910-2012.html.
36. Mary Janigan et al., "Gandhi's Reluctant Heir," *Maclean's*, November 12, 1984: 30.
37. Tariq Ali, *An Indian Dynasty: The Story of the Nehru-Gandhi Family* (New York: G. P. Putnam, 1985).
38. Nicholas Nugent, *Rajiv Gandhi: Son of a Dynasty* (London: BBC Books, 1990), 45.

39. Blema Steinberg, *Women in Power: The Personalities and Leadership Styles of Indira Gandhi, Golda Meir, and Margaret Thatcher* (Montreal: McGill-Queen's University Press, 2008), 45.
40. Ross Laver and David North, "India after Indira Gandhi," *Maclean's*, November 12, 1984: 24, 28.
41. Steinberg, *Women in Power*.
42. Darryl D'Monte, "Indira's Intrigues: India Elects a New Crown Prince," *The New Leader*, July 13, 1981.
43. Ali, *An Indian Dynasty*.
44. Joseph Lelyveld, "Rajiv the Son," *The New York Times*, December 2, 1984: 39, 43.
45. Laver and North, "India after Indira Gandhi," 24.
46. Janardan Thakur, *Prime Ministers: Nehru to Vajpayee* (Mumbai: Eeshwar Publications, 1999).
47. Lelyveld, "Rajiv the Son," 43.
48. Ibid., 40.
49. Ajoy Bose, "The End of a Dynasty?," *Maclean's*, June 3, 1991.
50. Bose, "The End of a Dynasty?," 36.
51. "Profile: Bashar al-Assad," *Al-Jazeera*, March 25, 2011, http://english.aljazeera.net/news/middleeast/2007/07/2008525185141454964.html.
52. Thomas Friedman, *From Beirut to Jerusalem* (New York: Anchor Books, 1989).
53. "Family Dynamics Drive Syrian President Assad," *BBC* News, April 30, 2011, www.bbc.co.uk/news/world-middle-east-13247375.
54. Eyal Zisser, *Commanding Syria: Bashar al-Assad and the First Years in Power* (London: I. B. Tauris, 2007).
55. "Profile: Bashar al-Assad."
56. Human Rights Watch, *A Wasted Decade: Human Rights in Syria during Bashar al-Assad's First Ten Years in Power* (New York, NY: Human Rights Watch, 2010).
57. Human Rights Watch, *A Wasted Decade*, 4.
58. Op. cit.
59. Flynt Leverett, *Inheriting Syria: Bashar's Trial by Fire* (Washington, D.C.: Brookings Institute Press, 2005).
60. Leverett, *Inheriting Syria*, 59.
61. Katherina Zoepf and Anthony Shadid, "Syrian Leader's Brother Seen as Enforcer of Crackdown," *The New York Times*, June 7, 2011, accessed June 8, 2011, www.nytimes.com/2011/06/08/world/middleeast/08syria.html.
62. Op. cit.
63. Zoepf and Shadid, "Syrian Leader's Brother."
64. Ibid.
65. "Profile: Rifaat al-Assad," *BBC News*, June 12, 2000, http://news.bbc.co.uk/2/hi/middle_east/788021.stm.
66. Joan J. Buck, "A Rose in the Desert," *Vogue*, 201, No. 3 (March 2011).
67. Salma Abdelaziz, "Flirtatious Emails Fill al-Assad's Inbox," *CNN*, March 21, 2012, http://articles.cnn.com/2012-03-21/middleeast/world_meast_syria-assad-emails_1_mails-al-assad-homs?_s=PM:MIDDLEEAST.
68. David W. Lesch, *The New Lion of Damascus: Bashar al-Assad and Modern Syria* (New Haven: Yale University Press, 2005).

Concluding Note

The quality of narcissism is not strained. It droppeth as the gentle rain from heaven. It floodeth the chambers of Congress and presidential palaces. 'Tis most dangerous in the mightiest, for it is enthroned in the hearts of kings and presidents.

With apologies to Shakespeare for this riff on Portia's eloquent soliloquy on mercy in the *Merchant of Venice*, in this age of narcissism, politicians with significant narcissistic personality features are apparently ubiquitous. The arena of politics is particularly attractive to narcissistic individuals who, if gifted with persuasive skills, can attract adoring followers. As the jury deliberated in the case of Senator John Edwards, accused of misuse of campaign funds to cover up an affair with a videographer with whom he had a child, an affair carried out while his wife was undergoing painful treatment for breast cancer, the gap between the glittering surface of the candidate and what lies beneath was all too palpable. The jury acquitted Edwards, saying the charges never should have been brought in the first place, and the Department of Justice dropped the case.

This raises an interesting and important question. Why do followers cling so long to narcissistic leaders whose grandiose façade is so patently false? "Leader" should be considered a plural noun because to be a leader, after all, requires at least one follower. This requires an examination of the psychology of followership. While one developmental pathway to the glittering grandiosity of the narcissistic leader is compensatory for the wounded self, another consequence of profound psychological wounds, of the wounded self, is to leave an individual feeling incomplete unto himself, forever searching to attach himself to an idealized other, the worshipful follower of the idealized leader. Dreams die hard and one does not easily give up an idealized rescuer, but when reality inevitably shatters that grandiose façade, the very magnitude of idealization is replaced by the rage of disillusion, and the search for new heroes goes on.

At the healthy end of the narcissistic spectrum are those bright, creative, and driven individuals who, from early on, are reaching for the stars. Ambitious and self-confident, whether in science, art and literature, or political leadership, they believe they have something special to contribute, and they pursue those lofty goals throughout their lives. Without reaching for the stars, their dreams of glory will not be achieved. Some carry a special sense of self, at times engendered by great expectations and sometimes leading to acts of remarkable heroism, especially when faced with mortal illness, as was the case with King Hussein of Jordan. When faced with terminal illness and dreams of glory still unfulfilled, it can lead some leaders to superimpose their foreshortened personal timetables on their nation's political timetable, sometimes with catastrophic results, as was the case with the terminal urgency of the Shah of Iran and Mao Zedong of the Peoples Republic of China.

Who shapes the dreams of glory will vary. For King Hussein, it was his grandfather King Talal, who engendered in his young grandson when but a boy his special sense of mission for his people. For others, like President Woodrow Wilson, General Douglas MacArthur, and President Franklin Delano Roosevelt, ambitious mothers played a special role in stimulating their sons' dreams of glory. In South Asia, two prominent female leaders, Indira Gandhi of India and Benazir Bhutto of Pakistan, early in life had great expectations set before them to carry on their families' legacies, pursuing and continuing familial dreams of glory. So, narcissistic dreams of glory can be "bred in the bone" and become self-fulfilling prophecies. In the ranks of political leaders, healthy narcissists pursuing dreams of glory have been associated with towering triumphs that have positively transformed history.

But consumed by dreams of glory, narcissistic leaders can also pursue dangerous paths that embroil their followers in violent conflict. In this study of narcissistic leaders, the factors that give rise to compensatory dreams of glory have been considered, as exemplified by Saddam Hussein, whose frustrated dreams of glory led to a violent course of action – and the world is still suffering the consequences. The traits underlying the grandiose façade have been detailed, including sensitivity to slight, which can distort the leader's relationship with his advisers, producing sycophants who tell the leader what he wants to hear rather than what he needs to hear. Thus, the narcissistic leader can progressively lose touch with reality as his inner circle shields him from the painful recognition of the failure of his dreams.

The retaliatory rage when dreams are thwarted has been considered. The difficulty of leaving the cynosure of power has been emphasized, with some leaders clinging too long to power and debasing all they have accomplished in the process, as exemplified by Habib Bourguiba, the founding father of Tunisia; Robert Mugabe of Zimbabwe; and Fidel Castro of Cuba. But, for the consummate narcissist, there is never enough glory, and he comes to think of himself as crucial for his nation's survival; his own identity and that of their nation become intertwined, leading some to become "president for life."

Putin the Great[a, 1]

While President Vladimir Putin has not designated himself President for life, he is behaving as if he believes he is indispensable to the leadership of his country and Russian speaking peoples.

Putin has been at the helm since 2000 and sees himself and Russia as one and the same. Believing only he can lead the former superpower, Putin created a political machine to ensure the survival of his rule for decades. In 2008, when Putin "stepped down" as president, his successor, Dimitry Medvedev, increased the presidential term to six years. Medvedev then resigned after one term, paving the way for then-Prime Minister Putin to regain the presidency in 2012, with the possibility of retaining power until 2024.

Putin is obsessed with masculinity, size, strength and power as evidenced by bare-chested photos of him with guns, and with a tranquilized tiger. These arranged stunts and photos convey the image of Putin as fearless, powerful and in control. It also is notable that these photo-shoots increased dramatically in 2008 when Putin became Prime Minister and was replaced by Medvedev. It appears this was a carefully calculated move to remind the Russian people and the world who was really in charge.

Putin's preoccupation with size and strength is overcompensation for his under-lying insecurity – that which may be a consequence of his small stature and his need to prove he cannot be pushed around. Standing 5'6", he was often bullied as a kid and picked on for his slight of build. In response to any insults or criticism, Putin responded viciously to his tormentors. He was also incapable of handling criticism from his teachers, openly expressing outrage at being reprimanded. As president, Putin continues to react intensely to criticism as any oligarch or journal-ist who criticizes or opposes him is likely to find themselves in prison or dead.

While Putin has publicly acknowledged that he does not want to restore the former Soviet Union, he does appear to view himself as a modern-day czar leading the Russian-speaking people (a portrait of Peter the Great is prominently displayed in his office). He thus finds threats to his crumbling empire intolerable. So when Ukraine turned to the EU, and the prospect of the West settling into his backyard became a genuine possibility, Putin acted quickly to forestall further erosion of his empire. He seized Crimea first and then orchestrated violence and unrest in southern and eastern Ukraine.

The quintessential narcissist, Putin is consumed with his image and how others perceive him. As evidenced by the extravagance of the Olympic games in Sochi, Putin yearns to be respected as a first-tier world leader and he under-stands that to earn this respect, his actions must appear reasonable and legit-imate. A brutally ruthless dictator masquerading as a principled democrat, Putin is determined to defend his power – so long as it does not damage his

---

[a] This section draws on an op-ed piece "Putin the Great: Struggling to Hold on to a Crumbling Empire," by Jennifer McNamara and Jerrold Post, M.D. from The Huffington Post.

international image and reputation. To achieve these two conflicting goals, Putin relies on his legal training and extremely calculating nature to fabricate meticulous pseudo-legal justifications for his actions.

It appears Putin has two goals that are difficult to pursue simultaneously. On the one hand, Putin yearns to be viewed as a respected first-tier world leader. On the other hand, "Putin the Great" views any potential loss of influence as an intolerable threat to Russian preeminence. Putin has continuously demonstrated his willingness to defend his power and influence at any cost. He believes the loss of Ukraine would be a death knell for his Russian empire, yet his aggressive destabilizing actions threaten to oust him from the community of respected world leaders.

Demonstrating the same pattern he showed in the takeover of Crimea, while steadfastly denying Russian involvement, Putin responded to Ukraine's turning the tide against the pro-Russian separatists in East Ukraine by introducing Russian military and weapons. U.S. Ambassador to the UN, Samantha Power, accused Russia of "manipulating," "obfuscating" and "outright lying" about its role in Ukraine. Putin in return defiantly warned NATO not to "mess with" "one of the leading nuclear powers," and stated that he could "take Kiev in two weeks." Taking off the mask of denial, Putin congratulated the pro-Russian separatists for their victory and then proposed a ceasefire. The ceasefire that went into effect on September 5 essentially diminished Kiev central control. In freezing the conflict, it could achieve permanent semi-autonomous status for the Russian separatist region and block NATO extension to the region, assuring Putin the level of influence and control over Ukraine he sees as his right. Thus Putin continued to project his carefully crafted image of legitimacy, whilst pursuing his own course of action.

Extreme narcissism is the driving force behind the recent actions of Russian President Vladimir Putin in Crimea and Ukraine. Predicting the future behavior of this former KGB operative must be based on his narcissistic personality and strong need for power and control.

The quality of advisers surrounding the leader, including wives, is critical in helping the leader either deal with reality and step down when his time is past or deny the spiraling difficulties and cling too long to power. These supporting cast members play what has been called a *selfobject* role. Mugabe's first wife played a remarkable role as first lady, bringing out the best in her husband and inspiring him to play a very positive role in the early years of Zimbabwe. Had he stepped down then, he would have gone down in his country's history as a heroic nation builder. But when she died, his second wife, consumed by greed, led Zimbabwe under Mugabe to become a virtual kleptocracy, destroying his legacy.

Still others attempt to extend their legacy through their progeny, as did Saddam Hussein of Iraq, Muammar Qaddafi of Libya, and Kim Il-sung and Kim Jong-il of North Korea. When the chosen successor dies and the ambitious father is forced to turn to a second-choice son, who then becomes leader by default, it places special burdens on these second-choice sons. Such was the case with U.S. President John

Fitzgerald Kennedy, Prime Minister Bibi Netanyahu of Israel, Prime Minister Rajiv Gandhi of India and President Bashar al-Assad of Syria.

Narcissism is at the heart of charismatic leader–follower relationships, associated with some of the most heroic moments in human history. Consider the reparative charismatic leadership of Mohandas Gandhi and Martin Luther King, who, to quote from the excerpt from the poem by Stephen Spender that introduced the chapter "Great Expectations," "left the vivid air signed with their honour."

But when a wounded followership follows as if hypnotized the siren song of the hate-mongering, destructive charismatic leader like Adolf Hitler or Osama bin Laden, as they pursue their grandiose narcissistic dreams of glory – it can produce nightmares for us all.

Notes

1. McNamara, Jennifer, and Jerrold Post: "Putin the Great: Struggling to Hold on to a Crumbling Empire." *Huffington Post*, January 4, 2014. www.huffingtonpost.com/jennifer-mcnamara/putin-the-great-strugglin_b_5072330.html.

Bibliography

Abdelaziz, Salma. "Flirtatious Emails Fill al-Assad's Inbox." *CNN*, March 21, 2012. http://articles.cnn.com/2012-03-21/middleeast/world_meast_syria-assad-emails_1_ mails-al-assad-homs?_s=PM:MIDDLEEAST.

Abend, Lisa. "Will Castro's Exit Change Cuba?" *Time*, February 19, 2008. http:// content.time.com/time/world/article/0,8599,1714323,00.html.

Abse, Wilfred, and Richard B. Ulman. "Charismatic Political Leadership and Collective Regression." In *Psychopathology and Political Leadership*, edited by Robert S. Robins. New Orleans: Tulane University, 1977, pp. 35–52.

Adams, Jad, and Phillip Whitehead. *The Dynasty: The Nehru-Gandhi Story*. London: Penguin Books, 1997.

Aderet, Ofer. "German Reporter: How I Got to Know Sara Netanyahu." *Haaretz*, June 9, 2012. www.haaretz.com/news/diplomacy-defense/german-reporter-how-i-got-to-know-sara-netanyahu.premium-1.435356.

"Ailing Chavez Has No Plans for Replacement Candidate." *Agence France Presse*, March 2, 2012(b). www.google.com/hostednews/afp/article/ALeqM5jcUTgIGLZ70nk 5y6cQCHxymf7jLg?docId=CNG.7dd23791b5739f8ecbd3acbo51c41676.2d1.

Alford, Fred. *Narcissism: Socrates, The Frankfurt School, and Psychoanalytic Theory*. New Haven: Yale University Press, 1988.

Al-Hayat. June 18, 2001. FBIS-NES GMP20010618000048. London.

Ali, Tariq. *An Indian Dynasty: The Story of the Nehru-Gandhi Family*. New York: G. P. Putnam, 1985.

Al-Jazeera. "Bhutto's Son Makes Debut in Pakistan Politics." *Al Jazeera*, December, 27, 2012. www.aljazeera.com/news/americas/2012/12/20121227145629622237.html.

American Psychiatric Association. *Diagnostic and Statistical Manual of Mental Disorders: DSM III*. Washington, D.C.: American Psychiatric Association, 1980.

American Psychiatric Association. *Diagnostic and Statistical Manual of Mental Disorders: DSM IV*. Washington, D.C.: American Psychiatric Association, 1994.

American Psychiatric Association. "The Principles of Medical Ethics: With Annotations Especially Applicable to Psychiatry." Last modified 2009. www. psych.org/mainmenu/psychiatricpractice/ethics/resourcesstandards/principlesofmedi calethics.aspx.

"Anders Behring Breivik: Oslo, Norway Bombing 'Necessary.'" *Huffington Post*, July 23, 2011. www.huffingtonpost.com/2011/07/23/anders-behring-breivik-oslo bombing_n_ 907880.html.

"An Italian Story." *The Economist*, April 28, 2001, pp. 23–28.

Anonymous. Personal Interview. "Benjamin Netanyahu." May 30, 2011.

"Assad: Duty to 'Annihilate Terrorists.'" *Reuters*, June 30, 2012. www.thehindu.com/ todays-paper/tp-in-school/assad-duty-to-annihilate terrorists/article3586545.ece.

Associated Press. "New Orleans' Madam Says Sen. David Vitter Used Her Brothel." *Fox News*, July 11, 2007. www.foxnews.com/story/0,2933,288868,00.html.

Associated Press. "John Ensign Affair, Apology & Drama: Timeline Leading to Senator's Resignation." *The Huffington Post*, April 21, 2011. www.huffingtonpost.com/2011/ 04/21/john-ensign-affair-apolog_n_852346.html.

Associated Press. "Petraeus Affair Timeline of Events." *POLITICO.com*, November 12, 2012. Accessed February 25, 2013. www.politico.com/news/stories/1112/.

Bacciagaluppi, Marco. "Fromm's Views on Narcissism and the Self." In *Narcissism and the Interpersonal Self*, edited by John Fiscalini and Alan Grey. New York: Columbia University Press, 1993, pp. 91–106.

Baram, Amazia. "Saddam Hussein as Wartime Decision Maker." Paper presented at the conference *The Iran-Iraq War: The View from Baghdad*, Woodrow Wilson International Center for Scholars, Washington, D.C., October 25–27, 2011.

Baughman, Duane, director. *Bhutto* [movie]. United States: First Run Features, 2010.

"Benazir Bhutto Interview." Academy of Achievement. October 27, 2000. Accessed December 10, 2010. www.achievement.org/autodoc/page/bhuoint-1.

Benedict, Ruth. *The Chrysanthemum and the Sword*. Boston: Houghton Mifflin, 1946.

"Berlusconi: The Power of Personality." *BBC News World Europe*, May 14, 2001. http:// news.bbc.co.uk/2/hi/europe/1298864.stm.

"Berlusconi's Legacy: The Cavaliere and the Cavallo." *The Economist*, June 9, 2011. www.economist.com/node/18780867

"Berlusconi's Wife to Divorce Him." *BBC News Europe*, May 3, 2009. http://news.bbc .co.uk/2/hi/8031520.stm.

Beyer, Lisa, and Eric Silver. "Israel: The Making of Bibi Netanyahu." *TIME*, June 10, 1996. Accessed January 28, 2011. www.time.com/time/magazine/article/0,9171,984667,00 .html.

"Bhutto." Accessed December 13, 2010. www.bhutto.org/1970–71.php.

Bhutto, Benazir. *Daughter of Destiny: An Autobiography*. New York: Simon and Schuster, 1989.

Bhutto, Benazir. *Daughter of the East: An Autobiography*. London: Simon & Schuster, 2007.

Bhutto, Fatima. *Songs of Blood and Sword: A Daughter's Memoir*. New York: Nation Books, 2010.

"Bhutto's Son Seeks Media Privacy." *BBC News*, January 8, 2008. Accessed June 6, 2011. http://news.bbc.co.uk/2/hi/7176743.stm.

Bion, Wilfred. *Experiences in Groups*. London: Tavistock Press, 1961.

"Bishop Eddie Long Tackles Controversy." *New Pittsburgh Courier*, May 17, 2006. Accessed April 12, 2011. www.highbeam.com/doc/1P3-1096044091.html.

Boadle, Anthony. "Fidel Castro, 20th Century Revolutionary." *Reuters*, February 19, 2008. www.reuters.com/article/2008/02/19/us-cuba-castro-profile idUSN1922504220080219.

"Bombing in Sacramento: The Letter; Excerpts from Letter by 'Terrorist Group,' FC, Which Says It Sent Bombs." *New York Times*, April 26, 1995. www.nytimes.com/1995/04/26/us/bombing-sacramento-letter-excerpts-letter-terrorist-group-fc-which-says-it-sent.html.

Borge, Tomas. "Part Six of Interview with Fidel Castro." *Excelsior*, June 4, 1992. http://lanic.utexas.edu/la/cb/cuba/castro/1992/19920607.

Bose, Ajoy. "The End of a Dynasty?" *Maclean's* 104, No. 22, June 3, 1991, p. 34.

"Bourguiba Returns; in Paris 6 Months." *New York Times*, June 2, 1970, p. 11

Bowden, Mark. "David Petraeus's Winning Streak." *Vanity Fair*, March 30, 2010. www.vanityfair.com/politics/features/2010/05/petraeus-exclusive-201005.

"'Breivik Manifesto' Details Chilling Attack Preparation." *BBC News*, July 24, 2011. www.bbc.co.uk/news/world-europe-14267007.

Broadwell, Paula. "General David Petraeus's Rules for Living." Newsweek, November 5, 2012. Accessed February 20, 2013. http://www.newsweek.com/general-david-petraeuss-rules-living-63791.

Broadwell, Paula, and Vernon Loeb. *All In: The Education of General David Petraeus*. New York: Penguin Press, 2012.

Brooke, James. "N. Koreans Talk of Baby Killings." *The New York Times*, June 10, 2002. www.nytimes.com/2002/06/10/world/n-koreans-talk-of-baby-killings.html?pagewanted=all&src=pm.

Brown, Mark. "Rod Blagojevich on the Stand Breathes Life into Retrial." *Chicago Sun-Times*, June 3, 2011. www.suntimes.com/news/watchdogs/6990852-452/with-rod-blagojevich-convicted-others-now-face-sentencing.html.

Bruck, Connie. "Profiles: Fault Lines." *The New Yorker*, May 21, 2007. Accessed April 6, 2011. www.newyorker.com/reporting/2007/05/21/070521fa_fact_bruck.

Bruni, Frank. "Gingrich Sees Echo of Ancient Rome in America Today." *The New York Times*, May 3, 1998. www.nytimes.com/1998/05/03/us/gingrich-sees-echo-of-ancient-rome-in-america-today.html?pagewanted=all&src=pm.

Bruni, Frank. "The Agony and the Bunga Bunga." *The New York Times*, September 12, 2011(a). www.nytimes.com/2011/09/13/opinion/bruni-the-agony-and-the-bunga-bunga.html.

Bruni, Frank. "The Affliction of Comfort." *The New York Times*, September 18, 2011(b). www.nytimes.com/2011/09/18/opinion/sunday/bruni-in-italy-and-america-the-affliction-of-comfort.html?_r=0.

Buck, Joan Juliet. "A Rose in the Desert." *Vogue*, 201, No. 3, March 2011, p. 528

Burki, Shahid J. *Pakistan under Bhutto, 1971–1977*. New York: St. Martin's Press, 1980.

Burns, James MacGregor. *Roosevelt: The Lion and The Fox*. New York: Harcourt, Brace & World, 1965.

Burns, John F. "House of Graft: Tracing the Bhutto Millions – A Special Report; Bhutto Clan Leaves Trail of Corruption." *New York Times*, January 9, 1998. Accessed June 16, 2011. www.nytimes.com/1998/01/09/world/house-graft-tracing-bhutto-millions-special- report-bhutto-clan-leaves-trail.html.

Butler, George. *Arnold Schwarzenegger: A Portrait*. New York: Simon & Schuster, 1990.

Bychowski, Gustav. *Dictators and Disciples: From Caesar to Stalin*. New York: International Universities Press, 1948.

Calabresi, Massimo. "Can Obama Escape the Taint of Blagojevich?" *TIME*, December 10, 2008. www.time.com/time/nation/article/0,8599,1865370,00.html.

Capps, Donald. *The Depleted Self: Sin in a Narcissistic Age.* Minneapolis: Fortress Press, 1992.

Caspit, Ben, and Ilan Kfir. *Netanyahu: The Road to Power.* Secaucus: Carol Publishing Group, 1998.

Castaneda, Ruben, and Miranda S. Spivack. "Former Prince George's County Executive Pleads Guilty to Extortion, Tampering." *The Baltimore Sun,* May 17, 2011. http://articles.baltimoresun.com/2011-05-17/news/bs-md-jack-johnson-plea-20110517_1_corruption-charges-guilty-plea-county-executive.

"Ceausescu, Nicolae." 2005. www.ceausescu.org.

Chandrasekaran, Rajiv, and Greg Jaffe. "Petraeus Scandal Puts Four-Star General Lifestyle under Scrutiny." *The Washington Post,* November 17, 2012. http://articles.washingtonpost.com/2012-11-17/world/35505221_1_robert-m-gates-commanders-joint-chiefs.

"Chavez Says Opposition Would Create 'War.'" *Agence France Presse,* February 17, 2012(a). www.google.com/hostednews/afp/article/ALeqM5htBi9ZLgzNmFllywREt3u VrpZ7bw?docId=CNG.b012575559d3dcf7e161312a2cd69fb9.2f1.

Church, George. "Targeting Gaddafi." *Time Magazine,* April 21, 1986.

Cillizza, Chris, and Paul Kane. "Republican Sen. John Ensign of Nevada Won't Seek Reelection." *The Washington Post,* March 7, 2011. www.washingtonpost.com/wp-dyn/content/article/2011/03/07/AR2011030704306.html.

Clifford, Garry, Alexandra Mezey, Susan Schindehette, and Margaret Bonnett Sellinger. "The Enigmatic Candidate: Friends and Family Portray Senator Gary Hart as a Shy Guy with a Private Wit and a Stormy but Loving Marriage." *People Magazine,* March 26, 1984. Accessed April 4, 2011. www.people.com/people/archive/article/0,,20087431,00.html.

Clinch, Nancy Gager. *The Kennedy Neurosis.* New York: Grosset & Dunlap, 1973.

Cohen, Richard. "Time for Netanyahu to Ditch His Do-Nothing Policy." *The Washington Post,* May 23, 2011. Accessed May 23, 2011. www.washingtonpost.com/opinions/time-for-netanyahu-to-ditch-his-do-nothing-policy/2011/05/23/AFHgP49G_story.html.

Cohn, Victor, and Susan Okie. "Doctors Say Shah Could Leave U.S. in Four Weeks." *Washington Post,* November 15, 1979, p. A33.

Collier, Peter, and David Horowitz. *The Kennedys: An American Drama.* New York: Summit Books, 1984.

Congress.org. March 3, 2011.

Cooper, Richard, and Chuck Neubauer. "Senator's Way to Wealth Was Paved with Favors." *Los Angeles Times,* December 17, 2003. Accessed May 11, 2011. http://articles.latimes.com/2003/dec/17/nation/la-na-stevens-favors-20031217.

Cornwell, Grant H., and Eve Walsh Stoddard. *Global Multiculturalism Comparative Perspectives on Ethnicity, Race, and Nation.* Lanham: Rowman & Littlefield Publishers, 2000.

Crayton, J. "Terrorism and Self-Psychology." In *Perspectives on Terrorism,* edited by Yonah Alexander and Lawrence Zelic Freedman. Wilmington: Scholarly Resources, 1983, pp. 33–51.

Criscione, Valeria. "Norwegian Terror Suspect Breivik Tells Court Today He Deserves a Medal." *Christian Science Monitor,* February 6, 2012. www.csmonitor.com/World/Europe/2012/0206/Norwegian-terror-suspect-Breivik-tells-court-today-he-deserves-a-medal.

Dallek, Robert. *An Unfinished Life: John F. Kennedy, 1917–1963*. Boston: Little, Brown and Company, 2003.

D'Alpuget, Blanche. *Robert J. Hawke: A Biography*. East Melbourne: Schwarts/ Landsdowne Press, 1982.

Damodaran, A. K., and U. S. Bajpai, eds. *Indian Foreign Policy: The Indira Gandhi Years*. New Delhi: Radiant Publishers, 1990.

Darman, Jonathan. "Spitzer in Exile." *Newsweek*, 153, No. 17, April 27, 2009, pp. 20–27.

"Deposed Pakistani PM Is Executed." *BBC News*, April 4, 1979. Accessed April 3, 2011. news.bbc.co.uk/onthisday/hi/dates/stories/april/4/newsid_2459000/2459507.stm.

Deming, Angus, Edward Behr, Sudip Mazumdar, Patricia J. Sethi, and Anne Underwood. "The Gandhi Legacy." *Newsweek*, 46, November 12, 1984, p. 59.

Dhar, P. N. *Indira Gandhi, The "Emergency," and Indian Democracy*. Oxford: Oxford University Press, 2000.

Dietz, Park. "Mass, Serial, and Sensational Homicides." *Bulletin of the New York Academy of Medicine* 62 (1986), pp. 477–491.

Dionne Jr., E. J. "Gary Hart the Elusive Front-Runner." *The New York Times*, May 3, 1987(a). www.nytimes.com/1987/05/03/magazine/garry-hart-the-elusive-front-runner.html?pagewanted=all&src=pm.

Dionne Jr., E. J. "Courting Danger: The Fall of Gary Hart." *The New York Times*, May 9, 1987(b). www.nytimes.com/1987/05/09/us/courting-danger-the-fall-of-gary-hart.html?pagewanted=all&src=pm.

D'Monte, Darryl. "Indira's Intrigues: India Elects a New Crown Prince." *The New Leader*, July 13, 1981, p. 10.

Donadio, Rachel, and Elisabetta Povoledo. "European Debt Crisis as Berlusconi's Last Stand." *The New York Times*, November 9, 2011(b), p. A1.

Donovan, Robert. *PT109: John F. Kennedy in World War II*. New York: McGraw-Hill, 1961.

Dowd, Maureen. "Bush, Taking Rival's Line, Says 'Labels' Don't Matter." *The New York Times*, November 4, 1988. www.nytimes.com/1988/11/04/us/bush-taking-rival-s-line-says-labels-don-t-matter.html?sec=&spon=&pagewanted=all.

Dreifus, Claudia. "Real-Life Dynasty; Benazir Bhutto." *The New York Times*, May 15, 1994. Accessed April 13, 2011. www.nytimes.com/1994/05/15/magazine/real-life-dynasty-benazir-bhutto.html.

Dugger, Celia. "Health in Doubt, Mugabe, 87, Vows to Stay in Power." *The New York Times*, May 20, 2011. www.nytimes.com/2011/05/21/world/africa/21zimbabwe.html?_r=1&pag wanted=all.

Edwards, John, Marion Crain, and Arne Kalleberg. *Ending Poverty in America: How to Restore the American Dream*. New York: New Press, 2007.

Eldar, Akiva. "Netanyahu's Historical Genes." *Ha'aretz.com*, August 15, 2005. Accessed January 29, 2011. www.haaretz.com/print-edition/opinion/netanyahu-s-historical-genes-1.166936.

Elson, Miriam, ed. *The Kohut Seminars on Self Psychology and Psychotherapy with Adolescents and Young Adults*. New York: W. W. Norton & Co., 1987.

Engel, Richard. "Petraeus' Biographer Paula Broadwell under FBI Investigation over Access to His Email, Law Enforcement Officials Say." *NBC News*, November 9, 2012. http://usnews.nbcnews.com/_news/2012/11/09/15056607-petraeus-biographer-paula-broadwell-under-fbi-investigation-over-access-to-his-email-law-enforcement-officials-say.

Epstein, Jason. "Personal History: The Eminent Publisher on His Teacher, Friend, and Political Opposite, Benzion Netanyahu," *Tablet*, July 6, 2010. Accessed June 3, 2011. www.tabletmag.com/news-and-politics/38335/personal-history/.

Erlanger, Steven. "Crisis in the Balkans: The Power Couple; The First Lady of Serbia Often Has the Last Word." *The New York Times*, May 31, 1999. www.nytimes.com/1999/05/31/world/crisis-balkans-power-couple-firstlady-serbia-often-has-last-word.html?pagewanted=all&src=pm.

Eya, Osamu. *Great Illustrated Book of Kim Jong Il*. [Translated in FBIS document KPP 2002 0501000062.] Tokyo: Shogakukan, 2000.

Faimberg, Haydée. *The Telescoping of Generations: Listening to the Narcissistic Links between Generations*. London: Routledge, 2005.

Faiola, Anthony. "Debt Finally Does in Italian Premier." *The Washington Post*, November 12, 2011, p. A1.

"Family Dynamics Drive Syrian President Assad." *BBC News*, April 30, 2011. www.bbc.co.uk/news/world-middle-east-13247375.

Farwell, Lisa, and Ruth Wohlwend-Lloyd. "Narcissistic Processes: Optimistic Expectations, Favorable Self-Evaluations, and Self-Enhancing Attributions." *Journal of Personality* 66 (1998), pp. 65–83.

Feiner, Arthur. "The Relation of Monologue and Dialogue to Narcissistic States and Its Implications for Psychoanalytic Therapy." In *Narcissism and the Interpersonal Self*, edited by John Fiscalini and Alan Grey. New York: Columbia University Press, 1993, pp. 254–292.

Fiscalini, John. "Interpersonal Relations and the Problem of Narcissism." In *Narcissism and the Interpersonal Self*, edited by John Fiscalini and Alan Grey. New York: Columbia University Press, 1993, pp. 318–348.

Fisher, Luchina, David Wright, and Kevin Dolak. "Mother of Arnold Schwarzenegger's Love Child Revealed." *ABC News*, May 18, 2010. Accessed November 19, 2010.

Frankel, Glen. "Zimbabwe Shifts Strategy to Tough Austerity Plan," *The Washington Post*, September 14, 1983, pp. A23–24.

Freud, Sigmund, "On Narcissism." In *The Standard Edition of the Complete Psychological Works of Sigmund Freud, Volume XIV (1914–1916): On the History of the Psycho-Analytic Movement, Papers on Metapsychology and Other Works*. London: Hogarth Press, 1958, pp. 67–102.

Freud, Sigmund. "Psychoanalytic Notes on an Autobiographical Account of a Case of Paranoia." In *The Standard Edition of the Complete Psychological Works of Sigmund Freud, Volume XII: The Case of Schreber, Papers on Technique, and Other Works, 1911*. London: Hogarth Press, 1958, pp. 9–82.

Friedman, Thomas. *From Beirut to Jerusalem*. New York: Anchor Books, 1989.

Foreign Broadcast Information Service. *North Africa Report*, January 4, 1978.

Foreign Broadcast Information Service. *Middle East Report*, July 7, 1980.

Foreign Broadcast Information Service. *Arab Africa Report*, November 9, 1987.

Forero, Juan. "Hugo Chavez May Have Aggressive Tumor, Cancer Experts Say." *The Washington Post*, February 15, 2012. www.washingtonpost.com/world/hugo-chavez-may-have-aggressive-tumor-cancer-experts-say/2012/02/25/gIQAgGuKaR_story.html.

Friedlander, Beau. "An Interview with a Madman: Breivik Asks and Answers His Own Questions." *TIME*, July 24, 2011. www.time.com/time/world/article/0,8599,2084895,00.html.

Fromm, Erich. *Man for Himself: An Inquiry into the Psychology of Ethics*. New York: Rinehart, 1947.

Fromm, Erich. *The Heart of Man: Its Genius for Good and Evil.* New York: Harper & Row, 1964.

Galanter, Mark. "The 'Relief Effect': A Sociobiological Model for Neurotic Distress and Large Group Therapy." *American Journal of Psychiatry* 135, No. 5 (1978), pp. 588–591.

Galanter, Mark. "The Moonies: A Psychological Study of Conversion and Membership in a Contemporary Religious Sect." *American Journal of Psychiatry* 136, No. 2 (1979), pp. 165–170.

Galanter, Mark. "Psychological Induction into the Large Group: Findings from a Modern Religious Sect." *American Journal of Psychiatry* 137, No. 12 (1980), pp. 1574–1569.

Galanter, Mark. "Engaged Members of the Unification Church: Impact of a Charismatic Large Group on Adaptation and Behavior." *Archives of General Psychiatry* 40, No. 11 (1983): 1197–1202.

Galanter, Mark. "'Moonies' Get Married: A Psychiatric Follow-Up Study of a Charismatic Religious Sect." *American Journal of Psychiatry* 143 (1986), pp. 1245–1249.

Garamone, Jim. "Petraeus Garners Praise at Retirement Ceremony." *United States Department of Defense,* August 31, 2011. www.defense.gov/News/NewsArticle .aspx?ID=65213.

"General Petraeus Remembers His Hometown." *Cornwall and Cornwall on Hudson,* February 2, 2007. Accessed February 24, 2013. www.cornwall-on hudson.com/busi ness.cfm?page=393.

Geoghegan, Tom. "Asma al-Assad and the Tricky Role of the Autocrat's Wife." *BBC News Magazine,* February 8, 2012. www.bbc.co.uk/news/magazine 16930738.

George, Alexander L., and Juliette L. George. *Woodrow Wilson and Colonel House: A Personality Study.* New York: John Day, 1964.

Gilani, Zulfiqar S. "Z. A. Bhutto's Leadership: A Psycho-Social View." *Contemporary South Asia* 94, No. 3 (1994), pp. 217–227.

"Gingrich Attacks Clinton on Lewinsky Matter, Foreign Policy." *CNN,* May 18, 1998. http://articles.cnn.com/1998-05-18/politics/gingrich.clinton_1_gingrich-foreign-policy-missile-technology?_s=PM:ALLPOLITICS.

Ginsborg, Paul. *Silvio Berlusconi: Television, Power, and Patrimony* (London: Verso, 2004).

GlobalSecurity.org. "Political Change in Cuba." Last modified May 7, 2011. www .globalsecurity.org/military/ops/cuba-intro.htm.

Globe Staff. "Eliot Spitzer to Lecture at Harvard Ethics Center." *Boston.com,* November 12, 2009. www.boston.com/news/local/breaking_news/2009/11/eliot_spitzer_t.html.

Goldman, Minton. *Revolution and Change in Central and Eastern Europe: Political, Economic, and Social Changes.* Armonk, NY: M. E. Sharpe, 1997.

Goren, B., & Berkowitz, E. "Mi ze? [6/26/2014?]." *Ha'ir,* June 21, 1996, pp. 34–43, 86–87.

"Governor Says Impeachment Vote Is Politically Driven." *CNN,* January 9, 2009. http:// articles.cnn.com/2009-01-09/politics/blagojevich.impeachment_1_impeachment-rod-blagojevich-illinois-house?_s=PM:POLITICS.

Greenwald, John, Kenneth Banta, and Rodman Griffin. "Rumania Mother of the Fatherland." *TIME Magazine,* July 14, 1986.

Grotstein, James S. "Meaning, Meaninglessness, and the 'Black Hole': Self and Interactional Regulation as a New Paradigm for Psychoanalysis and Neuroscience," 1987. Cited in Joan Lachkar, *The Narcissistic/Borderline Couple: A Psychoanalytic Perspective on Marital Treatment.* New York: Brunnel Mazel, 1992, pp. 28–29.

Habberman, Maggie. "Newt Gingrich: 'I Was Doing Things That Were Wrong.'" *POLITICO,* March 8, 2011. Accessed December 15, 2012. www.politico.com/news/ stories/031.

Habeeb, W. M. "Zine el Abidine Ben Ali," quoted from an interview in *Le Monde*, p. 82, November 8, 1987. In *Political Leaders of the Contemporary Middle East and North Africa: A Biographical Dictionary*, edited by B. Reich. New York: Greenwood, 1990, pp. 78–84.

Hakim, Danny, and William K. Rashbaum. "Spitzer Is Linked to Prostitution Ring." *New York Times*, March 10, 2008. Accessed April 6, 2011. www.nytimes.com/2008/03/10/nyregion/10cnd-spitzer.html?pagewanted=all.

Halper, Evan. "Schwarzenegger Approval Rating Hits New Low." December 16, 2009. Accessed November 12, 2010. http://latimesblogs.latimes.com/lanow/2009/12/schwar zeneggerapproval-rating-hits-new-low.html.

Hamby, Peter. "S.C. Attorney General to Review Sanford's Travel Records." *CNN*, July 1, 2009. http://articles.cnn.com/2009-06-30/politics/sanford_1_maria-belen-cha pur-sanford-spokesman-joel-sawyer-governor-sanford?_s=PM:POLITICS.

Hanley, Robert. "US Links Man with 3 Bombs to Terror Plot." *The New York Times*, February 4, 1989. www.nytimes.com/1989/02/04/nyregion/us-links-man-with-3-bombs-to-a terror-plot.html.

"'Hardball with Chris Matthews' for August 28." *MSNBC News*, August 29, 2007. Accessed April 12, 2011. www.msnbc.msn.com/id/20496581/ns/msnbc_tv hardball_with_chris_matthews/t/hardball-chris-matthews-august/.

"'Hardball with Chris Matthews' for October 3." *MSNBC News*, October 4, 2006, Accessed March 15, 2011. http://www.nbcnews.com/id/15128915/ns/msnbc-hard ball_with_chris_matthews/t/hardball-chris-matthews-oct/.U5iTKJRdVZY.

"In Public He Rails Against Immorality as the Voice of Christian Britain but in Private He Is a Wife Beater, Says His Former Partner." *Daily Mail (UK)*, January 28, 2011. Accessed April 10, 2011. www.dailymail.co.uk/news/article-1351585/Stephen-Green-rails-immorality-voice-Christian-Britan-private-wife-beater-says-partner.html.

Harper, Karen. "Senator John Ensign Should Resign from Senate." *Examiner.com*, N.d. Accessed March 25, 2011. www.examiner.com/article/senator-john-ensign-should-resign-from-senate.

"Hart First Withdrawal." *C-SPAN*, December 15, 1987. Accessed March 30, 2011. www.c-spanvideo.org/program/Wit&showFullAbstract=1.

Hastings, Michael. "The Runaway General." *Rolling Stone*, June 22, 2010. Accessed February 24, 2013. www.rollingstone.com/politics/news/the-runawaygen eral-20100622.

Healy, Rita. "A Mega-Scandal for a Mega-Church." *TIME*, November 3, 2006. Accessed April 20, 2011. www.time.com/time/nation/article/0,8599,1554388,00.html.

Hennessey, Kathleen. "Senate Confirms David Petraeus as CIA Director." *The Los Angeles Times*, June 30, 2011. http://articles.latimes.com/2011/jun/30/news/la-pn-petraeus-confirmed-20110630.

Hill, Melanie S., and Ann R. Fischer, "Does Entitlement Mediate the Link between Masculinity and Rape Related Variables?" *Journal of Counseling Psychology* 48 (2001), pp. 39–50.

Hirsch, Irwin. "The Ubiquity and Relativity of Narcissism: Therapeutic Implications." In *Narcissism and the Interpersonal Self*, edited by John Fiscalini and Alan Grey. New York: Columbia University Press, 1993, pp. 293–317.

Holmes, Dorothy. "The Wrecking Effects of Race and Social Class on Self and Success." *Psychoanalytic Quarterly* 75, No. 1 (2006), pp. 215–235.

Horney, Karen. *New Ways in Psychoanalysis*. New York: W. W. Norton, 1939.

"*Howard v. Arkansas* – George Rekers Fact Sheet." *American Civil Liberties Union (ACLU)*, October 4, 2004. Accessed April 21, 2011. www.aclu.org/lgbt-rights_hiv-aids/howard-v-arkansas-george-rekers-fact-sheet.

Human Rights Watch. *A Wasted Decade: Human Rights in Syria during Bashar al-Assad's First Ten Years in Power*. New York: Human Rights Watch, 2010.

Hussein, King of Jordan. *Uneasy Lies the Head: The Autobiography of His Majesty King Hussein I of the Hashemite Kingdom of Jordan*. New York: B. Geis Associates, 1962.

"In Quotes: Berlusconi in His Own Words." *BBC News*, May 2, 2006. http://news.bbc .co.uk/2/hi/3041288.stm.

"In Quotes: Italy's Silvio Berlusconi in His Own Words." *BBC News Europe*, November 8, 2011. www.bbc.co.uk/news/world-europe-15642201.

James, D. C. *The Years of MacArthur*. Boston: Houghton Mifflin, 1985.

James, Randy. "Senator John Ensign: 'I Had an Affair.'" *TIME*, June 18, 2009. www .time.com/time/nation/article/0,8599,1905351,00.html.

Janigan, Mary, et al. "Gandhi's Reluctant Heir." *Maclean's*, November 12, 1984.

Kaczynski, Theodore. "Industrial Society and Its Future." *The Washington Post*, September 19, 1995. www.washingtonpost.com/wpsrv/national/longterm/unabom ber/manifesto.text.htm.

Kakar, Sudhir. "Feminine Identity in India." In *Women in Indian Society: A Reader*, edited by Rehana Ghadially. New Delhi: Sage, 1988, pp. 44–68.

Kamen, Al. "Rumsfeld: The Boom Years." *The Washington Post*, March 11, 2011.

Kelley, Frank, and Cornelius Ryan. *MacArthur: Man of Action*. Garden City, N.Y.: Doubleday, 1950.

Kernberg, Otto. *Borderline Conditions and Pathological Narcissism*. New York: Jason Aronson, 1975.

Kernberg, Otto. *Object Relations Theory and Clinical Psychoanalysis*. New York: Jason Aronson, 1976, 1984.

Kernberg, Otto. *Internal World and External Reality*. New York: Jason Aronson, 1984.

Khalid, Mansour. *Nimeiri and the Revolution of Dis-May*. London: KPI, 1985.

Kim Myong Chol. "Kim Jong-il's Military Strategy for Reunification." *Comparative Strategy* 20, No. 4 (2001), pp. 303–420.

King, Wayne. "Swaggart Says He Has Sinned; Will Step Down." *New York Times*, February 22, 1998. Accessed April 12, 2011. www.nytimes.com/1988/02/22/us/swag gart-says-he-has-sinned-will-step-down.html?pagewanted=all&src=pm.

Klein Halevi, Yossi. "Bibi's Political Inheritance." *Tablet*, May 1, 2012. www.tabletmag .com/jewish-news-and-politics/98279/bibis-political-inheritance.

Knoll, James. "The 'Pseudocommando' Mass Murderer: A Blaze of Vainglory." *Psychiatric Times*, January 4, 2012. www.psychiatrictimes.com/display/article/ 10168/2013318.

Kohut, Heinz. *The Analysis of the Self*. New York: International Universities Press, 1971.

Kohut, Heinz. "Creativeness, Charisma, Group Psychology." *In Freud: The Fusion of Science and Humanism*, edited by John E. Gedo and George H. Pollock. Psychological Issues, 34/35. New York: International Universities Press, 1976, pp. 379–425.

Kohut, Heinz. *The Restoration of the Self*. New York: International Universities Press, 1977.

Kohut, Heinz. *The Search for the Self*. York: International Universities Press, 1978.

Kohut, Heinz. *How Does Psychoanalysis Cure?* Chicago: University of Chicago Press, 1984.

Kohut, Heinz. *Self-Psychology and the Humanities: Reflections on a New Psychoanalytic Approach*, edited by Charles B. Strozier. New York: W. W. Norton & Company, 1985.

Konigsmark, Anne Rochell. "A Week of Crisis Impeachment: The Speakership Livingston's Constituents Decision to Resign Jolts Home District." *The Atlanta Journal-Constitution*. December 20, 1998.

Krasniewicz, Louise, and Michael Blitz. *Arnold Schwarzenegger: A Biography*. London: Greenwood Press, 2006.

Kreisman, Stu. "Mark Sanford: Yet Another Lying Republican Creep." *The Huffington Post*, June 24, 2009. Accessed March 1, 2011. www.huffingtonpost.com/stu-kreisman/yet-another-lying-republi_b_220335.html.

Lachkar, Joan. *The Narcissistic/Borderline Couple: A Psychoanalytic Perspective on Marital Treatment*. New York: Brunnel Mazel, 1992.

LaCouture, Jean. *The Demigods: Charismatic Leadership in the Third World*. New York: Alfred A. Knopf, 1970.

Lasch, Christopher. *The Culture of Narcissism: American Life in an Age of Diminishing Expectations*. New York: W. W. Norton & Company, 1979.

Laver, Ross, and David North. "India after Indira Gandhi." *Maclean's*, November 12, 1984.

Lazarus, Jeremy. "Ethical Constraints in Leadership Profiling." Paper presented at the annual meeting of the American Psychiatric Association on "Psychiatric Contributions to the Study of Leadership," 1994.

Leamer, Laurence. *The Kennedy Men, 1901–1963: The Laws of the Father*. New York: Wm. Morrow, 2001.

Legum, Colin. "The New Statesman Profile – Robert Mugabe: Once Hailed as a New African Hero and a Non-racist, His Behaviour Is Now That of the Paranoid Pers." August 27, 2001. www.newstatesman.com/node/141018.

Leigh, Wendy. *Arnold: An Unauthorized Biography*. New York: Congdon & Weed, 1990.

Lelyveld, Joseph. "Rajiv the Son." *The New York Times*, December 2, 1984.

Lesch, David W. *The New Lion of Damascus: Bashar al-Assad and Modern Syria*. New Haven: Yale University Press, 2005.

Leverett, Flynt. *Inheriting Syria: Bashar's Trial by Fire*. Washington, D.C.: Brookings Institute Press, 2005.

Levy, Ariel. "Basta Bunga Bunga." *The New Yorker*, June 6, 2011. www.newyorker .com/reporting/2011/06/06/110606fa_fact_levy.

Levy, Steven T., Beth J. Seelig, and Lawrence B. Inderbitzin. "On Those Wrecked By Success: A Clinical Inquiry." *Psychoanalytic Quarterly* 64 (1995), pp. 639–657.

"Libya's Gaddafi: 'My people love me.'" *BBC News*, February 28, 2011. www.bbc.co .uk/news/world-africa-12603086.

Lichtblau, Eric, and Eric Lipton. "U.S. Scrutinized Ensign, but Senate Dug Deeper." *New York Times*, May 13, 2011. www.nytimes.com/2011/05/14/us/politics/14ensign.html? pagewanted=all.

Link, Arthur. *The Papers of Woodrow Wilson, Volume 5: 1885–1888*. Princeton, N.J.: Princeton University Press, 1968.

Loewenberg, Peter. "Psychoanalytic Models of History: Freud and After." In *Psychology and Historical Interpretation*, edited by William McKinley Runyan. New York: Oxford University Press, 1988, pp. 126–156.

Loewenberg, Peter. "The Psychohistorical Origins of the Nazi Youth Cohort." In *Decoding the Past: The Psychohistorical Approach*, edited by Peter Loewenberg. New York: Alfred A. Knopf, 1983, pp. 240–283.

Lush, Tamara, and Evan Berland. "AP Newsbreak: SC Gov 'Crossed Lines' with Women." *U-T San Diego*, June 30, 2009. Accessed December 16, 2013. www.utsan diego.com/news/2009/Jun/30/us-sc-governor-063009/.

MacArthur, Douglas. *Reminiscences*. New York: McGraw-Hill, 1964.

McNamara, Jennifer, and Jerrold Post: "Putin the Great: Struggling to Hold on to a Crumbling Empire." *Huffington Post*, January 4, 2014. www.huffingtonpost.com/jenni fer-mcnamara/putin-the-great-strugglin_b_5072330.html.

Maier, Anneli. "Enhanced Personality Cult for Elena Ceausescu." *Open Society Archives*, January 8, 1986. www.osaarchivum.org/files/holdings/300/8/3/text/53–863.shtml.

Malhotra, Inder. *Indira Gandhi: A Personal and Political Biography*. Sevenoaks: Coronet Books, 1991.

Malhotra, Inder. "Remembering Indira Gandhi." *The Hindu*, October 31, 2001. Accessed June 20, 2011. www.hindu.com/2001/10/31/stories/0531134c.htm.

Manso, Peter. "Arnold Schwarzenegger: The Man with the World's Most Perfectly Developed Physique Destroys a Few Myths about Body Building; He Smokes Dope, Stays Out Late and Forgets to Take His Vitamins." *Oui Magazine*, 1977. Accessed December 18, 2009. http://daggy.name/cop/effluvia/arnold.htm.

Margolick, David. "The Netanyahu Paradox." *Vanity Fair*, July 2012. www.vanityfair .com/politics/2012/07/benjamin-netanyahu-on-israel-mitt-romney.

Markus, Hazel R., and Shinobu Kitayama. "Culture and the Self: Implications for Cognition, Emotion, and Motivation." *Psychological Review* 98 (1991), pp. 224–253.

Marnham, Patrick. "In Search of Amin." *Granta Magazine* 17 (1985), pp. 69–82.

Martin, Jonathan. "Spokane Mayor West's Public and Private Lives Contrast." *The Seattle Times*, May 7, 2005. Accessed April 2, 2011. http://seattletimes.nwsource .com/html/localnews/2002266631_west07m.html.

Martin, Ralph G. *Seeds of Destruction: Joe Kennedy and His Sons*. New York: G. P. Putnam's Sons, 1995.

Masood, Salman. "Bhutto Assassination Ignites Disarray." *The New York Times*, December 28, 2007. Accessed June 16, 2011. www.nytimes.com/2007/12/28/world/ asia/28pakistan.html?pagewant.

Mathews, Joe. *The People's Machine*. New York: Public Affairs, 2006.

May, Caroline. "Petraeus' 'Other Woman' Reportedly a Married Mother of Two, under FBI Investigation." *The Daily Caller*, November 9, 2012. http://dailycaller.com/2012/ 11/09/petraeus-other-woman-a-married-mother-of-two-under-fbi-investigation/.

McKay, Mary-Jayne. "Turkmenbashi Everywhere." *CBS News 60 Minutes*. February 11, 2009. www.cbsnews.com/2100-18560_162-590913.html.

McWilliams, Nancy. *Psychoanalytic Diagnosis: Understanding Personality Structure in the Clinical Process*. New York: Guilford Press, 1994.

Mears, Walter R., and Hal Buell. *The Kennedy Brothers: A Legacy in Photographs*. New York: Black Dog and Leventhal, 2009.

Miller, Joshua D., and W. Keith Campbell. "Comparing Clinical and Social-Personality Conceptualizations of Narcissism." *Journal of Personality* 76 (2008), pp. 449–476.

Mitchell, Stephen. "The Wings of Icarus: Illusion and the Problem of Narcissism." *Contemporary Psychoanalysis* 22 (1986), pp. 107–132.

Mitchell, Stephen. *Hope and Dread in Psychoanalysis*. New York: Basic Books, 1993.

Mitchell, Stephen, and Lewis Aron. *Relational Psychoanalysis: The Emergence of a Tradition*. Hillsdale, N.J.: Analytic Press, 1999.

Mitzman, Dany. "Italy Wrestles with Berlusconi Legacy." *BBC News Europe*. January 12, 2012. www.bbc.co.uk/news/world-europe-16518599.

Moller, Jan. "David Vitter Sex Scandal Gets Spotlight Again in Debate with Charlie Melancon." *The Times-Picayune*, October 28, 2010. www.nola.com/politics/index .ssf/2010/10/david_vitter_sex_scandal_gets.html.

Monthly Chosun. April, 1997. Originally published in Korean. www.kimsoft.com/korea/ kjj-kisu.htm.

Moore, Clement Henry. *Tunisia Since Independence: The Dynamics of One-Party Government*. Westport: Greenwood Press, 1965.

Morgan, David. "Breivik's Father: I Wish My Son Killed Himself." *CBS News*, July 25, 2011. www.cbsnews.com/8301-503543_162-20082948-503543.html.

Morris, Betsy, Aida Gil, Patricia Neering, and Oliver Ryan. "Arnold Power He Accumulates It. He Wields It. He Wins Over Voters with It. But Is the Governator's Star Power Enough to Win the War of Wills with His California Opponents?" *Fortune Magazine*, August 2004. Accessed October 23, 2010. http://money.cnn.com/maga zines/fortune/fortune_archive/2004/08/09/377908/index.htm.

Morrison, Andrew (1989). *Shame: The Underside of Narcissism*. Hillsdale, N.J.: Analytic Press.

"Mugabe Marriage Splits Nation." *The Daily Telegraph*, August 16, 1996.

"Mugabe Rival Quits Election Race." *BBC News*, June 22, 2008. http://news.bbc.co.uk/ 2/hi/africa/7467990.stm.

"Mugabe's Wife on EU Sanctions List." *BBC News*, July 22, 2002. http://news.bbc.co .uk/2/hi/africa/2143442.stm.

Mujtaba, Hasan. "Bhutto: Man and Myth." *Newsline*, January, 1993, pp. 135–144.

Mullahy, Patrick. *The Contributions of Harry Stack Sullivan: A Symposium on Interpersonal Theory in Psychiatry and Social Science*. New York: Hermitage House, 1952.

Mullen, P. E. "The Autogenic (Self-Generated) Massacre." *Behavioral Sciences and the Law*, 22(2004), pp. 311–323.

Mutori, David. "The President's Office . . . The Albatross in Our Midst!" September 8, 2011. http://zimbabweinsights.blogspot.com/2011/09/presidentsoffice-albatross-in our.html.

Nadkarni, L., Janice M. Steil, J. Malone, and L. M. Sagrestano. "The Sense of Entitlement: The Development of a Self-Report Scale to Measure Personal Entitlement." 2014. Manuscript under review.

Natsios, Andrew. *The Great North Korean Famine: Famine, Politics, and Foreign Policy*. Washington, D.C.: United States Institute of Peace. 2001.

Netanyahu, Jonathan. *The Letters of Jonathan Netanyahu: The Commander of the Entebbe Rescue Force*. Jerusalem: Gefen Publishing House, 2001.

"Newt Gingrich Tells The Brody File He 'Felt Compelled to Seek God's forgiveness.'" *Christian Broadcasting Network*, March 8, 2011. http://blogs.cbn.com/thebrodyfile/ archive/2011/03/08/newt-gingrich-tells-brody-file-he-felt-compelled-to-seek.aspx.

Nimeiri, Jaafar. *The Islamic Way: Why?* Khartoum: Government Press, 1978.

"North Korea's Likely New Leader Seen as Bizarre." *St. Petersburg Times*, July 10, 1994.

"Norway Massacre: Breivik Disputes Psychiatric Report." *BBC News*, April 4, 2012. www.bbc.co.uk/news/world-europe-17613822.

Nugent, Nicholas. *Rajiv Gandhi: Son of a Dynasty*. London: BBC Books, 1990.

O'Connell, Jeff. "End of Days." *Muscle & Fitness*, January 2000. Accessed November 9, 2010. www.highbeam.com/doc/1P3-46630579.html.

Oh, Kong Dan, and Ralph Hassig. *North Korea Through the Looking Glass*. Washington D.C.: Brookings Institution Press, 2000.

Ovid (AD 8). *The Metamorphoses*, Book Three. Translated by Horace Gregory. New York: Viking, 1958, pp. 464–468.

Pahlavi, Mohammad Reza, Shah of Iran. *Mission for My Country*. New York: McGraw-Hill, 1961.

Park, Han. *North Korea: The Politics of Unconventional Wisdom*. Boulder, Colo.: Lynne Rienner, 2002.

Paulk, John, and Tony Marco. *Not Afraid to Change: The Remarkable Story of How One Man Overcame Homosexuality*. Mukilteo, Wash.: WinePress, 1998.

Photograph of Gary Hart and Donna Rice. *National Enquirer*, June 2, 1987. Front Cover.

Polman, Dick. "Those Aren't Rumors" *Smithsonian Magazine*, April 2008. Accessed June 2, 2011. www.smithsonianmag.com/people-places/presence-200804.html?c=y&page=4.

Porter, Mickey. "Newt's a Beaut." *Akron Beacon Journal*. July 25, 2000.

Post, Jerrold. "Woodrow Wilson Reexamined: The Mind-Body Controversy Redux and Other Disputations." *Political Psychology* 4, No. 2 (1983), pp. 289–306.

Post, Jerrold. "Dreams of Glory and the Life Cycle: Reflections on the Life Course of Narcissistic Leaders." *Journal of Political and Military Sociology* 12, No. 1 (1984), pp. 49–60.

Post, Jerrold. "Narcissism and the Charismatic Leader-Follower Relationship." *Political Psychology* 7, No. 4 (1986), pp. 675–688.

Post, Jerrold. "It's Us Against Them: The Basic Assumptions of Political Terrorists." In *Irrationality in Organizational Life*, edited by J. Krantz. Washington, D.C.: A. K. Rice Institute Press, 1987.

Post, Jerrold. "Saddam Hussein of Iraq: A Political Psychology Profile." *Political Psychology* 12, No. 2 (1991), pp. 279–289.

Post, Jerrold, and Robert Robins. *When Illness Strikes the Leader: The Dilemma of the Captive King*. New Haven: Yale University Press, 1993.

Post, Jerrold. "Current Concepts of Narcissism: Implications for Political Psychology." *Political Psychology* 14, No. 1 (1993b), pp. 99–121.

Post, Jerrold. "Publish or Perish: The Unabomber Papers." *Psychiatric Times* (November 1996).

Post, Jerrold. "Ethical Considerations in Psychiatric Profiling of Political Figures." In Vol. 25, No. 3 of *Psychiatric Clinics of North America*, edited by Glen Gabbard. Philadelphia: Saunders, 2002, pp. A635–A646.

Post, Jerrold, ed. *The Psychological Assessment of Political Leaders*. Ann Arbor: University of Michigan Press, 2003.

Post, Jerrold. *Leaders and Their Followers in a Dangerous World: The Psychology of Political Behavior*. Ithaca: Cornell University Press, 2004.

Post, Jerrold & Lara Panis. *Tyranny on Trial: Personality and Courtroom Conduct of Defendants Slobodan Milosevic and Saddam Hussein*. Cornell International Law Journal, 38, No. 3 (Fall 2005), pp 823–836.

Post, Jerrold. "Qaddafi Under Siege: A Political Psychologist Assesses Libya's Mercurial Leader." *Foreign Policy* (March 15, 2011). www.foreignpolicy.com/articles/2011/03/15/qaddafi_under_seige.

"Profile: Asif Ali Zardari." *BBC News*, 2007. Accessed January 20, 2011. http://news
.bbc.co.uk/2/hi/4032.
"Profile: Bashar al-Assad." *Al-Jazeera*, March 25, 2011. http://english.aljazeera.net/
news/middleeast/2007/07/200852518514154964.html.
"Profile: Rifaat al-Assad." *BBC News*, June 12, 2000. http://news.bbc.co.uk/2/hi/mid
dle_east/788021.stm.
"Raids Target Zimbabwe opposition." *CNN*, April 4, 2008. www.cnn.com/2008/
WORLD/africa/04/03/zimbabwe.election/index.html?eref=rss_topstories.
Ramos, Natalia. "'Don't Take Me Yet,' Ailing Chavez Begs God at Mass." *Agence
France Presse*, 2012. http://news.yahoo.com/dont-yet-ailing-chavez-begs-god-mass-
204022078.html.
Rawls, Oren. "In Other Words . . . " *The Forward*, August 15, 2003. http://forward.com/
articles/7892/in-other-words-/.
Reddy, C. K. C., et al. *Army Action in Punjab: Prelude & Aftermath*. New Delhi: Samata
Era, 1984.
Reeves, Thomas C. *A Question of Character: A Life of John F. Kennedy*. New York: Free
Press, 1991.
Reich, Wilhelm. *Character Analysis* (Revised 3rd edn.). New York: Farrar, Straus &
Giroux, 1972.
Renshon, Stanley A. *High Hopes: The Clinton Presidency and the Politics of Ambition*.
New York: New York University Press, 1996.
Rhodewalt, F., and C. C. Morf. "On Self-Aggrandizement and Anger: A Temporal
Analysis of Narcissism and Affective Reactions to Success and Failure." *Journal of
Personality and Social Psychology* 74 (1998), pp. 672–685.
Rick Wayne. "Reg Park . . . a Hero's Hero." *Muscle Builder/Power* (August/September
1976).
Ricks, Thomas E. *The Generals: American Military Command from World War II to
Today*. New York: Penguin Press, 2012.
Riding, Alan. "Clamor in the East; Rumanian Leader Refuses Changes." *The New York
Times*, November 21, 1989. www.nytimes.com/1989/11/21/world/clamor-in-the-east-
rumanian-leader-refuses-changes.html.
Robins, Robert. "Paranoia and Charisma." Paper presented at the annual meeting for the
International Society of Political Psychology, Toronto, Canada, 1984.
Robins, Robert, and Jerrold Post. *Political Paranoia: The Psychopolitics of Hatred*. New
Haven: Yale University Press, 1997.
"Romania Sells Ceausescu Luxuries from Communist Era." *BBC News*, January 27,
2012. www.bbc.co.uk/news/world-europe-16756590.
Romano, Lois. "Newt Gingrich, Maverick on the Hill: The New Right's Abrasive Point
Man Talks of Changing His Tone and Tactics." *The Washington Post*, January 3, 1985.
Roth, Alex, and Valeria Bauerlein. "Gov. Sanford Struggles to Hang On." *The Wall
Street Journal*, June 26, 2009. http://online.wsj.com/article/SB124596061328355673
.html.
Rothstein, Arnold. *The Narcissistic Pursuit of Perfection*. New York: International
Universities Press, 1980.
Rudoren, Jodi. "Unity Government in Israel Disbanding over Dispute on Draft." *The New
York Times*, July 17, 2012. www.nytimes.com/2012/07/18/world/middleeast/unity-gov
ernment-in-israel-disbanding-over-dispute-on-draft.html?pagewanted=all&_r=0.
Sahgal, Nayantara. *Indira Gandhi: Her Road to Power*. New York: F. Ungar, 1982.

Saint-Exupery, Antoine. *The Little Prince*. Translated by Katherine Woods. New York: Harcourt, Brace, and World, 1943.

"Sally Mugabe." *The Times*, January 30, 1992.

Salmon, Stephanie. "10 Things You Didn't Know About Benazir Bhutto." *U.S. News & World Report*, December 27, 2007. Accessed December 5, 2010. www.usnews.com/ news/world/articles/2007/12/27/10-things-you-didnt-know-about-benazir-bhutto.

Sass, Louis. "The Self and Its Vicissitudes: An 'Archaeological' Study of the Psychoanalytic Avante-Garde." *Social Research* 55, No. 4 (1988), pp. 551–607.

Scherzer, Amy. "Amy Scherzer's Diary." *Tampa Bay Times*, February 4, 2010. www .tampabay.com/news/humaninterest/amy-scherzers-diary/1070401.

Schiffer, Irvine. *Charisma: A Psychoanalytic Look at Mass Society*. Toronto: University of Toronto Press, 1973.

Schwarz, Gabriella. "Gingrich: I'm Not a Hypocrite." *CNN*, March 27, 2011. http:// politicalticker.blogs.cnn.com/2011/03/27/gingrich-i%E2%80%99m-not-a-hypocrite/.

Schwartz, Jonathan, and Tracy Tylka. "Exploring Entitlement as a Moderator and Mediator of the Relationship Between Masculine Gender Role Conflict and Men's Body Esteem." *Psychology of Men & Masculinity* 9 (2008), pp. 67–81.

Schwartz, Rhonda, Brian Ross, and Chris Francescani. "Edwards Admits Sexual Affair; Lied as Presidential Candidate." *ABC News*, August 8, 2008. Accessed April 6, 2011. http://abcnews.go.com/Blotter/story?id=5441195.

"Schwarzenegger Approval Rating: 39 Percent." *The Orange County Register*, April 13, 2006. www.ocregister.com/news/approval-188913-schwarzenegger-rating.html.

Schwarzenegger, Arnold. *Arnold: The Education of a Bodybuilder*. New York: Simon & Shuster, 1977.

"Schwarzenegger's Inauguration Speech." *CNN*, November 17, 2003. Accessed November 7, 2010. http://edition.cnn.com/2003/ALLPOLITICS/11/17/arnold.speech/.

"Schwarzenegger, Reagan Have a Lot in Common." *Fox News.com*, June 7, 2004. Accessed November 7, 2010. www.foxnews.com/story/0,2933,121970,00.html.

Sciolino, Elaine. "Blurred Images of North Korea's 'Junior.'" *The New York Times*, July 17, 1994. www.nytimes.com/1994/07/17/world/blurred-images-of-north-korea-s-jun ior.html?pagewanted=all&src=pm.

"Sen. Larry Craig's interview with Matt Lauer." *NBC News*, October 16, 2007. Accessed April 10, 2011. www.msnbc.msn.com/id/21303825/t/sen-larry-craigs-interview-matt-lauer/.

Seymour, Susan. *Women, Family and Child Care in India: A World in Transition*. Cambridge: Cambridge University Press, 1999.

Shaw, Angus. "Grace Mugabe Sues Paper over Wikileaks Diamond Story." *The Christian Science Monitor*, December 17, 2010. www.csmonitor.com/World/Latest-News-Wires/2010/1217/Grace-Mugabe-sues-paper-over-WikiLeaks-diamonds-story.

Sheehy, Gail. "The Inner Quest of Newt Gingrich." *Vanity Fair* 421, September 1995, pp. 147.

Shepherd, Lewis. "Petraeus as Ozymandias." *Shepherd's Pi*, November 10, 2012. http:// lewisshepherd.wordpress.com/2012/11/10/petraeus-as-ozymandias/.

Sherrill, Stephen. "The Year in Ideas: A to Z; Acquired Situational Narcissism." *The New York Times*, December 9, 2001. www.nytimes.com/2001/12/09/magazine/the-year-in-ideas-a-to-z-acquired-situational-narcissism.html.

Shindler, Colin. *Israel, Likud, and the Zionist Dream: Power, Politics, and Ideology from Begin to Netanyahu*. London: I. B. Tauris, 1995.

"Silvio Berlusconi & Family." *Forbes*, March 2013. www.forbes.com/profile/silviober lusconi/.

"Silvio Berlusconi Resigns After Italian Parliament Approves Austerity Measures." *The Huffington Post*, November 12, 2011. www.huffingtonpost.co.uk/2011/11/12/silvio-ber lusconi-resigns-after-italian-parliament-approves-austerity-measures_n_1090149.html.

"Silvio Berlusconi under Pressure: A Comedy that Has Gone on Too Long." *The Economist*, November 4, 2010. www.economist.com/node/17416756.

Simmons, Ann. "Norway Suspect Modeled His Writings after Unabomber Manifesto." *Los Angeles Times*, July 24, 2011. http://articles.latimes.com/2011/jul/24/world/la-fgw-norway-suspect-20110725.

"Simone Gbagbo: Profile of Ivory Coast's One-Time 'Iron Lady.'" *Newstime Africa*, April 12, 2011. www.newstimeafrica.com/archives/19278.

Singh, Khushwant. *A History of the Sikhs Volume II*. Oxford: Oxford University Press, 1990.

Smith, Amanda (ed.). *Hostage to Fortune: The Letters of Joseph P. Kennedy*. New York: Viking, 2001.

Smith, George Ivan. *Ghosts of Kampala: The Rise and Fall of Idi Amin*. London: Weidenfeld and Nicolson, 1980.

Smith, Jeffrey R. "N. Korean Strongman: 'Crazy' or Canny?" *The Washington Post*, September 26, 1993. www.washingtonpost.com/wpdyn/content/article/2006/10/18/AR2006101800821.html.

Squazzin, Antony, and Brian Latham. "Zimbabwe's Political Elite Profited from Gems, Wikileaks Says." *Bloomberg*, December 10, 2010. www.bloomberg.com/news/2010-12-10/zimbabwe-s-political-elite-profited-from-illicit-diamonds-wikileaks-says.html.

Stahl, Lesley. "Arnold Schwarzenegger: Success and Secrets." *CBS News*, September 30, 2012. www.cbsnews.com/8301-18560_162-57523140/arnold-schwarzenegger-suc cess-and-secrets/.

Steinberg, Blema. *Women in Power: The Personalities and Leadership Styles of Indira Gandhi, Golda Meir, and Margaret Thatcher*. Montreal: McGill-Queen's University Press, 2008.

Stein, Sam. "Ensign Whacked Bill Clinton for His Infidelities, Called Them 'Embarrassing' for Country." *The Huffington Post*, July 17, 2009. www.huffingtonpost.com/2009/06/16/ensign-whacked-clinton-fo_n_216508.html.

Stewart, Phil. "Italy's Berlusconi Wins Immunity from Prosecution." *Reuters*, July 22, 2008. www.reuters.com/article/2008/07/22/us-italy-immunity-idUSL22100720080722.

Stille, Alexander. *The Sack of Rome: How a Beautiful European Country with a Fabled History and a Storied Culture Was Taken Over by a Man Named Silvio Berlusconi*. New York: Penguin Press, 2006.

Stout, David. "Chavez Calls Bush 'the Devil' in UN Speech." *The New York Times*, September 20, 2006. www.nytimes.com/2006/09/20/world/americas/20cnd-chavez .html.

Subramanian, Courtney. "Top 10 Worst Silvio Berlusconi Gaffes." *TIME*. November 9, 2011. www.time.com/time/specials/packages/article/0,28804,1874098_1874099_20989 84,00.html.

Suh, Dae-Sook. *Kim Il Sung: The North Korean Leader*. New York: Columbia University Press, 1988.

Sullivan, Andrew. "Ben Zion Netanyahu 1910–2012." *The Daily Beast*. April 30, 2012. http://andrewsullivan.thedailybeast.com/2012/04/ben-zion-netanyahu-1910–2012.html.

Suvorov, Viktor. *Soviet Military Intelligence*. London: Grafton Books, 1986.
Tartakoff, Helen. "The Normal Personality in Our Culture and the Nobel Prize Complex." In *Psychoanalysis: A General Psychology*, edited by R. M. Loewenstein, L. M. Newman, M. Schur, & A. J. Solnit. New York: International Universities Press, 1966, pp. 222–252.
Taseer, Salmaan. *Bhutto: A Political Biography*. New Delhi: Vikas, 1980.
Thakur, Janardan. *Prime Ministers: Nehru to Vajpayee*. Mumbai: Eeshwar, 1999.
"The Arab Uprisings: Endgame in Tripoli." *The Economist*, February 24, 2011. www.economist.com/node/18239888.
"The Economist Wins Berlusconi lawsuit." *The Economist*, September 5, 2008. www.economist.com/node/12076765.
"The Enigmatic Candidate." *People Magazine*, March 26, 1984. www.people.com/people/archive/issue/0,7566840326,,00.html.
"The Genius of the Carpathians." *The New York Times*, March 15, 1989. www.nytimes.com/1989/03/15/opinion/the-genius-of-the-carpathians.html.
"The Great Mangyongdae Family." *NDSFK*, March 2001. http://ndfsk.dyndns.org/kuguk8/pym/nr3/Magdae.htm.
"The Hero of Perfected Mass." *Rolling Stone Archive*, June 1976. Accessed November 7, 2010. www.rollingstone.com.
The Jerusalem Post. December 15, 1981.
The Jerusalem Post. July 15, 1980.
The Oprah Winfrey Show. "Project Vote Smart." September 15, 2003. http://votesmart.org/public-statement/21364/the-oprahwinfrey-show bno.UrJRKShjNL4.
"The Prime Minister and the Press" (Original Title: "Citizen Berlusconi). First broadcast August 21, 2003 by PBS. Written and directed by Andrea Cairola and Susan Gray.
"The Secret of Silvio Berlusconi's Success." *BBC News Magazine*, November 12, 2011. www.bbc.co.uk/news/magazine-15629283.
Thornycroft, Peta. "Attack on Mugabe's Media Laws." *The Telegraph*, January 30, 2002. www.telegraph.co.uk/news/worldnews/africaandindianocean/zimbabwe/1383222/Attack-on-Mugabes-media-laws.html.
Thornycroft, Peta. "'Hitler' Mugabe Launches Revenge Terror Attacks." *The Telegraph*, March 26, 2003. www.telegraph.co.uk/news/worldnews/africaandindianocean/zimbabwe/1425727/Hitler-Mugabe-launches-revenge-terror-attacks.html.
"Transcript: Israeli Prime Minister Binyamin Netanyahu's Address to Congress." *The Washington Post*, May 24, 2011. www.washingtonpost.com/world/israeli-prime-minister-binyamin-netanyahus-address-to-congress/2011/05/24/AFWY5bAH_story.html.
"Transcript of Gary Condit Interview." *CNN*, August 23, 2001. http://edition.cnn.com/2001/US/08/23/condit.transcript/.
Twenge, Jean, and Campbell, Keith. *The Narcissism Epidemic: Living in the Age of Entitlement*. New York: Free Press, 2009.
Twenge, Jean, et al. "Egos Inflating Over Time: A Cross-Temporal Meta-Analysis of the Narcissistic Personality Inventory." *Journal of Personality* 76, No. 4 (2008), pp. 875–902.
Uncyclopedia. "Troy King's Letters to the Crimson White." http://uncyclopedia.wikia.com/wiki/Troy_King's_letters_to_the_Crimson_White.
"UPDATED: Sanford Says Mistress Is Soul Mate." *The Augusta Chronicle* [Columbia], June 30, 2009.
Vasudev, Uma. *Indira Gandhi: Revolution in Restraint*. Delhi: Vikas Publishing House, 1974.

Verkaik, Robert. "The Love That Made Robert Mugabe a Monster." *The Independent (UK)*, April 6, 2008. www.independent.co.uk/news/world/africa/exclusive-the-love-that-made-robert-mugabe-a-monster-804287.html.

Viroli, Maurizio. *The Liberty of Servants: Berlusconi's Italy*. Princeton: Princeton University Press, 2012.

Vitello, Paul. "Worried Town Recalls a Young Petraeus." *The New York Times*, September 12, 2007. www.nytimes.com/2007/09/12/washington/12petraeus.html?_r=0.

Volkan, Vamik. *Primitive Internalized Object Relations: A Clinical Study of Schizophrenic, Borderline, and Narcissistic Patients*. New York: International Universities Press, 1976.

Volkan, Vamik. "Narcissistic Personality Organization and Reparative Leadership." *International Journal of Group Psychotherapy* 30 (1980), pp. 131–152.

Volkan, Vamik. "Object and Self: A Developmental Approach." In *Object Relations and Self: A Developmental Approach*, edited by Edith Jacobson, Saul Tuftman, Carol Keye and Muriel Zimmerman. New York: International Universities Press, 1981, pp. 429–451.

Volkan, Vamik. "Narcissistic Personality Disorder." In *Critical Problems in Psychiatry*, edited by Jessie Cavenar & Keith Brodie. Philadelphia: J. B. Lippincott Co., 1982, pp. 332–350.

Volkan, Vamik and Norman Itzkowitz. *The Immortal Ataturk*. Chicago: University of Chicago Press, 1984.

Vulliamy, Ed. "Mira Cracked." *The Guardian*, July 7, 2001. www.guardian.co.uk/world/2001/jul/08/warcrimes.balkans?INTCMP=SRCH.

Waite, Robert. *The Psychopathic God: Adolf Hitler*. New York: Basic Books, 1977.

Walsh, Bill, and Bruce Alpert. "Senate Leader Wants 'Airing' of Vitter Scandal." *The Times Picayune*, July 17, 2007. http://blog.nola.com/times-picayune/2007/07/senate_leader_wants_airing_of.html.

Weber, Max. *The Sociology of Religion*. Boston: Beacon Press, 1922.

Whitney, Craig. "Bucharest Journal; To Rumanians, It Just Feels Like the Third World." *The New York Times*, July 20, 1989(a). www.nytimes.com/1989/07/20/world/bucharest-jour nal-to-rumanians-it-just-feels-like-the-third-world.html?pagewanted=all&src=pm.

Whitney, Craig. "Upheaval in the East: The Old Order, The Collapse of Stalinism." *The New York Times*, December 24, 1989(b). www.nytimes.com/1989/12/24/world/upheaval-in-the-east-the-old-order-the-collapse-of-stalinism.html?pagewanted=all&src=pm.

"Who We Are." *Exodus International*. www.exodusinternational.org/.

Wilner, Ann Ruth. *The Spellbinders: Charismatic Political Leadership*. New Haven: Yale University Press, 1984.

Winder, David. "Zimbabwe's Mugabe: Labels Like Marxist Don't Stick to Him," *Christian Science Monitor*, October 11, p. 183.

Witte, Griff. "Bhutto Assassination Sparks Chaos." *The Washington Post*, December 28, 2007. Accessed February 3, 2011. www.washingtonpost.com/wp-dyn/content/article/2007/12/27/A.

Wolfe, Thomas. *The Bonfire of the Vanities*. New York: Farrar, Straus, Giroux, 1987.

Woods, K. W. *Schwarzenegger: Muscleman to Terminator (An Unauthorized Biography)* Lincolnwood, Ill.: Publications International, 1991.

Wyatt, Kristen. "Suspect Anders Behring Breivik's Manifesto Plagiarized from the Unabomber." *The Huffington Post*, June 24, 2011. www.huffingtonpost.com/2011/07/25/suspect-anders-behring-br_n_909022.html.

Yeltsin, Boris. *Against the Grain: An Autobiography*. Translated by Michael Glenny. New York: Summit Books, 1990.

Young, J. T. "Zimbabwean Double Standard." *Washington Times*, January 14, 2003, p. A15

YouTube. "Larry Craig Interview Excerpts." Accessed April 10, 2011. www.youtube .com/watch?v=fwx8sViLViA.

Zisser, Eyal. *Commanding Syria: Bashar al-Assad and the First Years in Power.* London: I. B. Tauris, 2007.

Zoepf, Katherina, and Anthony Shadid. "Syrian Leader's Brother Seen as Enforcer of Crackdown." *The New York Times*, June 7, 2011. Accessed June 8, 2011 www .nytimes.com/2011/06/08/world/middleeast/08syria.html.

Zonis, Marvin. *Majestic Failure: The Fall of the Shah.* Chicago: University of Chicago Press, 1991.

Zonis, Marvin. "Shi'ite Political Activism in the Arab World." Draft manuscript, available from the author, Middle East Institute, University of Chicago, 1985.

Index

Printed in the USA
CPSIA information can be obtained
at www.ICGtesting.com
LVHW040604261223
767366LV00007B/65